The **Rough Guide** to

Toronto

written and researched by

Phil Lee and Helen Lovekin

ROUGH GUIDES

NEW YORK • LONDON • DELHI

www.roughguides.com

Contents

3

Introduction to

Toronto

In recent decades, Toronto has thrown itself into a spate of serious image-building, with millions of dollars lavished on glitzy architecture, slick museums, an excellent public transport system and the redevelopment of its waterfront. As a result, Toronto – the economic and cultural focus of English-speaking Canada, and the country's largest metropolis – has become one of North America's most likeable and attractive cities.

Toronto sprawls along the northern shore of Lake Ontario, its bustling, vibrant centre surrounded by a jingle and jangle of satellite townships and industrial zones that, as "Greater Toronto", cover no less than 600 square kilometres. In the centre, huge new shopping malls and high-rise office blocks reflect the economic successes of the last two or three decades, a boom that has attracted immigrants from all over the world, transforming an overwhelmingly Anglophone city into a cosmopolitan megalopolis of some seventy significant minorities. Indeed, getting the feel for Toronto's diversity is one of the city's great pleasures. Nowhere is this better experienced than in its myriad cafés and restaurants, where standards are high and prices are low. The city also boasts a pulsating club scene, not to mention a classy programme of performing arts, from dance to theatre and beyond.

Toronto also has its share of attention-grabbing sights, largely conveniently clustered in the city centre. The most celebrated of these is the CN Tower, the world's tallest free-standing structure, but much more enjoyable are the pick of the city's museums – for starters, there's the outstanding Art Gallery of Ontario and the delightful Gardiner Museum of Ceramic Art – and a brace of Victorian mansions. That said, these sights illustrate different facets of Toronto, but in no way do they crystallize its identity. The city remains opaque: too big and diverse to allow for a defining personality and too metamorphic to permit rigid definition. This, however, adds an air of excitement and unpredictability to the place. In fact, for many it's the surging vitality of the city that provides the most abiding memories.

▲ The Beaches waterfront

What to see

T oronto's central core is readily divided into three main areas: Downtown, Uptown and the waterfront. **Downtown**, bounded by Front Street to the south, Gerrard Street to the north, Spadina Avenue to the west and Jarvis Street to the east, is the most diverse of the three. Here you'll find the city's most visited attractions, kicking off with the famous **CN Tower** and the armadillo-like **Rogers Centre** (formerly the SkyDome) sports stadium next door. These two structures abut the **Banking District**, whose assorted skyscrapers display some of the city's most striking architecture, especially in the quartet of hulking black blocks that constitute the **Toronto Dominion Centre**. One of the four blocks holds the delightful **Gallery of Inuit Art**, an exemplary collection of Inuit sculpture gathered together from the remote settlements of the Arctic north in the 1960s. Close by, **St Andrew's Presbyterian Church** is a proud

▲ Fireworks over the Toronto skyline

Toronto past and present

Long before the Europeans arrived, the **Hurons** settled the northern shore of Lake Ontario and named the site of the city "Toronto", meaning "place of meeting". In the sixteenth century, British and French **fur traders** arrived in the area, and the French, who made their headquarters in Québec City, often canoed down to Toronto, which was an early portage route between Lake Ontario and Georgian Bay.

The French formed an **alliance** with the Hurons and ruled the area for over a century. It was only after success against the French in **The Seven Years' War** (1756-63) that control shifted in Britain's favour, and the arrival of several hundred United Empire Loyalists in the wake of the **American Revolution** further helped to strengthen the supremacy of the Crown. Tensions between the British and their American neighbours culminated here in the **War of 1812**, during which the American military briefly occupied Toronto twice, but ultimately the US was defeated, acknowledging Britain's role in North America with the signing of the Treaty of Ghent in 1814.

Today Toronto is the **provincial capital** of Ontario, one of ten provinces and three territories that make up Canada. The bicameral federal government meets at the nation's capital, Ottawa, on the Ontario/Québec border. The city achieved its **present geographical dimensions** in 1998 when, much to the chagrin of many locals, the six semi-independent boroughs of what had been Metropolitan Toronto were merged into one megacity. Its combined **population** is around 2.3 million, making it the largest city in Canada by a long chalk – its nearest rival being Montréal, with some 1,800,000 inhabitants.

reminder of the nineteenth-century city, its handsome neo-Romanesque stonework overlooking **Roy Thompson Hall**, the home of the Toronto Symphony Orchestra.

The Banking District fizzles out at Queen Street, giving way to **Nathan Phillips Square**, site of both the old and new city halls, and the sprawling **Eaton Centre**, Toronto's main shopping mall, which extends along Yonge as far as Dundas. Nearby is the much-lauded **Art Gallery of Ontario** (AGO), home to a first-rate selection of both European and Canadian works. Within easy striking distance is **Fort York**, the reconstructed British army outpost where Toronto began, and which is now stranded on the western edge of Downtown in the shadow of the Gardiner Expressway. In the opposite direction, the **St Lawrence** neighbourhood is one of the city's more distinctive, its main claim to fame being a clutch of fine old stone buildings. From here, it's another short hop east to the **Distillery District**, not actually a district at all, but rather Toronto's brightest arts and entertainment complex, which occupies a sprawling former distillery dating from the nineteenth century.

Moving north, **Uptown** runs from Gerrard as far as Dupont Street. With the exception of the **Ontario Legislative Assembly Building**, a whopping sandstone pile on University Avenue, the principal attractions here are the museums, beginning with the wide-ranging applied art of the **Royal Ontario Museum** (ROM), where pride of place goes to the Chinese collection. Smaller and more engaging are both the **Gardiner Museum of Ceramic Art**, which holds a connoisseur's collection of ceramics, and the fascinating range of footwear displayed at the **Bata Shoe Museum**. Also of interest are a pair of intriguing old houses: **Casa Loma**, a mock-Gothic extravagance dating from 1911, and **Spadina House**, whose studied charms are the epitome of Victorian gentility.

The third part of the city centre is the Lake Ontario **waterfront**. Formerly a grimy industrial strip of wharves and warehouses, it's now flanked by deluxe condominiums and bright office blocks. This is one of the smartest parts of the city and it comes complete with open-air performance areas, bars, restaurants, shops and a couple of art galleries, including the enterprising **Power Plant Contemporary Art Gallery**. The waterfront is also where

The Distillery District

In 1832, James Worts and William Gooderham, two immigrants from England, built a windmill beside Lake Ontario, in what is now central Toronto. Five years later, Gooderham added a distillery to produce whisky from Ontario grain and it was a great commercial success. By the 1860s the distillery was producing two and a half million gallons of whisky from a quarter of a million bushels of grain. In 1869, a fire destroyed most of the original works, but its replacement – a series of tidy brown–brick buildings – survives to this day, on Mill Street, just east of the foot of Parliament Street. The distillery, which at one time was the largest in the British Empire, closed in 1990, but the old works remains the best-preserved Victorian industrial complex in Canada. The complex has recently been revamped as the Distillery District (see p.61), which now holds, amongst much else, art galleries, independent designers, bakeries, shops, a microbrewery and no less than three performance venues – all without a multinational chain in sight, for which blessing the developers are due (at least) three hearty cheers.

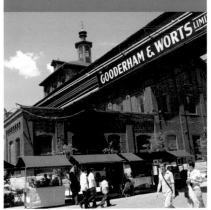

▲ Toronto Islands

ferries leave for the **Toronto Islands**, the low-lying, crescent-shaped sandbanks that shelter the harbour and provide opportunities for city folk to go walking, swimming and sailing amidst the woods and lawns.

To get the real flavour of Toronto's core, it's best to **explore on foot**, a perfectly feasible option as distances are quite manageable. However, visiting some of the more peripheral attractions – like Casa Loma and Spadina House – can be

Out of the city

Toronto is a convenient base for exploring southwest Ontario, a triangular tract of land that lies sandwiched between lakes Huron and Erie. Significant parts of the region are blotched by heavy industry, but there's also mile upon mile of rolling farmland and a series of excellent attractions, the best of which are within a two- to three-hour drive of Downtown. Potential destinations include Canada's premier tourist spot, Niagara Falls, as well as nearby Niagara-on-the-Lake, a beguiling town of leafy streets and charming colonial houses, as well as site of the renowned Shaw Festival and – within the vicinity – more than twenty wineries. There's also Goderich and Bayfield, two lovely little towns tucked against the bluffs of the Lake Huron shoreline, and Severn Sound, home to a pair of top-notch historical reconstructions, Discovery Harbour and Sainte-Marie among the Hurons. The sound is also the front door to the Georgian Bay Islands National Park, whose island-studded waters are strikingly beautiful. Beyond southwest Ontario, the most obvious target is Kingston, a lovely mid-sized town with a clutch of old stone buildings, about 260km east along the lake from Toronto.

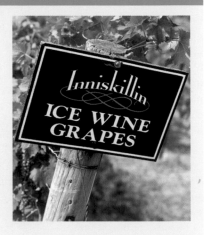

▲ Bloor Street

a bit of a trek, especially in the summer when the city is often unbearably humid. Fortunately, Toronto's **public transport** system is excellent, consisting of a comprehensive, safe and inexpensive network of streetcars, buses and subways that delves into every nook and cranny of the city. This system also brings most of the city's **suburbs** within easy striking distance. By and large they are of limited interest, the main exception being **The Beaches**, a delightful neighbourhood bordering Lake Ontario, just a twenty-minute streetcar ride east of Downtown.

When to go

Toronto has a harsh **climate**. In the winter, it's often bitterly cold, with sub-zero temperatures and heavy snowfalls. January and February are usually the coldest months, though real winter conditions can begin in early November and drag on into late March. Summers,

9

▼ Kew Beach Park

on the other hand, are hot and humid. July and August are consistently the hottest months, sometimes uncomfortably so. Spring and autumn offer the city's most enjoyable weather, with lots of warm, sunny days and balmy nights.

Toronto climate

	Jan	Feb	Mar	Apr	May	Jun	Jul	Aug	Sept	Oct	Nov	Dec
Average daily max temp												
°F	28	29	39	52	65	73	79	77	68	56	44	33
°C	-2.2	-1.7	3.9	11.1	18.3	22.8	26.1	25	20	13.3	6.7	0.6
Average daily min temp												
°F	15	15	24	35	45	54	60	58	50	39	31	20
°C	-9.4	-9.4	-4.4	1.7	7.2	12.2	15.6	14.4	10	3.9	-0.6	-6.7
Average rainfall												
in	1.9	1.8	2.3	2.6	2.6	2.6	2.8	3.2	2.8	2.5	2.6	2.4
mm	48.3	45.7	58.4	66	66	66	71	81.3	71	63.5	66	61

23

things not to miss

It's not possible to see everything Toronto has to offer in one trip – and we don't suggest you try. What follows is a selective taste of the city's highlights: first-class museums, great places to eat and drink and dynamic neighbourhoods to explore. Arranged in five colour-coded categories, you can browse through to find the very best things to see, do and experience. All highlights have a page reference to take you straight into the text, where you can find out more.

01 Ice skating at New City Hall Page **209** • Skate the winter blues away at this popular ice rink in front of New City Hall.

02 **The Art Gallery of Ontario** Page **67** • This prestigious gallery has a fabulous collection of Canadian art, a wealth of works by Dutch Golden Age and French Impressionist painters and the world's largest assemblage of Henry Moore sculptures.

04 **Casa Loma** Page **85** • Marvel at this outlandish behemoth of a building, conceived by the incorrigibly eccentric Henry Pellatt.

06 **Toronto Symphony Orchestra** Page **184** • Take in a performance by the internationally acclaimed orchestra, which performs in Downtown's Roy Thompson Hall.

03 **A game at the Rogers Centre** Page **50** • Baseball and football fans can revel in the Blue Jays and Argonauts games that are held here, in the former SkyDome.

05 **Exploring Chinatown** Page **72** • Enjoy the various sights and smells of Chinatown, the focus of Toronto's sizeable Chinese community, where scores of stalls selling every Asian delicacy you can imagine line the streets.

07 Cabbagetown Page **84** • Take a walk through this modish neighbourhood, with its trim Victorian terraces, named after its first occupants' habit of planting cabbages in the gardens.

08 Theatre Page **179** • You'll find everything from contemporary political satires to lavish, glitzy musicals making up Toronto's superb theatre scene.

09 The CN Tower Page **48** • Like it or lump it, the CN Tower is Toronto's mascot – and one of the world's best-known buildings.

10 Niagara Falls Page **111** • Get up-close to Niagara's roaring, crashing falls on a "Maid of the Mist" boat tour, making for a breathtaking experience.

12 High Park Page 107 • Hike, picnic or simply relax in this pick of the city's parks, a hilly expanse of lawn, lake, wood and garden.

11 Toronto International Film Festival Page 220 •
North America's largest film festival is a star-studded affair held over ten days in September.

14 Hockey Hall of Fame
Page 58 • Canada's Holy Grail is ice hockey's Stanley Cup, and the very first one is displayed in this museum.

15 Kensington Market
Page 72 • Check out everything from organic food to trendy clothes in Toronto's best open-air market.

13 Bata Shoe Museum
Page 83 • Indulge your fetish at this fun, inventive museum, dedicated to footwear of every description, from Ottoman platforms to French chestnut-crushing clogs.

16 **Georgian Bay Islands National Park** Page **128** • Wispy pines, rocky islets and placid waters make this spot a tranquil and beautiful retreat.

18 **The Beaches** Page **98** • This suburb of Toronto, with a 3km-long boardwalk, sits on the shores of Lake Ontario.

17 **The Royal Ontario Museum** Page **79** • Explore the city's largest and most diverse museum, noted for its outstanding Egyptian collection.

19 Arts festivals Pages **117** & **122** • Though not in Toronto, every year visitors and locals alike flock to the towns of Stratford and Niagara-on-the Lake to take in the top-notch Stratford and Shaw festivals, respectively.

21 St Lawrence District Page **59** • Striking architecture – some of the city's oldest buildings are here – plus a lively market, bar and restaurant scene make this neighbourhood a real draw.

22 Toronto Islands Page **93** • Enjoy the balmy summertime breezes that ripple across these low-slung Islands where, refreshingly, cars are forbidden.

20 The University of Toronto Page **77** • Escape from the buzz of modern-day city life on this Victorian-Gothic campus, home to one of North America's most respected universities.

23 Queen Street West Page **66** • Spend the day roaming about the grooviest place in town, awash with cafés, restaurants and designer shops – though it's the streetlife that really turns heads here.

Basics

Basics

Getting there

As Canada's commercial hub, Toronto is not at all difficult to reach. Flying is the most popular, time-effective option, unless you're already somewhat close to the city, in which case there are plenty of road and rail links to get you there. From outside of North America, flying is of course pretty much your only option. The main airport is Toronto Pearson International, just 25km northwest of the city centre (see "Arrival" for more information).

Airfares to Toronto from the UK, Australia and New Zealand vary depending on the **season**, with the highest prices applying from around mid-June to early September. You'll get the best deals during the low season, mid-November through to April (excluding Christmas and New Year, when seats are at a premium and prices are hiked up). Note also that flying on the weekend is generally more expensive than flying during the week. If you're flying from the US or from anywhere else in Canada, the same general strictures apply, though the market is more unpredictable, with airlines constantly moving their prices up and down.

Airfare costs can often be reduced by going through a **specialist flight agent** rather than an airline. These agents come in two main flavours: **consolidators**, who buy up blocks of tickets from the airlines and sell them at a discount, and **discount agents**, who, in addition to dealing with discounted flights, may also offer special student and youth fares, plus a range of other travel-related services such as insurance, car rental and the like. Some agents specialize in **charter flights**, which may well be cheaper than anything available on a scheduled flight – though be aware that departure dates are fixed and withdrawal penalties high.

Package deals from **tour operators** are rarely going to save you money in getting to Toronto. That said, several of the best do provide excellent city breaks at competitive prices, putting you up in good-quality accommodation.

Booking flights online

Most airlines and discount travel websites offer you the opportunity to book your tickets **online**, cutting out the costs of agents and middlemen, though many now charge a small handling fee. Good deals can also be found through auction sites, but you should read the fine print carefully. In the US, the airlines' own websites are becoming increasingly competitive with larger online travel bookers, so be sure to include them in your search.

Online travel and booking websites

🌐 **www.cheapflights.com** Bookings from the UK and Ireland only; for the US, visit 🌐 **www.cheapflight.com**; for Canada, 🌐 **www.cheapflights.ca**; for Australia, 🌐 **www.cheapflights.com.au**. All the sites offer flight deals, details of travel agents and links to other travel sites.

🌐 **www.cheaptickets.com** Hawaii-based discount flight specialists (US only) whose search engine claims to dig up the lowest possible fares worldwide; the one drawback is its cumbersome log-in procedure.

🌐 **www.counciltravel.com** If your journey originates in the US and you've some flexibility, this site can provide you with competitive deals.

🌐 **www.ebookers.com** Efficient, easy-to-use flight finder offering competitive fares.

🌐 **www.etn.nl/discount** A hub of consolidator and discount agent links, maintained by the nonprofit European Travel Network.

🌐 **www.expedia.com** Discount airfares, all-airline search engine and daily deals (US only; **for the UK** 🌐 **www.expedia.co.uk**; for Canada 🌐 **www.expedia.ca**).

🌐 **www.flights4less.co.uk** Does just what it says on the tin.

🌐 **www.flyaow.com** Online air travel info and reservations.

🌐 **www.gaytravel.com** US gay travel agent, offering accommodation, cruises, tours and more. Also at ☎ 1-800/GAY-TRAVEL.

Ⓦ **www.hotwire.com** Last-minute savings of up to forty percent on regular published fares. Travellers must be at least 18 years old. No refunds, transfers, or changes allowed. Bookings from the US only. If you're looking for the cheapest possible scheduled flight, this is probably your best bet.

Ⓦ **www.kelkoo.co.uk** Useful price-comparison site offering low-cost flights (and other goods and services) according to specific criteria. UK only.

Ⓦ **www.lastminute.com** UK site with good last-minute holiday package and flight-only deals; for Australia Ⓦ **www.lastminute.com.au**

Ⓦ **www.opodo.co.uk** Popular and reliable source for low UK airfares. Owned by nine major European airlines.

Ⓦ **www.orbitz.com** Comprehensive travel resource with great customer service.

Ⓦ **www.priceline.co.uk** (in UK), Ⓦ **www .priceline.com** (in US). Name-your-own-price website with discounts around forty percent off standard fares.

Ⓦ **www.qixo.com** Trawls through dozens of popular websites to find the best airfares and flight times.

Ⓦ **www.skyauction.com** Bookings from the US only. Auctions tickets and travel packages using a "second bid" scheme, just like eBay. You state the maximum you're willing to pay, and the system will bid only as much as it takes to outbid others, up to your stated limit.

Ⓦ **www.travelocity.com** and Ⓦ **www .travelocity.co.uk** Great resource for news on the latest airfare sales, cruise discounts, car hire and hotel deals. Provides access to the travel agent system SABRE, the most comprehensive central reservations system in the US.

Ⓦ **www.travelshop.com.au** Australian website offering discounted flights, travel packages, insurance, and online bookings.

Ⓦ **www.zuji.com.au (in Australia)** Destination guides, hot fares and great deals for car rental and accommodation.

From North America

For those coming from the **northern or northeastern US**, Toronto is eminently accessible – it's just a couple of hours' drive from the US/Canada border at Niagara Falls (near Buffalo, NY) and only a four-hour drive from Detroit, MI. **From further afield**, almost all major US cities have **direct flights** to Toronto, and service is characteristically frequent; about sixty percent of North America's population lives within a ninety-minute plane ride from the city.

Over the last few years, bus and train have become increasingly popular options for getting to Toronto from the US. **Canadians visiting Toronto** usually choose to drive or fly, though there are of course similar mass ground transit options.

By Plane

In addition to three Canadian carriers, sixty **international airlines** fly into Toronto Pearson International Airport. Of these, twelve are US carriers. The greatest number of daily flights between major US cities and Toronto occur during weekdays, reflecting the high volume of business travel.

Air Canada is the national carrier and offers the most number of direct flights to the US. **United Airlines** code-shares with Air Canada on major transporter routes to Toronto, such as those from New York, Chicago, Los Angeles and other major US cities. **American Airlines** and its subsidiary, American Eagle, have similar route structures.

Fares and fare structures on all airlines are extremely fluid, and travellers should consult airline and comparative travel websites for the best deals. As a rule, direct, nonstop flights on Air Canada are at a premium, with standard, return economy fare from New York, Chicago or Los Angeles in the area of Can$280–600, Can$300–620 and Can$350–890, respectively, for low season–high season. A rough range of flight costs between Toronto and Montréal, Ottawa, Halifax or Vancouver, under the same criteria, is Can$200–500, Can$120–280, Can$460–1200 and Can$480–1200, respectively.

Booking two or three weeks in advance of your trip is an immediate way to save money. Including a weekend in travel dates, on the other hand, no longer makes a difference. Air Canada offers five fare options: Executive, Latitude Plus, Latitude, Tango Plus and Tango. The variable is the degree of flexibility each ticket offers regarding changing flight dates and times, etc. Seat confirmations actually cost more, but without them passengers on over-booked flights can be bumped. Before booking your ticket, always enquire about the nature of your ticket's fare structure and the limitations involved, and if booking online pay close attention to the types of fares on offer.

The incentive driving Air Canada's recent interest in discount air service (via its Tango fares) is the brisk competition it is experiencing from the scrappy, Calgary-based WestJet (⊛ www.westjet.com), which innovated paperless, no-frills, book-online travel in Canada. Their core business is servicing the western part of the country, so it is a particularly good choice for Toronto/ Vancouver flights. New routes have been added to eastern Canada as well as US cities, notably in states such as Florida and Arizona. Prices for WestJet and Air Canada Tango fares are extremely competitive, and both airlines offer specials – which are invariably one-way and listed before taxes – on major routes, although price wars have subsided of late in view of the unpredictable cost of fuel.

For daily flight conditions, schedules and up-to-date airport information, travellers in Toronto can call the airline numbers listed below or tune into 1280 CFYZ Radio.

Airlines

Air Canada ☎ 1-888-247-2262, ⊛ www .aircanada.com. Canada's national airline flies to 30 US and 21 Canadian cities year round. The short-lived regional discount carrier Air Canada Jazz was consumed by its Air Canada parent and the discount fares now fall under the Tango rubric.
American Airlines ☎ 1-800/433-7300, ⊛ www .aa.com. Offers a number of flights to Toronto from major American cities, especially New York.
CanJet ☎ 1-866/656-3761, ⊛ www.canjet.com. The new discount kid in town, CanJet is an east coast-based, no-frills airline that runs three direct flights a week to Toronto from New York. It also delivers Canadian snowbirds to Florida resort towns and specializes in discount airfares to the Maritimes.
Continental Airlines ☎ 1-800/231-0856 or 1-800/784-4444, ⊛ www.continental.com. Provides one- and two-stop connecting flights to Toronto from US cities that have either no direct flights or only a limited number.
Delta Airlines ☎ 1-800/221-1212 domestic, international ☎ 1-800/241-4141, ⊛ www.delta .com. Daily, non-direct flights and multi-fare structures (three fares for coach; two for executive) from major cities, including New York, Chicago and Los Angeles.

Northwest Airlines ☎ 1-800/441-1818, ⊛ www .nwa.com. Sixteen flights daily from New York, Los Angeles and Chicago, though not one of them is direct. Detroit is the main connecting city to Toronto, followed by Minneapolis.
United Airlines domestic ☎ 1-800/241-6522, international ☎ 1-800/538-2929, ⊛ www.ual.com. Air Canada's code-share partner in the US. Direct flights from New York, Chicago and Los Angeles.
WestJet ☎ 1-800/538-5696, ⊛ www.westjet.com. Seasonal service to and from eight US cities – four direct (Ft Lauderdale, Phoenix, Orlando and Las Vegas), four with stopovers (San Francisco, LA, San Diego, Palm Springs) – plus domestic service across Canada.

By Bus

Toronto is a major hub for continental **bus** travel. Taking the bus is relatively inexpensive, and you arrive directly in the city centre, at the bus terminal at 610 Bay Street (☎ 416/393-7911). It goes without saying that travelling by bus is pretty much the slowest way possible, but if time isn't a consideration, it is a viable option.

Toronto is served from the US by **Greyhound** (US ☎ 1-800/229-9424; Canada ☎ 1-800/661-8747, ⊛ www.greyhound.com). Trips to Toronto from major cities such as New York, Detroit, Chicago and Montréal take eleven, six, fifteen and eight hours, respectively. From Los Angeles, it's about a two-and-a-half-day journey, so budget and time constraints are the determining factors here.

By Rail

Rail travel to Toronto has become more popular, given the increased amount of time spent in airport security lines over the last few years. As with buses, Toronto's train terminal, the graceful old Union Station, is conveniently located downtown. Train travel does takes time, however: a trip from New York City is thirteen hours (which includes a wait of about an hour and twenty minutes at the border) and it takes around fifteen hours from Chicago.

If you are coming to Toronto from a US city, you'll arrive on one of **VIA Rail** Canada's (☎ 1-888/842-7245, ⊛ www .viarail.com) passenger trains. **Fares** are roughly parallel to airfare, unless you book

The Natural Choice to Canada

Air Canada offers more daily direct flights between the U.K. and Canada than any other airline. With service to the most places in Canada, we're proud to fly you to over 70 destinations from coast to coast.

So if Canada's in your travel plans, fly with those who call it home.

Book your flights online at **aircanada.com**
Or contact your local travel agent or Air Canada Reservations on 0871 220 1111.

AIR CANADA ✦
STAR ALLIANCE ✸

about three weeks in advance. There are basically two fare structures, economy and first class, and special offers are available for seniors, students and families. Passengers returning to the US will be aboard **AMTRAK** (☎1-800/872-7245, ⓦwww.amtrak.com). Traditionalists will appreciate VIA's preference for paper tickets (there's an extra charge for etickets), though US passengers' tickets will be delivered by mail, so they should book several weeks in advance.

By Car

Getting to Toronto **by car** is easy enough but, like any other form of land travel, time is the critical factor. From **New York City to Toronto** you are looking at approximately 790km, which, assuming the border crossing is uneventful, translates to about ten hours' driving time. **Detroit** is 370km and roughly a four-hour drive away. From **Montréal**, it's about 540km, and driving will take you about five hours.

If you are driving a **rental car** in from the US, it may be helpful to let the agency know that you intend to cross the border into Canada with the car, to avoid any possible

misunderstandings concerning theft. A few major North American car rental companies are **National Car & Truck Rental** (Canada & US ☎1-888/501-9010, ⓦwww.nationalcar.com); **Budget Car Rental** (US ☎1-800/527-0700; Canada ☎1-800/268-8900, ⓦwww.budgetcar.com); and **Hertz** (US ☎1-800/654-3131, international ☎1-800/654-3001, ⓦwww.hertz.com). Bear in mind that once you reach Toronto, a car may be more of a hindrance than a help, as downtown parking and gas stations – both in short supply – are pricey.

Discount travel companies

Butte Travel Service Canada ☎1-866/656-3761 or 780/477-3561, ⓦwww.flyforless.ca. Edmonton-based specialists in discount flights and cruises around the world.
Educational Travel Center ☎1/800/747-5551 or 608/256-5551, ⓦwww.edtrav.com. Low-cost fares, student and youth discounts, car rental and tours.
Flight Centre US ☎1-866/967-5331, Canada ☎1-877/478-8747, ⓦwww.flightcentre.com. Guarantees lowest airfares.
STA Travel US ☎1-800/781-4040, Canada ☎1-800/427-5639, ⓦwww.sta-travel.com. Worldwide specialist in independent and student travel.

Crossing the US/Canada border

Recently there has been a lot of confusion in the US about what is needed to cross the **US/Canada border**. American visitors crossing the border in either direction do not need a **passport**. However, they may be asked to verify their citizenship with either a passport or a birth certificate, as well as a photo ID. Naturalized US citizens should carry a naturalization certificate, and permanent US residents who are not citizens should carry their Alien Registration Receipt Card (Green Card). Non-American visitors to Canada crossing into the US for a simple day-trip should be aware of all visa regulations and/or residency requirements for both countries and have the proper paperwork, or else risk being stranded at the border. Worthy sites to consult for relevant information include the **Ontario Ministry of Transportation** (ⓦ www.mto.gov.on.ca), **Canadian Boarder Service Agency** (ⓦ www.cbsa.gc.ca), and **US Department of State** (ⓦ travel.state.gov).

Student Flights ☎ 1-800/255-8000 or 480/951-1177, ⓦ www.isecard.com. Student and youth fares, plus student IDs and bus passes.

Travel Cuts Canada ☎ 1-800/667-2887, US ☎ 1-866/246-9762, ⓦ www.travelcuts.com. Student, youth and budget travel.

Worldtrek Travel ☎ 1-800/243-1723, ⓦ www .worldtrek.com. Discount travel agency for worldwide travel.

Tour Operators

American Express Vacations US ☎ 1-800/297-2777, Outside US ☎ 210/582-2716, ⓦ www .americanexpress.com/travel. Hotels, getaways, transportation and last-minute deals.

Brewster Tours Canada ☎ 1-800/661-1152 ⓦ www.brewster.ca. Vancouver-based rail specialists offering package tours from Toronto on VIA Rail's cross-country Canadian.

Collette Vacations US ☎ 1-800/321-8684, ⓦ www.collettvacations.com. Independent and escorted tours of Toronto and Niagara Falls.

Destinations Canada ☎ 1-888/475-4226 or 416/488-1169, ⓦ www.destinationcanada.com. Air-inclusive packages for Toronto and surrounding area.

Escape Tours Canada ☎ 1-866/607-4567, ⓦ www.escapetours.org. Central-Ontario specialists offering small, flexible tours to Algonquin Park, the Niagara region and smaller Ontario cities.

Fresh Tracks Canada ☎ 1-800/667-4744, ⓦ www.freshtracks.ca. Specialists in train travel packages with Toronto as the hub.

Gray Line ☎ 1-800/667-0882, ⓦ www.grayline .ca. The Gray Line bus company (Greyhound in the US) offers both day-trips and tour packages in and around Toronto. Packages are two- or three-night

affairs, with passes to attractions available at time of booking.

Maxxim Vacations ☎ 1-800/567-6666, ⓦ www .maxximvacations.com. Flexible, all-inclusive packages from the US to Toronto.

Odyssey Learning Adventures Canada ☎ 1-800/263-0050, ⓦ www.odysseylearningadvent ures.ca. Offers educational travel experiences and Elderhostel programmes. Toronto packages include either the Shaw Festival in Niagara-on-the-Lake or the Stratford Festival in Stratford.

Toronto Tours Canada ☎ 1-888/811-9247, ⓦ www.torontotours.com. Toronto and Niagara-region tours, plus various Toronto Harbour cruises.

Voyageur Quest ☎ 1-800/794-9660 or 416/486-3605, ⓦ www.voyageurquest.com. Adventure-travel company based in Toronto that takes you straight from Downtown to the forests edging Algonquin Provincial Park. Provides complete outfitting for three- to five-day wilderness experiences and also leads group canoe expeditions of Toronto Harbour.

Yankee Holidays US ☎ 1-800/225-2550, ⓦ www .yankeeholidays.com. Two- to five-day Toronto packages featuring theatre, restaurants, cultural attractions and neighbourhoods. Tours of Niagara region also available.

From the UK and Ireland

Toronto is easily reached **from the UK mainland** by either charter or scheduled flight. The majority of flights leave from London Heathrow, with other airports offering a slim to slender range of choices; Manchester and Glasgow have the most. **From Ireland** – north or south – there is only one seasonal scheduled direct, nonstop service to Toronto; the main options here are either charter flights or routings via the UK mainland or a US hub airport. Keep in mind that direct, nonstop flights can often – but certainly not always – be at a premium when compared with one-stop flights.

A standard return **fare** on a scheduled flight from London Heathrow direct to Toronto with **Air Canada**, the principal carrier, can range from £400–1200 (low season—high season). With restrictions, though, this can easily be trimmed to a very affordable £300–350. From **Ireland**, Air Canada's direct flights from Dublin and Shannon to Toronto (June–Sept only) can cost as little as €450, but without restrictions can weigh in at around €1750. Much more competitive, however, are the fares offered by the **budget airline** Zoom, whose going rate for a return from London to Toronto is between £200 and £300.

Airlines

Aer Lingus UK ☎0845/084 4444, Republic of Ireland ☎0818/365 000, ⓦwww.aerlingus.ie. Dublin to Boston; Boston to Toronto.
Air Canada UK ☎0871/220 1111, Republic of Ireland ☎01/679 3958, ⓦwww.aircanada.com. London Heathrow nonstop to Toronto; Manchester and Glasgow nonstop to Toronto (April–Oct only); Dublin and Shannon nonstop to Toronto (June–Sept only).

American Airlines UK ☎0845/7789 789 or 020/7365 0777, ⓦwww.americanairlines.co.uk; Republic of Ireland ☎01/602 0550, ⓦwww .americanairlines.ie. London Heathrow to Toronto via Boston, Chicago or New York; Glasgow and Manchester to Toronto via Chicago.
British Airways UK ☎0870/850 9850, Republic of Ireland ☎1890/626 747, ⓦwww.ba.com. London Heathrow to Toronto; Irish flight connections to Toronto via London Heathrow.
British Midland UK ☎0870/607 0222, from elsewhere UK ☎(0)1332/64 8181, ⓦwww.flybmi .com. In conjunction with Air Canada, flights from London Heathrow to Toronto.
Continental Airlines UK ☎0845/607 6760, ⓦwww.continental.com/uk; Republic of Ireland ☎1890/925 252, ⓦwww.continental.com/ie. From Birmingham, Bristol, Edinburgh, Glasgow, London Gatwick, London Heathrow and Manchester to Toronto via Newark, New Jersey. Also from Belfast, Dublin and Shannon to Toronto via Newark, New Jersey.
Delta UK ☎0800/414 767, Republic of Ireland ☎01/407 3165, ⓦwww.delta.com. London Gatwick to Toronto via Cincinnati or Atlanta, with connections to London Gatwick from several regional UK airports. Also Dublin to Toronto via Atlanta.
KLM/Northwest Airlines UK ☎0870/507 4074, ⓦwww.klm.com. KLM fly from a number of UK regional airports, principally Aberdeen, Birmingham, Edinburgh, Glasgow, Humberside, Leeds-Bradford, London City, London Gatwick, London Heathrow, Manchester and Norwich to Amsterdam. From

Amsterdam there are direct nonstop flights to Toronto.

Lufthansa UK ☎0845/7737 310, Republic of Ireland ☎01/844 5544, ⊛www.lufthansa.co.uk. Frankfurt to Toronto with connections from several UK airports, including London Heathrow.

United Airlines UK ☎0845/8444 777, ⊛www .unitedairlines.co.uk. London Heathrow to Toronto via Chicago or Washington DC; Manchester to Toronto via Chicago or via London Heathrow and Washington DC; Shannon to Toronto via Philadelphia.

Zoom ☎0870/240 0055, ⊛www.flyzoom.com. Scheduled flights from Belfast, Cardiff, Glasgow, London Gatwick, London Stansted and Manchester to Toronto. Also charter flights.

Discount travel and flight agents

Apex Travel Republic of Ireland ☎01/241 8000, ⊛www.apextravel.ie. Specialists in flights to Australia, Africa, the Far East, the US and Canada.

Aran Travel International Republic of Ireland ☎091/562 595, ⊛homepages.iol.ie/~arantvl /aranmain.htm. Low-cost flights worldwide.

CIE Tours International Republic of Ireland ☎01/703 1888, ⊛www.cietours.ie. General flight and tour agent.

Co-op Travel Care UK ☎0870/112 0085, ⊛www.travelcareonline.com. Flights and holidays around the world.

ebookers UK ☎0870/010 7000, ⊛www .ebookers.com, Republic of Ireland ☎01/241 5689, ⊛www.ebookers.ie. Low fares on an extensive selection of scheduled flights and package deals.

Flight Centre UK ☎0870/890 8099, ⊛www .flightcentre.co.uk. Rock-bottom fares worldwide.

Flights4Less UK ☎0871/222 3423, ⊛www .flights4less.co.uk. Airline consolidator and tour operator. Offers package deals and independent, tailor-made itineraries. Part of Lastminute.com.

Go Holidays Republic of Ireland ☎01/874 4126, ⊛www.goholidays.ie. City-break and package tour specialists.

Joe Walsh Tours Republic of Ireland ☎01/676 0991, ⊛www.joewalshtours.ie. Long-established travel agency and tour operator.

Lee Travel Republic of Ireland ☎021/427 7111, ⊛www.leetravel.ie. Comprehensive, independent travel agency.

McCarthy's Travel Republic of Ireland ☎021/427 0127, ⊛www.mccarthystravel.ie. Offers business, wedding, honeymoon, pilgrimage, skiing and other packages.

North South Travel UK ☎01245/608 291, ⊛www.northsouthtravel.co.uk. Friendly, competitive travel agency offering discounted fares worldwide.

Profits go to NST Development Trust, a charity that supports grass-roots projects in disadvantaged areas of Asia, Africa and Latin America.

Premier Travel Northern Ireland ☎028/7126 3333, ⊛www.premiertravel.uk.com. Group travel, business travel, car rentals, travel insurance and daily specials.

Rosetta Travel UK ☎028/9064 4996, ⊛www .rosettatravel.com. Travel bargains with flights leaving from Belfast.

STA Travel UK ☎0870/1600 599, ⊛www .statravel.co.uk. Worldwide specialists in low-cost flights and tours for students and under-26s, though other customers welcome.

Top Deck UK ☎020/8879 6789, ⊛www .topdecktravel.co.uk. Long-established agent dealing in discount flights.

Trailfinders UK ☎0845/0585 858, ⊛www .trailfinders.co.uk; Republic of Ireland ☎01/677 7888, ⊛www.trailfinders.ie. One of the best-informed and most efficient agents for independent travellers; they produce a very useful quarterly magazine worth scrutinizing for round-the-world routes.

USIT Republic of Ireland ☎01/602 1600, Northern Ireland ☎028/9032 7111, ⊛www.usit.ie. Specialists in student, youth and independent travel.

Tour operators

American Holidays Belfast ☎02890/238 762, Dublin ☎01/6733 840, ⊛www.american-holidays .com. Package deals from Ireland to all parts of the US and Canada.

Canada's Best UK ☎01502/565648, ⊛www .best-in-travel.com. Offers package and tailor-made holidays that include deals on Toronto hotels as well as Ontario cottages, resorts and inns.

TourWorld ⊛www.tourworld.com. Every sporting activity you can think of (and then some) is packaged-up on this comprehensive portal website.

Trek America UK ☎0870/444 8735, ⊛www .trekamerica.com. Youth-orientated camping and hiking trips throughout the US and Canada. Most of their Canadian holidays are in British Columbia, but they do offer a fourteen-day trip that includes New York, Toronto, Ottawa, Montréal, and New England.

From Australia and New Zealand

There are no direct, nonstop flights **from Australia and New Zealand** to Toronto; you will have to break your journey in either an Asian city, like Hong Kong, or in North America (usually Los Angeles or Vancouver);

the same applies to charter flights. **Fares** vary considerably, based on the restrictions attached to your ticket, rather than the time of year that you travel. A standard return fare from Sydney to Toronto (via Vancouver) with Air Canada costs around Aus$3000 – about the same from Auckland (via Los Angeles or San Francisco) – but special deals and discounts are commonplace.

Airlines

Air Canada Australia ℡1300/655 767, New Zealand ℡0508/747 767, ⓦwww.aircanada.com. Canada's principal domestic carrier offers flights from Sydney to Toronto via Vancouver and Los Angeles. Also Auckland to Toronto via San Francisco, Los Angeles or Vancouver.
Air New Zealand New Zealand ℡0800/737 000, ⓦwww.airnz.co.nz. Auckland and Wellington to Toronto via Los Angeles or Honolulu.
Cathay Pacific Australia ℡13 17 47, New Zealand ℡09/379 0861, ⓦwww.cathaypacific.com. Adelaide, Auckland, Brisbane, Melbourne, Perth and Sydney to Toronto via Hong Kong.
Japan Airlines Australia ℡02/9272 1111, New Zealand ℡09/379 9906, ⓦwww.japanair.com. Adelaide, Auckland, Brisbane, Cairns, Christchurch, Melbourne and Sydney to Toronto via Japan.
United Airlines Australia ℡13 17 77, New Zealand ℡0800/747 400, ⓦwww.unitedairlines.com.au. Sydney to Toronto via Los Angeles and Washington; Auckland to Los Angeles with onward flights to Toronto.

Discount travel and flight agents

Flight Centre Australia ℡13 31 33 or 02/9235 3522, ⓦwww.flightcentre.com.au; New Zealand ℡0800 243 544 or 09/358 4310, ⓦwww.flightcentre.co.nz. Discount flights.

Holiday Shoppe New Zealand ℡0800/808 480, ⓦwww.holidayshoppe.co.nz. Great deals on flights, hotels, packages and tours.
OTC Australia ℡1300/855 118, ⓦwww.otctravel.com.au. Cheap hotels, flights and getaway deals.
STA Travel Australia ℡1300/733 035 or 02/9212 1255, ⓦwww.statravel.com.au; New Zealand ℡0508/782 872 or 09/309 9273, ⓦwww.statravel.co.nz. Known as "the world's largest student travel organization". Specializes in independent travel.
Student Uni Travel Australia ℡02/9232 8444, ⓦwww.sut.com.au, New Zealand ℡09/379 4224, ⓦwww.sut.co.nz. Great deals for students.
Trailfinders Australia ℡1300/780 212, ⓦwww.trailfinders.com.au. One of the best-informed and most efficient agents for independent travellers.
travel.com.au and travel.co.nz Australia ℡1300/130 482, ⓦwww3.travel.com.au; New Zealand ℡0800/468 332, ⓦwww.travel.co.nz. Books flights, car rentals and accommodation; also offers tailor-made tours.

Tour operators

Adventure World Australia t02/8913 0755, ⓦwww.adventureworld.com.au, New Zealand ℡09/524 5118, ⓦwww.adventureworld.co.nz. Specializes in adventure travel throughout the world.
Canada & America Travel Specialists Australia ℡02/9922 4600, ⓦwww.canada-americatravel.com.au. Accommodation, train travel, adventure sports, car and RV rentals, bus passes, cruises, escorted tours and independent travel throughout North America.
Sydney Travel ℡02/925 09320, ⓦwww.sydneytravel.com. US and Canadian flights, accommodation, city breaks and car rental.

Red tape and visas

Citizens of the EU, the EEA and most Commonwealth countries travelling to Canada do not need an entry visa – all that is required is a valid passport. Technically at least, United States citizens only need some form of photo identification plus proof of US residence and citizenship (eg a birth certificate), but given the heightened state of security on all North American borders, you would be well advised to present a passport. Note that a US driver's licence alone is insufficient proof of citizenship.

All visitors to Canada have to complete a **customs declaration card**, which you'll be given on the plane or at the US/Canada border. At point of entry, the Canadian immigration officer will check the declaration card and decide the **length of stay permitted**, up to a maximum of six months, but usually not more than three. The officers rarely refuse entry, but they may launch into an impromptu investigation, asking how much money you have and what job you do; they may also ask to see a return or onward ticket or e-itinerary. If they ask where you're staying and you give the name and address of friends, don't be surprised if they check. Note also that, although passing overland between the US and Canada is usually straightforward, there can sometimes be long delays.

For visits of **more than six months, study trips** and stints of temporary **employment**, contact the nearest Canadian embassy, consulate or high commission for authorization prior to departure (see opposite for contact details). Once inside Canada, if an extension of stay is desired, written application must be made to the nearest **Canada Immigration Centre** well before the expiry of the authorized visit.

Duty-free

As for **duty-free allowances**, visitors arriving in Ontario who are 19 years of age or older may import, duty- and tax-free and

for personal use, either 1.5 litres of wine, 1.14l of liquor or spirits, or 24 x 355 ml cans or bottles of beer, ale or their equivalent. Visitors arriving in Ontario who are 19 years of age or older may also import, duty- and tax-free, 200 cigarettes, 50 cigars, 200 grams of manufactured tobacco and 200 tobacco sticks.

Canadian high commissions, consulates and embassies

An official list of all Canada's **high commissions, consulates** and **embassies** abroad, including email and postal addresses and telephone numbers, is to be found on ⑩www.dfait-maeci.gc.ca_/world /embassies/menu-en.asp.

Canadian consulates abroad

Australia Canberra High Commission ☏02/6270 4000; Melbourne Consulate ☏03/9653-9674; Perth Consulate ☏08/9322 7930; Sydney Consulate General ☏02/9364 3000.
Ireland Dublin Embassy ☏01/417 4100.
New Zealand Auckland Consulate ☏09/309 3690; Wellington High Commission ☏04/473 9577.
UK London High Commission ☏020/7258 6600.
USA Washington DC Embassy ☏202/682 1740. Consulates General in Atlanta, Boston, Buffalo, Chicago, Dallas, Denver, Detroit, Los Angeles, Miami, Minneapolis, New York and Seattle. Consulates in Anchorage, Houston, Raleigh, Philadelphia, Phoenix, San Diego and San Francisco.

Insurance

Prior to travelling, you should take out an insurance policy to cover against theft, loss and illness or injury. Before paying for a new policy, however, it's worth checking whether you already have some degree of coverage. Credit card companies, home-insurance policies and private medical plans sometimes cover you and your belongings when you're abroad. Most travel agents, tour operators, banks and insurance brokers will be able to help you, or you could consider the travel insurance offered by Rough Guides. Remember that when securing baggage insurance, make sure that the per-article limit – typically under £500/US$900 – will cover your most valuable possession.

After exhausting the possibilities above, you might want to contact a **specialist travel insurance company**. A typical travel insurance policy provides coverage for the loss of baggage, tickets and a certain amount of cash or traveller's cheques, as well as the cancellation or curtailment of your trip. Most policies exclude so-called **dangerous sports** unless an extra premium is paid. Many policies can be adapted to reflect the coverage you want – for example, sickness and accident benefits can often be excluded or included at will. If you do take medical coverage, verify if benefits will be paid during treatment or only after your return home, and whether there is a 24-hour medical emergency number. If you need to make a claim, keep receipts for medicines and medical treatment. Also, if you have anything stolen from you, you must file an official police report.

Rough Guides travel insurance

Rough Guides has teamed up with Columbus Direct to offer you **travel insurance** that can be tailored to suit your needs.

Readers can choose from many different travel insurance products, including a low-cost **backpacker** option for long stays; a **short break** option for city getaways; a typical **holiday package** option; and many others. There are also annual **multi-trip** policies for those who travel regularly, with variable levels of cover available. Different sports and activities (trekking, skiing, etc) can be covered if required on most policies.

Rough Guides travel insurance is available to the residents of 36 different countries with different language options to choose from via our website – ⓦwww .roughguidesinsurance.com – where you can also purchase the insurance.

Alternatively, UK residents should call ☎0800 083 9507; US citizens should call ☎1-800 749-4922; Australians should call ☎1 300 669 999. All other nationalities should call ☎+44 870 890 2843.

Health

It is vital to have travel insurance against potential medical expenses. Canada has an excellent health service, but non-residents are not entitled to free health care, and medical costs can be astronomical, depending on the treatment. If you have an accident, medical services will get to you quickly and charge you later.

Doctors and pharmacies

Doctors and dentists can be found listed in the *Yellow Pages*, though for **medical emergencies** (as well as fire and police) call ☎911. If you are bringing medicine prescribed by your doctor, carry a copy of the prescription – first, to avoid problems at customs and immigration; second, for renewing medication with Canadian doctors, as required.

As you would expect, Toronto has scores of **pharmacies.** In particular, Shopper's Drug Mart has several central pharmacy locations, including BCE Place, 161 Bay St at Front (☎416/777-1300); the Eaton Centre (☎416/979-9373); the Royal Bank Plaza, 200 Bay St (☎416/865-0001); and at 728 Yonge St and Charles (☎416/920-0098). For a **holistic apothecary**, try The Big Carrot, at 348 Danforth Ave (☎416/466-2129, ⓦwww .thebigcarrot.ca), a large whole-foods co-op with a wide selection of herbal remedies and health products; it is located three blocks east of Broadview Avenue.

Specific health problems

Canada requires no specific vaccinations, but problems can arise if you venture out into the backcountry; Algonquin Provincial Park (see p.133) is a case in point. Here, although tap water is generally safe to drink, it's prudent to ask first. You should also always **boil backcountry water** for at least ten minutes to protect against the **Giardia** parasite (or "beaver fever"). The parasite thrives in warm water, so be careful about swimming in hot springs – if possible, keep nose, eyes and mouth above water. Symptoms are intestinal cramps, flatulence, fatigue, weight loss and vomiting, all of which can appear up to a week after infection. If left untreated, more unpleasant complications can arise, so see a doctor immediately if you think you've contracted it.

Blackfly and **mosquitoes** are notorious for the problems they cause hikers and campers, and are especially bad in areas near standing water and throughout most of northern and much of central Ontario. **Horseflies** are another pest. Late April to June is the blackfly season, and the mosquito season is from June until about October. If you're planning an expedition into the wilderness, you'd be well-advised to take three times the recommended daily dosage of **vitamin B complex** for two weeks before you go, and to take the recommended dosage while you're in Canada; this cuts down bites by up to seventy-five percent.

Once you're there, **repellent creams** and **sprays** may help: the best are those containing DEET. The ointment version of Deep-Woods Off is the best brand, with 95 percent DEET. If you're camping or picnicking you'll find that burning coils or candles containing allethrin or citronella can help. If you're walking in an area that's rife with pests, it's well worth taking a gauze mask to protect your head and neck; wearing white clothes and no perfumed products also makes you less attractive to the insects. Once bitten, an **antihistamine cream** like phenergan is the best antidote. On no account go anywhere near an area marked as a blackfly mating ground – people have died from bites sustained when the creatures are in heat. Also dangerous, and recently arrived in Ontario, is **West Nile virus**, a mosquito-born affliction with life-threatening properties; up until now, the virus has only appeared in a handful of places in southern Ontario, but it may spread – so pay attention to local advice.

If you develop a large rash and flu-like symptoms, you may have been bitten by a tick carrying lyme borreliosis, or "**lyme disease**". This is easily curable, but if left untreated can lead to nasty complications, so again see a doctor as soon as possible. It's spreading in Canada, especially in the more southerly and wooded parts of the country and consequently it's a good idea to check on its prevalence with the local tourist authority. It may also be advisable to buy a strong **tick repellent** and to wear long socks, trousers and sleeved shirts when walking.

In backcountry areas, look out for **poison ivy**, which grows in many places, but particularly in a belt across southern Ontario. If you're likely to be walking in affected areas, ask at tourist offices for tips on where it is and how to recognize the plant, which causes itchy open blisters and lumpy sores up to ten days after contact. If you do come into contact with it, wash your body and clothes as soon as possible, smother yourself in calamine lotion and try not to scratch. In serious cases, hospital emergency rooms can give antihistamine or adrenalin jabs.

Information, websites and maps

Information on Toronto is easy to get hold of, either via the Internet, or, after arrival, from Downtown's Ontario Tourism Travel Information Centre. Maps are widely available from bookshops and newsagents.

Visitor information

The excellent **Ontario Tourism Travel Information Centre**, at street level inside the Atrium on Bay mall, 20 Dundas St West at Yonge (Mon–Fri 10am–9pm, Sat 10am–6pm & Sun noon–5pm; ☎1-800/ONTARIO, or within Toronto ☎1-905/282-1721), stocks a comprehensive range of information on all the **major attractions** in Toronto and throughout Ontario. Most of the stuff is free, including reasonably good-quality city **maps**, the *Ride Guide* to the city's transport system, and **entertainment** details in the monthly magazine *Where*. Ontario Tourism will also book hotel **accommodation** on your behalf both in Toronto and across all of Ontario. They also sell the City Pass (see p.47) and operate an all-encompassing website, ⓦwww.ontariotravel.net, which is particularly strong on practical information.

Alternatively, visit the **Info TO visitor information centre** (daily 9am–5pm), located in the city's Convention Centre at 255 Front St West, a couple of minutes' walk west from Union Station. Privately run, the TO centre is more geared-up for selling tour tickets than providing information, though they do have a reasonable supply of free literature on the city and its environs. They are not, however, nearly as good as the Ontario Tourism Travel Information Centre.

Surprisingly, **Tourism Toronto**, the city's official visitor and convention bureau, does not have an information office, but it does run a **telephone information line**, whose operators can handle most city queries and will make hotel reservations on your behalf (Mon–Fri 8.30am–6pm, Sat 9am–6pm, Sun 10am–6pm; ☎1-800/363-1990 or 416/203-2500). At time of writing, they are also planning to introduce an online accommodation booking service via their website, ⓦwww.torontotourism.com.

Useful websites

ⓦ**www.ago.net** The Art Gallery of Ontario comprehensive site provides high-quality reproductions of the gallery's key paintings and details of its temporary exhibitions. Plus, there's information regarding the museum's many programmes, including lectures, guided tours and art courses.

ⓦ**www.canada411.ca** Twelve million personal and business listings.

ⓦ**www.canadianhockey.ca** Proof positive that Canadians are passionate about their national sport, ice hockey.

ⓦ**www.city.toronto.on.ca** Official municipal site covering everything from living in Toronto through to tourist attractions. Has links to a series of city maps that you can use to pinpoint local amenities, and carries a guide to various concerts and events.

ⓦ**www.discoverniagara.com** Details of Niagara Falls' attractions, accommodation and restaurants.

ⓦ**www.gaytoronto.com** A useful starting point if you're looking to find out what's happening on the male scene, but it has precious little information for women. There's a useful bulletin board service, which has an accommodation section.

ⓦ**www.martiniboys.com** Perhaps the best online guide of Toronto's hottest and coolest bars and clubs, as well as intelligent, well-written restaurant reviews. The Martini Boys are invaluable in a town that takes eating and drinking so seriously.

ⓦ**www.moltencore.com** Molten Core, an admittedly partisan guide to the city's drinking, eating and, more especially, club and live music scene, features entertaining, provocative and well-informed reviews.

ⓦ**www.niagaraparks.com** The official website of the Niagara Parks Commission, providing information on all the major attractions in and around Niagara Falls. Has a link to a "falls cam", which broadcasts live pictures of the cascade.

ⓦ**www.ontariotravel.net** Whether you're planning a trip to Toronto or a more wide-ranging holiday in the province of Ontario, Ontario Tourism's excellent official site is regularly updated. Has an events calendar, maps, a travel tips section,

weather forecasts, and an accommodation feature that allows you to enter criteria and then book reservations.

ⓦ**www.thestar.com** The *Toronto Star* is the city's best newspaper; its website is strong on news, sports and weather updates. There's also a regularly updated "what's on" section covering local music, film and TV schedules.

ⓦ**www.toronto.com** One of the city's best and most comprehensive websites. Designed for people who live in Toronto, the site features plenty of good insider perspective. The online hotel reservations are handy for visitors, and if you decide you like the city well enough, you can always surf apartment availability.

ⓦ**www.tribemagazine.com** This free magazine, focusing on the dance-music scene in Canada, is available online in full, and gives frequently updated details on Toronto's clubland.

Maps

The **maps** in this guide should be perfectly adequate for most purposes, but if you want something a bit more comprehensive, best is the rip-proof, waterproof *Rough Guide Toronto Map* (1:16,000 to 1:27,000; Can$13.99/US$8.99/UK£4.99), which details the city's streets and pinpoints recommended restaurants, bars, sights and shops along the way.

If you plan to venture out into the wilds of Ontario, the best resource available is MapArt's excellent *Ontario Road Atlas* (mostly 1:250,000), a 100-page book that retails at Can$20; for shorter trips, the same company's *Ontario* map (1:750,000 to 1:1725,000; Can$5) is both clear and accurate.

Arrival

Located 25km northwest of the city centre, Toronto Pearson International Airport is linked to almost every important metropolis in the world, as well as every major Canadian town and city. The vast majority of visitors to Toronto arrive by plane.

Toronto's **bus and train stations** are conveniently located downtown and they link Toronto to a wide range of Canadian and American cities. Those arriving **by car** will find the city encircled by motorways, a straightforward drive except during rush hour when traffic congestion can be a real pain.

By air

Arriving by air, you'll almost certainly land at **Toronto Pearson International**, about forty minutes by car from Downtown. The airport is currently being renovated with the addition of a flashy new terminal, which will replace the oldest of the three existing terminals by 2007. In the meantime, two terminals are devoted to international flights, and one to domestic; in the long-term, there will just be two terminals – one for international, the other for domestic and US flights. Each terminal has – or will have – a full range of facilities, including money-exchange offices, ATMs and free hotel hotlines. A free, 24-hour airport coach shuttle – The Link – connects the terminals.

From the airport on the Airport Express bus

The **Airport Express bus** (daily, one every 20–30min, 5am–1am; T905/564-6333, W www .torontoairportexpress.com) picks up passengers outside all the terminals and heads toward Downtown, taking between forty and sixty minutes to get there – though heavy traffic can make the journey considerably longer. The bus drops passengers at the coach station and seven of Toronto's major hotels: the *Westin Harbour Castle*, *Fairmont Royal York*, *InterContinental*, *Sheraton Centre*, *Bond Place*, *Holiday Inn on King* and the *Delta Chelsea Inn*.

Tickets for the airport bus can be purchased either at the kiosks next to the bus stop outside each of the terminal buildings or from the driver. A one-way fare costs Can$15.50, and round-trip is Can$26.75.

From the airport by TTC bus

Much less expensive, if rather more time-consuming, are the several **bus services** linking the airport with the city's subway network. The two fastest are operated by the **TTC** (Toronto Transit Commission): the **Airport Rocket** (#192; Mon–Sat 5.30am–1.30am & Sun 8am–1am every 15–40mins; Can$2.50 one-way), takes about twenty minutes to reach Kipling subway station, at the west end of the subway network. From there, it takes another twenty minutes or so by subway (which operates Mon–Sat 6am–1am, Sun 9am–1am) to get downtown. The second option, TTC bus **#58A**, links the airport with Lawrence West subway station, to the north of Downtown (daily 5am–1am every 15–30mins; 45mins; Can$2.50 one-way). Buses leave from designated **stops** at each of the terminal buildings and payment can be made to the driver.

From the airport by limo and taxi

There's an airport **limo service** (a shared taxi system) next to each terminal's bus platform; limos cost about Can$46 per person for the journey from the airport to Downtown. Unlike taxis, the price is fixed – an important consideration if you arrive (or leave) during rush hour; the disadvantage is that they (mostly) only leave when they're full. Individual **taxis** charge about the same – say $50 from the airport to the city centre – but fares are metered.

Toronto City Centre Airport

On weekdays only, Air Canada (☎1-888/ 247-2262) operates flights from Ottawa and London, Ontario, into the much smaller **Toronto City Centre Airport**, which is on Hanlan's Point in Toronto's harbour, close to Downtown. From the airport, there's a free **minibus service** to the *Royal York Hotel*, on the corner of Front Street West and York Street.

By bus and by train

Toronto's **coach terminal** is located at 610 Bay Street, metres from Dundas Street West and a five-minute walk from the subway stop at the corner of Yonge and Dundas. If you're arriving late at night, note that the bus station's immediate environs are unsavoury – though it only takes a couple of minutes to reach more reassuring parts of Downtown. Nonetheless, if you're travelling alone and late at night, it's probably best to take a taxi to your ultimate destination.

All incoming trains arrive at **Union Station**, at the junction of Bay Street and Front Street West. The complex, which is the hub of the city's public transportation system, includes a subway station and holds the main terminal for the **GO trains and buses** that service the city's suburbs. Details of GO services are available at their station ticket offices, by phone on toll-free ☎1-888/438-6646 (within Toronto ☎416/869-3200) and on their website, ⊛www.gotransit.com.

By car

From Niagara Falls and points west along Lake Ontario, most traffic arrives via the **QEW** (Queen Elizabeth Way), which funnels into the **Gardiner Expressway,** an elevated motorway (notorious for delays) that cuts across the southern side of Downtown, just south of Front Street.

From the east, most drivers opt for the equally busy **Hwy-401**, which sweeps along Lake Ontario before veering off to slice through the city's suburbs north of Downtown. Driving in from the north, take **Hwy-400**, which intersects with Hwy-401 northwest of the centre, or **Hwy-404**, which meets Hwy-401 northeast of the centre. Note that on all routes you can expect delays during rush hours (roughly 7.30–9.30am and 4.30–6.30pm).

To relieve congestion on Hwy-401, an alternative motorway, **Hwy-407ETR**, has been built further north on the city's outskirts. It was North America's first all-electronic toll highway: instead of tollbooths, each vehicle is identified by an electronic tag (a transponder), and the invoice is posted later. **Toll charges** are fixed but vary – at peak times vehicles are charged 15¢ per kilometre – and there's also a small supplementary charge per trip for any vehicle without a transponder; these vehicles are identified by licence plate photos. If you rent a car, be aware that rental companies slap on an extra administration charge (of around $15) if you take their vehicles on this road.

City transport and guided tours

Fast, frequent and efficient, Toronto's public transportation system is operated by the Toronto Transit Commission (TTC), whose integrated network of subways, buses and streetcars, or trams, serves virtually every corner of the city. The TTC operates a 24-hour information line on ☎416/393-4636 with operator assistance available daily from 8am to 6pm; they also have a website, ⓦwww.ttc.ca.

With the exception of Downtown, where all the major sights are within easy walking distance of one another, your best option is to use public transport to hop between attractions – especially in the cold of winter or the sultry summertime. Much to its credit, the TTC has gone to great lengths to assure the safety of its passengers: all subway stations have well-lit **DWAs** (Designated Waiting Areas), intercom connections with TTC staff, and closed-circuit TV for monitoring. In addition, TTC buses operate a **Request Stop Program**, which allows women travelling alone late at night (9pm–5am) to get off buses wherever they want, and not just at regular TTC stops. A similarly positive approach has been adopted for passengers with disabilities, who can use a dedicated service, Wheel-Trans (see p.43).

On every part of the TTC system, a **single journey costs** Can$2.50 (local students and seniors Can$1.70; children ages 2–12 $0.60; children under two travel free). Paper **tickets** are available at all subway stations and from bus and streetcar drivers. Metallic **tokens** can also be used, but these are only issued at subway stations and they are impossibly small and difficult to keep track of. More economically, a batch of five tickets or tokens can be bought for Can$10, or Can$20 for ten, at any subway station and at many convenience stores and newsstands. Each ticket or token entitles passengers

to one complete journey of any length on the TTC system. If this involves more than one type of transport, it is necessary to get a paper **transfer** at your point of entry. Streetcar and bus drivers issue them, as do the automatic machines located at every subway station. A **day pass** costs Can$8 and provides one adult with unlimited TTC travel all day on Saturdays and Sundays, and after 9.30am on weekdays. On Sundays, the same pass can also be used as a family ticket, covering up to six people with a maximum of two adults.

The subway

Toronto's **subway**, the core of the city's public transportation network, is a simple, two-line system (see our map at the back of the book). One line cuts east to west along Bloor Street and Danforth Avenue, while the other forms a loop with Union Station at its head: north of Union, one part of this subway line runs along University Avenue, the other along Yonge Street. Transferring between the two subway lines is possible at three stations only: Spadina, St George and Bloor-Yonge. The subway operates Mon–Sat 6am–1.30am, Sun 9am–1.30am.

Buses and streetcars

The subway provides the backbone of the TTC system, but its services are faithfully

Orientation and street numbers

Yonge Street is Toronto's principal north–south artery. Main drags perpendicular to Yonge use this intersection to change from **west to east** – Queen Street West, for example, becomes Queen Street East when it crosses Yonge. Note, therefore, that 1000 Queen Street West, for example, is a long way from 1000 Queen Street East.

supplemented by **buses and streetcars**. The system couldn't be simpler, as a bus and/or streetcar station adjoins every major subway stop. Hours of operation vary with the route, but are comparable with subway times; there is also a limited network of **night buses** running along key routes hourly or so between 1am and 6am.

Commuter lines

In addition to subways, streetcars and buses, the TTC runs several **commuter lines**. The most useful is the **Scarborough Rapid Transit**, a streetcar service that picks up passengers at the eastern terminus of the Bloor-Danforth subway line and makes a five-stop trek to the heart of Scarborough, a Toronto suburb (see p.99). Transfers from the rest of the TTC network are valid on the Scarborough Rapid Transit. Finally, **GO trains** (☎416/869 3200, ⓦwww.gotransit.com) arrive and depart from Union Station, and link the city's various suburbs and satellite towns. There are no free transfers from the TTC system to GO train lines, though these are primarily used by commuters and little used by tourists based in the city.

Taxis

Taxis cruise the city in numbers and can be hailed from any street corner. Give the driver your destination and ask the approximate price before you start. Fares are generally reasonable, based on a fixed tariff of Can$2.75 for a pick-up and then 25¢ for every .19km thereafter. As an example, a ride from Union Station to the far side of Cabbagetown should cost around $10. Taxis can also be reserved in advance; of the multitude of companies to choose from, two of the most reliable are Co-op Cabs (☎416/504-2667) and Diamond Taxicab (☎416/366-6868). Toronto taxi drivers anticipate a tip of ten to fifteen percent on the total fare.

Guided tours

Guided tours are big business in Toronto and the range of what's on offer is exemplary – from heritage walks and boat cruises through to the more predictable coach tours. One of the best options is the free **Heritage Toronto Walks** (☎416/338-1338, ⓦwww.heritage toronto.org) organized by the city's Heritage Board. Running from late April to early July, about twenty different walks are offered once or twice each season, exploring everything from the old "Mansions of Jarvis Street" and "Nature on the Toronto Waterfront" to "The Yorkville Music Scene of the 1960s" and the neighbourhood of Cabbagetown (see p.84). No reservations are required, you just turn up at the appointed time and place; walks take between one and a half and two and a half hours.

Amongst the commercial guided tour operators, **Gray Line** (☎1-800/594-3310 or 416/594-3310, ⓦwww.grayline.ca) operates fairly enjoyable city **bus tours**, the most inexpensive of which is a two-hour zip round the main attractions for Can$37 (mid-May to Sept; one daily). They also run ten-hour coach trips to Niagara Falls (all year, one or two daily; Can$130) and twelve-hour excursions to Georgian Bay (see p.130), including an island cruise (June–Oct; one daily; Can$65). Perhaps of more appeal, Gray Line also operates **hop-on, hop-off tours of the city** in double-decker buses. These vehicles shuttle around the city centre between 9am and 4pm, appearing at regular intervals (thirty minutes to an hour) at about twenty major attractions. A ticket, valid for three days, costs Can$34. One good place to join the tour is the stop on the corner of York and Front streets, near the CN Tower. On all Gray Line trips, there are concessionary fares for seniors (age 60+) and children (ages 5–11).

Rather more intimate – and a good deal more economical – is **Travel Express** (☎905/855 5252), which operates guided minibus tours to (and of) Niagara Falls for Can$70. If you want to take a boat trip, the

Mariposa Cruise Line (☎416/203-0178; ⓦwww.mariposacruises.com) offers a good range of lake and harbour tours from mid–May to Sept; boats depart from the jetty beside the Queen's Quay Terminal building, at the foot of York St. Alternatively, the **Great Lakes Schooner Company** (☎416/203-2322; ⓦwww .greatlakesschooner.com) features genuine sailing trips on a three-master, the *Kajama* (June–Aug; one to three daily; Can$20). There are lots of other options and the annual *Visitor Guide*, available at either of the city's tourist offices (see p.30), outlines most of them.

Costs, money and banks

By western European standards, Toronto is very reasonably priced, with most basic items – from maps through to food and clothing – costing significantly less than back home. US residents and Australians, on the other hand, will find prices about the same, maybe a little higher, but not by much. As for dining and drinking, the sheer number of restaurants and bars keeps prices down. Less positively, accommodation, almost certainly your major outlay, is generally more expensive than in the rest of Canada, though there are plenty of bargains to be had. Throughout the guide, standard prices are given in Canadian dollars ($); where there might be any confusion between Canadian and American dollars, especially in the "Basics" section, we distinguish between the two (Can$ and US$).

Daily costs

If you're prepared to buy your own picnic lunch, stay in hostels, and stick to the least expensive bars and restaurants, you could scrape by on around Can$55/US$45/£25 per day. Staying in a good B&B, eating out in medium-range restaurants most nights and drinking often in bars, you'll go through at least Can$140/US$120/£65 per day, with the main variable being the cost of your room. On Can$220/$180/£100 per day and upwards, you'll be limited only by your energy reserves – though if you're planning to stay in the best hotels and to have a big night out pretty much every night, this still won't be enough. As always, if you're travelling alone you'll spend much more on accommodation than you would in a group

of two or more: most hotels do have single rooms, but they're fixed at about 75 percent (ie not half) of the price of a double.

Restaurants don't come cheap, but costs remain manageable if you avoid the extras and concentrate on the main courses, which start at around Can$11/US$9/£5 – though you can, of course, pay a lot more. **Tipping** at a restaurant is expected – between ten and fifteen percent – unless the service has been dire; taxi drivers expect a tip too, in the same percentages. **Museum admission prices** are mostly in the Can$7/US$5/£3 range, but discounts of at least fifty percent are routinely available for children, seniors and students; indeed, **concessionary fares and rates** are offered on all sorts of things, including public transport (which is already fairly inexpensive, at Can$2.50 a ride).

Finally, a word about **taxation**. Virtually all prices in Canada for everything from bubble-gum to hotel rooms are quoted without tax, which means that the price you see quoted is not the price you'll end up paying. Across the province of Ontario, which includes Toronto, there's a **Provincial Sales Tax** (PST) of eight percent on most goods and services, including hotel and restaurant bills; this is supplemented by the **Goods and Services Tax** (GST), a seven percent levy applied nationwide. As a small mercy, visitors can claim a **GST and PST rebate** on certain outgoings. The rules are complicated, but broadly GST rebates are available on payments of Can$50 and over that involve hotel accommodation and goods you are taking home with you; the total claimed must be at least Can$14. PST rebates apply on shopping receipts where you have spent Can$625 or more. **Claim forms** are available at many hotels, shops and airports. Return them, with **all original receipts**, to the address given on the form. Those returning overland to the US can claim their rebate at selected border duty-free shops. For more information, call either ☎905/791-5007, or consult ⓦwww.nationaltaxrefund.com.

Currency

Canadian currency is the dollar ($), made up of 100 cents (¢) to the dollar. Coins are issued in 1¢ (penny), 5¢ (nickel), 10¢ (dime), 25¢ (quarter), $1 and $2 denominations; the $1 coin is known as a "loonie", after the bird on one face, the newer $2 coin is mostly called the "twoonie". Paper currency comes in $5, $10, $50, $100, $500 and $1000 denominations. Although US dollars are widely accepted, it's mostly on a one-for-one basis, and as the US dollar is worth more than its Canadian counterpart, it makes sense to exchange US currency at a bank or similar, rather than going shopping with it.

As regards **exchange rates**, at the time of writing Can$1 is worth US$0.83, £0.46, AUS$1.08, and €0.67. For the most up-to-date rates, check the currency converter website ⓦwww.oanda.com.

Traveller's cheques

The main advantage of buying **traveller's** cheques is that they are a safe way of carrying funds. All well-known brands in all major currencies are widely accepted in Toronto, with US dollar and Canadian dollar cheques being the most common. The usual fee for their purchase is one to two percent of face value, though this fee is often waived if you buy the cheques through a bank where you have an account. Be sure to have plenty of the $10 and $20 denominations for everyday transactions, and keep the purchase agreement and a record of **check serial numbers** safe and separate from the checks themselves. In the event that checks are lost or stolen, the issuing company will expect you to report the loss immediately; most companies claim you'll have replacements within 24 hours.

ATMs and debit and credit cards

Toronto has plenty of **ATMs**, with a particular concentration in the city centre. Most ATMs accept a host of **debit cards**, including all those carrying the Cirrus coding. If in doubt, check with your bank to find out whether the card you wish to use will be accepted – and if you need a new (international) PIN. You'll rarely be charged a transaction fee, as the banks make their profits from applying different exchange rates. **Credit cards** can be used in ATMs too, but in this case transactions are treated as loans, with interest accruing daily from the date of withdrawal. All major credit cards, including American Express, Visa and MasterCard, are widely accepted in Toronto.

Banks and exchange

If you need to change money, Toronto's **banks** offer reasonable rates. Banks are legion and, although opening hours vary, all are open Mon–Fri 10am–3pm at the very least. Two central locations for the Toronto Dominion (TD) bank, one of the city's largest, are 77 Bloor St at Bay St and 65 Wellesley

Lost or stolen credit card contact numbers

American Express ☎905/474-9280
MasterCard ☎1-800/361-0070
Visa ☎1-800/847-2911

St East. Outside regular banking hours, you might consider a **bureau de change**. One of the most reliable is the Travel Information Centre Currency Exchange (Mon–Fri 10am–9pm, Sat 10am–6pm & Sun noon–5pm), 20 Dundas St West at Yonge St, adjacent to Ontario Tourism. Alternatively, try Thomas Cook, 10 King St E (☎416/863-1611), or Calforex, whose main branch is at 170 Bloor St W (☎416/921-4872). American Express cheques can be cashed at their downtown office, 50 Bloor St W (☎416/967-3411).

Wiring money

Having **money wired** from home using one of the companies listed below is costly, and should only be considered as a last resort. It can be slightly cheaper to have your own bank send the money through, but for that you'll need to nominate a receiving bank in Toronto and confirm the arrangement with them before you set the wheels in motion back home; any large branch will do. The sending bank's fees are geared to the amount being transferred and the urgency of the service you require – the fastest transfers, taking two or three days, start at around £25/US$45 for the first £300–400/US$540–725.

Money-wiring companies

Travelers Express/MoneyGram US ☎1-800/444-3010, Canada ☎1-800/933-3278, UK, Ireland and New Zealand ☎00800/6663 9472, Australia ☎0011800/6663 9472, ⓦwww .moneygram.com.
Western Union US and Canada ☎1-800/CALL-CASH, Australia ☎1800/501 500, New Zealand ☎0800/005 253, UK ☎0800/833 833, Republic of Ireland ☎66/947 5603, ⓦwww.westernunion .com. (Customers in the US and Canada can send money online.)

Post, phones and email

Canada in general and Toronto in particular has an efficient postal system. Also, after a tardy start, mobile phone coverage across the city and the rest of southern Ontario is fairly comprehensive. Telephone booths and mailboxes are liberally distributed across the city, and charges for both types of service are very reasonable. Internet and email access presents few problems: there is a scattering of Internet cafés, most hotels provide access of some description for their guests and the main reference library has a whole bank of public-access PCs.

Post

Canada Post operates branches in scores of locations, mostly as a discrete part of a larger retail outlet, principally pharmacies and stationery stores. Usual opening hours are Mon–Fri 9am–6pm and Sat 9am–noon. Specific **post offices** are thinner on the ground, but there are a number dotted across the city centre. One of the handiest is inside the Atrium on Bay mall, 20 Dundas St West at Yonge St (Mon–Fri 9am–6pm & Sat 9am–5pm). If you're posting letters to a Canadian address, always include the **postcode** or your mail may never get there. Apart from Canada Post branches or offices, **stamps** can be purchased from the lobbies of larger hotels, airports, train stations, bus terminals and many retail outlets and newsstands. Current **postal charges** are 50¢ for letters and postcards up to 30g within Canada, 85¢ for the same weight to the US, and Can$1.45 for international mail (also up to 30g).

Telephones

Public telephones are commonplace in Toronto, though the rise of the mobile phone means that their numbers will not increase and may well diminish. All are equipped for the hearing-impaired, and for making domestic or international calls; most accept pre-paid calling cards and credit cards in addition to coins. Local calls cost 25¢ from a public phone, but are free on private phones (though not usually hotel phones). All **phone books** contain maps of the Downtown core and display Toronto Transit Commission (TTC) routes; the *Yellow Pages*, a compendium of all business phone numbers, grouped by service, are especially informative.

When **dialling** any Canadian number, either local or long-distance, you must include the area code – ☎416 or ☎647 in Toronto. Long-distance calls beyond the area code from which you're dialling must be prefixed with "1". On public telephones, this "1" secures an operator intercept; the operator will tell you how much money you need to get connected. Thereafter, you'll be asked to shovel money in at regular intervals – so unless you're making a reverse-charge/ collect call you'll need a stack of quarters (25¢ pieces) handy, if your call will be of any length.

To confuse matters, some connections within a single telephone code area are charged at the long-distance rate, and thus need the "1" prefix; a recorded message will tell you this is necessary as soon as you dial the number. To save the hassle of carrying all this change, you could consider either buying a telephone card back home (see opposite) or here in Toronto. In Toronto, there are a number of telephone charge cards to choose from, with one of the more widely available being Bell's **Prepaid Calling Card**, sold in denominations of Can$5, Can$10 and Can$20. For further details of this and other Bell phone cards, contact their customer service department on ☎1-800/668 6878, ⓦwww.bell.ca.

As for **tariffs**, the cheap-rate period for calls is between 6pm and 8am during the week and all the weekend. Detailed rates are listed at the front of the Toronto telephone directory. Note also that many businesses, especially hotels, have **toll-free numbers** (prefixed by ☎1-800 or 1-888). Some of these can only be dialled from phones in the

same province, others from anywhere within Canada, and a few from anywhere in North America; as a rough guideline, the larger the organization, the wider its toll-free net. Finally, remember that although most hotel rooms have phones, there is almost always an exorbitant surcharge for their use.

Useful phone numbers

Directory enquiries from private phones local, regional and long-distance within North America ☎411; international, call the operator ☎0.
Directory enquiries from public phones local or regional ☎411; long-distance within North America ☎1+ area code + 555-1212; international, call the operator ☎0.
Emergencies (police, fire and ambulance) ☎911.
Operator (domestic and international) ☎0.
Phoning abroad from Toronto To Australia: ☎011 + 61 + area code minus zero + number; to the Republic of Ireland: ☎011 + 353 + area code minus zero + number; to New Zealand: ☎011 + 64 + area code minus zero + number; to the UK: ☎011 + 44 + area code minus zero + number; to the US: ☎1 + area code + number.
Phoning Toronto from abroad Dial your country's international access code for Canada, then the area code, followed by the number.

Telephone charge card

One of the most convenient ways of phoning home from abroad is via a **telephone charge card** issued by your home phone company. Using a PIN number and the card, you can make calls from most hotels and public and private phones that will be charged to your home telephone account. Since most major charge cards are free to obtain, it's certainly worth getting one at least for emergencies. Bear in mind, however, that rates aren't necessarily cheaper than calling from a Toronto public phone – it's just more convenient, not having to carry quarters around.

Mobile phones

If you want to use your **mobile phone** in Toronto, you may need to set up international cellular access with your phone provider before you set out. Also check out their **call charges**, as these can be exorbitant – especially as you are likely to be charged extra for incoming calls that originate from back home as the people calling you will be paying the usual (national) rate. The same sometimes applies to text messages, though in many cases these can now be received with the greatest of ease (no fiddly codes and so forth) and at ordinary rates. In Toronto, the mobile network covers almost all of the city and all but the remotest parts of Ontario. It works on GSM 1900, which means that mobiles bought in **Europe** need to be **triband** to gain cellular access.

Email

Toronto is well geared-up for Internet and email access with a healthy supply of **Internet cafés**. In addition, note that most of the better hotels provide email and Internet access for their guests free or at reasonable rates, as does Uptown's **Toronto Reference Library,** 789 Yonge St at Cumberland (Mon–Thurs 10am–8pm, Fri & Sat 10am–5pm, plus mid-Sept to late June Sun 1.30–5pm; ☏416/393-7131, ⓦwww .torontopubliclibrary.ca).

One of the best ways to keep in touch while travelling is to sign up with one of the free, **web-based email** providers like Yahoo! and Hotmail, accessible through ⓦwww .yahoo.com and ⓦwww.hotmail.com, respectively. In addition, ⓦwww.kropla.com is a useful website giving details of how to plug your laptop in when abroad; it also lists international phone codes and provides information about electrical systems in different countries.

Selected Internet cafés

Cyber Orbits 1 Gloucester ☏416/920-5912. Open 24 hrs.
Internet Café 370 Yonge St ☏416/408-0570. Open daily 6am–1am.
Net Space 275 Queen St W ☏416/597-2005. Open daily 8am–1am.
Net Space 2 2305 Yonge St ☏416/486-9071. Open daily 8am–1am.

The media

Toronto does well for newspapers and magazines, some of which are free, as well as for radio stations. By contrast, the TV channels on offer, both broadcast and cable, are largely uninspiring until after 11pm, at which point any number of truly strange and exotic programmes are launched at the unwary. Many shows that are deemed too risqué for general North American audiences find their previews on Toronto TV channels during the wee hours.

Newspapers and magazines

Toronto has two first-rate daily **newspapers**: the *Globe and Mail* and the *Toronto Star*. Both provide insight into every facet of the city, but the *Globe and Mail* is better for international coverage. The *Globe* is also Canada's main nationwide newspaper, its only rival being the comparable, if more rightist, *National Post*.

The **magazine** locals rush to is *Toronto Life* (ⓦwww.torontolife.com), which also does an excellent line of listings publications; "Where to Get Good Stuff Cheap" is a particular favourite and tends to sell out quickly.

A few **literary publications** deserve special note: the twice-yearly *Brick* (ⓦwww .brickmag.com) serves up an eclectic mix of book reviews, poetry, essays, memoirs and interviews, or you could burrow into *Blood & Aphorisms* (ⓦwww.strategicink.com/banda), which – despite its gothic title – publishes new writers of speculative fiction and has somehow managed to stay afloat for over a decade. For serious aficionados of local 'zines and comics, **The Beguiling**, 601 Markham St (℡416/533-9168, ⓦwww .beguiling.com) is a must-visit, as it stocks most of the indie publications.

TV and radio

Canadian TV is dominated by US sludge, though the publicly-subsidized **Cana-dian Broadcasting Corporation** (CBC) does fight a rearguard action for quality programmes, from drama through to documentary. The main local TV station is the chatty and rather inconsequential **City TV**. **Cable television** is commonplace, both in private homes and in the vast majority of hotel and motel rooms.

As regards **radio**, CBC Radio One (99.1 FM) is Toronto's frequency for the Canadian Broadcasting Corporation, an excellent source for public affairs, news and arts programming. For just news, try CFTR (680 AM) or CFRB (1010 AM). For easy rock, tune in to CHUM (104.5 FM) or MIX (99.9 FM). Harder rock is found on Q 107 (107.1 FM), and alternative sounds are on CFNY (102.1 FM). CISS (92.5 FM) does country, and CFMX (96.3 FM) or CBC Two (94.1 FM) are good for classical. There are also two excellent student stations that feature alternative and world artists, as well as news and events: CKLN (88.1 FM) from Ryerson Polytechnic, and CIUT (89.5 FM) from the University of Toronto.

Opening hours and public holidays

Shopping is a major Toronto pastime and opening hours are therefore very generous, though many places are closed on public holidays – excluding bars, restaurants and hotels. Public transport keeps moving on holidays, too, operating a skeleton service.

Opening hours

Most **shops** are open seven days a week, usually from 10am until anywhere from 8pm to 10pm Monday to Thursday; on Friday quite a few places close a little earlier, at 6pm or 7pm; weekend hours are usually Saturday 10am to 6pm or 7pm, and Sunday noon to 6pm. In addition, convenience stores, like 7-11, are routinely open much longer, often round the clock. **Office hours** are more restricted, characteristically Monday–Friday 9/9.30am–4.30/5pm. Most major **museums** are open daily from around 10am to 5pm or 5.30pm, with one late night a week, usually Thursday until 8pm or 9pm. As for **restaurants**, these are usually open daily from

Subterranean Toronto

For better or worse, Toronto has the world's largest **underground shopping complex**, over one thousand shops and stores spread out along a seemingly endless network of subterranean pedestrian walkways and mall basements. The network links over forty office towers and several major hotels and, best of all, keeps city folk well away from the extremes of their climate. The network stretches north from Union Station to the Eaton Centre and the coach terminal, and west–east from the CBC Broadcasting Centre to the King Street subway; access points – of which there are many – sport a multi-coloured sign inscribed "**PATH**".

11am to 11pm, with or without an afternoon break, from around 2.30/3pm to 5/6pm. **Bars** are open daily from 11am to 2am.

Public holidays

New Year's Day Jan 1
Good Friday varies; March/April
Easter Sunday varies; March/April
Victoria Day third Monday in May
Canada Day July 1

Labour Day first Monday in Sept
Thanksgiving second Monday in Oct
Christmas Day Dec 25
Boxing Day Dec 26
Also widely observed, but not official public holidays are:
Easter Monday varies; March/April
Simcoe Day first Monday in Aug
Remembrance Day Nov 11

Crime and personal safety

There's little reason why you should ever come into contact with either the Toronto Police Service or the Ontario Provincial Police, who safeguard the rest of the province: Toronto is one of the safest cities in North America and although there are a few crime hotspots, these are mostly on the city's peripheries.

Few citizens carry arms, muggings are uncommon, and street crime less commonplace than in many other major North American cities – though the usual cautions about poorly lit urban streets and so forth stand. Note also that the police are diligent in enforcing traffic laws.

Petty crime

Almost all the problems tourists encounter in Toronto are to do with **petty crime** – such as pickpocketing and bag-snatching – rather than more serious physical confrontations. As such, it's good to be on your guard and know where your possessions are at all times. Thieves often work in pairs and, although **theft** is far from commonplace, you should be aware of certain ploys, such as: the "helpful" person pointing out "birdshit" (actually shaving cream or similar) on your coat, while someone else relieves you of your money; being invited to read a card, map or newspaper on the street to distract your attention; or someone in a café moving for your drink with one hand while the other goes for your bag. If you're in a crowd of tourists, watch out for people moving in unusually close.

Sensible **precautions** against petty theft include: carrying bags slung across your neck and not over your shoulder; not carrying anything in pockets that are easy to dip into; and carrying photocopies of your passport, airline ticket and driving licence, while leaving the originals in your hotel safe, if possible. When you're looking for a hotel room, never leave your bags unattended, and, similarly, if you have a car, don't leave anything in view when you park: vehicle theft is still fairly uncommon, but luggage and valuables do make a tempting target.

If you are robbed, you'll need to go to the **police** to report it, not least because your insurance company will require a police report. Remember to make a note of the report number – or, better still, ask for a copy of the statement itself. Don't expect a great deal of concern if your loss is relatively small, and don't be surprised if the process of completing forms and formalities takes ages.

Personal safety

Although generally you can walk around the city without fear of **harassment or assault**, certain parts of Toronto are decidedly shady and neither is the overall Downtown atmosphere improved by the large number of (sometimes aggressive) beggars. There are no clearly defined "no-go" areas as such – though Sherbourne Street to the south of Queen Street East comes close – but on the other hand, pockets of seedy roughness are dotted here and there seemingly at random. Consequently, and especially until you are familiar with the city's layout, it's always best to err on the side of caution. Using **public transport**, even late at night, isn't usually a problem – but if in doubt take a taxi.

In the unlikely event that you are **mugged**, or otherwise threatened, never resist, and try to reduce your contact with the robber to a minimum; either just hand over what's wanted, or throw money in one direction and take off in the other; afterwards go straight to the police.

For **police emergencies** (as well as fire and ambulance), call ☎911. To reach the police in a **non-emergency situation**, call ☎1-888/310 1122 (24hr), or TDD ☎1-888/310- 1133.

Being arrested

If you're **detained** by the police, the arresting officer must identify him/herself. At the police station, detainees have the right to free but reasonable use of a telephone and legal counsel. For certain sorts of suspected offence – primarily gun- and drug-related – the police are likely to strip-search detainees, though these searches, and the frequency of them, remain controversial.

Travellers with disabilities

Toronto is one of the best places in the world to visit if you have mobility problems or other physical disabilities. All public buildings are required to be wheelchair-accessible and provide suitable toilet facilities, almost all street corners have dropped kerbs, and public telephones are specially equipped for hearing-aid users.

Operated by the TTC, the city's public transport system (see p.34) is disability-friendly, its bespoke **Wheel-Trans** operation providing a door-to-door transit service seven days a week (Mon–Fri 6am–1am, Sat & Sun 7am–1am). Further Wheel-Trans information is available on ☎416/393-4111 (Mon–Fri 8am–4pm). For other TTC route, fare and schedule information, call either ☎416/393-4636 or TTY ☎416/481-2523.

Information and contacts

Australia and New Zealand

ACROD (Australian Council for Rehabilitation of the Disabled) PO Box 60, Curtin ACT 2605; ☎02/6282 4333 (also TTY), ⊛www.acrod.org.au. Provides lists of travel agencies and tour operators.

Disabled Persons Assembly 4/173-175 Victoria St, Wellington, New Zealand ☎04/801 9100 (also TTY), ⊛www.dpa.org.nz. Resource centre with lists of travel agencies and tour operators.

UK and Ireland

Access Travel 6 The Hillock, Astley, Lancashire M29 7GW ☎01942/888 844, ⊛www.access-travel.co.uk. Helps travellers secure wheelchair-accessible accommodation, adapted vehicles, nursing services and more.

Holiday Care 2nd floor, Imperial Building, Victoria Rd, Horley, Surrey RH6 7PZ ☎0845/124 9971 or 0208/760 0072, ⊛www.holidaycare.org.uk. Offers free lists of accessible accommodation abroad – including North American destinations – plus a list of manageable attractions in the UK. Provides information on supplemental funding for vacations.

43

Irish Wheelchair Association Blackheath Drive, Clontarf, Dublin 3 ☎01/818 6400, ⓦwww.iwa .ie. Useful information about travelling abroad with a wheelchair.

Tripscope The Vassall Centre, Gill Ave, Bristol BS16 2QQ, ☎0845/7 58 56 41 ⓦwww.tripscope .org.uk. Provides a national telephone information service with free advice on UK and international travel.

US and Canada

Access-Able ⓦwww.access-able.com. Puts people with disabilities in contact with each other.

Directions Unlimited 123 Green Lane, Bedford Hills, NY 10507 ☎1-800/533-5343 or 914/241-1700. Travel agency specializing in bookings for people with disabilities.

Mobility International USA 451 Broadway, Eugene, OR 97401 ☎541/343-1284, ⓦwww .miusa.org. Answers travel questions and operates an exchange programme for the disabled. Annual membership includes quarterly newsletter.

Society for the Advancement of Travelers with Handicaps 347 5th Ave, New York, NY 10016 ☎212/447-7284, ⓦwww.sath.org. Nonprofit organization comprising travel agents, tour operators, hotels and airlines and travellers with disabilities.

Wheels Up! ☎1-888/38-WHEELS, ⓦwww .wheelsup.com. Provides discounted airfares, tours and cruises. Publishes a free monthly newsletter.

The City

The City

Downtown Toronto

T he skyscrapers etched across **Downtown Toronto**'s skyline witness the clout of a city that has discarded the dowdy provincialism of its early years to become the economic and cultural focus of English-speaking Canada. There's no false modesty here, kicking off with Toronto's mascot, the **CN Tower**, and continuing with the **Rogers centre**, formerly the **SkyDome**, the flashy stadium built for the Blue Jays and Argonauts sports teams. Close by, the plush and extravagant *Royal York* hotel marks the start of the **Banking District**, a brisk and bustling part of the city whose herd of tower blocks proceeds north to Queen Street. Here, modern behemoths like the **Toronto Dominion Centre** and the gold-coated **Royal Bank Plaza** are beacons of modern-day prosperity, but there are older high rises too, like the **Dominion Bank** and the **Canada Permanent Trust building**, whose sumptuous designs (circa 1920) trumpet the aspirations of previous generations. Toronto's business elite also funded Downtown's most enjoyable art gallery, the outstanding **Toronto Dominion Gallery of Inuit Art**.

At Queen Street, the Banking District gives way to the central **shopping** area, which revolves around the sprawling **Eaton Centre**. Immediately to the west is **City Hall**, another striking example of modern design, and the **Art Gallery of Ontario**, which houses the province's finest collection of paintings, as well as an entire gallery of sculptures by Henry Moore. Finally, on the western periphery of Downtown is **Fort York**, an accurate and intriguing reconstruction of the British garrison established here in 1793.

Downtown is best explored on **foot**, though the tower blocks can be a bit claustrophobic and local complaints that the city centre lacks a human dimension are legion. To be fair, this sentiment has been taken into account, and although it's a bit late in the day, efforts have been made to make the downtown core more people-friendly, with plazas, pavement cafés and street sculptures.

Toronto City Pass

If you are a diligent sightseer, you may be able to save money with the **Toronto City Pass**. Valid for nine days, the pass entitles visitors to free entrance to six of the city's most popular attractions – the CN Tower (see p.48), the Art Gallery of Ontario (see p.67), the Royal Ontario Museum (see p.79), Casa Loma (see p.85), the Ontario Science Centre (see p.104) and Toronto Zoo (see p.99). It costs $47 ($29.75 for 4–12 year olds) and can be purchased at any of the six sights.

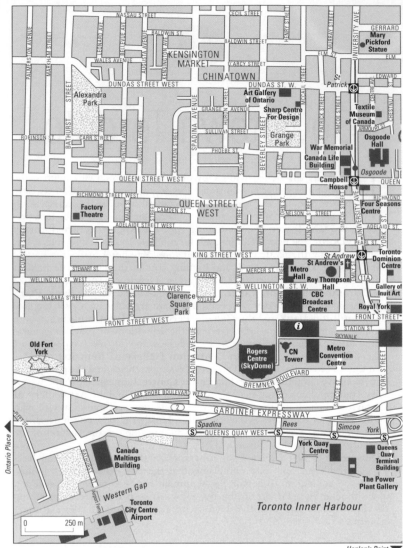

The CN Tower

Much to the dismay of many Torontonians, the **CN Tower**, 301 Front St West (daily: Sun–Thurs 9am–10pm, Fri & Sat 9am–10.30pm, sometimes later; observation deck & glass floor $20, Sky Pod $6 extra; ☏416/868-6937, ⊛www .cntower.ca; Union Station subway), has become the city's symbol. It's touted on much of the city's promotional literature, features on thousands of postcards and holiday snaps and has become the obligatory start to most tourist itineraries.

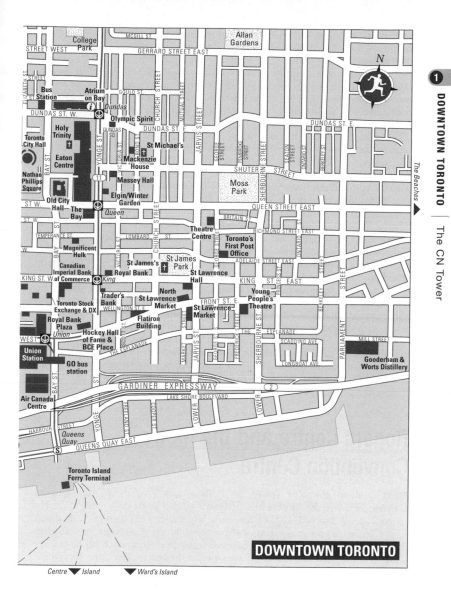

The Beaches ▶

Centre ▼ Island   ▼ Ward's Island

DOWNTOWN TORONTO

From anywhere in the city, it's impossible to miss its slender form poking high above the skyline, reminding some of French novelist Guy de Maupassant's quip about another famous tower: "I like to lunch at the Eiffel Tower because that's the only place in Paris I can't see it."

Unlikely as it may seem, the celebrity status of the CN Tower was entirely unforeseen, its origins plain and utilitarian. In the 1960s, the Canadian Broadcasting Company (CBC) teamed up with the railway conglomerate Canadian National (CN) to propose the construction of a bigger and better transmission antenna. CBC eventually withdrew from the project, but CN, who owned the land and saw a chance for profit, forged ahead. Much to the company's surprise, they found that the undertaking stirred intense public interest – so much so that long before the tower was completed, in April 1975, it was clear that its potential as a tourist sight would be huge: today, broadcasting only accounts for about twenty percent of the tower's income, with the rest provided by the two million visitors who throng here annually. Come early (especially on school holidays) to avoid the crowds.

The tallest structure in the world, the sleek, elegant tower tapers to a minaret-thin point 553m (1815ft) above the city centre; details of its construction are provided in a series of **photographs** and **touch-screen displays** on the mezzanine level just beyond the main access ramp and security check-in. This background information is extremely interesting, revealing all sorts of odd facts and figures, though it is hardly reassuring to know that the tower is hit by lightning between sixty and eighty times a year.

From the foot of the tower, **glass-fronted elevators** whisk you up the outside of the structure to the indoor and outdoor **Look Out level** galleries at 346m. These circular galleries provide views over the whole of the city, which appears surprisingly leafy, and markers help by pointing out the most conspicuous sights. This is also where you'll find the *360 Restaurant* (which slowly revolves around the tower, taking 72 minutes to make one revolution), and the reinforced **glass floor** – a vertigo thrill that goes some way to justifying the tower's pricey admittance fee. You are, however, still 100m from the top of the tower, with a separate set of lifts carrying visitors up to the **Sky Pod**, a confined little gallery that, frankly, doesn't justify the extra expense. On the way down, the lifts deposit passengers at the ground-floor souvenir shop, which adjoins an arcade full of (eminently missable) simulated film rides of bungee jumping and so on; there is an extra charge for these.

Rogers Centre and the Metro Convention Centre

Next door to the CN Tower, at 1 Blue Jays Way, stands the **Rogers Centre**, formerly the **SkyDome** (frequent guided tours depending on event schedules; call ☎416/341-2770 for latest timetable; $12.50; ⊛www.skydome.com), home to two major Toronto sports teams: the Argonauts, of Canadian football fame, and the Blue Jays baseball team (for more on both teams, see Chapter 14, Sports and outdoor activities). Opened in 1989, the SkyDome seats 53,000 and is used for special events and concerts, as well as sports. It was the first stadium in the world to have a fully retractable roof, an impressive feat of engineering with four gigantic roof panels mounted on rail tracks that together take just twenty minutes to cover the stadium's eight acres of turf and terrace. With every justification, the SkyDome was much heralded by the city, but however ingenious the design, the building itself is really rather ugly, and, despite the best efforts of artist **Michael Snow** – who added a pair of giant cartoon sculptures to the exterior: *The Audience Part 1* and *Part 2* – when the roof is closed it looks like a giant armadillo. (For more of Snow's work, check out the Eaton Centre, p.63.) Hour-long **guided tours** begin with a ten-minute **film** about the stadium's construction and continue with a

△ Michael Snow's *The Audience*

walking tour that takes in a team dressing room, the Blue Jays Memorabilia Suite and a stroll on the playing field.

On the other side of the CN Tower, the **Metro Convention Centre** straddles the rail lines into Union Station (see below), with the dreary North Building on one side, and the smart, chic South Building, with its acres of glass and steel, on the other. The former faces onto Front Street West, and the latter onto Bremner Boulevard. The South Building has the main entrance, where the foyer displays *The Turtle Pond* – a delightful mosaic of frogs, frogspawn and turtles. Here also, just outside the building, is an engaging sculpture of two whopping woodpeckers pecking away at a steel tree.

Union Station and the Air Canada Centre

A sheltered walkway called the **Skywalk** leads from the Metro Convention Centre to **Union Station** (Front St W and Bay St), a distinguished Beaux Arts structure designed in 1907 and finally completed in 1927. The station's exterior is imposing, with its long serenade of Neoclassical columns, but the interior is the real highlight, the vast **main hall** boasting a coffered and tiled ceiling of graceful design. Like other North American railway stations of the period, Union Station has the flavour of a medieval cathedral, with muffled sounds echoing through its stone cloisters, and daylight filtering through its high arched windows. The station's grandiose quality was quite deliberate. In the days when the steam train was the most popular form of transport, architects were keen to glorify the train station, and, in this case, to convey the idea of Canada's vastness – a frieze bearing the names of all the Canadian cities reachable by rail at the time of construction runs around the hall.

A short walk south from Union Station, the **Air Canada Centre**, 40 Bay St (☎416/815-5500, ⊕www.theaircanadacentre.com), is home to hockey's Maple Leafs and basketball's Raptors; see Chapter 14, Sports and outdoor activities, for more on these two teams. Hour-long **tours** of the Air Canada Centre ($12) are available, and include a visit to a dressing room and the Maple Leafs Memories and Dreams Suite, which looks at the team's history.

The Royal York hotel

Directly opposite the west end of the railway station, the **Royal York** hotel, 100 Front St W, was the largest and tallest building in the British Empire when it opened in 1929. The architects, Montreal's Ross and Macdonald, opted for the Beaux Arts style, so as to match the hotel with Union Station, but in lieu of the formal symmetries of its neighbour, the *Royal York* has a cascading, irregular facade with stylistic flourishes reminiscent of a French chateau. Originally, the hotel had its own concert hall, mini-hospital and 12,000-book library, and each of its one thousand rooms had a radio, private shower and bath. The hotel soon became a byword for luxury, where every well-heeled visitor to the city stayed, and although other, newer hotels have usurped its pre-eminent position in the last decade or two, a recent refurbishment has restored it as a favourite with visiting bigwigs. For full contact details, as well as what it costs to stay here, see p.140.

The Banking District

Opposite the east end of Union Station, the **Banking District,** whose skyscrapers march north as far as Adelaide, kicks off with the **Royal Bank Plaza**, 200 Bay St, where the two massive towers were designed by local architect Boris Zerafa during the architectural boom of the mid-1970s. Each tower is coated with a thin layer of gold, and despite Zerafa's assertion that the gold simply added texture to his creation, it's hard not to believe that the Royal Bank wanted to show off a bit too.

In between the *Royal York* hotel and the Royal Bank, a gated **stone stairway** climbs up from Front Street West to a tiny plaza overseen by a phalanx of skyscrapers. It's a delightful spot, in a heart-of-the-city sort of way, and Catherine Widgery's *City People* (1989), a folksy set of life-size metal figures attached to the stairway's walls, adds a touch of decorative élan. The walkway continues down to Wellington Street West, just a few metres from the southern tower – now the Waterhouse Tower – of the **Toronto Dominion Centre**, whose four reflective black blocks straddle Wellington Street between Bay and York. Arguably the most appealing of the city's modern skyscrapers, the four towers are without decoration, though as an ensemble they achieve an austere beauty that can't help but impress. Begun in 1964, they were designed by **Ludwig Mies van der Rohe** (1886–1969), one of the twentieth century's most influential architects. Rohe was influenced by a wide range of architectural styles,

> ## Selling air
>
> In one of the city's stranger ordinances, Toronto's buildings were once decreed to have a "notional maximum altitude". Owners of historic properties were not allowed to extend their buildings upwards, but they were permitted to sell the empty space between their roofs and the notional maximum to builders of new structures. Consequently, developers literally bought empty space and added it on to the maximum height they were already allowed for their buildings, thus creating the skyscrapers that the ordinance seemed to forbid.
>
> The arrangement enhanced neither the old nor the new buildings, and was quickly followed up by an even stranger agreement. By the late 1980s, preservationists had convinced the city that no more of the city's old buildings should be demolished. Developers, however, still wanted to build new Downtown buildings, and several deals emerged where a new complex would incorporate or literally engulf the old – the most extreme example being BCE Place at the corner of Yonge and Front streets (see p.58).

including Prussian Classicism and Russian Constructivism; he also served as the director of Bauhaus. In his last decades, he refined his architectural vision, seeking to establish contemplative, neutral spaces guided by his maxim-cum-motto "Less is more"; the Toronto Dominion Centre is a case in point.

The Toronto Dominion Gallery of Inuit Art

An outstanding collection of over a hundred pieces of inuit sculpture is spread over two levels at the **Toronto Dominion Gallery of Inuit Art**, in the (Mon–Fri 8am–6pm, Sat & Sun 10am–4pm; free) in the south – or Waterhouse Tower of the Toronto Dominion Cenre. The collection is owned by the Dominion Bank, who commissioned a panel of experts to celebrate Canada's Centennial in 1965 by collecting the best of postwar Inuit art. All the favourite themes of Inuit sculpture are here, primarily **animal and human studies** supplemented by a smattering of **metamorphic figures**, in which an Inuit adopts the form of an animal, either in full or in part. Other sculptures depict **deities**, particularly Nuliayuk the sea goddess (also known as Sedna). Inuit religious belief was short on theology, but its encyclopedic animism populated the Arctic with spirits and gods, the subject of all manner of Inuit folk tales. Christianity destroyed this traditional faith, but the legends survived and continue to feature prominently in Inuit art. Most of the sculptures are in **soapstone**, a greyish-blue stone that is easy to carve, though there are bone, ivory and caribou-antler pieces too. The only problem is the almost total lack of labelling, but a free **introductory booklet**, available from the rack at the start of the gallery, does provide some assistance.

In the **foyer**, beside the revolving doors, the gallery begins with **Johnny Inukpuk**'s raw, elemental *Mother Feeding Child* (1962), an exquisite piece in which a woman holds her child in an all-encompassing embrace. Hailing from Port Harrison, on the eastern shores of Hudson Bay, Inukpuk was one of the first Inuit sculptors to establish a reputation in the south, and his work has been collected since the late 1950s. There's another of his soapstone sculptures in the foyer as well – the *Tattooed Woman* is a fine, almost fierce portrayal of a woman in traditional attire, whose eyes stare out into the distance.

Upstairs, distributed among a dozen glass cabinets, is a superb selection of soapstone sculptures. In the first cabinet are two striking representations of Sedna, one by **Saggiak**, the other by **Kenojuak Ashevak**, both carved in Cape Dorset in 1965. Half-woman, half-seal, **Sedna**, the goddess of the sea and sometimes of life itself, is one of the key figures of Inuit mythology. Her story is a sad one. She was deceived by a young man who posed as a hunter, but was in fact a powerful shaman. Sedna married him and he promptly spirited her away from her family. Sedna's father gave chase and rescued his daughter, but on the return journey they were assailed by a violent storm conjured by the shaman. Terrified, the father threw his daughter overboard, and when she repeatedly attempted to get back into the boat, he chopped off her fingers and then her hands. These bits and pieces became whales, seals, walruses and fish, but Sedna herself sank to the depths of the ocean, where she remains.

Other striking works to look for include the magnificent *Bear*, by Cape Dorset's **Pauta Saila**, located four cabinets along from the Sedna sculptures. The bear is crudely carved, but the jaws are all that's needed to convey the animal's ferocity, and the blurring of the trunk and the legs gives the appearance of great strength. There's also a wise-looking, but somehow anguished,

Fort York

Modern-day Toronto traces its origins to **Fort York** (late May to Aug daily 10am–5pm; Sept to late May Mon–Fri 10am–4pm, Sat & Sun 10am–5pm; $6; ☎416/392-6907), a colonial stockade built in 1793 on the shores of Lake Ontario to bolster British control of the Great Lakes. Since then, landfill has pushed the lakeshore southwards and today the fort, which has been attractively reconstructed, is unlucky to be marooned in the shadow of the Gardiner Expressway just to the west of Bathurst Street. There are **two entrances** to the fort – a (well-signed) main entrance off Lakeshore Boulevard West along Fleet St and then Garrison Rd; and a pedestrians' back entrance via a path off Bathurst Street. To get to the latter, head west along Front Street from the CBC Broadcasting Centre (see p.56), turn left onto Bathurst, walk over the bridge and the path is on the right; to shorten the walk, take the King Street tram west to King and Bathurst. To reach the front entrance, take either the Bathurst streetcar (#511) or streetcar #509 from Union Station, and get off on Fleet Street at the foot of Garrison Road; from here the fort is a ten-minute walk.

Fort York was initially a half-hearted, poorly fortified affair, partly because of a lack of funds, but mainly because it was too remote to command much attention – never mind that the township of York was the capital of Upper Canada. However, in 1811, a deterioration in Anglo-American relations, which was to soon lead to war, put it on full alert. There was a sudden flurry of activity as the fort's ramparts and gun emplacements were strengthened, but it was still too weak to rebuff the American army that marched on York in 1813. Hurriedly, the British decided to evacuate and blow up the gunpowder magazine to stop its contents falling into enemy hands. Unfortunately, they completely underestimated the force of the explosion, and killed or wounded ten of their own men in addition to 260 of the advancing enemy, the fatalities including the splendidly named American general Zebulon Montgomery Pike. After the war, Fort York, which the Americans occupied only briefly before abandoning it, was rebuilt and its garrison made a considerable contribution to the development of Toronto, as York was renamed in 1834. The British army moved out in 1870 and their Canadian replacements stayed for another sixty years; the fort was opened as a **museum** in 1934. Throughout the summer, **costumed guides** give the low-down on colonial life and free plans of the fort are issued at reception.

half-crow, half-human figure another couple of cabinets down, also dating from the 1960s, though not attributed to any particular sculptor.

To St Andrew's Presbyterian Church

Crossing over Wellington Street, and walking between the other three towers of the Toronto Dominion Centre, you soon pass **Joe Fafard**'s herd of grazing cows – seven extraordinarily realistic **bronze statues** that have proved immensely popular with the city's office workers. From here, it's a short detour west along King Street to **St Andrew's Presbyterian Church**, 75 Simcoe St (daily: 9am–3pm; free; St Andrew subway). Marooned among the city's skyscrapers, this handsome sandstone structure is a reminder of an older Toronto, and its Roman-esque Revival towers and gables have a distinctly Norman appearance. Built in 1876 for a predominantly Scottish congregation, the church has a delightful interior, its cherrywood pews and balcony sloping down towards the chancel with dappled light streaming in through the stained-glass windows. Additionally, St Andrew's has an admirable history of social action. Since the earliest days of the city's settlement, St Andrew's, along with many other Toronto churches, has played a leading role in the campaign against poverty and homelessness.

The fort

The fort's carefully restored earth and stone **ramparts** are low-lying and thick and constructed in a zigzag pattern, both to mitigate against enemy artillery and to provide complementary lines of fire. They enclose a haphazard sequence of log, stone and brick buildings, notably a couple of well-preserved **blockhouses**, complete with heavy timbers and snipers' loopholes. In one of them – **Building No.5** on the plan – an introductory **video** outlines the history of the fort and an **exhibit** explores the various military crises that afflicted Canada from the 1780s to the 1880s, especially the War of 1812. Here also is a small but particularly good display on late eighteenth- and early nineteenth-century **artillery**. The prize pieces include a 1793 British rampart gun, a cross between a rifle and an artillery piece, and a hot-shot furnace for heating cannon balls. There's also a feature on **Lieutenant Colonel Shrapnel**, who saw military service in Canada but wasn't at all impressed by cannon balls and invented his own much more lethal shell, which fragmented on impact. To prove his invention, Shrapnel arranged a test firing at the arsenal in Woolwich, back in London, and a card copy of the results is displayed here; needless to say, the top brass were suitably persuaded.

Moving on, **Building No.6** started out as a magazine but ended up as a storehouse. Its ground floor now holds a modest display on the role of black soldiers and settlers in the early history of Ontario. The Upper Canada legislature actually banned the importation of slaves in 1793, forty years before it was abolished right across the British Empire. Up above, an archeological section displays the various bits and pieces unearthed at the fort – buckles, brooches, plates, clay pipes, tunic buttons and so forth. The most interesting piece is a "Sacred to Love" stick pin, an example of the mourning jewellery that was popular amongst Victorians. Across the fort, **Building No.4**, the Blue Barracks, is a 1930s reconstruction of the junior officers' quarters, whilst **Building No.3** is the former Officers' Quarters and Mess. The latter boasts several period rooms and two original money vaults, hidden away in the cellar. Opposite, the stone and brick powder magazine – **Building No.8** – has two-metre-thick walls and spark-proof copper and brass fixtures.

Roy Thompson Hall, Metro Hall and the CBC Broadcasting Centre

Across Simcoe Street from St Andrew's, **Roy Thompson Hall**, the home of the Toronto Symphony Orchestra (see p.184), was completed in 1982 to a design by Canada's own Arthur Erickson. The hall looks like an upturned soup bowl by day, but at night its appearance is transformed, its glass-panelled walls radiating a skein of filtered light high into the sky. Next door, **Metro Hall**'s trio of glass-and-steel office blocks is set around an attractive plaza of water fountains and lawns. Built in the early 1990s, the complex represents a break from the brash architectural harshness of previous decades and a move toward more fluid, people-friendly designs.

To the south, Metro Hall abuts the **CBC Broadcasting Centre**, 250 Front St West, a ten-storey edifice whose painted gridiron beams make the building aesthetically bearable, but not much more. Since its foundation in 1936, **CBC** (the Canadian Broadcasting Company) has built up an international reputation for the impartiality of its radio and television news and, although it carries commercials unlike the UK's BBC, it remains in public ownership and is directly responsible to Parliament. CBC used to offer guided tours of the Broadcasting Centre, but these have been discontinued, at least for the moment. You can, however, still visit the **CBC museum** (Mon–Fri 9am–5pm, Sat noon–4pm; free; ⑩www.cbc.ca/museum), where, amongst a series of modest exhibits, vintage CBC TV shows are shown in a mini-theatre. In addition, three sets of push-buttons – one set each for public affairs, news and kids' programmes – access about forty brief programme clips, from perceptive comments on the US war in Vietnam to the heart-rending moment in 1980 when Terry Fox, who had lost a leg from cancer, had to abandon his attempt to run across Canada. Less impressive is the 1969 report on Toronto's Yorkville (see p.83), a particularly potty piece of social scaremongering in which the reporter claims – amongst much else – that the assorted drug-addled hippies would "make love to anyone".

From the CBC Broadcasting Centre, it's a brief stroll east to the former Toronto Stock Exchange (see p.57) or a twenty-minute hoof west to Fort York (see pp. 54–55).

The Fenian raids

During the American Civil War, the British continued to trade with the Confederacy, much to the chagrin of the Union army. After the war, tensions between the two countries abated, though many northerners still hankered for retribution – no group more so than the **Fenian Brotherhood**, formed by Irish exiles in New York in 1859. Many of these Irishmen had a deep and abiding hatred for the British, whose cruel administration of their homeland had caused the Catholic population endless suffering. To the Brotherhood, Britain's continued control of Canada was unbearable, and they hoped to capitalize on the residue of ill-feeling left from the Civil War to push the US into military action against its northern neighbour. Their tactics were simple: they organized a series of cross-border raids, several of which were aimed against Fort York, hoping that if they provoked a military retaliation from the British, the US government would feel obliged to come to their aid and invade Canada. The most serious Fenian raid crossed the border in 1866 with a thousand men. The British drove the Fenians out without too much difficulty, and although there were significant casualties, Congress didn't take the military bait.

The Toronto Stock Exchange

Doubling back from the CBC Centre along Wellington Street West, it's a brief walk to the old **Toronto Stock Exchange**, 234 Bay St at King St, whose crisp architectural lines have been badly compromised by its incorporation within a tower block that imitates – but doesn't match – the sober blocks of the adjacent Toronto Dominion Centre (see p.52). Nevertheless, the original facade has survived, its stone lintel decorated with muscular Art Deco carvings of men at work. Curiously enough, and seemingly unnoticed by the captains of capital, an unknown stonemason couldn't resist adding a subversive subtext when he carved the main frieze: look closely and you'll see that the top-hatted figure – the capitalist – is dipping his hand into a worker's pocket. Inside, the routinely modern ground floor is used to accommodate the **temporary exhibitions** of the **Design Exchange** (Mon–Fri 10am–6pm, Sat & Sun noon–5pm; admission charged for some exhibitions), or "**DX**", whose purpose is to foster innovative design. Displays may cover everything from local furniture design to prototype plans for making the city more environmentally friendly. Very different is the **trading floor** up above, which has been preserved in all its Art Deco pomp, its geometric panelling decorated with a series of delightful ribbon murals celebrating industry.

The CIBC buildings

Across the street from the Exchange, the formidable (and formidably named) **Canadian Imperial Bank of Commerce**, 243 Bay St, is a stainless-steel behemoth erected in the 1970s to a design by renowned architect **I.M. Pei** (born 1917). Hailing from China, where his father was a prominent banker, Pei moved to the United States in the 1930s, and it was there that he eventually established a worldwide reputation for sleek modern designs, seen in buildings such as the John Hancock Tower in Boston and the glass pyramids at the Louvre museum in Paris. Pei's CIBC tower is typical of his work, its sheer, overweening size emphasized by its severe angles and sleek trajectory. The tower stands in sharp contrast to the former **CIBC building**, next door to the north at 25 King St West. This older structure, erected just after the stock market crash of 1929, has a restrained stone exterior, where the cathedral-like doors, draped with carved reliefs, merely hint at the magnificent chandeliers, gilt-coffered ceilings and precise marble tracery within.

The Bay-Adelaide development

Walking north up Bay Street from King Street West, turn right on Temperance Street for a glimpse of the **Bay-Adelaide development**, the city's biggest real-estate fiasco. The big wheels of the business community decided to plonk a mammoth office complex here in the mid-1980s, when property speculation was at a fever pitch. Millions of dollars were invested, but in 1988 the bottom fell out of the office rental market just as construction had begun. In a panic, the developers cancelled further work on the project, leaving a scattering of foundations and a rough, concrete block six storeys high that was intended to be the core of the main skyscraper. Many Torontonians were delighted by the collapse of the project, and a *Toronto Star* columnist promptly christened the concrete stump the "**Magnificent Hulk**" – and the name stuck. What will happen to the site now is anybody's guess, but further development seems unlikely.

The Royal and Trader's banks

At the east end of Temperance Street, turn right down Yonge Street and you'll soon reach the **Royal Bank**, 2 King St East, which was designed by Ross and Macdonald, also the creators of Union Station and the *Royal York* hotel. Clumsily modernized on the ground floor, the austere symmetries of the building as a whole still impress, as do the classical columns and decorative motifs that were gracefully worked into the lower floors of the main facade.

A quick step to the south, **Trader's Bank**, 67 Yonge St at King (no public access), was **Toronto's first skyscraper**, a fifteen-storey structure completed in 1906. The owners were apprehensive that the size of the building might prompt accusations of vanity, so they insisted on overhanging eaves and stumpy classical columns in an effort to make it look shorter. They need not have bothered: as soon as it was finished visitors thronged the bank and the top floor was turned into an observation deck. Newer skyscrapers now dwarf Trader's, of course, and the once unhindered view is long gone.

The Hockey Hall of Fame

From Trader's Bank, it's a short haul south to the **Hockey Hall of Fame**, 30 Yonge St at Front St West (Sept to late June Mon–Fri 10am–5pm, Sat 9.30am–6pm, Sun 10.30am–5pm; late June to Aug Mon–Sat 9.30am–6pm, Sun 10am–6pm; $12, children 4–13 years old & seniors $8; ☎416/360-7765, ⊛www.hhof.com), a highly commercialized, ultra-modern tribute to Canada's national sport – though you wouldn't think so from the outside. The only part of the Hall visible from the street is the old **Bank of Montréal building**, a Neoclassical edifice dating back to 1885. The bank is actually one of Toronto's finer structures – its intricately carved stonework is adorned by a dainty sequence of pediments and pilasters – but its incorporation into the Hall of Fame is awkward. The bank's entrance has been blocked off and the interior bowdlerized to house a collection of hockey trophies.

The **entrance** to the Hockey Hall of Fame is below ground in the adjacent **BCE Place**, a glitzy retail complex on the west side of Yonge St between Front and Wellington streets. Inside the museum are a series of **exhibition areas**, featuring a replica of the Montréal Canadiens' locker room, copious biographical details of the sport's great names and descriptions of the various National Hockey League (NHL) teams. Much of this is geared toward the enthusiast, but there's plenty to keep the less-obsessed entertained as well, notably the mini **ice-rink**, where visitors can blast away at hockey pucks, and two small theatres showing **films** of hockey's most celebrated games. The film of the 1972 "World Summit Series" between the USSR and Canada records what must rank as one of the most gripping sporting events ever, a tense confrontation infused with Cold War resonances. Finally, the **trophy room**, located inside the old bank building, contains the very first **Stanley Cup**, donated by Lord Stanley, the Governor General of Canada, in 1893. An English aristocrat, Stanley was convinced that sports raised the mettle of the men of the British Empire. Concerned that Canadian ice hockey lacked a trophy of any stature, he inaugurated the Stanley Cup, which has become the defining emblem of the sport. For more on ice hockey, see Sports and outdoor activities, p.205.

The St Lawrence District

One of the city's oldest neighbourhoods, the **St Lawrence District**, lying just to the east of Yonge St, between The Esplanade, Adelaide Street East and Frederick Street, enjoyed its first period of rapid growth after the War of 1812. In Victorian times, St Lawrence became one of the most fashionable parts of the city, and although it hit the skids thereafter, it was revamped and (partly) gentrified in the late 1990s.

The best approach is along Front Street East, heading east from Yonge. From this direction, you'll soon spot the distinctive trompe l'oeil **mural** on the back of the **Flatiron building**, a sturdy office block of 1892, which fills in the narrow triangle of land between Wellington and Front streets. From here, it's a short hop to **St Lawrence Market** (Tues–Thurs 8am–6pm, Fri 8am–7pm & Sat 5am–5pm), at Front and Jarvis, a capacious 1844 red-brick building that holds the city's best food and drink market. Spread out across the main and lower levels, there are stalls selling everything from fish and freshly baked bread to international foodstuffs, all sorts of organic edibles and Ontario specialities – cheese, jellies, jams and fern fiddleheads to name but a few. The market is at its busiest on Saturday. Up above, and reachable by the elevator beside the main entrance, is the old city council chamber – the front part of today's market served as the town hall from 1845 to 1899 – where you'll find the **Market Gallery** (Wed–Fri 10am–4pm, Sat 9am–4pm & Sun noon–4pm; free). This displays regularly rotated **exhibitions**, often of sketches and photographs drawn from the city's archives. Visiting the market on Saturdays also means that you can drop by the **North St Lawrence Market**, an authentic farmers' market (Sat 5am–5pm) housed in the long brick building opposite, on the north side of Front Street.

St Lawrence Hall

Palatial **St Lawrence Hall**, whose columns, pilasters and pediments are surmounted by a dinky little cupola, is one of the city's most attractive Victorian buildings. Dating from 1850, the hall which is located behind North St Lawrence Market, just along Jarvis Street, was built as the city's main meeting-place, with oodles of space for balls, public lectures and concerts. Some performances were eminently genteel, others decidedly mawkish – it was here that the "Swedish songbird" **Jenny Lind** (1820–1887) made one of her Canadian appearances – and yet others more urgent, like the anti-slavery rallies of the 1850s. The bad taste award goes to the American showman and circus proprietor **P.T. Barnum** (1810–1891), one-time mayor of his hometown of Bridgeport, Connecticut, and author of the bizarre *The Humbugs of the World*. It was Barnum who saw the potential of his fellow Bridgeportonian, the diminutive Charles Sherwood Stratton, aka **Tom Thumb** (1838–1883), exhibiting him as a curiosity here in St Lawrence Hall as well as anywhere else where people were willing to pay. Stratton was just 60cm (2ft) tall when he first went on tour.

St James Cathedral

On the other side of King Street, a couple of hundred metres west from St Lawrence Hall, rises the graceful bulk of **St James Anglican Cathedral**, whose yellowish stone is fetchingly offset by copper-green roofs and a slender spire. An excellent example of the neo-Gothic style once popular in every corner of the British Empire, the cathedral boasts scores of pointed-arch windows and acres of sturdy buttressing. Inside, the nave is supported by elegant high-arched pillars and flanked by an ambitious set of **stained-glass windows** that attempts to trace the path by which Christianity reached Canada from Palestine via England. It's all a little confusing, but broadly speaking, the less inventive windows depict Biblical scenes, whereas those that focus on English history are the more ingenious. These stained-glass windows were inserted at the end of the nineteenth century, but those of **St George's Chapel**, in the southeast corner of the church, were added in 1935 to celebrate the Silver Jubilee of King George V. They exhibit an enthusiastic loyalty to the British Empire that is echoed in many of the cathedral's funerary plaques: take, for example, that of a certain **Captain John Henry Gamble**, who was born in Toronto in 1844 but died on active service in the Khyber Pass in 1879; his stone is in the west transept. Spare a

△ St James Cathedral

thought also for poor old **William Butcher**, a native of Suffolk, in England, who fell to his death from the scaffolding erected during the construction of the cathedral spire when he was just 27; his stone is in the main entrance way.

Toronto's First Post Office

Located about five minutes' walk northeast of St James Cathedral, in a tatty part of town, **Toronto's First Post Office**, 260 Adelaide St East (Mon–Fri 9am–4pm, Sat & Sun 10am–4pm; free), occupies an old brick building that dates back to 1833. Returned to something approaching its original appearance, and staffed by costumed volunteers, the **museum** gives the flavour of the times and features displays on postal history. It also doubles up as a working post office, where visitors can write a letter with a quill pen, seal it with wax and tie it up with a ribbon.

From the post office, it takes about twenty minutes to walk west to Nathan Philips Square (see below) or, heading southeast, around fifteen minutes to reach the Distillery District.

The Distillery District

The **Distillery District** (☎416/866-8687, ⊛www.distillerytours.ca) is home to Toronto's newest arts and entertainment complex, sited in the former **Gooderham and Worts distillery**, an extremely appealing industrial "village" on Mill Street, near the foot of Parliament Street. In use as a distillery until 1990, this rambling network of over forty brick buildings once constituted the largest distillery in the British Empire. It was founded in 1832, when ships could sail into its own jetty, though landfill subsequently marooned it in the lee of the railway lines and the tail end of the Gardiner Expressway. Since its demise, the distillery has been sympathetically redeveloped by a small group of entrepreneurs, who chose to integrate many of the original features into the revamp – including its quirky walkways and bottle runways – and, with refreshing integrity, to exclude all multinational chains. One of the architectural highlights is the **Pure Spirits building**, which features French doors and a fancy wrought-iron balcony.

Not all the prospective tenants have moved into the complex yet, but when the work is completed in the next year or so, the space will hold, amongst much else, over thirty art galleries and artists' studios, furniture designers, a chocolatier, bakeries, shops, a microbrewery, a visitor centre (offering guided tours) and a couple of performance venues. As for **opening times**, most of the galleries and shops start daily at 10am and close down at 6pm, whereas the cafés and bars hang on till 8pm.

To get to the Distillery District by **public transport**, take the King Street streetcar (#503 or #504) east to Parliament and walk from there – it takes about five minutes. Try not to miss it.

Nathan Phillips Square and City Hall

Back in the city centre of Queen St, **Nathan Phillips Square**, One of Toronto's most distinctive landmarks was designed by the Finnish architect

The Hudson's Bay Company

Across the street from the Old City Hall, The Bay department store (see p.198), at Queen and Yonge sts, is the present incarnation of the **Hudson's Bay Company**, which played a crucial role in the development of colonial Canada. The story begins in 1661, when two Frenchmen, Medard Chouart des Groseilliers and Pierre-Esprit Radisson, reached the southern end of Hudson Bay overland and realized this was the same vast and icy inland sea described by earlier seafaring explorers, and now at the northern edge of Ontario. They returned to Québec laden with **furs** – and the French governor arrested them for trapping without a licence. Understandably peeved, they turned to England, where Charles II's cousin, Prince Rupert, persuaded the king to finance and equip two ships, the *Eaglet* and the *Nonsuch*. After a mammoth voyage, the *Nonsuch* returned with a fantastic cargo of furs and this led to the incorporation of the Hudson's Bay Company by Charles II on May 2, 1670. The Company was granted wide powers, including exclusive trading rights to the entire Hudson Bay watershed – to be called Rupert's Land.

The HBC was a joint-stock company, the shareholders annually electing a governor and committee to hire men, order trade goods and arrange fur auctions and shipping. By 1760, **trading posts** had been built at the mouths of all the major rivers flowing into the bay; these were commanded by factors, who took their policy orders from London. The orders were often unrealistic and based on the concept of native trappers bringing furs to the posts – whereas the rival Montréal-based North West Company operated with mainly Francophone employees spending months in the wilderness working with the natives. Unsurprisingly, the NWC undercut the Company's trade and there was intense competition between the two across the north of the continent, occasionally resulting in violence. In 1821 a compromise was reached and the two companies merged. They kept the name Hudson's Bay Company and the British parliament granted the new, larger company a commercial monopoly from Hudson Bay to the Pacific. However, the administrative structure of the Company was changed. A North American chief factor was appointed and his councils dealt increasingly with local trading concerns, though the London governor and committee continued to have the last word.

The extensive **monopoly** rights ceded to the new company were fiercely resented by local traders, and, in a landmark case of 1849, a Canadian jury found a trader by the name of Sayer guilty of breaking the monopoly, but simultaneously refused to punish him. Thereafter, in practice if not by law, the Company's stranglehold on the fur trade was dead and buried. Furthermore, the HBC's quasi-governmental powers seemed increasingly anachronistic and when a company official, James Douglas, became governor of British Columbia in 1858, the British government forced him to resign from the HBC. This marked the beginning of the end of the Company's colonial role.

In 1870 the HBC sold Rupert's Land to Canada. In return it received a cash payment, but, more importantly, retained the title to the lands on which the trading posts had been built. Given that the trading posts often occupied land that was the nucleus of the burgeoning western cities, this was a remarkably bad deal for Canada – and a great one for the HBC. Subsequently, the HBC became a major real-estate developer and **retail chain**, a position it maintains today.

Viljo Revell (1910–1964). It is framed by an elevated walkway and focuses on a reflecting pool, which becomes a skating rink in winter. The square is overlooked by Revell's **City Hall**, whose twin curved glass and concrete towers stand behind and to either side of a mushroom-topped entrance. In front of this is *The Archer*, a **Henry Moore** sculpture resembling nothing so much as a giant propeller. Surprising as it seems today, when such architectural designs are fairly commonplace, Revell won all sorts of awards for this project, which was considered the last word in 1960s dynamism – though its weather-stained blocks now look rather dejected. In its creation, however, the square became a catalyst for change. Named after its sponsor, Nathan Phillips, Toronto's first Jewish mayor, the space suddenly provided the kind of public gathering place the city so sorely lacked, kick-starting the process by which the private Toronto of the 1950s became the extrovert metropolis of today.

Standing in the southwest corner of Nathan Phillips Square, a statue of **Winston Churchill** (1874–1965) recalls Toronto's British connection. Inscribed upon the statue are five famous quotations, one of which is drawn from the speech Churchill delivered to the Canadian House of Commons on December 30, 1941 in the dark days of World War II: "[The losing French] generals advised France's divided cabinet 'In three weeks, the English will have their necks wrung like a chicken'. Some chicken! Some neck!"

Had Revell's grand scheme been fully implemented, the city would have bulldozed the **Old City Hall** – it wasn't, though, and so the imposingly flamboyant pseudo-Romanesque building on the east side of the square still stands. Completed in 1899, it was designed by **Edward J. Lennox**, who developed a fractious relationship with his paymasters on the city council. They had a point: the original cost of the building had been estimated at $1.77 million, but Lennox spent an extra $750,000 and took all of eight years to finish the project. Nevertheless, Lennox had the last laugh, carving gargoyle-like representations of the city's fathers on the capitals of the columns at the top of the front steps and placing his name on each side of the building – something the city council had expressly forbidden him to do. Lennox was also responsible for the construction of Casa Loma (see p.85).

The Eaton Centre

A second-floor walkway crosses Queen Street to connect The Bay department store with the **Eaton Centre** (Mon–Fri 10am–9pm, Sat 9.30am–7pm, Sun noon–6pm; Queen or Dundas subways), a three-storey assortment of shops and restaurants spread out underneath a glass-and-steel arched roof. By shopping-mall standards, the design is appealing, and the flock of fibreglass Canada geese suspended from the ceiling adds a touch of flair; they are the work of **Michael Snow**, who also spruced up the SkyDome (see p.50). Maps of the shopping mall are displayed on every floor, but the general rule is: the higher the floor, the more expensive the shop. The centre takes its name from **Timothy Eaton**, an immigrant from Ulster who opened his first store here in 1869. His cash-only, fixed-price, money-back-guarantee merchandising revolutionized the Canadian market and made him a fortune. Soon a Canadian institution, Eaton kept a grip on the pioneer settlements in the west through his mail-order catalogue, known as the "homesteader's bible" – or the "wish book" among native peoples – whilst Eaton department stores sprang up in all of Canada's big cities. In recent years, however, the company has struggled to maintain its profitability and the branch in the Eaton Centre has been taken over by Sears.

About two-thirds of the way along the Eaton Centre from Queen Street – just before Sears – a side exit leads straight from Level 3 to the **Church of the Holy Trinity**, a quirky nineteenth-century structure whose yellow brickwork is surmounted by a flourish of matching turrets and chimneys. Much to its credit, the church campaigns hard on issues of poverty, and beside its entrance stands the **Toronto Homeless Memorial**, which lists those who have died as a result of their homelessness. The church also figures in Canadian movie history. It was here, with the church set against the skyscrapers that crowd in on it, that Canadian director **David Cronenberg** filmed the last scene of *Dead Ringers*. The dubious moral content of the film – the unscrupulous exploits of twin rogue gynaecologists, both played by Jeremy Irons – prompted Cronenberg to defend his subject matter coyly: "I don't have a moral plan. I'm a Canadian."

The Dundas and Yonge intersection

The Eaton Centre ends (or begins) at the corner of **Dundas and Yonge** streets, once the city's main intersection and long a popular rendezvous. By the 1990s, the junction looked tatty and neglected, but thereafter the city council began a thoroughgoing revamp, the first part of which was the construction of a public piazza, **Dundas Square**, with water jets and a giant video screen showing ads and promotional videos. Further redevelopment is currently being planned.

Dundas Square is overlooked by **Olympic Spirit** (daily: 10am–6pm; $21, 13–17 year olds & seniors $17.50; children 4–12 $12; ☎1-888/466-9991, ⓦwww.olympicspirit.ca), at 35 Dundas St East, the self-billed "first and only permanent entertainment complex themed around the Olympic Games". There are two floors – one each for the summer and winter games – and the idea is that, through a series of interactive simulators (bobsleigh, long jump, sprint and so forth) visitors can come close to experiencing the Games from an athlete's perspective. Perhaps.

Mackenzie House and St Michael's Cathedral

It's hardly an essential visit, but the **Mackenzie House** (Jan–April Sat & Sun noon–5pm, May–Aug Tues–Sun noon–5pm, Sept–Dec Tues–Fri noon–4pm, Sat & Sun noon–5pm; $4, $5.50 on public holidays; Dundas subway), a brief walk east of the Dundas and Yonge intersection at 82 Bond St, is of some interest as the home of **William Lyon Mackenzie** (1795–1861). Born in Scotland, Mackenzie moved to Toronto where he scraped together a living publishing *The Colonial Advocate*, a radical anti-Tory newspaper. Frustrated with the politics of the colony's early leaders, Mackenzie was one of the instigators of the Rebellion of 1837 (see p.230), after which he was exiled to the US for twelve years before being pardoned. Mackenzie lived in this house between 1859 and 1861, and it has been restored to an approximation of its appearance at the time, complete with a print shop (circa 1845) whose workings are demonstrated by costumed guides.

From the Mackenzie House, it's a few paces south to **St Michael's Cathedral** (Mon–Sat 6am–6pm, Sun 6am–10pm; free), an imposing neo-Gothic edifice whose sturdy brickwork dates back to the middle of the nineteenth century. Broadly patterned on York Minister, in this UK, this Catholic cathedral boasts a soaring, crocketted spire, good-looking pointed windows along the nave, attenuated buttresses and perky dormer windows – though somehow the whole caboodle still manages to look a tad sullen. Inside, the capacious three-aisled nave is flanked by mini-shrines and permeated with the whiff of burning candles. The **stained-glass windows** are the church's pride and joy and they divide into two types: machine-embossed windows made in the US and Canada and hand-blown, more subtly coloured windows imported from France. The three (French) windows at the east end of the church, above the high altar, are particularly fine, the central one of the three depicting the Crucifixion set against a deep blue background.

The Elgin and Winter Garden Theatre Centre

Across from the Eaton Centre, just north of Queen St at 189 Yonge, the **Elgin and Winter Garden Theatre Centre** (guided tours only, Thurs 5pm & Sat 11am; 90min; $7; ☎416/597-0965; Queen subway) is one of the city's most unusual attractions. The first part of the **guided tour** covers the **Elgin**, an old vaudeville theatre whose ornate furnishings and fittings, including a set of splendid gilt mirrors, have been restored after years of neglect. The Elgin was turned into a cinema in the 1930s and, remarkably enough, its accompaniment, the top-floor **Winter Garden**, also a vaudeville theatre, was sealed off. Such double-decker theatres were first introduced in New York in the late nineteenth century, and soon became popular along the whole of the east coast, but only a handful have survived. When this one was unsealed, its original decor was found to be intact, the ceiling hung with thousands of paint-preserved beech leaves, illuminated by coloured lanterns. In the event, much of the decor still had to be replaced, but the restoration work was painstakingly thorough and the end result is delightful. Vaudeville was an informal business, with customers coming and going as they saw fit and performances following each other nonstop. Consequently, every vaudeville theatre had a ready supply of **backcloths**, and several were discovered when the Winter Garden was unsealed; they are now a feature of the tour.

Osgoode Hall, Campbell House and Queen Street West

Immediately to the west of Nathan Phillips Square, along Queen Street, stands **Osgoode Hall** (no public access), an attractive Neoclassical pile built in the nineteenth century for the Law Society of Upper Canada. Looking like a cross between a Greek temple and an English country house, its immaculate lawns and gardens are protected by a sturdy wrought-iron fence with fancy gates that was designed to keep cows and horses off the lawn. Across Queen Street, at the corner of University, the brand new **Four Seasons Centre for the Performing**

Arts will be the home of the Canadian Opera Company (see p.182) and the National Ballet of Canada when it is completed in 2006. Close by, in the middle of University Avenue, stands a **War Memorial** honouring those Canadians who fought for the British imperial interest in the South African (or Boer) War at the start of the twentieth century. The memorial features two Canadian soldiers of heroic disposition, and the column is engraved with the names of the battles where Canadian regiments fought.

The elegant Georgian mansion on the west side of University Avenue is **Campbell House** (late May to early Oct daily 9.30am–4.30pm, early Oct to late May Mon–Fri 9.30am–4.30pm; ☎416/597-0227; $4.50; Osgoode subway), originally built on Adelaide Street for Sir William Campbell, Chief Justice and Speaker of the Legislative Assembly. The house was transported to its current location in 1972. There are regular **guided tours** of the period interior, which is distinguished by the immaculately carved woodwork and sweeping circular stairway. The tours also provide a well-researched overview of early nineteenth-century Toronto, in which Campbell was a surprisingly progressive figure: he eschewed the death penalty whenever possible, and even awarded the radical William Mackenzie (see p.64) damages when his printing press was wrecked by a mob of Tories in 1826.

Beyond the Campbell House, **Queen Street West** between University and Spadina is one of the grooviest parts of the city, its assorted cafés and bars attracting the sharpest of dressers. Meanwhile, the alternative crew of students and punks who once hung around here have moved further west, out to what is known as **Queen West West**, between Spadina and Bathurst. In the daytime, this whole section of Queen Street is a great place to be – but at night it's even better.

The Canada Life building and the Textile Museum of Canada

The monumental Neoclassical lines of the **Canada Life building**, which stands behind Campbell House, are capped by a chunky Art Deco tower-cum-weather beacon – the cube on top signifies white for snow, red for rain and green for sun. The Canada Life building is, however, but one of a long sequence of bristling tower blocks, which march up **University Avenue** as it slices across the city, running north from Front Street to the Ontario Legislative Assembly Building (see p.73). Strolling north up University from Queen Street West, it only takes a couple of minutes to reach **Armoury Street**, the site of the old city armoury and the spot where the province's soldiers mustered before embarking overseas for the battlefields of both world wars. Just off Armoury Street, the **Textile Museum of Canada**, housed in part of an office block at 55 Centre Ave (daily: 11am–5pm, Wed till 8pm; $10; ☎416/599-5321, ⓦwww.textilemuseum.ca), offers a rolling programme of **temporary exhibitions**. International in outlook, the museum has featured everything from contemporary domestic textile pieces to traditional work such as Oriental rugs and the hooked mats that were once handmade in Newfoundland and Labrador. The displays are often very good and are frequently supplemented by practical **demonstrations** of different textile techniques.

North of the Textile Museum, back on the east side of University Avenue, just beyond Elm Street, look for the bust of **Mary Pickford** (1893–1979). Pickford was born in Toronto, but left on a theatrical tour at the tender age of eight. She dropped her original name – Gladys Mary Smith – when she began working as a motion-picture extra in Hollywood in 1909. Renowned as "America's sweetheart", she earned the cinematic sobriquet with her cute face and fluffy mop of hair, which enabled her to play little-girl roles well into her thirties.

From the Pickford statue, it's a short walk north to the Ontario Legislative Assembly building (see p.73) and a similarly brief excursion southwest to the Art Gallery of Ontario (see below).

The Art Gallery of Ontario

Just west of University Avenue along Dundas Street West, the **AGO**, the **Art Gallery of Ontario** (opening hours liable to change, but currently Wed–Fri 10am–9pm, Sat & Sun 10am–5.30pm; $8, plus extra for special exhibitions; St Patrick subway; ☎416/979-6648, ⊛www.ago.net), is celebrated both for its wide-ranging collection of **foreign and domestic art** and its excellent temporary exhibitions; they also run a first-rate programme of **free guided tours**. The gallery is, however, in the throes of a **major overhaul**, which will continue until 2008, and, in the intervening period, only parts of the gallery will be open at any one time. The account below describes some of the more important elements of the collection, at least parts of which should be displayed, but for the moment it is all rather hit and miss. For better or worse, one thing that will probably stay the same is the matching pair of **Henry Moore sculptures** that stand outside the museum on Dundas Street, large and chunky bronzes uninspiringly called *Large Two Forms*. Museum **maps**, showing the current state of display, are issued free at reception; there is a **café** and a large **gift and bookshop** on the ground floor.

Canadian eighteenth-century paintings

The AGO owns a small but intriguing assortment of paintings by **eighteenth-century Canadians**. One noteworthy canvas is a curiously unflattering *Portrait of Joseph Brant* by **William Berczy** (1748–1813). A Mohawk chief, **Joseph Brant** (1742–1807) was consistently loyal to the British, his followers fighting alongside them during the American War of Independence. Brant's reward was a large chunk of Ontario land and a string of official portraits; this was one of them. Brant is shown in a mix of European and native gear; he carries an axe and has a Mohawk hairdo, but wears a dress coat with a sash – an apt reflection of his twin loyalties. Brant spoke English fluently, even translating parts of the Bible into Mohawk, and was a Freemason and Anglican to boot, feted by high society during a visit to England in 1776. At the same time, under his Mohawk name, Thayendanega (Two Bets), Brant was a powerful figure in the Iroquois Confederacy, leading one of its four main clans in both war and peace.

Canadian nineteenth-century paintings

Early to mid-nineteenth-century Canadian paintings at the AGO include the cheery *Passenger Pigeon Hunt* by **Antoine Plamondon** (1802–1895). Trained in Paris, Plamondon worked in the Neoclassical tradition, but

Cornelius Krieghoff

Born in Amsterdam, **Cornelius Krieghoff** (see below) trained as an artist in Düsseldorf before emigrating to New York, where, at the tender age of 21, he joined the US army, serving in the Second Seminole War in Florida. Discharged in 1840, Krieghoff immediately re-enlisted, claimed three months' advance pay and deserted, hotfooting it to Montréal with the French-Canadian woman he had met and married in New York. In Montréal, he picked up his brushes again, but without any commercial success – quite simply no one wanted to buy his paintings. That might have been the end of the matter, but Krieghoff moved to Québec City in 1852 and here he found a ready market for his paintings among the well-heeled officers of the British garrison, who liked his folksy renditions of Québec rural life. This was the start of Krieghoff's most productive period. Over the next eight years he churned out dozens of souvenir pictures – finely detailed, anecdotal scenes that are his best work. In the early 1860s, however – and for reasons that remain obscure – he temporarily packed in painting, returning to Europe for five years before another stint in Québec City, though this time, with the officer corps gone, he failed to sell his work. In 1871, he went to live with his daughter in Chicago and died there the following year, a defeated man.

here he allows some freedom of movement amongst the young hunters, with the St Lawrence River as the backdrop. From eastern Canada comes **John O'Brien** (1832–1891), who is well represented by *The Ocean Bride leaving Halifax Harbour*. Self-taught, O'Brien specialized in maritime scenes, turning out dozens of brightly coloured pictures of sailing ships and coastal settings. Look out also for the canvases of one of the era's most intriguing figures, Irish-born **Paul Kane** (1810–1871), notably his *Landscape in the Foothills with Buffalo Resting* and *At Buffalo Pound*, where bison are pictured in what looks more like a placid German valley than a North American prairie and *Indian encampment on Lake Huron*, a softly hued oil on canvas painting dating to 1845. Equally interesting is the work – and life – of the prolific **Cornelius Krieghoff** (1815–1872). The AGO owns a healthy sample of Krieghoff's paintings, including characteristic winter scenes like his *Settler's Log House* and *The Portage Aux Titres*, whose autumnal colours surround a tiny figure struggling with a canoe, and the humorous *Toll Gate*.

Folksy and/or romanticized country scenes and landscapes ruled the Canadian artistic roost from the 1850s through to the early twentieth century. By and large this is pretty dull stuff, but **Homer Watson**'s (1855–1936) glossy Ontario landscapes, with their vigorous paintwork and dynamic compositions, made him a popular and much acclaimed artist – Queen Victoria even purchased one of his paintings, and Oscar Wilde dubbed him "the Canadian Constable". The AGO possesses several Watson paintings, most memorably *The Old Mill* and *The Passing Storm*, two especially handsome and well-composed canvases, but his *Death of Elaine* – inspired by a Tennyson poem – is a bizarrely unsuccessful venture into ancient legend, the eponymous maiden looking something like a stick insect. From the same period come a couple of important paintings by the Newfoundlander **Maurice Cullen** (1866–1934), beginning with the precise angles and dappled brushwork of *Moret in Winter*, which is generally regarded as the beginning of Canadian Impressionism. Cullen was trained in Paris, where he was greatly influenced by the work of Monet, producing this French riverscape just before he returned to Canada, where he applied a similar approach to the landscapes of the St Lawrence River, as in his *The Last Loads*.

Paul Kane

Born in Ireland, **Paul Kane** emigrated to Toronto in the early 1820s. In 1840, he returned to Europe, where, curiously enough, he was so impressed by a touring exhibition of paintings on the American Indian that he promptly decided to move back to Canada. In 1846, he wrangled a spot on a westward-bound fur-trading expedition, beginning an epic journey: he travelled from Thunder Bay to Edmonton by canoe, crossed the Rockies by horse, and finally returned to Toronto two years later. During his trip, Kane made some seven hundred sketches, which he then painted onto canvas, paper and cardboard. Like many early Canadian artists, Kane's paintings often displayed a conflict in subject and style – that is, the subject was North American but the style European; indeed, it wasn't until the Group of Seven (see p.70) that a true Canadian aesthetic emerged.

In 1859, Kane published *Wanderings of an Artist among the Indian Tribes of North America*, the story of his long travels. It includes this account of Christmas dinner at Fort Edmonton: "At the head, before Mr Harriett, was a large dish of boiled buffalo hump; at the foot smoked a boiled buffalo calf...one of the most esteemed dishes among the epicures of the interior. My pleasing duty was to help a dish of mouffle, or dried moose nose [while] the worthy priest helped the buffalo tongue and Mr Randall cut up the beaver's tails. The centre of the table was graced with piles of potatoes, turnips and bread conveniently placed, so that each could help himself without interrupting the labours of his companions. Such was our jolly Christmas dinner at Edmonton."

The Group of Seven at the AGO

One of the most distinctive artists of the Group of Seven (see box, p.70) was **Lawren Harris** (1885–1970), whose 1922 *Above Lake Superior* is a pivotal work, its clarity of conception, with bare birch stumps framing a dark mountain beneath Art Deco clouds, quite exceptional. Equally stirring is his surreal *Lake Superior* (1923), one of several paintings inspired by the wild, cold landscapes of the lake's north shore. Harris was also partial to urban street scenes and the AGO has several – including two of Toronto – each painted in a careful pointillist style very different from his wilderness works.

The *West Wind* by **Tom Thomson** (1877–1917) is another seminal work, an iconic rendering of the northern wilderness that is perhaps the most famous of all Canadian paintings. Thomson was the first to approach the wilderness with the determination of an explorer and a sense that it could encapsulate a specifically Canadian identity. A substantial sample of his less familiar (but no less powerful) works are part of the AGO collection, including the moody *A Northern Lake*, the Cubist-influenced *Autumn Foliage 1915*, the sticky dabs of colour of *Maple Springs*, and his *Autumn's Garland*, an oil on panel finished the year before he died. There is also a whole battery of preparatory sketches of lakes and canyons, waterfalls and forests, each small panel displaying the vibrant, blotchy colours that characterize Thomson's work.

J.E.H. MacDonald (1873–1932) was fond of dynamic, sweeping effects, and his panoramic *Falls, Montreal River* sets turbulent rapids beside hot-coloured hillsides. MacDonald also produced the startling sweep of *October Shower Gleam* and the superbly observed *Rowan Berries*. His friend **F.H. Varley** (1881–1969) dabbled in portraiture and chose soft images and subtle colours for his landscapes, as exemplified by the sticky-looking brushstrokes he used for *Moonlight after Rain*. The talents of **A.J. Casson** (1898–1992) are perhaps best recalled by the jumble of snow-covered roofs of his *House Tops in the Ward*, and his bright and rather formal *Old Store at Salem*, which offers

The Group of Seven

In the autumn of 1912, a commercial artist by the name of **Tom Thomson** returned from an extended trip to the Mississauga country, north of Georgian Bay, with a bag full of sketches that were to add new momentum to Canadian art. His friends, many of them fellow employees of the art firm of Grip Ltd in Toronto, saw Thomson's naturalistic approach to indigenous subject matter as a pointer away from the influence of Europe, declaring the "northland" as the true Canadian "painter's country". World War I and the death of Thomson – who drowned in 1917 – delayed these artists' ambitions, but in 1920 they formed the **Group of Seven**. Initially, the group comprised Franklin H. Carmichael, Lawren Harris, A.Y. Jackson, Arthur Lismer, J.E.H. MacDonald, F.H. Varley and Frank Johnston; later, they were joined by A.J. Casson, L.L. Fitzgerald and Edwin Holgate. Working under the unofficial leadership of **Lawren Harris**, they explored the wilds of Algoma in Northern Ontario in the late 1910s, travelling around in a converted freight car, and later foraged even further afield, from Newfoundland and Baffin Island to British Columbia.

They were immediately successful, staging forty shows in eleven years, a triumph due in large part to Harris's many influential contacts. However, there was also a genuine popular response to the intrepid **frontiersman element** of their aesthetic. Art was a matter of "taking to the road" and "risking all for the glory of a great adventure", as they wrote in 1922, whilst "nature was the measure of a man's stature", according to Lismer. Symbolic of struggle against the elements, the Group's favourite symbol was the lone pine set against the sky, an image whose authenticity was confirmed by reference to the "manly" poetry of Walt Whitman.

The **legacy** of the Group of Seven is, however, somewhat double-edged. On the one hand, they rediscovered the Canadian wilderness and established the autonomy of Canadian art. On the other, their contribution was soon institutionalized, and well into the 1950s it was difficult for Canadian painters to establish an identity that didn't conform to the group's precepts. Among many later painters, the Group was – and remains – unpopular, but the Ontario artist Graham Coughtry was generous, saying: "They are the closest we've ever come to having some kind of romantic heroes in Canadian painting."

a break from the scenic preoccupations of the rest of the Seven. There are also the vital canvases of **A.Y. Jackson** (1882–1974), most notably the bold colours and forms of his *Yellowknife Country* and the carpet-like surface of *Algoma Rocks, Autumn*, painted in 1923. Yet another member of the Group of Seven, **Arthur Lismer** (1885–1969), spent every summer at his cottage in Georgian Bay, north of Toronto, where he concentrated on painting shoreline and island vistas; the AGO has several prime examples. A contemporary of the Group – but not a member – the gifted **Emily Carr** (1871–1945) focused on the Canadian west coast in general, and its dense forests and native villages in particular, as in her dark and haunting *Thunderbird* of 1930 and the deep green foliage of both *Indian Church* and *Western Forest*, dating to 1929.

Inuit art

Soapstone sculptures form the bulk of the AGO's collection of **Inuit art**. Highlights here include **Pauta Saila**'s (born 1916) light-hearted *Dancing Bear* and **Joe Talirunili**'s (1906–1976) *Migration*, in which a traditional Inuit boat – an *umiak* – is crowded with Inuit seemingly bent on escaping danger. Talirunili carved a large number of migration boat scenes throughout his long career, the inspiration derived from a dramatic incident in his childhood when the break-up of the pack ice caught his family unawares, forcing them to hurriedly evacuate their encampment. Look out also for the work of **John Tiktak** (1916–1981), generally regarded as one of the most talented Inuit sculptors of his generation. The death of Tiktak's mother in 1962 had a profound effect on him, and his *Mother and Child* forcefully expresses this close connection, with the figure of the child carved into the larger figure of the mother. Tiktak's *Owl Man* is another fine piece, an excellent example of the metamorphic – half-human, half-animal – figures popular amongst the Inuit, as is **Thomas Sivuraq**'s (born 1941) *Shaman Transformation*.

The European collection

The AGO possesses a marvellous sample of **European fine and applied art**, including ivory and alabaster pieces, exquisite cameos and fine porcelain, as well as **European sculptures** by the likes of Barbara Hepworth. Early paintings include some rather pedestrian Italian altarpieces, Pieter Brueghel the Younger's incident-packed *Peasant Wedding*, and a strong showing of **Dutch painters** of the Golden Age – Rembrandt, Van Dyck, Frans Hals and Goyen to name but four. Look out also for Carel Fabritius's exquisite *Portrait of a Lady with a Handkerchief*, one of only a few of the artist's works to have survived the powder-magazine explosion that killed him in Delft in 1654 – though the authorship of the painting has been disputed. **French painters** are much in evidence, too, with distinguished works including *St Anne with the Christ Child* by Georges de la Tour and *Venus Presenting Arms to Aeneas* by Poussin. Amongst the **Impressionists,** there's Degas's archetypal *Woman in the Bath*, Renoir's screaming-pink *Concert*, and Monet's wonderful *Vétheuil in Summer*, with its hundreds of tiny jabs of colour. **Modern art** is represented by such luminaries as Picasso and Francis Bacon, among many others.

Contemporary art and Henry Moore

The AGO's collection of **contemporary art** showcases work by European, British and American artists. Prime pieces include Andy Warhol's *Elvis I* and *II*, Mark Rothko's strident *No.1 White and Red* and Claes Oldenburg's quirky if somewhat frayed *Giant Hamburger*. The AGO also possesses the world's largest collection of **Henry Moore** (1898–1986) plaster casts and bronzes, though it was actually something of an accident that his work ended up here at all. In the 1960s, Moore had reason to believe that London's Tate Gallery was going to build a special wing for his work. When the Tate declined, Moore negotiated with the AGO instead, after being persuaded to do so by the gallery's British representative, Anthony Blunt – the art expert who was famously uncovered as a Soviet spy in 1979. Given the sheer size and volume of Moore's AGO sculptures, it is likely that, at the end of all the rebuilding, he will still have a gallery to himself.

The Grange

Attached to the back of the AGO is **The Grange**, an early nineteenth-century brick mansion with Neoclassical trimmings built by the Boultons, one of the city's most powerful families. The last of the line, William Henry – "a privileged, petted man...without principle", according to a local journalist – died in 1874, and his property passed to his widow, Harriette, who promptly married an English expatriate professor named Goldwin Smith. The latter enjoyed Toronto immensely, holding court and boasting of his English connections, and when he died in

1910 (after Harriette) he bequeathed the house to the fledgling Art Museum of Toronto, the predecessor of the AGO. The Grange remains part of the AGO and it is currently being restored to its mid-nineteenth-century appearance. **Guides** dressed in period costume will show you around, enthusiastically explaining the ins and outs of life in nineteenth-century Toronto. Several of Harriette's **paintings** have survived, and while the **antique furnishings** and fittings are appealing, it's the beautiful wooden staircase that really catches the eye.

The Sharp Centre for Design

Immediately to the south of the AGO, along McCaul St, the Ontario College of Art and Design occupiedy a plain brick building until the extraordinary **Sharp Centre for Design** was added to it in 2004. Created by the English architect Will Alsop – his first building in North America – the centre comprises a giant black-and-white-panelled rectangular "table-top", perched high up at roof level and supported by mammoth multi-coloured steel legs; it holds art studios, theatres and so forth and has variously been described as "adventurous" and "ludicrous". Regardless, it certainly is big.

Chinatown and Kensington Market

Back on Dundas, the Art Gallery of Ontario is fringed by **Chinatown**, a bustling, immensely appealing neighbourhood cluttered with **shops**, **restaurants** (for recommendations, see p.157) and **street stalls** selling any and every type of Asian delicacy. The boundaries of Chinatown are somewhat blurred, but its focus, ever since the 1960s, when the original Chinatown was demolished to make way for the new City Hall, has been Dundas Street West between Beverley Street and Spadina Avenue. The first Chinese to migrate to Canada arrived in the mid-nineteenth century to work in British Columbia's gold fields. Subsequently, a portion of this population migrated east, and a sizeable Chinese community sprang up in Toronto in the early twentieth century. Several more waves of migration – the last influx following the handing over of Hong Kong to mainland China by the British in 1997 – have greatly increased the number of Toronto's Chinese, bringing the population to approximately 250,000 (about eight percent of the city's total).

Next door to Chinatown, just north of Dundas Street West, between Spadina and Augusta avenues, lies Toronto's most ethnically diverse neighbourhood, pocket-sized **Kensington Market**. It was here, at the turn of the twentieth century, that Eastern European immigrants squeezed into a patchwork of modest little brick and timber houses that survive to this day. On Kensington Avenue they established an **open-air street market**, the main feature of the neighbourhood ever since, a lively, entertaining bazaar whose stall owners stem from many different backgrounds. The lower half of the market, just off Dundas Street, concentrates on **secondhand clothing**, while the upper half is crowded with **fresh food stalls and cafés**. Even if you don't want to actually buy anything, Kensington Market is one of the city's funkiest neighbourhoods, a great place to hang out.

Uptown Toronto

S preading north from Gerrard Street, **Uptown Toronto** is something of an architectural hodgepodge, with perhaps the handiest starting point being **University Avenue**, whose bristling, monochromatic office blocks stomp up towards the imposing Victorian stonework of the **Ontario Legislative Assembly Building**, one of the city's most distinctive structures. The Assembly Building marks the start of a small **museum district**, made up of the delightful **Gardiner Museum of Ceramic Art** and the large but somewhat incoherent **Royal Ontario Museum**, which possesses one of the country's most extensive collections of applied art; both museums, however, are being thoroughly revamped – the first for a grand reopening in 2006, the second for 2007. The Assembly Building is also close to the prettiest part of the sprawling **University of Toronto** campus, on and around King's College Circle.

Moving north, office blocks and shops choke Bloor Street West, though it's here you'll find the fanciful **Bata Shoe Museum**, as well as the ritzy little neighbourhood of **Yorkville**. From here, it's a short subway ride or a thirty-minute walk to the city's two finest historic homes: the neo-baronial **Casa Loma** and the debonair **Spadina House** next door, both covered by the **Toronto City Pass** (see p.47).

Uptown's principal east–west corridor, **Bloor Street**, intersects with **Yonge Street**, the main north–south drag, which cuts a lively, if somewhat seedy, route north from Gerrard Street, lined along the way with **bars, cafés and shops**. At Wellesley Street, Yonge makes its way through the edge of the **Gay Village**, but the only sights hereabouts are further east in **Cabbagetown**, a pleasant old neighbourhood of leafy streets and terrace houses.

The Ontario Legislative Assembly Building

Peering down University Avenue, from just north of College Street, the pink sandstone mass of the **Ontario Legislative Assembly Building** dates to the 1890s (frequent 30min guided tour from late May to early Sept daily 10am–4pm, late Sept to late May Mon–Fri 10am–4pm; free; ☎416/325-7500, ✉www .ontla.on.ca; Queen's Park subway). Elegant it certainly isn't, but although the building is heavy and solid, its ponderous symmetries do have a certain appeal, with block upon block of roughly dressed stone assembled in the full flourish

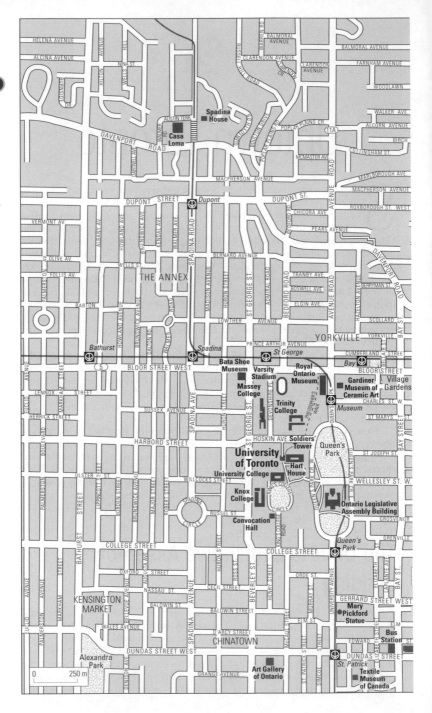

HELENA AVENUE
ALCINA AVENUE
NINA ST.
WELLS ST.
HILTON
AVENUE
BALMORAL
AVENUE
BALMORAL AVENUE
CLARENDON AVENUE
CLARENDON
AVENUE
FARNHAM AVENUE
WOODLAWN
WALKER AVE
ALCORN AVENUE
BIRCH
DAVENPORT ROAD
Spadina
House
Casa Loma
AUSTIN TERR.
POPLAR PLAINS CR.
11A
McMASTER AVE.
COTTINGHAM ST.
MACPHERSON AVENUE
MARLBOROUGH AVE.
MACPHERSON AVENUE
ROXBOROUGH ST. WEST
DUPONT STREET
Dupont
DUPONT ST.
CHICORA AVE.
PEARS AVENUE
VERMONT AV
ALBANY AV
HOWLAND AVE.
RYDSWICK AVE.
KENDAL AVE.
WALMER AVE.
SPADINA ROAD
BERNARD AVENUE
BERNARD AVENUE
DAVENPORT ROAD
AVENUE ROAD
V. OLIVE AV.
FOLLIS AV.
WELLS ST.
THE ANNEX
MADISON AVENUE
HURON STREET
ST. GEORGE ST.
ADMIRAL ROAD
BEDFORD ROAD
TRANBY AVE.
BOSWELL AVE.
ELGIN AVE.
HAZELTON AVENUE
BERRYMAN ST.
BARTON
PALMERSTON
HOWLAND AVENUE
BRUNSWICK AVENUE
DALTON RD.
WALKER
LOWTHER AVENUE
SCOLLARD
YORKVILLE
YORKVILLE
BAY ST.
Bathurst
Spadina
St George
PRINCE ARTHUR AVENUE
CUMBERLAND STREET
Bay
Bata Shoe
Museum
Varsity
Stadium
Royal
Ontario
Museum
BLOOR STREET
BLOOR STREET WEST
Gardiner
Museum of
Ceramic Art
Village
Gardens
Massey
College
DEVONSHIRE PL.
Trinity
College
PHILOSOPHER'S WALK
Museum
CHARLES ST. W
ST MARYS
SUSSEX AVENUE
HARBORD STREET
HOSKIN AVE.
Soldiers'
Tower
Queen's
Park
ST JOSEPH ST.
University
of Toronto
Hart
House
University College
WELLESLEY ST. W.
ULSTER ST.
WILLCOCKS STREET
Knox
College
KING'S COLLEGE RD.
QUEEN'S PARK CR. W.
Ontario Legislative
Assembly Building
GROSVENOR
SPADINA
CIRCLE
RUSSEL ST.
KING'S COLLEGE
CIRCLE
Convocation
Hall
GRENVILLE
COLLEGE STREET
COLLEGE STREET
Queen's
Park
KENSINGTON
MARKET
OXFORD STREET
NASSAU ST.
BALDWIN STREET
WALES AVENUE
AUGUSTA AVE.
CECIL STREET
ROSS ST.
BEVERLEY STREET
HURON ST.
BALDWIN STREET
D'ARCY STREET
CHINATOWN
ORDE ST.
MURRAY ST.
MCCAUL STREET
UNIVERSITY AVENUE
GERRARD STREET WEST
Mary
Pickford
Statue
ELM ST.
ELM
Bus
Station
ELIZABETH ST.
BAY ST.
EDWARD ST.
DUNDAS STREET WEST
DUNDAS STREET
Alexandra
Park
GRANGE AVENUE
Art Gallery
of Ontario
St Patrick
Textile
Museum
of Canada
ST PATRICK STREET
SIMCOE

0   250 m

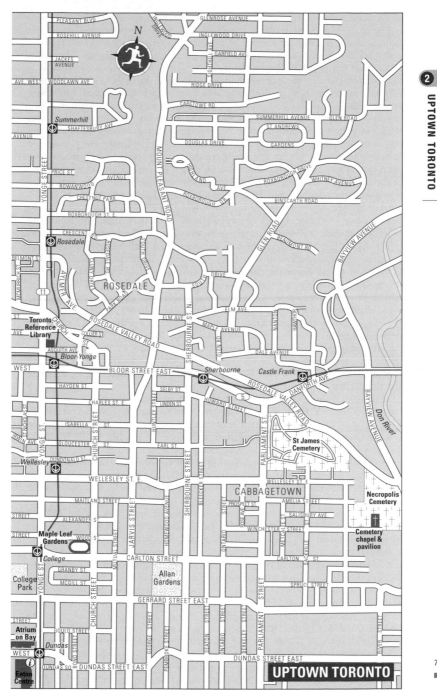

UPTOWN TORONTO

of the Romanesque Revival style. Seen from close up, the design is even more engaging, its intricacies a pleasant surprise: above the chunky columns of the main entrance is a sinuous filigree of carved stone, with mythological creatures and gargoyle-like faces poking out from every nook and cranny. The main facade also sports a Neoclassical frieze in which the Great Seal of Ontario is flanked by allegorical figures representing art, music, agriculture and so forth.

Inside, the foyer leads to the wide and thickly carpeted **Grand Staircase**, whose massive timbers are supported by gilded iron pillars. Beyond is the capacious **Legislative Chamber**, where the formality of the mahogany and sycamore panels is offset by a series of whimsical little **carvings** – look for the owl overlooking the doings of the government and the hawk overseeing the opposition benches. Under the Speaker's gallery, righteous **inscriptions** have been carved into the pillars, which is a bit of a hoot considering the behaviour of the building's architect, Richard Waite. Waite was chairman of the committee responsible for selecting an architect, and, as chairman, he selected himself.

A fire burned down the building's **west wing** in 1909, and to avoid a repeat performance, Parliament had its replacement built in marble the following year. No expense was spared in the reconstruction, so there was an awful fuss when one of the MPPs (Members of the Provincial Parliament) noticed what appeared to be blemishes in the stone on several of the pillars. The blotches turned out to be **dinosaur fossils**, and nowadays they are pointed out on the **guided tour**. The provincial assembly typically sits from late September to late June, with breaks at Christmas and Easter, and although guided tours avoid the chamber when the body is in session, the **visitors' gallery** is open to the public during its deliberations Monday through Thursdays; call for further details and times.

Back outside, in front of the main entrance, are a pair of Russian **cannons** that were captured during the Crimean War. Queen Victoria gave them to the city in 1859 in honour of those Canadian regiments who had fought alongside the British during the siege of Sevastopol. The cannons are flanked by a series of **statues** of politicians and imperial bigwigs that spread across the manicured lawns of **Queen's Park**. Two of the more interesting are just a few metres to the east of the assembly's main entrance, beginning with **Queen Victoria**, who sits on her throne with a rather paltry crown on her head. Strangely, Victoria looks very male and, as if to compensate, her bust appears much too large for her slender frame. The adjacent statue of **John Graves Simcoe** (see p.229) is a much happier affair, with the one-time lieutenant-governor of Upper Canada cutting a dashing figure with a tricorn hat in one hand and a cane, held at a jaunty angle, in the other.

On the west side of the building stands a **bust** of anti-Tory radical William Lyon Mackenzie (see p.64 & p.230) and immediately behind it is an over-blown **memorial** to "The struggle for responsible government" – that is, the campaign for representative government as opposed to rule by British appoint-ees. Mackenzie was one of the first figures of any note to champion this cause. Behind the memorial is a **plaque** honouring the **Mac-Paps**. Named after the joint leaders of the Rebellion of 1837 – Mackenzie and Louis Joseph Papineau – the Mac-Paps were a 1500-strong Canadian battalion of the International Brigades, who fought for the Republicans against Franco and the Fascists in the Spanish Civil War of the 1930s. The plaque is attached to a hunk of rock from the Spanish town of Gandesa, scene of some of the war's bloodiest fighting.

There's more **statuary** behind the Legislative Building on the other section of Queen's Park. Here, right in the middle of the greenery, lording over the pigeons and the squirrels, is a heavyweight equestrian statue of King Edward VII in full-dress uniform. Originally plonked down in Delhi, this imperial leftover looks a bit forlorn – and you can't help but feel the Indians must have been pleased to off-load it.

University of Toronto

The sprawling campus of the **University of Toronto**, which extends south-north from College to Bloor and east-west from Bay to Spadina, is dotted with stately college buildings and halls of residence. The best-looking (and most interesting) are to be found close to the Legislative Assembly Building at the west end of Wellesley Street, beginning on **Hart House Circle**. Here, the ivy-covered walls, neo-Gothic architecture and cloistered quadrangles of **Hart House** are reminiscent of Oxford and Cambridge – just as they were designed to be. Primarily a students' social and cultural facility, Hart House dates from the early twentieth century, its communal rooms culminating in the cavernous **Great Hall**, with its high timber ceiling and acres of wood panelling.

Hart House is named after **Hart Massey** (1823–1896), a member of the Massey family that made a vast fortune from the manufacture of farm machinery. One of the last of the family to be directly associated with the company was **Vincent Massey** (1887–1967), an extraordinarily influential man, sometimes ribbed as Canada's representative in heaven. Vincent was the one-time Chairman of the National Gallery, Chancellor of the University of Toronto, and the first native-born Governor-General of Canada from 1952 to 1959. Hart House was built at Vincent's instigation, and he also

John Strachan

Toronto's first Anglican bishop was the redoubtable **John Strachan**, a one-time schoolmaster who made a name for himself in the War of 1812. The Americans may have occupied Toronto easily enough, but Strachan led a spirited civil resistance, bombarding the occupiers with a deluge of requests and demands about everything from inadequate supplies to any lack of respect the Americans showed to private property. Perhaps surprisingly, the Americans treated Strachan's complaints very seriously, though they did get mightily irritated. After the war, Strachan turned his formidable energies to education. All of bourgeois Toronto believed in the value of university education, but the problem was agreeing on who should provide it, as Canada's various religious denominations all wanted a piece of the educational action.

In 1827, Strachan obtained a royal charter for the foundation of Toronto's first college of higher education, but his plans for an Anglican-controlled institution were resisted so forcibly that **King's College**, as Strachan's college was called, didn't open its doors until 1843. Even then, Strachan's triumph was short-lived: Anglican control lasted just six years before the provincial government secularized the institution and renamed it the **University of Toronto**.

Over the ensuing decades the university was browbeaten by theological colleges that considered a secular university to be immoral, but by the turn of the twentieth century the University of Toronto had made a name for itself, ultimately becoming one of North America's most prestigious educational institutions. It was here that **insulin** was discovered in 1921, and here that **Marshall McLuhan**, who taught at the university, wrote his seminal *The Medium is the Massage*.

△ University of Toronto

helped equip it with a sizeable collection of **modern Canadian paintings**, in which the Group of Seven (see box p.70) makes a strong showing. The collection is too large to display at any one time, so the exhibits are regularly rotated, and they can be viewed both in some of the public rooms of Hart House and sometimes in its **Justina M. Barnicke Gallery** (July–Aug Mon–Fri 11am–6pm & Sat 1–4pm; Sept–June Mon–Fri 11am–7pm, Sat 1–4pm; free; ☎416/978-8398). The gallery, which has just two small rooms, runs a lively programme of temporary exhibitions and has a sound reputation for showcasing the work of less well-known, modern Canadian painters from the 1920s onwards.

The Soldiers' Tower

Hart House is attached to the **Soldiers' Tower**, a neo-Gothic memorial erected in 1924 to honour those students who had died in World War I. It adjoins an arcaded **gallery**, which is inscribed with a list of the war dead as well as Canadian **John McCrae**'s *In Flanders Fields*, arguably the war's best-known poem: "...We are the Dead. Short days ago/We lived, felt dawn, saw sunset glow,/Loved and were loved, and now we lie,/In Flanders fields...". Optimistically, the builders of the memorial didn't leave any space to commemorate the dead of any future war – so the names of the university students killed in World War II had to be inscribed on the walls under the arches at the foot of the tower.

King's College Circle

Hart House Circle leads into the much larger **King's College Circle**, where an assortment of university buildings flanks a large field. On the north side of the field stands **University College**, a rambling Romanesque-style structure, whose arcades and rotunda, turrets and dormer windows frame an imposing if somewhat surly central tower. Further around the circle, the rough sandstone masonry of **Knox College**, dating from 1874, repeats the studied Gothicism of its neighbours, whereas the adjacent **Convocation Hall** makes a break for a lighter tone, its elegant rotunda having been erected in the 1920s.

Philosopher's Walk

Backtracking to Hart House Circle, walk through the arch of the Soldiers' Tower, turn right along Hoskin Avenue and – just before you reach the traffic island – watch for the footpath on the left. This is **Philosopher's Walk**, an easy, leafy stroll, which leads north, slipping around the back of (but still giving access to) the Royal Ontario Museum on the way to Bloor Street West.

The Royal Ontario Museum

From both the Legislative Assembly Building and Hart House Circle, it's a short walk north along the boulevard to the **Royal Ontario Museum**, at 100 Queen's Park (Mon–Thurs 10am–6pm, Fri 10am–9.30pm, Sat & Sun 10am–6pm; $15, seniors $12, children 5–14 years $10, free after 4.30pm on Fri; ☎416/586-5549, ⊛www.rom.on.ca; Museum subway). The ROM is Canada's largest and most diverse museum and, among much else, possesses a vast collection of fine and applied art drawn from every corner of the globe.

Opened in 1914, the ROM's **main building** is a serious-minded stone structure whose precise neo-Gothic symmetries have been embellished with Art Deco flourishes. The main doors are imposingly large and above them a complement of muses, astrological symbols and mythological beasts stands guard. Just beyond is the domed and vaulted **entrance hall** whose ceiling is decorated with a brilliant mosaic of imported Venetian glass; bolted into the adjacent stairwells are four colossal and stunningly beautiful Native Canadian **crest poles** (commonly but erroneously referred to as totem poles). Dating from the 1880s, and the work of craftsmen from the Haida and Nisga'a peoples of the west coast, these poles – the tallest is 24.5 metres high – are decorated with stylized carvings representing the supernatural animals and birds that were associated with particular clans.

Currently the museum is in the midst of being entirely **restructured**, a process that includes the addition of a large and flashy new extension, whose six crystal-shaped, aluminium-and-glass cubes are the brainchild of the architect **Daniel Libeskind**. Work is well under way and the redevelopment should be completed by the beginning of 2007, but in the meantime visitors can only see a small fraction of the collection and have to take pot luck as to what's displayed and when. What follows are some general hints as to the ROM's most impressive sections, notably its internationally acclaimed Chinese collection and the assorted fossils of the Dinosaurs' gallery. **Museum plans** are available for free at the entrance.

Canadiana

Scheduled to be displayed on Level 1, the ROM's **Canadian collection** is strong on prehistoric archeology and late eighteenth- and early nineteenth-century **trade silver**, an intriguing assortment of ornaments – brooches, earrings, crucifixes, medals and the like – which European traders swapped with natives for furs. This section also includes the iconic *Death of Wolfe* by **Benjamin West**. The British general James Wolfe inflicted a crushing defeat on the French outside Québec City in 1759, but was killed during the battle. West's painting transformed this grubby colonial conflict into a romantic extravagance, with the dying general in a Christ-like pose, a pale figure held tenderly by his subordinates. West presented the first version of his painting to the Royal Academy of Arts in 1771 and it proved so popular that he spent much of the next decade painting copies.

The Chinese collection

The ROM owns an exquisite collection of **Chinese Temple Art**, most notably three large and stunningly beautiful Daoist and Buddhist wall paintings dating from around 1300 AD. Two of them are a matching pair of Yuan Dynasty **murals** depicting the lords of the Northern and Southern Dipper, each of whom leads an astrological procession of star spirits. There is also a superb sample of Buddhist temple figures dating from the twelfth to the fourteenth centuries.

The museum's **East Asian** collection spans six millennia, from 4500 BC to 1900 AD. Among the most important pieces is a remarkable collection of toy-sized **tomb figurines** – a couple of hundred ceramic pieces representing funerary processions of soldiers, musicians, carts and attendants. Dating from

Ethnic
Toronto

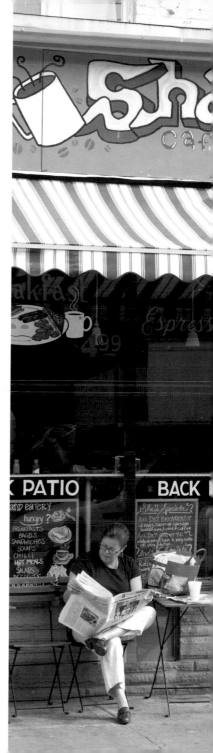

In travel guidebooks (not unlike this one) and nearly any other place Toronto is written about, you're likely to come across Peter Ustinov's hoary old chestnut about the city being like "New York run by the Swiss". It is undoubtedly true that Toronto boasts a crisp efficiency, but, as a clever-sounding comment on the city's alleged sterility, the quote irritates many Torontonians no end – and with justification. After all, every major city in the West is, to a lesser or greater degree, now cosmopolitan and multi-ethnic, and this applies to Toronto in full measure.

Toronto's particular **multiculturalism** has some of the qualities of a well-considered project, in which the different groups both share a common (Canadian) identity and maintain their own – the so-called "fruit cake" approach, as distinct from the USA's "melting pot". At heart, this tolerant flexibility has much to do with Canada's own lack of a clear identity, but the differences are elusive and their own bigwigs are prone to dodge the issue as speedily as they can: "A true Canadian is one who can make love in a canoe without tipping", declared the historian Pierre Berton, while filmmaker David Cronenberg has quipped, "I don't have a moral plan. I'm a Canadian". Whatever the reasons, the results of this tolerance are almost all positive and, for the most part at least, Toronto simply revels in its diversity, living up to its designation by UNESCO as the "world's most multicultural city".

Festivals

It is in the city's headliner **festivals** that its true cosmopolitanism reveals itself, sometimes placidly and calmly, sometimes with a great, noisy jolt. To be sure, the boisterous café, bar, club and street scenes are effortlessly, seamlessly multicultural, but their liveliness can hardly measure up to events like the two-week-long **Caribana Festival**, a high-energy, Caribbean extravaganza culminating in one of the biggest street parties anywhere, with an eye-popping parade featuring hundreds of floats, dazzling costumes and jaw-dropping dancing. Other quite varied highlights abound: African Heritage Month is celebrated throughout February with festivals like **Kuumba: Jambalaya Jump Up**; South Asian artists are introduced to large audiences as part of the **Masala! Mheendi! Masi!** festival in the first week of August; and over the last weekend in November the Canadian Aboriginal Festival features everything from music and theatre through to dancing competitions.

Neighbourhoods

Immigrants who have settled here over the years have helped shape one of Toronto's most striking features – its division into sharply distinct **neighbourhoods**. Many of these are based on ethnic origin (some by sexual preference or income), albeit with the occasional artificiality to the nomenclature – Chinatown, for example, has hundreds of Vietnamese residents, while Little Italy is home to a large contingent of Portuguese. Nevertheless, the demarcations provide a handy way of knowing the best places to go for some kielbasa (Little Poland) or five element theory acupuncture (Koreatown) – or just the locations of places where you can bet the atmosphere will have a distinctive jig and jive.

Thanks to a swelling population (and equally swelling real estate prices), Toronto is home to not one, but four **Chinatowns.** Chinese people first arrived in Toronto in the early twentieth century, and subsequent waves of immigration – the last influx following the handing over of Hong Kong to mainland China by the British in 1997 – have brought the local population to approximately 250,000. The oldest and best known of the city's Chinatowns, concentrated along Dundas Street West, between Bay Street and Spadina Avenue, is also one of Toronto's most distinctive neighbourhoods. The area is packed with busy restaurants and stores selling anything from porcelain and jade to herbs and pickled seaweed.

A more recently burgeoning neighborhood, **Greektown**, is located along Danforth Avenue, between Pape and Woodbine. Although a handful of Greeks resided in Toronto at the turn of the twentieth century, it wasn't until after World War II that a real community began to flourish. Currently home to the largest Greek population in North America, this is definitely the place to go for Greek food.

Italians constitute Toronto's largest non-Anglo group, and **Little Italy** – the so-called Corso Italia, which runs along College Street between Bathurst and Clinton – is one of Toronto's liveliest neighbourhoods, filled with bustling cafés, restaurants, nightclubs and high-end

Little Portugal

clothing stores. Although not too visually appealing, **Little India**, along Gerrard Street East, running one block west from Coxwell Avenue, also has a number of fine restaurants that are worth checking out, while **Little Portugal**, focused on Dundas Street West, west of Bathurst Street as far as Dovercourt Road, is a crowded, vital area packed with shops and local food joints. The heart of Toronto's large **Polish** community is found along **Roncesvalles Avenue**, the main drag of the High Park neighbourhood, which takes its name from the stretch of greenery that overlooks the Gardiner Expressway to the west of Downtown.

Little India

Spadina Avenue, Chinatown

Kensington Market

Although the enclaves may consist of just a few streets and, architecturally speaking, can seem indistinguishable from their surroundings, they still manage to sustain a flavour all their own. The most ethnically diverse of the bunch is **Kensington Market**, just north of Dundas Street West between Spadina and Augusta avenues, where Portuguese, West Indian and Jewish Canadians pack the streets with many tiny shops and open-air stalls. The lower half of the market, just off Dundas, concentrates on secondhand clothing, while the upper half is crowded with fresh food stalls and cafés. Even if you're not looking to buy anything, this funky area is a great place to hang out.

Food

Perhaps the most obvious manifestation of Toronto's diversity is the variety of **cuisines** on offer. Whether you have a craving for a Sri Lankan crepe, a large-platter Ethiopian dish or a fragrant, multi-course Persian feast, you are sure to find it here. One real surprise is that Toronto, or more precisely the Greater Toronto area (GTA), is the only city outside Asia to offer examples of all schools of **Chinese** cuisine. The truly adventurous can investigate this boast by heading off to a slew of restaurants in both the city and in the malls of its northern suburbs. There's everything from glitzy dim sum palaces to high quality restaurants showcasing exotic regional fare such as Hakka, Tianjin and spicy Yunnan dishes alongside the more familiar Cantonese and Szechuan classics. **Indian** cuisine also plays a particularly strong hand in Toronto, from the eye-watering dishes of Kashmir to the vegetarian specialities of Madras, while popular **Italian** restaurants range from street-corner pizza and pasta joints through to deluxe establishments, offering fresh, made-on-the-spot food subtly seasoned in true Mediterranean style.

Toronto's thriving **café scene** is the seam in the city's social fabric, where locals share a quick meal, an evening drink or a lazy morning latte. One of the latest trends is the appearance of **grazing menus**, with Asian, Spanish, Greek and other foods sampled via dim sum, tapas, meze and the like. In a nod to both its Anglo past and its multicultural present, a formidable **tea culture** embraces everything from high tea, offered in four-star hotels, to bubble tea, a Taiwanese mixture of sweet, iced and Technicolour teas with globules of tapioca sitting at the bottom.

Dim sum

the early sixth to the late seventh century, they re-create the habits of early China: how people dressed, how horses were groomed and shod, changes in armoury and so forth. There is also a fabulous collection of **snuff bottles**, some carved from glass and rock crystal, others from more exotic materials like amber, ivory, bamboo and even tangerine skin. Europeans introduced tobacco to China in the late sixteenth century, and although smoking did not become popular in China until recent times, snuff went down a storm and anyone who was anybody at court was snorting the stuff by the middle of the seventeenth century. Perhaps the most popular component of the Chinese collection, however, is its **Ming Tomb**. The aristocracy of the Ming Dynasty (1368–1644 AD) evolved an elaborate style of monumental funerary sculpture and architecture, and the ROM holds the only example outside of China, though it is actually a composite tomb drawn from several sources rather than an intact, original whole. Central to the Ming burial conception was a Spirit Way, an avenue with large-scale carved figures of guards, attendants and animals placed on either side. At the end of the alley was the tumulus, or burial mound – in this case the tomb house of a seventeenth-century Chinese general by the name of Zu Dashou.

The Age of Dinosaurs' gallery

When the redesigned ROM is up and running, most of Level 2 will be devoted to the natural world, with separate galleries for evolution, mammals, birds and the like. The highlight will almost certainly be the **Age of Dinosaurs' gallery**, which will hold dioramas and simulations as well as the ROM's splendid assortment of **fossil-skeletons**, the pick being those retrieved from the Alberta Badlands, near Calgary. These Badlands are the richest source of dinosaur fossils in the world, having yielded over 300 complete skeletons and 35 dinosaur species – ten percent of all those known today. Many of the Alberta dinosaur fossils have been dispatched to museums across the world, but the ROM still has a superb collection; the rampant herd of **Allosaurus** – a Jurassic-period carnivore of large proportions and ferocious appearance – commands the most attention.

Also in this section there will likely be a large display on Canada's **insects** (a fearsome-looking bunch, including the No-see-um, which drives caribou to distraction by burrowing into their nostrils) and a revamped **Discovery Gallery**: the existing version is one of the best education facilities in Toronto, giving children the opportunity to handle and study museum artefacts at their own pace. Currently, children under ten visiting the Discovery Gallery will have to be accompanied by an adult, while ten- to twelve-year-olds must have an adult supervisor on the premises.

Europe and the Mediterranean World

The ROM's **European Collection** includes a string of period rooms, mostly English, from the sixteenth to the eighteenth century, as well as eclectic collections of Arms and Armour, Art Nouveau and Art Deco, metalwork, glass and ceramics. Amongst the latter is a superb collection of Delftware and Italian majolica (see p.82, under the Gardiner Museum, for more on majolica).

As regards the **Mediterranean World**, there is much from Imperial Rome, Mesopotamia, Nubia, classical Greece and Etruria, but the ROM is at its strongest when it comes to **Ancient Egypt**, owning several finely preserved mummies, including the richly decorated sarcophagus of a certain Djedmaatesankh, a court musician who died around 850 BC. Even more unusual is the assortment of mummified animals, including a crocodile, a hawk and a weird-looking cat. There is also the intriguing **Punt Wall**, a 1905 plaster cast of the original in Queen Hatshepsut's temple in Deir el-Bahri, Egypt. The events depicted on the wall occurred in the year 1482 BC, and represent a military expedition to Punt, which lay south of Egypt near present-day Somalia.

The George R. Gardiner Museum of Ceramic Art

Named after its wealthy founding patron, the **George R. Gardiner Museum of Ceramic Art** (℡416/586-8080, ⊛www.gardinermuseum.on.ca; Museum subway), just across the street from the ROM at 111 Queen's Park, possesses a superb connoisseur's collection of ceramics, though the museum is currently **closed for redevelopment** and will not reopen until the spring of 2006. The new, expanded museum will feature a contemporary ceramics gallery and a gallery for temporary exhibitions; if the old museum is anything to go by, you can expect the exhibits to be beautifully presented and both well labelled and well explained.

The Gardiner has an especially fine collection of **pre-Columbian** artefacts, comprising of over three hundred pieces from regions stretching from Mexico to Peru. One of the most comprehensive collections of its kind in North America, it provides an intriguing insight into the lifestyles and beliefs of the Maya, Inca and Aztec peoples. The **sculptures** are all the more remarkable for the fact that the potter's wheel was unknown in pre-Columbian America, and thus everything was hand-modelled. While some of the pieces feature everyday activities, it is the **religious sculptures** that mostly catch the eye, from wonderfully intricate Mexican incense burners to the fantastical zoomorphic gods of the Zapotecs.

The museum also owns an exquisite sample of fifteenth- and sixteenth-century tin-glazed **Italian majolica**, consisting mostly of dishes, plates and jars depicting classical and Biblical themes designed by Renaissance artists. The early pieces are comparatively plain, limited to green and purple, but the later examples are brightly coloured, for in the second half of the fifteenth century Italian potters learnt how to glaze blue and yellow, and ochre was added later. Perhaps the most splendid pieces are those from the city – and pottery centre – of Urbino, including two wonderful plates portraying the fall of Jericho and the exploits of Hannibal.

Amongst the Gardiner's collection of eighteenth-century **European porcelain**, there are fine examples of hard-paste wares (fired at very high temperatures) from Meissen, Germany, as well as an interesting sample of Chinese-style blue and white porcelain, long the mainstay of the European ceramic industry. There is also an unusual collection of English ware, which features both well-known manufacturers – notably the ornate products of Royal Worcester – as well as less familiar pieces, including the demure and modest crockery produced in the village of Pinxton, on the edge of Sherwood Forest, in the eighteenth century. Another key part of the collection is a charming menagerie of Italian *commedia dell'arte* figurines, doll-sized representations of theatrical characters popular across Europe from the middle of the sixteenth to the late eighteenth century.

Bata Shoe Museum

Within easy walking distance of the Gardiner, the **Bata Shoe Museum**, 327 Bloor St West at St George St (Tues, Wed, Fri & Sat 10am–5pm, Thurs 10am–8pm, Sun noon–5pm, plus June–Aug Mon 10am–5pm; $8; ☎416/979-7799, ⓦwww.batashoemuseum.ca; St George subway), was designed by **Raymond Moriyama**, the much-lauded Canadian architect whose other creations include the Ontario Science Centre (see p.104), the Scarborough Civic Centre and the Toronto Reference Library (see p.84). Moriyama is not without his architectural critics, but his accomplished designs demonstrate a soft and subtle charm in their preference for unusual angles and wavy, rounded lines. For the Bata Museum, which opened in 1995, Moriyama chose to make the exterior look like a shoe box, the roof set at a jaunty angle to suggest a lid resting on an open box. It is not, perhaps, one of his most successful creations, but it seems to have satisfied the woman who was funding it all – **Sonja Bata** of the Bata shoe manufacturing family – who had the museum built to display the extraordinary assortment of footwear she had spent a lifetime collecting.

A leaflet issued at reception steers visitors around the museum, starting with an introductory section on Level B1 entitled "**All About Shoes**", which presents an overview on the evolution of footwear and includes a plaster cast of the oldest human footprint ever discovered (roughly 3,700,000 years old). Among the more interesting exhibits in this section are pointed shoes from **medieval Europe**, where different social classes were allowed different lengths of toe, and tiny **Chinese silk shoes** used by women whose feet had been bound. Banned by the Chinese Communists when they came to power in 1949, foot binding was common practice for over a thousand years, and the "ideal" length of a woman's foot was a hobbling three inches. Here also is an assortment of **specialist footwear**, most memorably French chestnut-crushing clogs from the nineteenth century, inlaid Ottoman platforms designed to keep aristocratic feet well away from the mud and a pair of US army boots from the Vietnam War with the sole shaped to imitate the sandal prints of the Vietcong.

The stairs leading up from Level B1 are flanked by a small but unusual collection of **stirrups** – the iron ones look spectacularly uncomfortable – and at the top, on Level G, a large glass cabinet showcases all sorts of **celebrity footwear**. The exhibits are rotated regularly, but look out for Buddy Holly's loafers, Eminem's sneakers, Marilyn Monroe's stilettos, Princess Diana's red court shoes, Shaquille O'Neal's colossal Reebok trainers and Elton John's ridiculous platforms. Level 2 and Level 3 are used for **temporary exhibitions** – some of which are very good indeed – and there's also a small section explaining the museum's role in restoring and repairing old footwear.

Yorkville

From both the Bata Museum and the Gardiner, it's the briefest of walks to the chic and well-heeled **Yorkville neighbourhood**, whose epicentre is Cumberland Street and Yorkville Avenue between Bay Street and Avenue Road. Jam-packed with chichi **cafés, restaurants and shops**, Yorkville makes for a pleasant stroll (especially if you've got some spare cash), one of its most agreeable features being the **old timber-terrace houses** that are still much in evidence. These same houses have actually seen much grimmer days: in the late 1950s, Yorkville was run down and impoverished, but then the hippies arrived and soon turned the area into a countercultural enclave – a diminutive version of Haight-Ashbury, with Joni Mitchell and Gordon Lightfoot in attendance. Things are much less inventive today – big cars and big jewellery – but the **Village Gardens**, at the corner of Cumberland and Bellair streets, is a particularly appealing and cleverly designed little park. The centrepiece is a hunk of granite brought from northern Ontario, and around it are arranged a variety of neat little gardens, displaying every native Ontario habitat from forest to wetlands.

The Toronto Reference Library

At the east end of Cumberland Street, east of Yorkville at 789 Yonge St, the **Toronto Reference Library** (Mon–Thurs 10am–8pm, Fri & Sat 10am–5pm, plus mid-Sept to late June Sun 1.30–5pm; ☎416/393-7131, ⓦwww .torontopubliclibrary.ca) occupies a striking modern building designed by Canada's own **Raymond Moriyama** (see p.83). The exterior is actually a good deal less becoming than the interior, whose five floors are arranged around a large and airy floor-to-ceiling atrium with a pool and waterfall. As you would expect, the library possesses an enormous stock of books, CDs and audiobooks, as well as around 100 public-access PCs, which are divided into two groups – those which can be booked ahead of time and those which are used instantly for a maximum of fifteen minutes; Internet access on all the computers is free.

Amongst the library's many sections, the fourth-floor **Periodicals Centre** has Canadian source materials dating back to the eighteenth century, as does the adjoining **Special Collections, Genealogy and Maps Centre**, comprising the library's rare and specialized research collections. The latter covers a wide range of subject areas from local history through to rare books. Regular **exhibitions** illustrate various aspects of the special collections, but it's the fifth-floor **Arthur Conan Doyle Room** (Tues, Thurs & Sat 2–4pm; free) that steals the show, boasting the world's largest collection of books, manuscripts, letters and so forth written by Conan Doyle, including of course the illustrious Sherlock Holmes series.

Cabbagetown

The precise boundaries of **Cabbagetown**, southeast of the Toronto Reference Library, continue to be a matter of dispute between local historians and real estate agents – the former try to narrow the area and the latter try to expand it – but, roughly speaking, this Victorian neighbourhood is bounded by Dundas Street to the south, Parliament Street to the west, Wellesley Street to the north, and the Don River valley to the east.

Cabbagetown got its name from nineteenth-century Irish immigrants who grew cabbages in their yards instead of (the more traditional) flowers. Contemporary residents have embraced the vegetable and even have their own flag with a large, leafy cabbage prominently displayed at the centre. The neighbourhood once had a reputation for substandard homes and dire living conditions, prompting novelist Hugh Garner to anoint it "the largest Anglo-Saxon slum in North America". Today, however, most of the houses have been renovated by their more prosperous owners, and cabbagetown has become a haven for the city's hip and moderately well-to-do.

Specific sights in Cabbagetown are thin on the ground, but **Metcalfe Street**, running one block east of Parliament Street, does possess a particularly appealing ensemble of **Victorian houses**, as does adjoining **Winchester Street**. Common architectural features include high-pitched gables, stained-glass windows, stone lintels and inviting timber verandas. At the east end of Winchester Street, the entrance to one of the city's oldest cemeteries is marked by a handsome Gothic Revival **chapel** and matching **pavilion**, whose coloured tiles and soft yellow brickwork date to the middle of the nineteenth century. Inside the **cemetery**, the gravestones are almost universally modest and unassuming, but their straightforward accounts of the lives of the dead give witness to the extraordinary British diaspora that populated much of Victorian Canada. Cabbagetown is also home to the **oldest neighbourhood festival** in Toronto; for details, see p.220.

Casa Loma

On the other end of Uptown, northwest of the Yorkville neighbourhood, it's a five-minute walk from Dupont subway station up the slope of Spadina Road to the corner of Davenport Road, where a flight of steps leads to Toronto's most bizarre attraction: **Casa Loma**, at 1 Austin Terrace (daily: 9.30am–5pm, last admission 4pm; $12, parking $2.75 per hour; ☎416/923-1171, ⓦwww .casaloma.org). A folly to outdo almost every other folly, Casa Loma is an

---

Sir Henry Pellatt

Sir Henry Pellatt (1859–1939) made a fortune by pioneering the use of hydroelectricity, harnessing the power of Niagara Falls (see p.111) to light Ontario's expanding cities. Determined to become a man of social standing, Pellatt threw his money around with gusto. He levered his wife into a key position as a leader of the Girl Guides and managed to become a major general of the Queen's Own Rifles, bolstering his appointment by taking 640 soldiers to a military training camp in Aldershot, in England, at his own expense. Pellatt's enthusiasm for the British interest went down well, and he even secured a knighthood, though he was never fully accepted by the old elite – for one thing, he was fond of dressing up in a costume that combined a British colonel's uniform with the attire of a Mohawk chief.

In 1911, Pellatt started work on Casa Loma, gathering furnishings from all over the world and even importing Scottish stonemasons to build a wall around his six-acre property, the end result being an eccentric mixture of medieval fantasy and early twentieth-century technology. Pellatt spent more than $3 million fulfilling his dream, but his penchant for reckless business dealings finally caught up with him, forcing him to move out and declare himself bankrupt in 1923. He died penniless sixteen years later, his dramatic fall from grace earning him the nickname "Pellatt the Plunger".

enormous towered and turreted mansion built to the instructions of Sir Henry Pellatt and his architect Edward J. Lennox between 1911 and 1914. A free map of the house is available at the reception, as are **audioguides**.

A clearly numbered route around the house goes up one side and down the other. It begins on the ground floor in the **Great Hall**, a pseudo-Gothic extravaganza with an eighteen-metre-high cross-beamed ceiling, a Wurlitzer organ and enough floor space to accommodate several hundred guests. Hung with flags, heavy-duty chandeliers and suits of armour, it's a remarkably cheerless place, but, in a touch worthy of Errol Flynn, the hall is overlooked by a balcony at the end of Pellatt's second-floor bedroom; presumably, Sir Henry could, like some medieval baron, welcome his guests from on high.

Pushing on, the **library** and then the walnut-panelled **dining room** lead to the **conservatory**, an elegant and spacious room with a marble floor and side-panels set beneath a handsome Tiffany domed glass ceiling. Well-lit, this is perhaps the mansion's most appealing room, its flowerbeds kept warm even in winter by the original network of steam pipes. The nearby **study** was Sir Henry's favourite room, a serious affair engulfed by mahogany panelling and equipped with two secret passageways, one leading to the wine cellar, the other to his wife's rooms – a quintessential dichotomy. Also of note is the ground-floor **Oak Room**, which comes complete with an elaborate stucco ceiling and acres of finely carved oak panelling.

On the second floor, **Sir Henry's Suite** has oodles of walnut and mahogany panelling, which stands in odd contrast to the 1910s white-marble, high-tech bathroom, featuring an elaborate multi-nozzle shower. **Lady Pellatt's Suite** wasn't left behind in the ablutions department either – her bathroom had a bidet, a real novelty in George V's Canada – though she had a lighter decorative touch, eschewing wood panelling for walls painted in her favourite colour, Wedgwood Blue, with pastel furniture to match. This suite also contains a small display on Lady Pellatt's involvement with the Girl Guides, a uniformed organization encouraging good imperial habits: self-reliance, honesty, self-discipline and so forth. In the photos, Lady Pellatt looks serious and concerned, the girls suitably keen and dutiful.

At the other end of the main second-floor corridor are the **Round Room**, with its curved doors and walls, and the smartly decorated **Windsor Room**, named after – and built for – the Royal Family, in the rather forlorn hope that they would come and stay here. Of course they never did; Pellatt was much too parvenu for their tastes. Up above, the third floor holds a mildly diverting display on Pellatt's one-time regiment, the **Queen's Own Rifles**, tracing their involvement in various campaigns from the suppression of the Métis rebellion in western Canada in 1885 through to World War I and beyond. The most interesting features are the old photographs and the potted biographies of some of the regiment's bravest, medal-winning soldiers. From the third floor, wooden staircases clamber up to two of the house's **towers**, where you'll have pleasing views over the house and gardens.

Back on the ground floor, stairs lead down to the Lower Level, which was where Pellatt's money ran out and his plans ground to a halt. Work never started on the bowling alley and shooting range he had designed, and the **swimming pool** only got as far as the rough concrete basin that survives today – never mind that Pellatt conceived a marble pool overlooked by golden swans. Pellatt did, however, manage to complete the 250-metre-long **tunnel** that runs from the house and pool to the **carriage room** and **stables**, where his thoroughbred horses were allegedly better-treated than his servants, chomping away at their oats and hay in splendid iron and mahogany stalls.

The stables are a dead end, so you'll have to double back along the tunnel to reach the house and the exit. Before you leave, spare time for the **terraced gardens** (May–Oct daily 9.30am–4pm; no extra charge), which tumble down the ridge at the back of the house. They are parcelled up into several different sections and easily explored along a network of footpaths, beginning on the terrace behind the Great Hall. Highlights include the Rhododendron Dell, the lily pond and waterfall of the Water Garden and the Cedar Grove, a meadow garden flanked by cool, green cedars.

Spadina House

What the occupants of **Spadina House** (guided tours only, April–Aug Tues–Sun noon–5pm plus holiday Mon noon–5pm; Sept–Dec Tues–Fri noon–4pm, Sat & Sun noon–5pm; Jan–March Sat & Sun noon–5pm; $6, $6.75 on public

△ Spadina House

holidays; ☎416/392-6910; Dupont subway) thought when Casa Loma went up next door can only be imagined, but there must have been an awful lot of curtain-twitching. The two houses are a study in contrasts: Casa Loma a grandiose pile and Spadina an elegant Victorian property of genteel appearance dating from 1866.

Spadina was built by James Austin, an Irish immigrant from County Armagh who was a printer's apprentice before becoming a successful businessman and a co-founder of the Toronto Dominion Bank. After his death, Spadina House passed to Albert Austin, who enlarged and modernized his father's home, adding billiard and laundry rooms, a garage and a refrigerator room to replace the old ice house. Albert's property eventually passed to his three daughters, who lived in the house until the last of the sisters, Anna Kathleen, moved out in 1983, the year before she died. Anna bequeathed Spadina House to the City of Toronto, which now manages and maintains the place. The Austins' uninterrupted occupation of the house means that its furnishings are nearly all genuine family artefacts, and they provide an intriguing insight into the family's changing tastes and interests.

Narrated by enthusiastic volunteers, the **guided tour** is a delight. Particular highlights include the conservatory trap door that allowed the gardeners to come and go unseen by their employers, an assortment of period chairs and sofas designed to accommodate the largest of bustles, the original gas chandeliers and a couple of canvases by **Cornelius Krieghoff** (see p.68). Pride of place, however, goes to the **Billiard Room**, which comes complete with an inventive Art Nouveau decorative frieze dating from 1898, and the **library**, equipped with a sturdy oak bureau and a swivel armchair in the manner of the designs of England's William Morris. On the first floor, look out for the unusual arcaded arches and wooden grills above the bedroom doors. These were installed in the 1890s as part of a scheme to improve the circulation of air as recommended by Florence Nightingale (1820–1910), who became famous in every corner of the British Empire as the nurse who took over the military hospital at Scutari during the Crimean War of the 1850s.

After touring the house, be sure to wander the **garden** (same times; no extra cost), with its neat lawns and colourful borders.

The waterfront and the Toronto Islands

There is much to enjoy on the shore of **Lake Ontario**, despite its industrial blotches and the heavy concrete brow of the Gardiner Expressway. Footpaths and cycling trails nudge along a fair slice of the **waterfront**, and the **Harbourfront Centre** offers a year-round schedule of activities – music festivals, theatre, dance and the like. Here also is the adventurous **Power Plant Contemporary Art Gallery**, as well as **Ontario Place**, a leisure complex spread over three man-made islands that provides all sorts of kids' entertainment throughout the summer.

Even better are the **Toronto Islands**, whose breezy tranquillity attracts droves of city-dwellers during Toronto's humid summers. It only takes fifteen minutes to reach them by municipal ferry, but the contrast between the city and the islands could hardly be more marked, not least because the islands are almost entirely **vehicle-free**; many locals use wheelbarrows or golf buggies to move their tackle, while others walk or cycle.

The waterfront and around

Toronto's grimy docks – a swathe of warehouses and factories that was unattractive and smelly in equal measure – once blighted the shoreline nearest the city centre. Today it's another story: the port and its facilities have been concentrated further east, beyond the foot of Parliament Street, while the **waterfront** west of Yonge Street has been redeveloped in grand style, sprouting luxury condominium blocks, jogging and cycling trails, offices, shops and marinas. The focus of all this activity is the **Harbourfront Centre**, whose various facilities include an open-air performance area and the **Power Plant Contemporary Art Gallery**. To reach the Harbourfront Centre by public transport, take streetcar #509 or #510 from Union Station and get off at Queens Quay Terminal, the second stop.

The Harbourfront Centre

The centrepiece of Toronto's downtown waterfront is the ten-acre **Harbourfront Centre**, an expanse of lakefront land stretching from the foot of York Street in

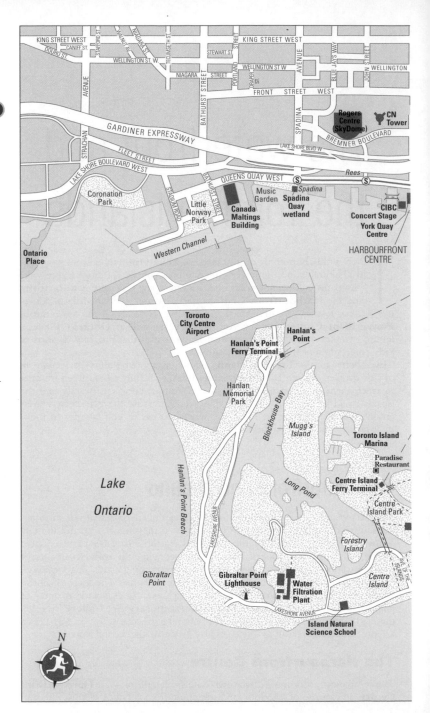

KING STREET WEST
CANIFF ST
DOURO ST
WALNUT AV
STAFFORD ST
NIAGARA ST
TECUMSETH ST
KING STREET WEST
STEWART ST
STREET
WELLINGTON ST W
AVENUE
BLUE JAYS WAY
JOHN STREET
WELLINGTON
WELLINGTON ST W
NIAGARA STREET
PORTLAND ST
DRAPER ST
FRONT STREET WEST
BATHURST STREET
SPADINA
Rogers
Centre
(SkyDome)
CN Tower
GARDINER EXPRESSWAY
FLEET STREET
STRACHAN
BREMNER BOULEVARD
LAKE SHORE BLVD W
LAKE SHORE BOULEVARD WEST
Rees
QUEENS QUAY WEST
Coronation Park
SPADINA AVENUE
Little Norway Park
Canada Maltings Building
Music Garden
Spadina
Spadina Quay wetland
CIBC Concert Stage
York Quay Centre

HARBOURFRONT CENTRE

Ontario Place

Western Channel

Toronto City Centre Airport

Hanlan's Point Ferry Terminal

Hanlan's Point

Hanlan Memorial Park

Blockhouse Bay

Mugg's Island

Toronto Island Marina

Paradise Restaurant

Centre Island Ferry Terminal

Lake Ontario

Hanlan's Point Beach

LAKESHORE AVENUE

Long Pond

Centre Island Park

AVE. OF THE ISLANDS

Forestry Island

Gibraltar Point

Gibraltar Point Lighthouse

Water Filtration Plant

Centre Island

LAKESHORE AVENUE

Island Natural Science School

N

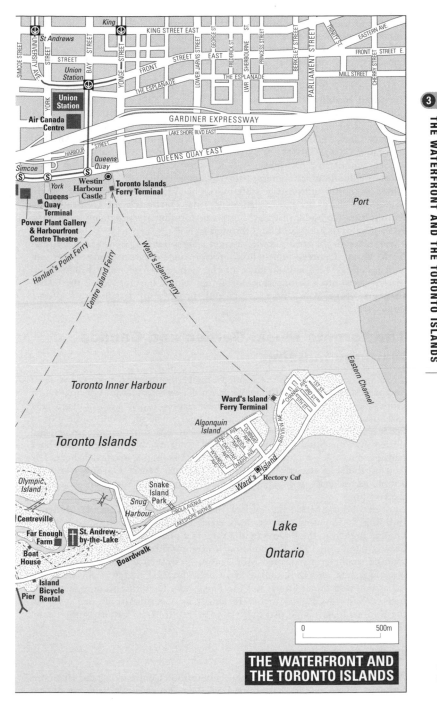

THE WATERFRONT AND
THE TORONTO ISLANDS

the east to the conspicuous outdoor Harbourfront Concert Stage, about five minutes' walk away to the west. This is one of Toronto's most creative quarters, and many of the city's artistic and cultural events are held here, either outside or indoors at one of several venues, principally the Harbourfront Centre Theatre.

The east end of the Harbourfront Centre is marked by the **Queens Quay Terminal building**, a handsome, glassy structure built as a combined warehouse and shipping depot in 1927. Attractively refurbished, it now holds cafés, offices and smart shops. Next door, the **Power Plant Contemporary Art Gallery** (Tues & Thurs–Sun noon–6pm, Wed noon–8pm; $4, but free on Wed after 5pm; ☎416/973-4949, ⊛www.thepowerplant.org) is housed in an imaginatively converted 1920s power station. Every year, the gallery presents about a dozen exhibitions of contemporary art, often featuring emerging Canadian artists. It's mostly cutting-edge stuff; indecipherable to some, exciting to others. The gallery shares the power station with the **Harbourfront Centre Theatre**, a former ice house that now hosts a performing arts programme featuring everything from poetry readings through to ballet.

Next door to the west, another former warehouse has been turned into the **York Quay Centre**, which holds performance areas, meeting spaces and craft galleries. The south entrance of the Centre lets out to a shallow pond that converts into a skating rink during the winter. Further west is the **CIBC Concert Stage**, which boasts a graceful fan-like roof designed to suggest a ship's deck.

The Toronto Music Garden and Canada Maltings building

Cross the footbridge on the west side of the Harbourfront Centre and you're a few metres from **Queens Quay West**, once a busy boulevard but now much more subdued, separated from the Gardiner Expressway by a raft of brand-new apartment blocks. Walking west along the road, it's about 600m to the foot of Spadina Avenue, where a tiny slice of old industrial land has been reclaimed and turned into the **Spadina Quay wetland** – not much to write home about perhaps, but still a minor concession to the lakeshore's original habitat. The wetland abuts the attractively landscaped **Toronto Music Garden**, essentially a series of rockeries with vague musical allusions, which meanders west along the lakeshore.

Just beyond the Music Garden lurk the giant silos of the **Canada Maltings building**, an imposing concrete hulk erected in 1928 for the storage of barley brought here from the Prairies by the ships that once thronged the St Lawrence Seaway. Closed in 1987, the building is derelict today, but architecturally – as a prime example of industrial Modernism – it's much too fine a structure to be demolished, and Torontonians have been debating its future for years. On its far side is Bathurst Street, and the dinky little ferry that shuttles across the narrow Western Channel to the Toronto City Centre Airport (see p.33) on the Toronto Islands; note that there is no access from the airport to the rest of the Toronto Islands.

Ontario Place

A couple of kilometres west of the Harbourfront Centre along the lakeshore, **Ontario Place**, at 955 Lakeshore Blvd West (late May & Sept Sat & Sun

10am–6pm; June–Aug mostly, though times can vary, daily 10am–8pm; day pass covering most rides $32, children ages 4–5 & seniors $17; ☎416/314-9900, ⓦwww.ontarioplace.com), rises out of the lake like some sort of postmodern Atlantis. Architect Eberhard Zeidler was given a mandate to create "leisure space in an urban context", and he came up with these three man-made islands, or "pods", covering ninety-five acres with landscaped parks, lagoons and canals. The attractions here are almost entirely themed around water, and rides like the Rush River Raft Ride, the Purple Pipeline and the Pink Twister provide exciting ways to get dizzy and wet. Visitors looking for less frenetic activities can rent **pedal boats** (available at all of the park's various lagoons) or two-seater aquatic bicycles, which are used to thrash through the canals that separate the pods.

Both an amusement park and an entertainment complex, Ontario Place was the template for facilities like Disney's EPCOT Center in Florida, and it teems with young families and teenagers during the day. The atmosphere at night tends to be a bit more mature, particularly at the **Molson Amphitheatre**, which puts on a series of summer concerts dominated by headliner rock groups. In addition, every June and July a spectacular international fireworks competition called **Symphony of Fire** overwhelms Ontario Place. Pyrotechnic teams congregate at the water's edge and try to beat out their rivals with creative routines and sheer firepower.

Also at Ontario Place is the **Cinesphere**, whose distinctive geodesic dome, containing a 750-seat theatre with a curved, six-storey screen, was the world's first IMAX theatre when it opened in 1971; IMAX technology was developed by the Toronto-based IMAX Corporation in 1967. Distinguishing IMAX from normal cinema, the frames of an IMAX film are physically larger than in any other processing format. The film runs through a behemoth projector at twenty-four frames per second and the screens average 20m (65 feet) in height. The cumulative sensation is one of being immersed in the film, and it has certainly proved a popular formula – there are now IMAX theatres all over the world. To see an IMAX film here, it is a good idea to book ahead, either online or by phone; tickets cost $7–10 each.

To get to Ontario Place by **public transport**, take the Harbourfront streetcar, #509, from Union Station to Exhibition Place, then walk south through the Exhibition grounds, over the Lakeshore bridge and into Ontario Place; the walk takes about ten minutes.

The Toronto Islands

Originally a sandbar peninsula, the **Toronto Islands**, arching around the city's harbour, were cut adrift from the mainland by a violent storm in 1858. First used as a summer retreat by the Mississauga Indians, the islands went through various incarnations during the twentieth century: they once hosted a baseball stadium, where slugger Babe Ruth hit his first professional home run, saw fun fairs featuring horses diving from the pier and even served as a training base for the Norwegian Air Force during World War II. Today, this archipelago, roughly 6km long and totalling around 800 acres, seems worlds away from the bustle of Downtown, a haven for rest and relaxation – and a place where visitors' **motor cars are banned**.

The city side of the archipelago is broken into a dozen tiny islets dotted with cottages, leisure facilities, verdant gardens and clumps of wild woodland.

Mrs Simcoe and the Toronto Islands

Mrs Elizabeth Simcoe (1766–1850), the energetic wife of the lieutenant-governor of Upper Canada, John Graves Simcoe, arrived in York, today's Toronto, in 1793 and returned to England three years later. An avid diarist, Mrs Simcoe recorded the day-to-day happenings of colonial life in her diary, a lively, attractively illustrated text dotted with shrewd observations and descriptions of Canada's flora. Mrs Simcoe took a shine to the Toronto Islands – or the peninsula, as it was then – and rode there frequently. Her first jaunt is recorded as follows: "We met with some good natural meadows and several ponds. The trees are mostly of the poplar kind, covered with wild vines, …[and] on the ground were everlasting peas creeping in abundance, of a purple colour. I am told they are good to eat when boiled…The diversity of scenes I met with this morning made the ride extremely pleasant. I was very near riding into what appeared a quicksand…[which was]…the only unpleasant incident that occurred this day." If this extract whets your appetite, *The Diary of Mrs John Graves Simcoe* is available at the World's Biggest Bookstore (see p.195), even though it's currently out of print.

By comparison, the other side of the archipelago is a tad wilder and more windswept, consisting of one long sliver of land, which is somewhat arbitrarily divided into three "islands": from the east, these are **Ward's Island**, a quiet residential area with parkland and wilderness; **Centre Island**, the busiest and most developed of the three; and **Hanlan's Point**, which leads round to Toronto's pint-sized City Centre Airport (see p.33). Hanlan's Point also holds the city's best **sandy beach** – though, as Lake Ontario is generally regarded as being too polluted for swimming, most visitors stick to sunbathing.

Practicalities

Passenger **ferries** bound for the Toronto Islands depart from the mainland **ferry terminal**, which is located behind the conspicuous *Westin Harbour Castle Hotel*, between the foot of Yonge and Bay streets. To get to the ferry terminal from Union Station, take the #509 or #510 streetcar and get off at the first stop – Queen's Quay (Ferry Docks). The islands have three **ferry docks** – one each on Ward's Island, Centre Island and Hanlan's Point. The ferries to Ward's Island and Hanlan's Point run year-round, while the ferry shuttling visitors over to Centre Island only operates from spring to fall. During peak season (May to early Sept), ferries to all three islands depart at regular intervals, either every half-hour, every forty-five minutes, or every hour; at other times of the year, it's usually hourly. Ferries begin running between 6.30am and 9am and finish between 9pm and 11.30pm, depending on the service and the season. For schedule details, telephone ☎416/392-8193. Regardless of the time of year, a return **fare** for adults is $6, or $3.50 for seniors and students. Cyclists are allowed to take their **bikes** with them unless the ferry is jam-packed, and **rollerblades** are permitted, but must be removed while on board.

From May to October, **bike rental** is available on Centre Island from **Island Bicycle Rental** (☎416/203-0009), a five- to ten-minute walk from the Centre Island ferry dock at the foot of the pier. They open daily at around 10.30am and stock ordinary bicycles, tandems and even quadracycles, but the only reservations they accept are for groups of ten or more. Ordinary bikes cost $6 per hour plus a fully refundable deposit of $10; photo ID is required. **Canoe and paddle boat rental** is available on Centre Island too, from the **Boat House**, a five- to ten-minute walk from the Centre Island ferry dock.

Hiring a boat allows you to paddle round the islands' network of mini-lagoons and reach a couple of tiny wooded islets that are otherwise impossible to reach. Aside from walking, cycling and rowing, the other means of conveyance is a free and fairly frequent trackless **train** that runs across the islands throughout the summertime; you can board the train at any point along its circuitous route. As regards eating and drinking, it's all fast-food stuff except for the **Rectory Café** (Mon–Thurs 11am–6pm, Fri–Sun 11am–8pm; high season daily 10am–10pm), on Ward's Island, where they serve tasty snacks and light meals. Finally, note that **cars** are not allowed on the Toronto Islands without a special permit and these are only available to island residents.

Several hours are needed to explore the islands by bike, a full day if you are on foot, or you can overnight at the islands' one and only B&B (see p.144).

Ward's Island

Named after the Ward family, who settled on the then-peninsula in 1830, **Ward's Island** holds the coziest little hamlet, whose narrow lanes are flanked by antique wooden cottages that seem to blend seamlessly into the surrounding greenery. The island is home to approximately 700 full-time residents, but remains one of the least-developed of the chain – the landscape is still dominated by primeval-looking scrub, reed and birches mixed with wild apple trees and grape vines. The cottages edge up towards a curving, sandy beach and a pleasant boardwalk, which scoots along the Lake Ontario side of the island, with a network of paths exploring the rest of the terrain. A trio of narrow footbridges connects Ward's with its tiny neighbours – **Algonquin Island**, with yet more dinky little cottages, wild **Snake Island** and private **Snug Harbour**, the first of three inter-connected islets that are owned by the Canadian yacht club. The **Rectory Café**, easily the best place to eat on the islands and with an attractive patio, is metres from the Algonquin footbridge.

Centre Island

Most of the summer season's action takes place on **Centre Island**, with ferries arriving at its dock carrying boatloads of day-trippers. The first things you'll see as the ferry sails in is the landscaped gardens abutting the dock and the *Paradise Restaurant*, a favourite watering hole for the thirsty sailors of the adjacent Toronto Island Marina. From the dock, it's a five-minute walk east to **Centreville** (June–Aug daily, plus May & Sept weekends, 10.30am–5pm, 6pm, 7pm or 8pm; ☎416/203-0405, ⊛www.centreisland.ca), a children's amusement park with charmingly old-fashioned rides. There are around thirty rides altogether, including paddle boats shaped as swans, a carousel, a Ferris wheel and a rollercoaster. Each ride costs a specified number of tickets, from two to board the carousel up to a maximum of six to experience the rollercoaster. Individual tickets are 75¢, or you can splash out on an all-day pass costing $25 for adults (and anyone over four feet tall), or $17.50 for kids under four feet. At the east end of Centreville is the **Far Enough Farm**, a small farm and petting zoo popular with very young children.

Just to the south of Centreville, a footbridge spans the narrow waterway that bisects Centre Island to reach the **Avenue of the Islands**, a wide walkway surrounded by trim gardens. At its southern end, this walkway extends into a forked **pier** that pokes out beyond the stone breakwater into the lake. Island Bicycle Rental (see opposite) is located at the foot of the pier and boat rental is available from the Boat House, near to – and clearly signposted from – the

△ Gibraltar Point Lighthouse

Avenue of the Islands; from the Boat House you can paddle off through the islands and get to places, like wooded and uninhabited **Forestry Island**, which are otherwise inaccessible.

One other minor attraction, just east of the Avenue of the Islands, across the water from Far Enough Farm, is the Anglican **St Andrew-by-the-Lake**, a long and slender clapboard church dating from 1884.

Hanlan's Point

Hanlan's Point is named after another old island family, who first settled here at Gibraltar Point, on the island's southwestern tip, in 1862. The most famous member of the family was **Edward "Ned" Hanlan**, who earned Canada's first Olympic gold medal as a champion rower, a skill he honed rowing back and forth to the mainland. The Hanlans built a hotel-resort on the island and others followed, though none has survived and neither has an old amusement park, which was demolished in the 1930s to make way for what is now the Toronto City Centre Airport (see p.33); there's a **statue** of Ned in his pomp by the Hanlan's Point ferry dock.

Ferries arrive on the northeast side of the island just beyond the airport. From here, a combined **footpath and bicycle trail** runs south, passing behind – and just east of – **Hanlan's Point Beach**, a long, stretch of tawny sand which is generally regarded as one of the city's best beaches. Frankly, this is not much of a boast, but it is enough to attract a fair few sunbathers, though swimmers – given the polluted nature of the lake – are few and far between. Part of the beach is for the clad; in the other part – in the ungainly words of the park's department signs – "clothing [is] optional". Altogether, the beach is perhaps more valued as an environmentalist's haven, and generations of budding biologists have been nurtured at the nearby Toronto Islands Natural Science School, which teaches city children about the flora and fauna of both the islands and Lake Ontario.

The school is on the south side of the island, beyond the **Gibraltar Point Lighthouse**, a sturdy limestone structure with a dark pink iron top. Erected at the beginning of the nineteenth century, the original lighthouse was sixteen metres high, and equipped with a lamp that burned sperm oil. This setup was updated in the 1830s, when the lighthouse was heightened by about four metres and its lamp replaced by one fuelled by coal oil; an electric lamp was installed in 1916. In its early days, when Toronto harbour was crowded with sailing ships, the Gibraltar was a vitally important beacon. It also achieved notoriety when its first keeper, a certain Radan Muller, disappeared in 1815. The *York Gazette* was quick to pronounce Muller of "inoffensive and benevolent character", and was pleased to report that the police had detained two suspects in his disappearance. In the event, the suspects – two soldiers from Fort York (see p.54) – were never charged, but popular legend continued to assert their guilt. The story went that they dropped in on Radan for a drinking session, and a quarrel ensued in which the lighthouse keeper was accidentally killed. More murkily, it's possible that Radan was a whisky smuggler, and the fight started over the profits of some contraband booze. Whatever the truth, the remains of Radan's body were finally discovered by a later keeper in 1893, buried in a shallow grave just to the west of the lighthouse – quite enough to fuel endless ghost stories.

The suburbs

Venturing outside the city centre is certainly worth your while, especially since many major attractions – like the **Toronto Zoo**, the **Ontario Science Centre** and **Black Creek Pioneer Village** – are found in the suburbs, notably **Scarborough** and **North York**. Large swaths of undeveloped, natural parkland ring the suburbs and provide opportunities for outdoor sporting activities usually associated with the hinterlands rather than major cities. Additionally, far from being monochromatic stretches of urban sprawl, Toronto's suburbs echo the cultural diversity so prevalent downtown. In particular, they are great places to experience **ethnic cuisines**, such as regional classics from China as well as Persian dishes served during long, multi-coursed feasts.

Toronto's extensive **transit system** takes passengers to the city's perimeters for the single (adult) flat rate of $2.50. In most cases it is better to take public transport than to drive, as the fares are always cheaper than parking, and the arterial roadways can be a scary prospect during rush hour traffic if you are unfamiliar with them. On weekends, suburban bus and train schedules operate less frequently; contact the Toronto Transit Commission (TTC) for route information: ☎416/393-4636 or ⊛www.city.toronto.on.ca/ttc.

A century ago, **The Beaches**, located to the east of Downtown, was what the Toronto Islands are today: a summer vacation area used for frolicking about the shores of **Lake Ontario**. The Beaches are now more a residential than a holiday spot, but its overall atmosphere has retained the look and feel of a turn-of-the-century seaside resort. It has a three-kilometre **boardwalk**, ample Queen Anne-style houses with generous front porches, and a charming **bandshell** in Kew Beach Park, which serves as the main stage for the neighbourhood's many **festivals**. The fact that The Beaches has been so successfully preserved is remarkable, especially considering that Toronto's Downtown core is only twenty minutes away by streetcar.

In the 1880s, the Toronto Street Railway Company (the predecessor to the Toronto Transit Commission) installed a **streetcar** line that ran east along

The Mega City

In 1998, Ontario's provincial government decided that the City of Toronto and its suburban municipalities would amalgamate into one huge city. This "Mega City", as it was colloquially known, has a population of about 2.5 million people, and the region known as the Greater Toronto Area (GTA) is home to over 5 million people and covers an area of 632 square kilometres. The consolidation was a major social and political controversy, leading to the virtual shutout in Toronto's municipal, provincial and federal elections of the individuals and party seen as most responsible.

Queen Street and led to the sparsely settled Beaches. Initially, the churchgoing city was scandalized by the TSR's idea to run its trams on Sundays, so that the city's working people could get out in the fresh air and visit the amusement parks that were springing up in the area. But commerce and recreation triumphed, and the line – which continues running to this day – spurred the growth of The Beaches community. In 1903, the city began a thirty-year project to acquire the private parks clustered along the waterfront; the consolidation of these parks led to the opening of the public **Beaches Park**, whose nature trails, boardwalks and unspoiled beaches offer rest and relaxation to all the city's residents.

Kew, Balmy and Cherry beaches

There are two main sections to The Beaches community – **Kew Beach** and **Balmy Beach**, and neither wants to be thought of as subordinate to the other, hence the insistence on pluralization ("The Beaches"). Kew, however, is probably the most popular. Here, **Kew Beach Park**, situated just below Queen Street, is a picture-perfect spot with rolling, grassy hills and a sandy beachfront that is delightful even on a packed Sunday afternoon. Balmy Beach is separated from Kew Beach by a tiny inlet at the foot of Silverbirch Avenue, but there is very little distinction between the two – despite what some locals may say, Balmy's beach and parklands are just as nice as Kew's.

Slightly west of Kew Beach, unspoiled, car-free **Cherry Beach** is a favourite among hikers, birdwatchers and cyclists. It begins at **Ashbridges Bay Park**, which is at the corner of Lakeshore Boulevard East and Coxwell Avenue. Signs inside the park point out the **Martin Goodman Trail**, a hiking route that spans the entire Toronto waterfront.

Scarborough

Of all Toronto's suburbs, **Scarborough** is perhaps, on a number of levels, the most diverse. Noted for its striking bluffs and accessibility to undeveloped stretches of Lake Ontario, it is also marred by dreary strip malls and ubiquitous doughnut shops. Some of Toronto's wealthiest enclaves are tucked away in the suburb's ravines and swath of lakefront, but the unchecked sprawl of the 1960s led to Scarborough being given the unfortunate nickname "Scarberia" by other Torontonians. Nevertheless, old-money members of the country-club set share the town with new-money entrepreneurs from Hong Kong and mainland China, who have infused Scarborough's infamous strip malls with restaurants, herbalists and feng shui practitioners.

Toronto Zoo

When it reopened in 1974 after several years' closure, the **Toronto Zoo** (daily: Jan to mid-March 9:30am–4:30pm, mid March to late May 9:30am–6pm, late May to early Sept 9am–7pm, mid-Oct to Dec 9.30am–4.30pm; last admission an hour before closing; closed Dec 25; $19, children ages 4–12 $11, children ages 3 and under free, seniors $13; ☎416/392-5900, ☜www.torontozoo.com), formerly the Riverdale Zoo, emerged onto the scene as the first zoo without cages. Instead, its occupants were housed in either naturalistic pavilions or

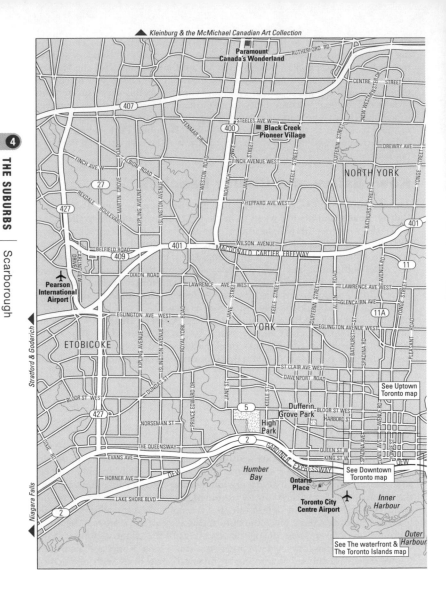

outdoor enclosures that replicated the animals' indigenous environments as closely as possible. Although this layout is now the norm in any credible institution, it was a huge innovation at the time, replacing the sad, menagerie type of display of the past.

With over 5000 animals representing 460 species, the zoo, set on the hilly edge of the Rouge Valley, takes up a lot of room, requiring a 710-acre site that makes it one of the world's largest zoos. Six **pavilions** or biospheres (the Gorilla Rainforest Exhibit, African Rainforest, Indo-Malayan, Americas, Malayan Woods, and Australasian) are filled with **flora** indigenous to the

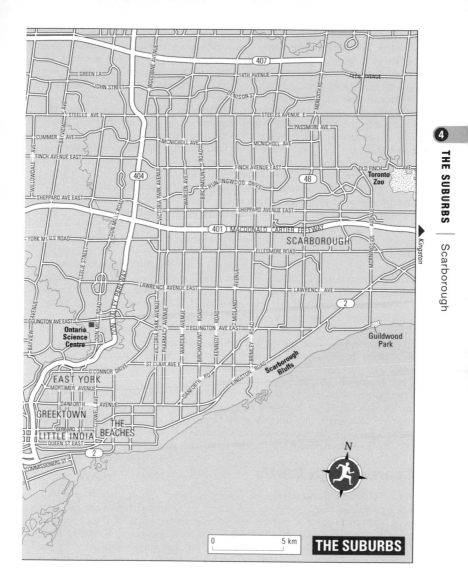

resident **fauna**, and hardier species – such as moose, Siberian tigers, snow leopards, elk, camels and wolves – live outdoors in large, naturalistic paddocks and enclosures. An open train, the **Zoomobile** ($5), zips around the vast site for those opposed to hiking the 10km worth of **trails** between pavilions and enclosures. In addition to grizzly bears, musk oxen and tapirs, a variety of Toronto's wildlife (raccoons, chipmunks and foxes) drop in from the woodland surrounding the zoo for frequent visits.

The most popular pavilion by far is the two-acre **gorilla habitat**. Tragically, most of the world's gorilla population lives in zoos, so endangered is the species in its natural habitat in the mountains of central Africa. The Toronto Zoo has an active **breeding programme** that works in concert with an international campaign to prevent gorillas from becoming extinct. Apart from devising the surroundings of these magnificent primates to support their social needs and give them room to roam, viewing facilities and a research station have been put in place to raise visitors' awareness of conservation needs.

Gorillas are social creatures with an elaborate family structure, and the youngest members of the population were born here – something the Toronto Zoo is inordinately proud of. The zoo's media relations go on overdrive when **zoo babies** are born, and highly publicized naming contests greet photogenic new arrivals. Other successful breeding programmes have included ones for Sumatran tigers and – a Canadian first – Komodo dragons.

Though not a habitat-related site, **Discovery Zone** is basically an educational playground for children, featuring a water play area, an outdoor theatre and a petting zoo; the attendant **Kid's Zoo** offers camel and pony rides and face painting ($5). Another popular attraction is the **polar bear pool**, which features a step-down glass wall that allows you to view the cavorting bears underwater.

Adults may be more interested in learning about the zoo's extensive **conservation programmes**, which, as previously mentioned, include breeding, habitat recovery and a highly respected species-reintroduction programme. The Vancouver Island marmot, trumpeter swan, black-footed ferret and Mexican axolotl are four species benefiting from these programmes.

If you want to eat while at the zoo, the majority of your **dining** choices will revolve around fast-food outlets. The zoo also has the expected **gift shops**, but in addition there is a **plant nursery** that reflects the zoo's activities in habitat restoration, and a new **Special Events Pavilion** that houses the human species when headliner music and variety acts play here.

Arriving by **car**, take Hwy-401 to Scarborough (exit 389) and drive north on Meadowvale Road, following the signs for the zoo. Via **public transport** – which takes about fifty minutes from Downtown – catch the Sheppard East (#85B) bus from the Sheppard subway station year-round or the Scarborough (#86A) bus from Kennedy during the summer season.

Scarborough Bluffs

When Elizabeth Simcoe, wife of Upper Canada's first lieutenant-governor, sailed past these bluffs, she remarked how they reminded her of the Scarborough cliffs in England – and hence the most easterly part of Toronto got its name. The **Scarborough Bluffs** are indeed a beautiful and significant geological feature, and they have been preserved from rampant development by the Toronto and Region Conservation Authority (☎416/661-6898, ⓦwww.trca .on.ca), which has created three parks, the most significant of which is **Bluffer's Park**, a 473-acre waterfront space featuring supervised beaches (July & August), picnic areas sheltered in groves, snack bars, sports facilities – with everything from cricket and lacrosse to bocce and soccer – a public marina for recreational sailors and a private yacht club. Smaller and less developed but nevertheless impressive, **Cathedral Bluffs Park** has spires of eroded sandstone cliffs rising more than 90m above Lake Ontario, a natural phenomenon echoed to the park's immediate north by the Gothic coils of a huge Augustinian seminary.

To reach Bluffer's Park **by car**, simply follow Brimley Road south from Kingston Road straight downhill towards Lake Ontario. If using **public transport** take the Kingston Road (#12) bus to the Brimley Road stop. The **waterfront**

△ Bluffer's Park

is a short walk south that pleasantly turns from cityscape to country meadow. For more information about these or any of Toronto's parks call ☎416/392-8186 or visit ⓦwww.city.toronto.on.ca/parks.

Guildwood Park

Another scenic stop along the bluffs, **Guildwood Park**, on the grounds of a former estate, is accessible either by turning south onto Guildwood Parkway from Kingston Road, or by taking the Morningside (#116) bus, which departs from the Kennedy subway station and heads east into the park. Although a succession of people have owned the property since the eighteenth century, its name and reputation were established in 1932, when Spencer and Rosa Clark decided to turn their 36-acre manor into a "Guild of all arts", and established a rent-free colony for artists and craftspeople. During World War II, **Guildwood** became an infirmary for victims of battle fatigue (today known as post-traumatic stress syndrome) and the artists' residence programme was permanently suspended – though the **Ontario Crafts Council's Guild Shop** on Cumberland Avenue in Yorkville (see p.198) continues as part of its legacy.

The Clarks also had a collection of over seventy **architectural ornaments** from many of the historic Toronto buildings that were torn down to make way for the skyscrapers that dominate the skyline today. Huge keystones and fanciful patios, arches and doorways (minus their buildings) dot the Guildwood Park grounds. Ironically, the Clarks' pseudo-Georgian house, until recently an inn and restaurant, is currently boarded up and is itself awaiting demolition. Guildwood Park's stunning **view of Lake Ontario** amid the eclectic, even surrealistic collection of architectural fragments and sculpture makes it a popular spot for film shoots and photographers of all kinds. The **gardens** are laid out country-estate style, containing some interesting varieties of tulips, iris and lilies, while the **wetlands and woods** that surround Guildwood have a good cross-section of local flora and some fauna, including increasingly rare woodpeckers.

North York

Just as Scarborough was parodied by native-son Mike Myers in *Wayne's World*, **North York** got skewered on the long-running hit *Second City TV* (or SCTV), where it was repackaged as Mellville – Torontians' nickname for North York thanks to the two-decade-long reign of mayor Mel Lastman. The suburb finds itself on many itineraries because of the **Toronto Centre for the Arts**, which hosts some of the city's biggest musicals and theatrical productions. The most popular attraction in North York, however, is the **Ontario Science Centre**, a sprawling testament to the notion that science and technology can be fun.

To reach North York from Downtown, take the Yonge subway line north to the North York Centre stop.

The Ontario Science Centre

On a mission "to delight, inform and challenge visitors through engaging and thought-provoking experiences in science and technology", the **Ontario Science Centre**, 770 Don Mills Rd (daily: July to early Sept 10am–6pm; early Sept to June 10am–5pm; $14, seniors $10, children ages 13–17 $10, children ages 4–12 $8, children under 4 free; OMNIMAX Theatre tickets can be purchased separately or together with admission for reduced prices; special exhibits are extra; ☎416/696-1000, ⊛www.ontariosciencecentre.ca), is up to the task with over six hundred exhibits in ten exhibition halls. Almost everything is interactive, and topics at the forefront of scientific enquiry are not only prominently featured but in fact placed within a social context, a notable example being the exhibit on the Genome Project and an ancillary exhibit on notions of race and racism.

A $40 million renovation titled "Agents of Change" is currently underway and due to be completed in late 2006. The project will remake more than thirty percent of the OSC's public spaces, and the new content will focus on "Solving Twenty-First Century Problems". The OSC hopes to bring in more adult visitors with this renovation, though their chief function remains exposing children and teenagers to the workings – for good or for ill – of science and technology.

An example of the OSC's forward approach to topical science is the **Question of Truth** hall, which considers how the supposed empiricisms of science have been used to validate errors in reasoning, such as the Ptolemaic universe or, far more perniciously, eugenics. One of the most popular exhibits is **The Human Body**, where visitors can discern the inner workings of human biology through life-sized three-dimensional displays and various quizzes and games. Similarly, though more explicit and adult-oriented, Gunther von Hagens's BodyWorlds 2 exhibit is a fascinating display of two hundred plastinated bodies and body parts posed, exposed or sliced very finely to give us an in-depth understanding of our bodies. The OSC also showcases complex medical advances like bioengineering, DNA fingerprinting and immunology, all presented in an easily accessible format. Other halls focus on subjects like communications, space and sport; additionally, the "Kid Spark" programme encourages children to learn-through-play, and the Weston Family Innovation Centre focuses on the latest innovations, debates and challenges in science today.

The 320-seat **OMNIMAX Theatre** (call ☎416/696-1000 for show schedules) is another big draw, with its 24-metre-high wraparound screen and digital sound that creates an enveloping cinematic experience. Admissions to the OMNIMAX shows are either separate from the general admission ($11) or can be combined with general admission ($20, seniors $14, children ages 13–17 $14, children ages 4–12 $10).

To reach the Science Centre by **car** from Downtown, take the Don Valley Parkway and follow the signs from the Don Mills Road North exit. By **public transport**, take the Yonge Street subway line north to Eglington station and transfer to the Eglington East (#34) bus; get off at Don Mills Road or take the Bloor Danforth line east to Pape and take the Don Mills (#25) bus to St Dennis Drive, right in front of the OSC. The trip should take about thirty minutes from the vicinity of Downtown's Union Station.

Black Creek Pioneer Village

A distant second in popularity to the Ontario Science Centre, North York's **Black Creek Pioneer Village**, 100 Murry Ross Parkway at Jane Street and Steels Avenue West (May–June Mon–Fri 9.30am–4pm, Sat & Sun 10am–5pm, July–Sept daily 10am–5pm, Oct–Dec Mon–Fri 9.30am–4pm, Sat & Sun 10am–4.30pm; $10, children $6, students and seniors $9; ☎416/736-1733, ⊕www .trca.on.ca/parks_and_recreation), appeals to those with an interest in pioneer history. Like the Fort York "living history" site in Downtown Toronto, Pioneer Village is staffed by interpreters dressed in **period costume** performing daily tasks, in this case all the activities of an 1860s Ontario village, such as open-hearth cooking, blacksmithing, milling, printing and various farming chores. The site has over 35 buildings restored to historical specifications, as well as **heritage gardens**. If romanticizing mid-nineteenth-century household drudgery and small-town Victoriana is of interest, BCPV does what it does very well. From late November through December, special holiday events are presented.

Arriving by **car**, travel north on Hwy-400 and exit on Steels Avenue East. From here, turn west on Murray Ross Parkway, which is one block east of Jane Street, to find the Village's car park. Via **public transport** (about forty minutes from Downtown), take the Yonge subway line to Finch station and board the Steels bus (#60 B, D or E).

Paramount Canada's Wonderland

Canada's de facto Disney World, **Paramount Canada's Wonderland**, Hwy-400, Rutherford exit (May–Oct, opening hours vary; one-day pass covering all rides $37.99, two days for $51.99, children ages 3–6 and seniors $26 one-day pass; tax not included; ☎905/832-7000, ⊕www.canadas-wonderland.com) is a theme park featuring over two hundred attractions and sixty different rides, spread over a large chunk of land about 30km north of Downtown in the suburb of **Vaughan**. Visiting the park is an all-day affair: among the many attractions here are thirteen **rollercoasters**, a twenty-acre **water park** called Splash Works (with sixteen water slides and the country's largest outdoor wave pool), souped-up go-karts, **mini-golf** and roaming cartoon characters, such as Fred Flintstone and SpongeBob SquarePants. The **thrill rides**, with aggressive names like Top Gun, Drop Zone and Cliff Hanger, are enough to make the strongest stomachs churn, if the kitsch of the place doesn't do it first. During the peak summer season, big-name **rock concerts** and "extreme" special events, such as stunt shows put together by Hollywood crews, are scheduled. This being Toronto, there is also a roster of **cultural festivals** featuring food, music and family activities during the summer.

If you're travelling here by **public transport**, catch the Wonderland Express GO bus from the Yorkdale or York Mills subway stations; buses leave every hour and take forty minutes.

McMichael Canadian Art Collection

Situated in the village of Kleinburg, the **McMichael Canadian Art Collection**, 10365 Islington Ave (daily May–Oct 10am–5pm, Nov–April Tues–Sat 10am–4pm, Sun 10am–5pm; $15; ☎905/893-1121 or 1-888/213-1121, ⓦwww.mcmichael.com), is housed in a series of handsome log and stone buildings in the wooded Humber River valley. Robert and Signe McMichael, devoted followers of the Group of Seven (see p.70), opened their home and art gallery to the public in the early 1960s, and in 1965 they turned their property over to the Province of Ontario.

On the collection's **Lower Level**, a series of small galleries focuses on various aspects of the **Group of Seven**'s work. Gallery Two, for example, begins with the artistic friends and contemporaries who influenced the Group's early style, while Gallery Three zeroes in on the Group's spiritual founder, Tom Thomson, who died in a canoeing accident three years before the Group showed as a collective. The galleries boast fine paintings here by J.E.H. MacDonald, Lawren Harris, Edwin Holgate, F.H. Varley and L.L. Fitzgerald, as well as works by their talented contemporary Emily Carr. Other artists who later became associated with the Group of Seven, notably A.J. Casson, are also strongly represented. For those unfamiliar with the Group's work, Lawren Harris's huge, luminous canvases of icebergs, mountains and increasingly abstract depictions of the far north are a revelation. People already familiar with the Group might want to check out the gallery section highlighting their portraiture, which encourages a deeper appreciation of their talents.

The museum's **Upper Level** is devoted primarily to modern **First Nations Art** and **Inuit sculpture and prints**. Rotating **temporary exhibitions** on this floor currently focus solely on the Group of Seven and their contemporaries.

When you've finished with what's inside the McMichael, allow a little time to stroll the footpaths that weave through the **woods** surrounding the gallery and the outbuildings. **Maps** are provided free at reception, and as you wander around you'll bump into various pieces of **sculpture**, as well as Tom Thomson's old wooden shack, moved here from Rosedale in 1962. For true Group of Seven devotees wishing to pay their respects, the grounds also contain the **graves** of five Group members.

To get here by **driving** from Downtown, take Hwy-401 to Hwy-400 north to Major Mackenzie Drive. Turn left (west) on Major Mackenzie Drive to Islington Avenue. Turn right (north) on Islington Avenue to the village of Kleinburg. **Public transport** requires a few transfers: from the Islington subways take the

TTC (#37) bus north to Steels and Islington, then transfer to the York Region (#13) bus, continuing up Islington to the McMichael Collection entrance. Alternatively, a taxi ride from Islington subway station is about $24.

High Park district

Poles began immigrating to Toronto in the middle of the nineteenth century, but the first major influx came in the 1890s, when their homeland was wracked by famine. These early immigrants were reinforced on several subsequent occasions, notably during and immediately after World War II, when the Germans and then the Russians occupied Poland, driving thousands into exile. In the 1950s, Poles, along with other Eastern Europeans (particularly Ukrainians) gravitated to Toronto's **High Park district**, about 5km west of Yonge Street. Architecturally undistinguished, the neighbourhood consists for the most part of a low tangle of early twentieth-century brick buildings. Lately it has been evolving into a great area for **alternative clubs and bars**, and **cafés** with espresso machines are replacing little bakeries specializing in rye bread. Despite this demographic shift, the long main street – **Roncesvalles Avenue** – is still lined with Eastern European eateries and shops.

High Park

On Roncesvalles's western edge, the hilly expanse of **High Park** is a 161-hectare (399-acre) rectangle of greenery running north from the Gardiner Expressway to Bloor Street West. Attracting over a million visitors annually, it is the apex of Toronto's excellent parks system. The park traces its origins to John George Howard, an Englishman who bought the land shortly after his arrival in Toronto in 1832. The Howard family later bequeathed their estate to the city, and the old family home, **Colborne Lodge** (☎ 416/392-6916; call for hours and admission), still stands, tucked away among the wooded ravines on the southern edge of the park. The Regency-era lodge is rare for Toronto, and its interior has been delightfully restored to its mid-nineteenth-century appearance. John Howard was a keen watercolourist, and a regularly rotated selection of his work is displayed at the lodge. Although he was hardly an outstanding artist, his paintings are enjoyable, especially in the eccentric way he manages to squeeze a jubilant animal (or two) into each and every one of his paintings. John and his wife, Jemima Francis, were buried a short stroll north of the lodge beneath the large **stone cairn**. A children's garden, allotment gardens and a municipal **greenhouse** are also nearby.

The flatter, northern half of the park is prime **picnic** territory, with primly mown lawns and a scattering of **sports facilities**. While two thirds of High Park remains in its natural oak savannah, the park's southwest corner boasts the charming **Hillside Gardens**, a manicured stretch that borders the wooded slopes above **Grenadier Pond**. The pond was supposedly named after the British grenadiers who paraded here on the winter ice, though there are more lurid theories: the most widely believed has a young skater spotting a grinning grenadier frozen under the ice. Currently, the pond – really a mini-lake – is in a state of recovery, its ecosystem unbalanced by a surfeit of saline storm water from the drain runoffs of the surrounding neighbourhoods. Efforts to rectify matters by integrating water treatment facilities into the natural environment, and introducing controls to improve the quality of runoff, have had a noticeable effect on the pond's bass and pike population. Flora repopulation is taking a bit longer but appears to be progressing. The reclamation of the landscape can be scrutinized from a nearby teahouse and **café**. Midway through the park is the **amphitheatre and stage** for the much-loved Dream in High Park, a summertime staging of Shakespeare (see p.219) as well as an annual poetry event called Scream in High Park

The north side of the park is a short walk from the High Park **subway** station; the south and east sections are readily reached on **bus** #80, which leaves Keele subway station and travels down the eastern edge of the park along Parkside Drive.

Dufferin Grove Park

In 1995 a group of people living near the west-end **Dufferin Grove Park** (875 Dufferin St. Subway: Dufferin) attempted to raise funds for a much-needed community centre. When that didn't work out, they built a communal, **wood-fired oven** inside the park instead. Today there are two large, brick, wood-burning ovens about the size of low-slung garden sheds. From June to September, bread is baked by a volunteer organization called Friends of Dufferin Grove Park, and food from the **farmers' market** is cooked up into a Friday Night Supper that you can enjoy for $6; on Saturday there is a bake sale. Learn how to **bake bread** merely by watching the regulars or, if you're a do-it-yourselfer, you can give it a go after 3pm on Thursdays. Pizza dough, tomato sauce and cheese (bring your own toppings) can be bought from the volunteers for $2 on Sunday, Tuesday and Wednesday throughout the summer, and group **pizza-making parties** can be scheduled, with prices adjusted accordingly. For more information, call ☎416/392-0913 or visit ⊛www.dufferinpark.ca /oven/bakeoven.html.

Day-trips

One of the most celebrated sights in North America, **Niagara Falls** is without a doubt the most popular day-trip destination from Toronto. A vast arc of water crashing over a 52-metre cliff, the falls are just 130km south of the city, along and around the heavily industrialized Lake Ontario shoreline. They adjoin the uninspiring **town of Niagara Falls**, which bills itself as the "Honeymoon Capital of the World" – and its hotels and motels have the heart-shaped double beds to prove it. Much more enticing, especially as a place to overnight, is the beguiling little town of **Niagara-on-the-Lake**, whose colonial villas abut Lake Ontario 26km downstream from the falls.

Less familiar, to foreigners at least, is the **Lake Huron shoreline**, 210km west of Toronto across a thick band of fertile farmland, whose southern reaches are dotted with pretty little country towns, most memorably **Goderich** and **Bayfield**. The first possesses a charming small-town air and one key sight, the fascinating **Huron Historic Gaol**, the second is graced by leafy streets and elegant clapboard villas, a far cry from the fast-food joints and neon billboards of many a Canadian town. In between Toronto and the Lake Huron shoreline is **Stratford**, a pleasant, middling little village, which puts on North America's largest classical theatre festival every year from May to November.

A couple of hours north of Toronto by car is **Severn Sound**, the southeastern inlet of **Georgian Bay**, whose bare, glacier-shaved rocks, myriad lakes and spindly pines were immortalized by the Group of Seven painters (see p.70). This is one of the most beautiful parts of southern Ontario, and, although the region is dotted with country cottages, its pristine landscapes have been conserved in the **Georgian Bay Islands National Park**, accessible by water taxi from the tiny resort of **Honey Harbour**. Also on Severn Sound are two outstanding historical reconstructions: the seventeenth-century Jesuit complex of **Sainte-Marie among the Hurons** and the British naval base at **Discovery Harbour**, founded outside Penetanguishene in 1817.

Finally, east from Toronto, it's a fast 260km along the Lake Ontario shoreline to **Kingston**, a handsome old town with a clutch of attractive colonial buildings, a genial lakeshore setting and excellent freshwater diving.

Buses and trains link Toronto with Niagara Falls and Kingston, but otherwise you'll be struggling to reach any of the other destinations mentioned above by **public transportation**; car rental is, however, reasonably priced – see p.222 for contact info.

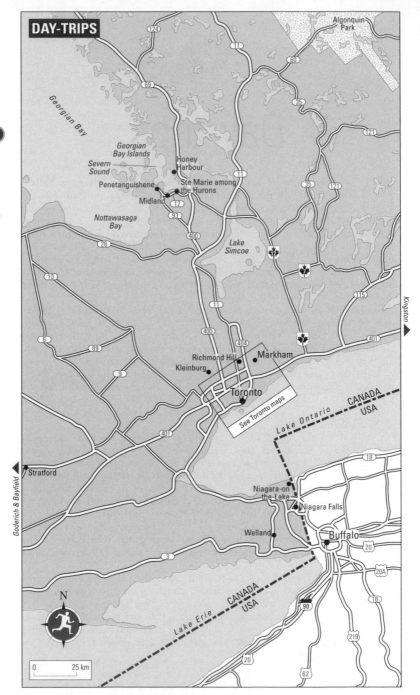

DAY-TRIPS

Algonquin Park

Georgian Bay

Georgian Bay Islands

Severn Sound

Honey Harbour

Penetanguishene

Ste Marie among the Hurons

Midland

Nottawasaga Bay

Lake Simcoe

Kingston

Richmond Hill

Markham

Kleinburg

Toronto

See Toronto maps

Goderich & Bayfield

Stratford

CANADA
USA

Lake Ontario

Niagara-on-the-Lake

Niagara Falls

Welland

Buffalo

CANADA
USA

Lake Erie

N

0   25 km

Niagara Falls

In 1860, thousands watched as **Charles Blondin** walked a tightrope across **Niagara Falls**. Midway, he paused to cook an omelette on a portable grill, and then had a marksman shoot a hole through his hat from the *Maid of the Mist* boat, fifty metres below. As attested by Blondin's antics, and by the millions of waterlogged tourists who jam the tour boats and observation points, Niagara Falls is a dramatic attraction – but the stupendous first impression doesn't last long. To prevent each year's crop of visitors from getting bored, the Niagarans have created an infinite number of vantage points. You can take in the 52-metre drop from boats, viewing towers, helicopters, cable cars and even tunnels in the rock face behind the cascade. Of these options, the tunnels and boats best capture the extraordinary force of the waterfall, a perpetual white-crested thundering pile-up that had composer Gustav Mahler bawling "At last, fortissimo!" over the din.

Arrival, information and transport

From Toronto's main bus terminal (see p.33), there are regular **Coach Canada buses** (hourly; 1hr 30min to 2hrs; ☎1-800/461-7661) to Niagara Falls; there is also a less frequent **VIA train** service (2 daily; 2hrs; ☎1-888/842-7245) from Toronto's Union Station (see p.33). The train trip is the more pleasant journey of the two, though delays on the return leg – on the once daily train originating in New York City – can be a real pain. If you're travelling by **car**, a day is more than enough time to see the falls and squeeze in a visit to Niagara-on-the-Lake, just 26km downstream; allow an hour and a half for the drive from Toronto to the falls.

Trains to the town of Niagara Falls pull in at the **VIA train station**, on Bridge Street, in the commercial heart of the town, about 3km north of the falls. The **bus station** is across the street, at 420 Bridge St at Erie Ave. From the bus station, **Niagara Transit** (☎905/356-1179) operates the **Falls Shuttle bus service** (daily: May–Sept every 30min, Oct–April hourly; single ticket $3.50, all-day pass $6), which runs across town, stopping – amongst many other places – at the foot of Clifton Hill (see p.113) and beside the falls. The Shuttle links with the Niagara Parks' **People Mover** system (mid-May to late Oct daily 10am–6pm; winter service under review), whose buses travel 30km along the riverbank between Queenston Heights Park, north of the falls, and the Rapids' View car park to the south, pausing at all the major attractions in between. People Movers appear at twenty-minute intervals and an all-day pass costs $7.50. Car drivers should be aware that **parking** anywhere near the falls can be a major hassle in the summer; try to get there before 10am, when tourists begin to arrive in hordes. Another hassle can be crossing the border over to the US: it only takes a few minutes to walk across the Rainbow Bridge from near the falls, but coming back can take literally hours, depending on border controls.

For **visitor information**, steer clear of the gaggle of privately run tourist centres that dot the area and head instead for the main **Niagara Parks information centre** (☎905/371-0254 or 1-877/642-7275, ⊛www.niagaraparks .com), at the Table Rock complex beside the falls. Here, and elsewhere, from mid-May to late October, you can purchase the **Niagara Falls Great Gorge Adventure Pass**, a combined ticket covering four of the main attractions (the Journey Behind the Falls, Maid of the Mist, White Water Walk and the Butterfly Conservatory; see below for info on these) plus all-day transportation on the People Mover system; it costs $35 for adults, or $22 for children ages 6–12.

Other places to pick up visitor information include the municipal **Niagara Falls Visitor and Convention Bureau**, just off Hwy-420 as you head into town from the QEW, at 5515 Stanley Ave (Mon–Fri 8am–6pm, Sat & Sun 10am–6pm; ☏905/356-6061 or 1-800/563-2557, ✆www.discoverniagara .com), and the **Ontario Welcome Centre** (daily: generally at least 8.30am–5pm; ☏905/358-3221), which is well-stocked with literature on the whole of the province. The Welcome Centre is located beside Hwy-420 at the Stanley Avenue intersection.

Accommodation

Niagara's most expensive **hotels** line up along Fallsview Boulevard, on top of the ridge directly above the falls. Almost all of them are chain hotels, and the same applies down below on and around Clifton Hill, which is a less expensive and rather more convenient area to stay. **Prices** vary enormously depending on availability – if there is a convention in town, the cost of a room with a view of the falls can be wallet emptying; at other times you can get some real bargains.

Brock Plaza Hotel 5685 Falls Ave ☏905/374-4444 or 1-800/263-7135, ✆www.niagarafalls hotels.com/brock/. Just metres from the foot of Clifton Hill, this is one of Niagara's older and most attractive hotels, a tidy tower block with Art Deco flourishes whose upper storeys (and more expensive rooms) have splendid views over the American Falls. Marilyn Monroe stayed here, in Room #801, while filming *Niagara*. $120.

Comfort Inn – Clifton Hill 4960 Clifton Hill ☏905/358-3293 or 1-800/263-2557, ✆www .comfortniagara.com. Nothing extraordinary perhaps, but this chain motel has entirely adequate rooms decorated in a brisk, modern style, and is handily located near the falls. $120.

Quality Inn – Clifton Hill 4946 Clifton Hill ☏905/358-3601 or 1-800/263-7137, ✆www .qualityniagara.com. Motel-style rooms just one block from the falls. $120.

Sheraton on the Falls 5875 Falls Ave ☏905/374-4444 or 1-800/263-7135, ✆www .niagarafallshotels.com. Walloping high rise whose upper floors have wondrous views of the American Falls. Large, well-appointed rooms have supremely comfortable beds. $150.

Water's Edge Inn 4009 River Rd ☏905/356-3306 or 1-800/565-0035, ✆www.niagara watersedgeinn.com. Comfortable if unexceptional motel in attractive location, flanked by parkland near the Spanish Aero Car (see p.113). $60.

The falls

Though you can hear the growl of the **falls** from miles away, nothing quite prepares you for your first glimpse – the fearsome white arc shrouded in clouds of dense spray, with riverboats struggling far below. There are actually two cataracts, as tiny Goat Island (which must be one of the wettest places on earth) divides the accelerating water into two channels: on the American side, the river slips over the precipice of the **American Falls**, 320m wide but still only half the width of **Horseshoe Falls**, on the Canadian side. The spectacle is even more extraordinary in winter, when snow-covered trees edge a jagged armoury of freezing mist and heaped ice blocks.

This may look like a scene of untrammelled nature, but it isn't. Since the early twentieth century, hydroelectric schemes have greatly reduced the water flow, and all sorts of tinkering has spread what's left of the Niagara River more evenly across the falls' crest line. As a result, the process of erosion – which has moved the falls some 11km upstream in twelve thousand years – has slowed from one metre a year to just 30cm. This obviously has advantages for the tourist industry, but the environmental consequences of harnessing the river in such a way are still unclear.

Beside Horseshoe Falls, **Table Rock House** has a small, free **observation platform** and elevators that travel to the base of the cliff, where **tunnels** (Mon–Thurs 9am–8.30pm, Fri–Sun 9am–9.30pm; $10), grandly named the **"Journey Behind the Falls"**, lead to points directly behind the waterfall, where you really do get a sense of its power. For a more panoramic view, a small **Incline Railway** ($2) takes visitors up the hill behind Table Rock House to the **Minolta Tower**, 6732 Fallsview Boulevard (daily: June–Sept 9am–11pm, Oct–May 9am–10pm; $7), which has its own elevated observation decks.

Back at Table Rock House, a wide and often crowded path leads north along the cliffs above the gorge, with the manicured lawns of **Queen Victoria Park** to the left and views of the American Falls to the right. At the end of the park is **Clifton Hill**, the main drag linking the riverside with the town of Niagara Falls, and the jetty from where **Maid of the Mist boats** edge out into the river and push up towards the Falls – an exhilarating and extremely damp trip that no one should miss (daily: May to mid-June 9.45am–4.45/5.45pm, late June to July 9am–7.45pm, Aug 9am–7pm, Sept to late Oct 9.45am–5pm; boats leave every 15mins in high season, otherwise every 30mins; $13, $8 for children ages 6–12, including waterproofs; ☎905/358–5781, ⓦwww.maidofthemist.com).

Clifton Hill itself is a tawdry collection of fast-food joints and bizarre attractions, like the eminently missable Ripley's Believe It or Not! Museum and the House of Frankenstein. If you stick to the river's edge, though, you can avoid both this unattractive side of Niagara and the area's second-biggest crowd-puller, one of the town's two 24-hour **casinos**: this one is near the Rainbow Bridge over to the United States; the other is up on Fallsview Boulevard.

Eating and drinking

Big Anthony's 5677 Victoria Ave ☎905/354-9844. Good, reasonably priced Italian food at this small, well-known restaurant named after a one-time professional wrestler, pictures of whom decorate the walls. Pizzas from $12. Close to Clifton Hill.

Remington's of Montana 5675 Victoria Ave ☎905/356 4410. The restaurant scene in Niagara Falls is hardly pulsating, but this bright, new spot partly fills the gap. Serves tasty and well-prepared steaks (from $15) and seafood.

Around Niagara: downstream from the falls

The **Niagara River Recreation Trail** is a combined bicycle and walking track that travels the entire length of the Niagara River from Lake Ontario to Lake Erie, running parallel to the main road, the **Niagara Parkway**. Downstream from the falls, the trail cuts across the foot of Clifton Hill before continuing north for a further 3km to the **White Water Walk** (May–Oct daily dawn–dusk; $7.50). This comprises an elevator and then a tunnel leading to a boardwalk that overlooks the Whirlpool Rapids, where the river seethes and fizzes as it makes an abrupt turn to the east. From here, it's a further 1km along the parkway now to the brightly painted **Spanish Aero Car** (June–Aug daily 9am–7.45pm; $10; rest of year call ☎905/371-0254 for times), a cable-car ride across the gorge that's as close as you'll come to emulating Blondin's

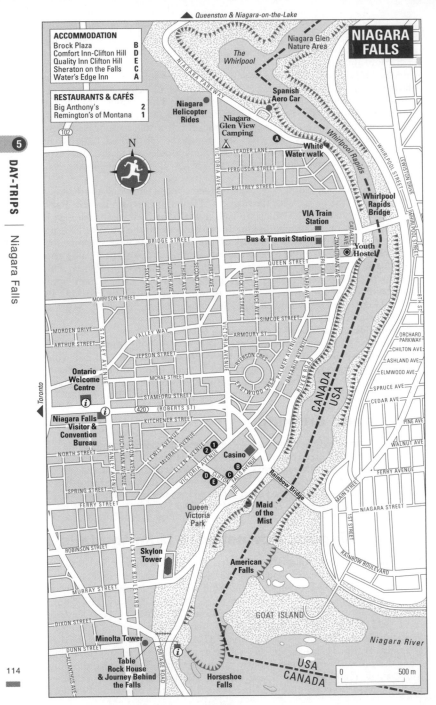

ACCOMMODATION
Brock Plaza   B
Comfort Inn-Clifton Hill   D
Quality Inn Clifton Hill   E
Sheraton on the Falls   C
Water's Edge Inn   A

RESTAURANTS & CAFÉS
Big Anthony's   2
Remington's of Montana   1

NIAGARA FALLS

Queenston & Niagara-on-the-Lake

Niagara Glen
Nature Area

The Whirlpool

Spanish Aero Car

Niagara Helicopter Rides

Niagara Glen View Camping

White Water walk

Whirlpool Rapids

Whirlpool Rapids Bridge

VIA Train Station

Bus & Transit Station

Youth Hostel

NIAGARA PARKWAY

WHIRLPOOL RAPIDS

LEADER LANE

FERGUSON STREET

BUTTREY STREET

VICTORIA AVENUE

LEWISTON DRIVE

WHIRLPOOL STREET

8TH ST

ORCHARD PARKWAY

CHILTON AVE

ASHLAND AVE

ELMWOOD AVE

SPRUCE AVE

CEDAR AVE

PINE AVE

WALNUT AVE

FERRY AVENUE

NIAGARA STREET

1ST STREET

RAINBOW BOULEVARD

BRIDGE STREET

SIXTH AVE
FIFTH AVE
FOURTH AVE
THIRD AVE
SECOND AVE
FIRST AVE

QUEEN STREET

ST LAURENCE AVE

BUCKLEY STREET

ONTARIO AVE

ERIE AVE

CATARACT AVE

ZIMMERMAN AVE

MORRISON STREET

SIMCOE STREET

VALLEY WAY

ARMOURY ST

RYERSON CRES

EASTWOOD CRES

ONTARIO AVENUE

PALMER AVENUE

RIVER ROAD

JEPSON STREET

MCRAE STREET

STAMFORD STREET

MORDEN DRIVE

ARTHUR STREET

Ontario Welcome Centre

Niagara Falls Visitor & Convention Bureau

STANLEY AVENUE

102

N

Toronto

420 (ROBERTS ST)

KITCHENER STREET

LEWIS AVENUE

MCGRAIL AVENUE

ELLEN AVENUE

VICTORIA AVENUE

CLIFTON HILL

CANADA
USA

DESSON AVENUE

BUCHANAN AVENUE

NORTH STREET

SPRING STREET

FERRY STREET

Casino

1
2
B
C
D E

Rainbow Bridge

Maid of the Mist

MAIN STREET

ROBINSON STREET

Skylon Tower

Queen Victoria Park

FALLSVIEW BOULEVARD

American Falls

MURRAY STREET

DIXON STREET

Minolta Tower

Table Rock House & Journey Behind the Falls

DUNN STREET

ALLANTHUS AVE

PORTAGE ROAD

GOAT ISLAND

Horseshoe Falls

Niagara River

USA
CANADA

0   500 m

tightrope trick. Another 1.5km brings you to **Niagara Helicopter Rides**, 3731 Victoria Ave (☎905/357-5672, ⊛www.niagarahelicopters.com), which offers a twelve-minute excursion over the falls for $105 per person, though costs can be reduced significantly if you are in a group (four people costs $370). You don't need to book ahead, as the helicopters whiz in and out with unnerving frequency from 9am to sunset, weather permitting.

Pushing on, the trail soon reaches the parklet that introduces the **Niagara Glen Nature Area** (daily dawn to dusk; free), where paths lead down from the clifftop to the bottom of the gorge. It's a hot and sticky trek in the height of the summer, and strenuous at any time of the year, but rewarding: here at least (and at last) you get a sense of what the gorge was like before all the tourist hullabaloo. Nearby, about 800m further downstream along the parkway, lie the immaculately manicured **Niagara Parks Botanical Gardens** (daily dawn to dusk; free), whose various themed gardens – parterre, rose, bog and so forth – flank the **Butterfly Conservatory** (daily: May–Sept 9am–9pm, Oct–April 9am–6pm or dusk; $10), which attracts visitors in droves.

About 3km further on, **Queenston Heights Park** marks the original location of the falls, before the force of the water eroded the riverbed to its present point, 11km upstream. Soaring above the park is a grandiloquent **monument** to Sir Isaac Brock, the Guernsey-born general who was killed here in the War of 1812, leading a head-on charge against the Americans. Brock is depicted standing on top of an enormous Neoclassical plinth with guardian lions at the base. From beside the park, the parkway begins a curving descent down to the little village of **Queenston**, whose importance as a transit centre disappeared when the falls were bypassed by the Welland Canal, running west of the river between lakes Erie and Ontario and completed in 1829. In the village, on Queenston Street, the **Laura Secord Homestead** (guided tours late May to late Sept Mon–Fri 9.30am–3.30pm, Sat & Sun 11am–5pm; $3.75) is a reconstruction of the substantial timber-frame house of Massachusetts-born Laura Ingersoll Secord (1775–1868). It was from here, during the War of 1812, that Secord proved her dedication to the imperial interest by walking 30km through the woods to warn a British platoon of a surprise attack planned by the Americans. As a result, the British and their native allies laid an ambush and captured over 500 Americans at the Battle of Beaver Dams. Secord had good reason to loathe the Americans – during the war they looted her house and her husband was badly wounded at the battle of Queenston Heights – but in the years following her dramatic escapade she kept a low profile, possibly fearing reprisals in what was then a wild, frontier area. Indeed, it was only in 1861, after her deeds came to the attention of the Prince of Wales, the future King Edward VII, that she received any real credit, plus a reward of one hundred golden sovereigns. The house itself is of elegant proportions and equipped with period furnishings and fittings; the tour provides an intriguing insight into Secord's frontier life in colonial times.

Niagara-on-the-Lake

Boasting elegant clapboard houses and well-kept gardens, all spread along tree-lined streets, **Niagara-on-the-Lake**, 26km downstream from the falls, is one of Ontario's most charming little towns, much of it dating from the early nineteenth century. The town was originally known as Newark and

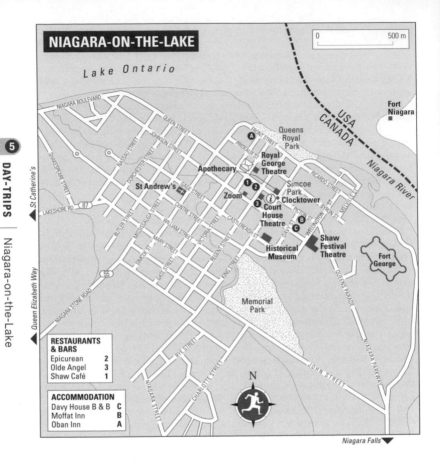

NIAGARA-ON-THE-LAKE

0   500 m

Lake Ontario

Fort
Niagara

USA
CANADA

Niagara River

NIAGARA BOULEVARD

QUEEN STREET

JOHNSON STREET

NASSAU STREET

St Catherine's

Queen Elizabeth Way

SHAKESPEARE STREET

DORCHESTER STREET

LAKESHORE RD   87

BUTLER STREET

MISSISSAUGA STREET

MARY STREET

SIMCOE ST

NIAGARA STONE ROAD

55

GATE STREET

WILLIAM STREET

CENTRE STREET

VICTORIA STREET

REGENT STREET

KING STREET

PRIDEAUX ST

FRONT STREET

GAGE STREET

Royal
George
Theatre

Apothecary

St Andrew's

Zoom

Queens
Royal
Park

Simcoe
Park

Clocktower

Court
House
Theatre

CASTLEREAGH ST

RICARDO STREET

BYRON ST

MELVILLE ST

JUNCTION ST

DAY ST

WELLINGTON

Historical
Museum

Shaw
Festival
Theatre

Fort
George

QUEENS PARADE

NIAGARA PARKWAY

Memorial
Park

RYE STREET

NIAGARA STREET

CHARLOTTE STREET

JOHN STREET

N

**RESTAURANTS
& BARS**
Epicurean   2
Olde Angel   3
Shaw Café   1

ACCOMMODATION
Davy House B & B   C
Moffat Inn   B
Oban Inn   A

Niagara Falls ▼

became the first capital of Upper Canada in 1792, but four years later it lost this distinction to York (Toronto) because it was deemed too close to the American frontier, and therefore vulnerable to attack. The US army did, in fact, cross the river in 1813, destroying the town, but it was quickly rebuilt and renamed. Even better, it has managed to avoid all but the most sympathetic of modifications ever since, except just away from the centre down on Melville Street, where a rash of new development and a marina add nothing to the appeal of the place. Niagara-on-the-Lake attracts a few too many day-trippers for its own good, but the crowds are rarely oppressive, except on weekends in July and August. The town is also popular as the location of one of Canada's most acclaimed theatre festivals, the **Shaw Festival**, which celebrates the works of George Bernard Shaw with performances from April to late October.

Arrival, information and transport

A reliable **minibus service** linking Niagara Falls and Niagara-on-the-Lake is provided three or four times daily by 5-0 Transportation (☎905/358-3232),

The Shaw Festival

The only festival in the world devoted solely to the works of George Bernard Shaw and his contemporaries, the **Shaw Festival** is mandated to produce only plays written in the playwright's lifetime (1856–1950), which the company refer to as "plays about the beginning of the modern world". Performances are held in **three theatres.** The largest is the Festival Theatre, a modern structure seating 850 people at 10 Queen's Parade, and the other two theatres – the Court House, a nineteenth-century stone building at 26 Queen Street, and the Royal George, with its fancy Edwardian interior at 85 Queen Street – both hold around 320. **Ticket prices** for the best seats at prime weekend performances hit $82, but most seats go for $50–60. The box office for all three theatres is ☏1-800/511-7429, or book online at ⓦwww.shawfest.com. The festival runs from April to late November.

who charge $10 for the one-way fare, $18 return. The Niagara-on-the-Lake **tourist office** is on the main drag at 26 Queen St, in the lower level of the Court House (daily: May to mid-Oct 10am–7.30pm, mid-Oct to April 10am–5pm; ☏905/468-1950, ⓦwww.niagaraonthelake.com). They issue town maps and operate a free **room reservation service**, which can be a great help in the summer when the town's hotels and B&Bs – of which there are dozens – get very busy.

It only takes a few minutes to stroll from one end of town to the other, but to venture further afield – especially to the falls – you might consider renting a **bicycle** from Zoom, plumb in the centre of town at 42 Market St (☏905/468-2366 or 1-866/811-6993, ⓦwww.zoomleisure.com).

Accommodation

Davy House B&B 230 Davy St ☏905/468-5307 or 1-888/314-9046, ⓦwww.davyhouse.com. Cosy two-storey clapboard house with a veranda for relaxing. Within easy strolling distance of the town centre. $175.

Moffat Inn 60 Picton St ☏905/468-4116, ⓦwww.moffatinn.com. Rooms in this modest hotel close to the centre of town are pleasant but undistinguished; the prices are therefore lower than most of its rivals' and there is sometimes space here when everyone else is full. $100.

Oban Inn 160 Front St ☏905/468-2165 or 1-866/359-6226, ⓦwww.obaninn.ca. A delightful and luxurious hotel across from the lake and within easy walking distance of the town centre. The original *Oban* burnt to the ground in 1992, but its replacement was built in true colonial style, with an elegant wooden veranda. The gardens are beautiful and the breakfasts are first-rate. $265.

The Town

It's the general flavour of Niagara-on-the-Lake that appeals, rather than any specific sight, but **Queen Street**, the main drag, does hold the **Apothecary** (mid-May to Sept daily noon–6pm; free), which is worth a look for its beautifully carved walnut and butternut cabinets and porcelain jars. There is also the **Niagara Historical Museum**, at 43 Castlereagh St and Davy (daily: May–Oct 10am–5pm, Nov–April 1–5pm; $5), whose accumulated tackle relates the early history of the town and includes mementoes of the Laura Secord family (see p.115). Also of interest is the fenced **burial plot in**

Simcoe Park, at King and Byron streets, which holds the earthly remains of 25 Polish soldiers who died here during the great influenza epidemic of 1918–1919.

Fort George

There is more military stuff not too far away at the one-time British outpost of **Fort George** (May–Oct daily 10am–5pm; $8), 700m southeast of the town centre via Picton Street. In the early nineteenth century, so many of the fort's soldiers were hightailing it off to the States that the British had to garrison it with the Royal Canadian Rifle Regiment, a troop of primarily

△ Niagra-on-the-Lake

Polish soldiers in Niagara-on-the-Lake

In the later stages of World War I, over twenty thousand Poles mustered in the US to form a Polish brigade. It was a delicate situation, as the Allies needed the soldiers but the Poles were committed to the creation of an independent Poland at a time when their country was ruled by Russia, an ally of the US. In the event, policy differences with the US government prompted the Poles to move to Niagara-on-the-Lake, where they established a base camp. The Poles were trained by Canadian officers and paid and equipped by France, and they were subsequently shipped off in batches to fight on the Western front, deferring their attempts to create an independent Poland. At the end of the war, with the tsar gone and the Bolsheviks in control of Russia, the Polish brigade – or "Blue Army" as it was called from the colour of their uniform – crossed Germany to return to their homeland, where they played a key role in the foundation of an independent Poland. The graves of the 25 soldiers here in Niagara recall these historical complexities, and a wooden shrine has been erected in their honour.

married men approaching retirement who were unlikely to forfeit their pensions by deserting. If they did try and were caught, they were branded on the chest with the letter "D" (for "Deserter"), and were either lashed or transported to a penal colony – except in wartime, when they were shot. The fort was destroyed during the War of 1812, but today's site is a splendid reconstruction. The palisaded **compound** holds about a dozen buildings, among them two log blockhouses and the officers' quarters; a tunnel links the main part of the fort with an exterior bastion, or ravelin, which is the site of a third, even stronger blockhouse. The only original building is the **powder magazine**, whose interior was equipped with wood and copper fittings to reduce the chances of an accidental explosion; as an added precaution, the soldiers working in here went barefoot. There are also ninety-minute lantern-light **ghost tours** of the fort – good fun with or without an apparition (May–June Sun 8.30pm; July–Aug Sun, Mon, Wed & Thurs 8.30pm; Sept Sun 7.30pm; $10; ☎905/468-6621). Tours leave from the car park in front of the fort; **tickets** can be purchased either in advance at the fort's **gift shop**, or from the guide at the beginning of the tour.

Eating and drinking

By sheer weight of numbers, the day-trippers set a mediocre gastronomic tone here in Niagara-on-the-Lake, but one or two good **cafés** and **restaurants** have survived the deluge to offer tasty meals and snacks.

Epicurean 84 Queen St. Inexpensive but very competent café featuring Mediterranean dishes. Vegetarian options are offered on most days; sandwiches are $6–9. Daily 9am–9pm.

Olde Angel Inn 224 Regent St. With its low-beamed ceilings and flagstone floors, this is the town's most atmospheric pub, serving a first-rate range of draught imported and domestic beers. Also offers filling and very affordable bar food – Guinness steak-and-kidney pies and so forth from $8 – and has a smart á la carte restaurant at the back. Just off Queen St.

Shaw Café and Wine Bar 92 Queen St at Victoria. This café-restaurant caters to theatre-goers rather than day-trippers. The decor is a tad overdone, but the pastas and salads (from $9) are tasty and well prepared. Closes at 8pm.

5

Ontario wines

Until the 1980s **Canadian wine** was something of a joke. The industry's most popular product was a sticky, fizzy concoction called "Baby Duck", and other varieties were commonly called "block-and-tackle" wines, after a widely reported witticism of a member of the Ontario legislature: "If you drink a bottle and walk a block, you can tackle anyone." This state of affairs was, however, transformed by the **Vintners Quality Alliance** (VQA), who have, since 1989, come to exercise tight control over wine production in Ontario, which produces around eighty percent of Canadian wine. The VQA's appellation system distinguishes between – and supervises the quality control of – two broad types of wine. Those wines carrying the **Provincial Designation** on their labels must be made from one hundred percent Ontario-grown grapes, and those grapes must be from an approved list of European varieties and selected hybrids; those bearing the **Geographic Designation** (ie Niagara Peninsula, Pelee Island or Lake Erie North Shore), by comparison, can only use *Vitis vinifera*, the classic European grape varieties, such as Riesling, Chardonnay and Cabernet Sauvignon. As you might expect from a developing wine area, the results are rather inconsistent, but the **Rieslings** have a refreshingly crisp, almost tart flavour with a mellow, warming aftertaste – and are perhaps the best of the present range, white or red.

More than twenty **wineries** are clustered in the vicinity of Niagara-on-the-Lake, and most are very willing to show visitors around. Local tourist offices carry a full list with opening times, but one of the most interesting is **Inniskillin**, Line 3 (Service Road 66), just off the Niagara Parkway, about 5km south of Niagara-on-the-Lake (daily: May–Oct 10am–6pm, Nov–April 10am–5pm; ☎905/468-3554, ⒲www .inniskillin.com). Here you can follow a self-guided tour or take a free guided tour, sip away at the tasting bar and buy at the wine boutique. Inniskillin has produced a clutch of award-winning vintages and played a leading role in the improvement of the industry. They are also one of the few Canadian wineries to produce **ice wine**, an outstanding sweet dessert wine made from grapes that are left on the vine till December or January, when they are hand-picked at night while frozen; there is also a slightly tarter sparkling ice wine. The picking and the crushing of the frozen grapes is a time-consuming business and this is reflected in the price – from about $55 per 375ml bottle of either sparkling or regular.

Stratford, Goderich and Bayfield

Heading west from Toronto, you eventually escape the city's sprawling suburbs and satellite townships to emerge in rural Ontario, a sprawling chunk of flat and fertile farmland that extends as far as the shores of Lake Huron. The first place that calls for a stop is **Stratford**, an attractive little town about 160km from Toronto that is celebrated for its theatre festival and has a goodly crop of B&Bs. From here it is another short haul (about 60km) to the **Lake Huron shoreline**. Popular with holidaying Canadians, the lakeshore is trimmed by sandy beaches and a steep bluff that's interrupted by the occasional river valley. Lake Huron is much less polluted than Lake Ontario, the sunsets are beautiful, and in **Goderich** and neighbouring **Bayfield**, it possesses two of the most appealing places in the whole of the province.

Stratford makes for an easy day-trip, but Lake Huron is a tad too far for comfort and it's better to stay the night – Bayfield has the choicer accommodation. There are good **bus and train** services from Toronto to Stratford, but there is no **public transport** to either Goderich or Bayfield.

Stratford

A homely and likeable town of 30,000 people, **STRATFORD** is brightened by the **River Avon** as it meanders through the centre and by its grandiose **city hall**, a brown-brick confection of cupolas, towers and limestone trimmings. More importantly, the town is home to the **Stratford Festival**, which started in 1953 and is now one of the most prestigious theatrical occasions in North America, attracting no fewer than half a million visitors each and every year.

Arrival and information

From Stratford **train and bus stations**, on Shakespeare Street, it's a fifteen-minute stroll north via Downie Street to the centre of town on the south bank of the River Avon. There are two **tourist offices**: the main one is Tourism Stratford, at 47 Downie St (Mon–Sat 9am–5pm, closed Sat Sept–May; ☎519/271-5140 or 1-800/561-7926, ✆www.city.stratford.on.ca), and the other is the Visitor Information Centre (May–Sept Mon–Fri 9am–5pm, Sat & Sun 9am–6pm), located by the river on York Street, immediately northwest of the town's main intersection, where Erie, Downie and Ontario streets all meet.

Accommodation

Stratford has over 250 guesthouses and B&Bs plus around a dozen hotels and motels, but **accommodation** can still be hard to find during the Festival's busiest weekends, usually in July and August. The walls of the tourist offices are plastered with pictures and descriptions of many of these establishments, and standards (and prices) are high. Both offices will help you find somewhere to stay.

Avonview Manor B&B 63 Avon St ☎519/273-4603 ✆www.bbcanada.com/avonview. Occupying an expansive Edwardian villa overlooking the north bank of the River Avon, this enjoyable B&B has four tastefully decorated and immaculately maintained bedrooms. $100.
Deacon House B&B Inn 101 Brunswick St ☎519/273-2052 ✆www.bbcanada.com/1152 .html. Six lovely guest rooms – all en suite –

in a good-looking, centrally located Edwardian villa with a wide veranda. $110.
Duggan Place B&B Inn 151 Nile St ☎519/273-7502 or 1-888-394-1111, ✆www.dugganplace .com. Well-kept Victorian villa with four en suite rooms; two have private balconies overlooking a splendid garden. A five-minute walk from the town centre. $140.

Eating

Stratford has plenty of excellent **cafés and restaurants**, with one of the best being *Fellini's Italian Café & Grill*, 107 Ontario St, which offers a good range of fresh pizzas and pastas at reasonable prices. There are tasty snacks and light meals at *Tango Coffee Bistro*, 104 Ontario St, which also has live music on the weekend, and more of the same at the homely *Let Them Eat Cake*, 82 Wellington St. *Rundles*, 9 Cobourg St (May–Oct Tues & Sun 5–7pm, Wed–Sat 5–8.30pm, also Sat & Sun 11.30am–1.15pm; ☎519/271-6442), is arguably the classiest restaurant in town, serving up imaginatively prepared French-style cuisine at finger-burning prices; the strikingly modern surroundings help compensate.

Goderich

Perched on the edge of Lake Huron, **Goderich** is a delightful country town of eight thousand inhabitants. It began life in 1825 when, amid rumours of

The Stratford Festival

Each season, North America's largest classical repertory company puts on the **Stratford Festival** (☎ 1-800/567-1600, ⓦ www.stratfordfestival.ca), featuring two of Shakespeare's tragedies and two of his comedies; this programme is augmented by other classical staples – the works of Moliere, Sheridan, Johnson and so forth – as well as by the best of modern and musical theatre. The festival also hosts a lecture series, various tours (of backstage and a costume warehouse, for example), music concerts, an author reading series and meet-and-greet sessions with the actors. The festival runs from mid-April to early November and there are performances in three downtown locations: the Festival, Tom Patterson and Studio theatres. Regular **tickets** cost anywhere between $45 and $100, depending on the performance and seat category, though there are all sorts of discounts for students, seniors, same-day performances and previews; many plays are, however, sold out months in advance. Call or consult the website for the latest news.

bribery and corruption, the British-owned Canada Company bought two and a half million acres of fertile southern Ontario – the so-called Huron Tract – from the government at the ridiculously low rate of twelve cents an acre. Today, the wide tree-lined avenues of the geometrically planned centre of Goderich radiate from a grand **octagonal central circus**, which is dominated by a white stone courthouse. From the circus, the four main streets follow the points of the compass, with North Street leading to the compendious **Huron County Museum** (Mon–Sat 10am–4.30pm & Sun 1–4.30pm; $5, $7.50 with jail, see below), which concentrates on the exploits of the district's pioneers. Highlights include a fantastic array of farm implements, from simple hand tools to gigantic, clumsy machines like a steam-driven thresher. There's also a beautifully restored Canadian Pacific steam engine, as well as exhibition areas featuring furniture and military memorabilia.

From the museum, it's a ten-minute walk to the high stone walls of the **Huron County Gaol**, at 181 Victoria St (mid-May to early Sept daily 10am–4.30pm; $5): to get there, walk up to the far end of North Street, then turn right along Gloucester Terrace and it's at the end of the street on the right. This joint courthouse and jail was constructed between 1839 and 1842, but the design was very unpopular with local judges, who felt threatened by the proximity of those they were sentencing. The other problem was the smell: several judges refused to conduct proceedings because of the terrible odour coming from the privies in the exercise yard below and, in 1856, the administration gave in and built a new courthouse in the middle of the central circus. On a visit, don't miss the original **jailer's apartment** and a string of well-preserved **prison cells**, which reflect various changes in design between 1841 and 1972, when the prison was finally closed. The worst is the leg-iron cell for "troublesome" prisoners, where unfortunates were chained to the wall with neither bed nor blanket.

Back in the centre, West Street leads the 1km through a cutting in the bluffs to the harbour and salt workings on the Lake Huron shoreline. From here, a footpath trails north round the harbourside silos to the **Menesetung Bridge**, a former railway crossing that is now a pedestrian walkway spanning the Maitland River. On the far side of the river, you can pick up the **Maitland Trail**, which wanders down the north bank of the river as far as the marina. In the opposite direction, the shoreline has been tidied up to create a picnic area, but, although the sunsets are spectacular, the beach itself is a tad scrawny.

Practicalities

The Goderich **tourist office** (mid–May to Aug daily 9am–7pm; Sept to mid–May Mon–Fri 9am–4.30pm; ☎519/524-6600 or 1-800/280-7637, ⊛www .town.goderich.on.ca) is at Nelson and Hamilton streets, beside Hwy-21, a couple of minutes' walk northeast of the central circus. They have details of the town's **bed-and-breakfasts**, which average about $75 for a double.

The *Colborne Bed & Breakfast*, at 72 Colborne St (☎519/524-7400 or 1-800/390-4612, ⊛www.colbornebandb.com), has four pleasantly appointed guest rooms in an early twentieth-century home. All are en suite and have air conditioning. A gourmet breakfast is included in the price ($110), and the place is just a short walk from the central circus. The distinctive *Bedford Hotel*, at 92 The Square (☎519/524-7337, ⊛www.hotelbedford.on.ca) is directly on the circus. Built in 1896, the *Bedford* has a grandiose wooden staircase just like a saloon in a John Ford movie – though the unimaginatively modernized rooms ($90) at the top are something of a disappointment.

For **eating and drinking**, you can get big pizzas, starting at $9, and steaks at the inexpensive *Big Daddy's Pizza & Grill*, located at 42 West St (☎519/524-7777). Filling pub food (main courses from $9) and views of the lake can be had at *Park House*, 168 West St (☎519/524-4968), the liveliest bar in town. *Thyme on 21*, in the centre of town at 80 Hamilton St (☎519/524-4171) is situated in a restored Victorian house and serves an imaginative menu featuring local ingredients. Main courses average around $12. Reservations are advised.

Bayfield

Pocket-sized **Bayfield**, just 20km south of Goderich, is a well-heeled town with handsome timber villas nestling beneath a canopy of ancient trees. The towns-folk have kept modern development at arm's length – there's barely a neon sign in sight, never mind a concrete apartment block – and almost every house has been beautifully maintained. Historical plaques give the low-down on the older buildings that line Bayfield's short **Main Street**, and pint-sized **Pioneer Park**, on the bluff overlooking the lake, is a fine spot to take in the sunset. Bayfield is mainly a place to relax and unwind, but you can also venture down to the **harbour** on the north side of the village, where, in season, you can pick wild mushrooms and fiddleheads along the banks of the Bayfield River.

Practicalities

The Bayfield **tourist office** (May–Sept daily 10am–6pm; ☎519/565-2499, ⊛www.bayfieldchamberofcommerce.on.ca), in the village hall beside the green at the end of Main Street, will help you find **accommodation** – though their assistance is only necessary in July and August, when vacancies can get thin on the ground.

The first-rate **bed-and-breakfast** *Clair on the Square*, at 12 The Square (☎519/565-2135, ⊛www.claironthesquare.ca) occupies a charming Victorian villa right in the town centre. It offers comfortable, attractive double rooms ($130), all en suite and decorated in a crisp, modern-meets-traditional style. The best **hotel** for miles around is *Little Inn of Bayfield*, at 26 Main St (☎519/565-2611 or 1-800/565-1832, ⊛www.littleinn.com). Housed in a modernized nineteenth-century timber-and-brick building with a lovely wraparound veranda, most of the delightfully furnished rooms ($175), with their pastel shades and bright and airy demeanour, have whirlpool baths, and many have balconies.

The *Little Inn of Bayfield* also has a superb **restaurant** (☎519/565-2611), whose speciality is fresh fish from Lake Huron – perch, pickerel and steelhead.

Though informal, it's still expensive: seafood dishes cost about $25, and chicken and duck about the same. A nice bar is attached.

For more casual dining, try the *Albion Hotel* on Main St (☎519/565-2641), where you'll find tasty bar food and a good range of beers at reasonable prices.

Severn Sound

One of the most delightful parts of Ontario, the sheltered southern shore of **Severn Sound**, some 150km north of Toronto along Hwy-400, is lined with tiny ports, and its deep-blue waters are studded by thousands of rocky little islands. There's enough here for several day-trips, beginning with two of the province's finest historical reconstructions: **Discovery Harbour**, a British naval base, and **Sainte-Marie among the Hurons**, a Jesuit mission. Be sure, also, to spare some time for the wonderful scenery of the **Georgian Bay Islands National Park**, whose glacier-smoothed, Precambrian rocks and wispy pines were so marvellously celebrated by the Group of Seven painters (see p.70) and by the likes of the Canadian author Alice Munro, one of whose characters revels "What drew her in – enchanted her actually – was the very indifference, the repetition, the carelessness and contempt for harmony, she found on the scrambled surface of the Precambrian shield."

In conjunction with Greyhound, PMCL (☎1-800/661-8747, ⓦwww .greyhound.ca) runs several **buses** daily from Toronto to the regional towns of **Penetanguishene** and **Midland**. Beyond that, however, local bus services are very patchy, and your best bet is to **rent a car** in Toronto.

Penetanguishene

Homely **Penetanguishene** ("place of the rolling white sands") is the westernmost town on Severn Sound, and site of one of Ontario's first European settlements – a Jesuit mission founded in 1639 and then abandoned a decade later. Thereafter, in the eighteenth century, Europeans established a trading station here, but the settlement remained insignificant until the British built a naval dockyard following the War of 1812. This attracted both French- and English-speaking shopkeepers and suppliers, and even today Penetanguishene is one of the few places in southern Ontario to maintain a bilingual tradition.

The town's primary thoroughfare, **Main Street**, is a pleasant place for a stroll, its shops and cafés installed behind sturdy redbrick facades, which slope down towards the waterfront. Take a peek also at the **Centennial Museum**, 13 Burke St (Mon–Sat 9am–4.30pm & Sun 12–4.30pm; $4.50; ⓦwww.pencemuseum .com), a couple of minutes' walk east of Main Street along the waterfront's Beck Boulevard. The museum occupies the old general store and offices of the Beck lumber company, whose yards once stretched right along the town's lakeshore. The company was founded in 1865 by Charles Beck, a German immigrant who made himself immensely unpopular by paying his men half their wages in tokens that were only redeemable at his stores. The museum has examples of these "Beck dollars", as well as a fascinating selection of old photographs featuring locals at work and at play in the town and its forested surroundings.

From the jetty at the north end of Main Street, the MS *Georgian Queen* (☎705/549-7795 or 1-800/363-7447, ⓦwww.georgianbaycruises.com) offers an enjoyable programme of **summer cruises**. The pick are the two-and-a-half-hour

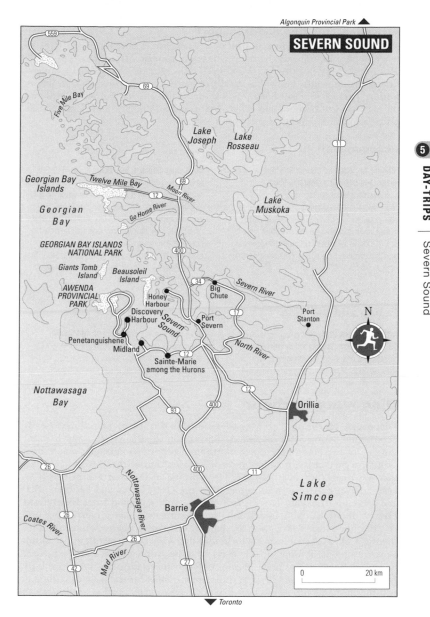

559

69

Five Mile Bay

Lake
Joseph   Lake
Rosseau

11

Georgian Bay
Islands   Twelve Mile Bay   69   Moon River

Georgian
Bay   12   Go Home River   Lake
Muskoka

GEORGIAN BAY ISLANDS
NATIONAL PARK   400

Giants Tomb
Island   Beausoleil
Island   34   Big
Chute   Severn River

AWENDA
PROVINCIAL
PARK   Honey
Harbour

Discovery   Severn   Port
Harbour   Sound   Severn   17   Port
Stanton

Penetanguishene
Midland   12   North River

N

Sainte-Marie
among the Hurons   12

Nottawasaga
Bay   400   Orillia

93

26   400   11

26   Lake
Simcoe

Coates River   26   Barrie

Nottawasaga River

Mad River   26

42   27

0   20 km

excursion to Cedar Springs, on Beausoleil Island in the Georgian Bay Islands National Park (July to mid-Aug, 2 weekly; $22), and the three-and-a-half-hour cruise to Minicognashene, amongst the Thirty Thousand Islands, the collective name for the myriad islets that confetti the southern reaches of Georgian Bay (July to early Sept, 4 weekly; $22). It's advisable to make **reservations** at least a day ahead of time; for more on Georgian Bay Islands National Park, see p.128.

Arrival, information and transport

Penetanguishene's tiny **bus depot** is at Main Street and Robert, a five- to ten-minute walk from the harbour, where the **tourist office** (May–Aug daily 10am-6pm, Sept to early Oct Mon–Fri 11am-4pm; ℡705/549-2232, ✑www .southerngeorgianbay.on.ca) has details of local hotels and bed-and-breakfasts. **Union Taxi** (℡705/549-7666), next door to the bus station, will whisk you off to Discovery Harbour and Sainte-Marie among the Hurons if required (see p.127 below and opposite respectively).

Accommodation

Hillside Inn B&B 27 Church St at Brock ℡705/549-5462 or 1-866/806-3508, ✑www.hillsideinnbandb.com. This attractive old house with a wraparound veranda has a handful of cozy, well-appointed guest rooms with shared facilities. It stands on a wooded ridge with views out across the bay, near the centre of town. Around $70.

No. 1 Jury Drive 1 Jury Drive ℡705/549-6851, ✑www.jurydrbb.huronia.com. A delightful bed-and-breakfast in a leafy suburban setting at the entrance to Discovery Harbour. The immaculate modern house, built in the style of a Victorian clapboard, has five extremely comfortable en-suite rooms, all with deep and downy mattresses. A fantastic breakfast is provided – ask for the carrot muffins. Highly recommended. $100.

Eating and drinking

Arthur's 3 Beck Blvd. Not exactly haute cuisine, but this harbourside bar-cum-restaurant offers seafood dishes from as little as $12. Very popular with the locals.

Blue Sky Family Restaurant 48 Main St. Agreeable small-town diner offering good-quality snacks and meals at very affordable prices. Great place for a gossip, too.

Discovery Harbour

Discovery Harbour (late May to June Mon–Fri 10am–5pm; July to early Sept daily 10am–5pm; $6.50; ℡705/549-8064, ✑www.discoveryharbour .on.ca), located about 5km north along the bay from Penetanguishene's town centre on Jury Drive, is an ambitious reconstruction of the British naval base that was established here in 1817. The purpose of the base was primarily to keep an eye on American movements on the Great Lakes, and between 1820 and 1834 up to twenty Royal Navy vessels were stationed here. **Lieutenant Henry Bayfield**, who undertook the monumental task of surveying and charting the Great Lakes, used the base as his winter quarters, informing his superiors of his determination "to render this work so correct that it shall not be easy to render it more so". He lived up to his word, and his charts remained in use for decades. The naval station, unfortunately, was more short-lived. By 1834, relations with the US were sufficiently cordial for the navy to withdraw, and the base was turned over to the army, who maintained a small garrison here until 1856.

Staffed by enthusiastic **costumed guides**, the sprawling site spreads along a hillside above a tranquil inlet, its green slopes scattered with accurate recon-structions of everything from a sailors' barracks to several period houses, the prettiest of which is the **Keating House**, named after the base's longest-serving adjutant, Frank Keating. Only one of the original buildings survives, the dour limestone **Officers' Quarters**, which dates from the 1840s, but the complex's pride and joy is the working harbour-cum-dockyard. Here, a brace of fully rigged **sailing ships**, the HMS *Bee* and HMS *Tecumseth*, have been rebuilt to their original nineteenth-century specifications. Both schooners take on volunteers as members of their crews and make occasional outings; for sailing times and prices, call ahead.

Sainte-Marie among the Hurons

One of Ontario's most arresting historical attractions, the reconstructed Jesuit mission of **Sainte-Marie among the Hurons** (early to mid-May & mid to late Oct Mon–Fri 10am–5pm; late May to mid-Oct daily 10am–5pm; early to late May & mid Sept to late Nov $8.50, late May to mid-Sept $11; ☎705/526-7838, ⊛www.saintemarieamongthehurons.on.ca) marks the site of a crucial episode in Canadian history.

In 1608, the French explorer **Samuel de Champlain** returned to Canada convinced that the only way to make the fur trade profitable was by developing partnerships with native hunters. Three years later, he formed an alliance with the **Huron** of southwest Ontario, cementing the agreement with a formal exchange of presents. However, his decision to champion one tribe against another – and particularly his gift of firearms to his new allies – disrupted the balance of power among the native societies of the St Lawrence and Great Lakes areas. Armed with Champlain's rifles, the Huron attacked their ancient enemies, the **Iroquois**, with gusto, inflicting heavy casualties; the Iroquois licked their wounds, determined to get even whenever they could. Meanwhile, in 1639, the **Jesuits** had established their centre of operations here at Sainte-Marie. They converted a substantial minority of the native people to Christianity, thereby undermining the social cohesion of the Huron – but much more importantly they had unwittingly infected and enfeebled the Huron with three European sicknesses: measles, smallpox and influenza.

In 1648, the Dutch, copying Champlain, began to sell the Iroquois firearms, and in March of the following year the Iroquois launched a full-scale invasion of Huron territory, or **Huronia**, slaughtering their enemies as they moved in on Sainte-Marie. Fearing for their lives, the Jesuits of Sainte-Marie burned their settlement and fled. Eight thousand Hurons went with them; most starved to death on Georgian Bay, but a few made it to Québec. During the campaign, two Jesuit priests, fathers **Brébeuf and Lalemant**, were captured at the outpost of Saint-Louis (near present-day Victoria Harbour), where they were bound to the stake and tortured – as per standard Iroquois practice. Despite the suffering brought upon the Hurons, it was the image of Catholic bravery and Iroquois cruelty that long lingered in the minds of French Canadians.

Today the mission is located 8km southeast of Penetanguishene off Hwy-12; there are **no buses**, but Penetanguishene's Union Taxi (☎705/549-7666) charges about $14 each way to make the trip.

The Mission

A visit to Sainte-Marie starts in the impressive **reception centre**. An audio-visual show provides some background information, ending with the screen lifting dramatically away to reveal the painstakingly restored **Mission**. The twenty-odd wooden buildings are divided into two sections: the Jesuit area with its watchtowers, chapel, forge and farm buildings; and the native area, including a hospital and a pair of bark-covered long houses – one for Christian converts, the other for heathens. Relatively spick-and-span today, it takes some imagination to see the long houses as they appeared to Father Lalemant, who saw "a miniature picture of hell...on every side naked bodies, black and half-roasted, mingled pell-mell with the dogs...you will not reach the end of the cabin before you are completely befouled with soot, filth and dirt".

Costumed **guides** act out the parts of Hurons and Europeans with vim, answering questions and demonstrating crafts and skills, though they show a reluctance to eat the staple food of the region, *sagamite*, a porridge of cornmeal seasoned with rotten fish. The cemetery contains the remains of several Hurons who died here, and in the adjacent wooden church of St Joseph is the **grave** where the remains of Brébeuf and Lalemant were interred. At the end of the tour, a path leads from the site to the excellent **museum**, which traces the story of early Canada with maps and displays on such subjects as fishing and the fur trade.

Martyrs' Shrine

Overlooking Sainte-Marie from across Hwy-12, the twin-spired church of the **Martyrs' Shrine** (late May to mid-Oct daily 8.30am–9pm; $3) was built in 1926 to commemorate the eight Jesuits who were killed in Huronia between 1642 and 1649. Blessed by Pope John Paul II in 1984 – when he remarked that it was "a symbol of unity of faith in a diversity of cultures" – the church is massively popular with pilgrims, who have left a stack of discarded crutches in the transept, in sight of the assorted reliquaries that claim to contain the body parts of the murdered priests. The most conspicuous reliquary is the skull of Brébeuf, which is displayed in the glass cabinet near the transept door.

Georgian Bay Islands National Park

Georgian Bay Islands National Park consists of a scattering of about sixty islands spread between Severn Sound and Twelve Mile Bay, approximately 50km to the north. The park's two distinct landscapes – the glacier-scraped rock of the Canadian Shield and the hardwood forests and thicker soils of the south – meet at the northern end of the largest and most scenic island, **Beausoleil**. This beautiful island is a forty-minute boat ride west of **Honey Harbour**, the park's nearest port, which contains little more than a jetty, a couple of shops and a few self-contained hotel resorts.

Beausoleil has eleven short **hiking trails**, including two that start at the Cedar Spring landing stage on the southeastern shore: Treasure Trail (3.8km), which heads north behind the marshes along the edge of the island, and the Christian Trail (1.5km), which cuts through beech and maple stands to balsam and hemlock groves overlooking the rocky beaches of the western shoreline. At the northern end of Beausoleil, the Cambrian (2km) and Fairy trails (2.5km) are delightful routes through harsher glacier-scraped scenery, while, just to the west, the Dossyonshing Trail (2.5km) tracks through a mixed area of wetland, forest and bare granite that covers the transitional zone between the two main landscapes.

Practicalities

Honey Harbour is around 170km north of Toronto – take Hwy-400 and watch for the turn-off onto Route 5 (Exit 156), just beyond Port Severn. The **national park visitor reception** in Honey Harbour (late June to early Sept Sun–Thurs 9am–5pm, Fri & Sat 10am–6pm; ⑦705/526-9804) provides a full range of information on walking trails and flora and fauna.

There's no public transport to Honey Harbour, so having your own car is essential. Several Honey Harbour operators run **water taxis to Beausoleil**, with a one-way trip costing about $40 in summer, a few dollars less in spring and fall. Among them, Honey Harbour Boat Club (☎705/756-2411), about 700m beyond the park office, is probably your best bet. There are no set times, but in summer boats leave for Beausoleil quite frequently. Fares to several of the park's other islands are negotiable. In all cases, advance **reservations** are required, and you should be sure to agree on a pick-up time before you set out. With less time to spare, the national park's **Georgian Bay Islands Day Tripper boat** leaves from Honey Harbour three times daily in July and August bound for Beausoleil, where passengers get four hours' hiking time. The round-trip fare is $16; for further details and reservations, contact the main national park office (☎705/756-2415). Prospective hikers and campers bound for Georgian Bay Islands National Park need to come properly equipped – this is very much a wilderness environment. And whatever you do, don't forget the insect repellent.

If you decide to stay overnight, Beausoleil has eleven small **campsites**. The charge is $14 a night and all operate on a self-registration, first-come, first-served basis, with the exception of Cedar Spring ($23), where the **visitor centre** (☎705/756-5909) near the main boat dock takes reservations for an additional $10. The campsites can get packed to the gills, so check availability before departure. Less arduously, Honey Harbour has one good **hotel**, the seasonal, lakeshore *Delawana Inn Resort* (☎705/756-2424 or 1-888/335-2926, ☒www .delawana.com), which has spacious chalet-cabins dotted round its extensive, pine-forested grounds – though note that the resort is geared up for family holidays rather than overnight travellers. In high-season chalets start at about $800 for two nights for two people, including meals. Guests have use of the resort's canoes, kayaks and windsurfing equipment. A more economical option – and one where overnight stays are more usual – is *Rawley Lodge* (☎705/538-2272 or 1-800/263-7538, ☒www.rawleylodge.on.ca; $200 including breakfast & dinner). This pleasantly old-fashioned, 1920s timber hotel is located on the water's edge in the hamlet of **Port Severn**, some fifteen kilometres from Honey Harbour, just off Hwy-400 (Exit 153 or 156). **Restaurants** hereabouts are few and far between – the pick is *The Inn at Christie's Mill* (☎705/538-2354), at Port Severn, where the modern and reasonably priced restaurant offers tasty steaks and seafood; reservations are advised.

Kingston

Birthplace of Bryan Adams but prouder of its handsome limestone buildings, the town of **Kingston**, a fairly quick 260km east of Toronto along Hwy-401, is the largest and most enticing of the communities along the northern shore of Lake Ontario. It occupies an attractive and once strategically important position where the lake narrows into the St Lawrence River, its potential first recognized by the French who built a fortified fur-trading post here in 1673. It was not a success. The commander, the Comte de Frontenac, managed to argue with just about everybody, and his deputy, Denonville, pursued a risky sideline in kidnapping, inviting local Iroquois to the fort and then forcibly shipping them to France as curiosities.

The British succeeded the French in the middle of the eighteenth century, and shortly afterwards there was an influx of **United Empire Loyalists** – that is, those Americans who had no truck with their compatriots' struggle for independence against Britain. These Loyalists promptly developed Kingston into a major shipbuilding centre and naval base. In 1841, the city became the capital of Upper Canada, and although it lost this distinction just three years later, it remained the region's most important town until the 1880s. In recent years, Kingston has had its economic ups and downs, though it benefit continually from the presence of **Queen's University**, one of Canada's most prestigious academic institutions, and of the **Royal Military College**, the country's answer to Sandhurst and West Point.

Attractions in Kingston include a cluster of especially fine nineteenth-century limestone buildings – most notably **City Hall** and the **Cathedral of St George** – as well as the first-rate **Agnes Etherington Art Centre** gallery and **Bellevue House**, once the home of Prime Minister Sir John A. Macdonald. Additionally, with several wonderful **B&Bs**, a handful of good **restaurants** and scenic **boat trips** round the **Thousand Islands** just offshore, Kingston is well worth a visit of at least a day or two.

Arrival, information and transport

Trains from Toronto (4–6 daily; 2hrs 20mins) terminate at the **VIA Rail station** on Hwy-2, an inconvenient 7km northwest of the city at the junction of Princess and Counter streets; Kingston Transit bus #4 (Mon–Sat only; every 30mins) connects with downtown Kingston. The terminus for long-distance **Coach Canada buses** is on the corner of Division and Counter streets, about 6km to the north of the city centre; Kingston Transit bus #2 (Mon–Sat only; hourly) runs downtown from here. Kingston Transit's **local bus** information line is ☎613/546-0000.

A helpful **tourist office** is in the city's centre, across from the waterfront at 209 Ontario St (☎613/548-4415 or 1-888/855-4555, ⊛www.visitkingston .ca). They have a wide range of local and regional information and operate a free room-reservation service. Kingston in fact has an excellent range of accommodation, from hotels through to hostels, but it is mainly noted for its **B&Bs**, the pick of which occupy grand Victorian mansions; advance reservations are advised in high season.

Accommodation

Alexander Henry Bed and Breakfast 55 Ontario St ☎613/542-2261, ⊛www.marmus .ca/marmus/alexhenry.html. Kingston's most unusual lodgings are provided in this former coastguard icebreaker, moored downtown next to the town's workaday Marine Museum. Berths vary from a bunk in a tiny cabin ($35 per person) to more comfortable quarters ($80–95 for a two-person cabin). The ship itself dates from the 1960s and is a sturdy affair with narrow stairways and corridors and the salty taste of the sea. Open mid-May to Sept.

Freshwater diving

In the 1950s, the creation of the St Lawrence Seaway regulated the depth of Lake Ontario and flooded its various rapids. Before then, the waters off Kingston had been extremely treacherous, and the bottom of the lake is still dotted with **shipwrecks**. The tourist office (see above) publishes an excellent booklet explaining what is where and several companies rent out **diving** gear and organize diving trips. One of them is Kingsdive Limited, 121 Princess St (☎613/542-2892).

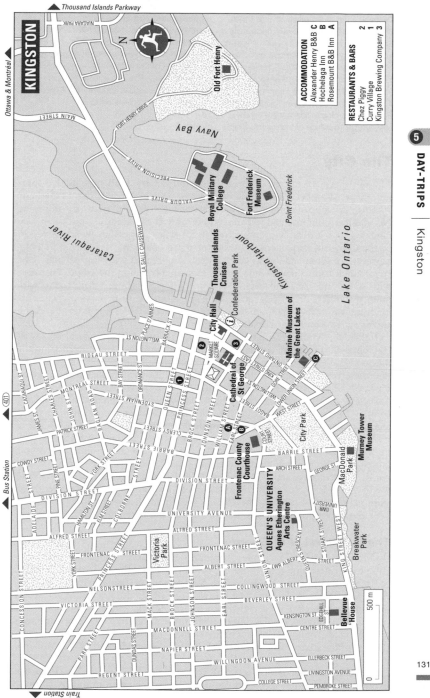

KINGSTON

Thousand Islands Parkway

Ottawa & Montréal

Main Street

NIAGARA PARK

N

Old Fort Henry

FORT HENRY DRIVE

Navy Bay

PRECISION DRIVE

VALOUR DRIVE

Royal Military College

Fort Frederick Museum

Point Frederick

Cataraqui River

LA SALLE CAUSEWAY

Thousand Islands Cruises

City Hall

Confederation Park

i

Kingston Harbour

Lake Ontario

Marine Museum of the Great Lakes

WELLINGTON ST

BARRACK ST

PLACE D'ARMES

RIDEAU STREET

BAY STREET

ORDNANCE ST

QUEEN STREET

MARKET SQUARE

Cathedral of St George

2

3

KING STREET EAST

ONTARIO STREET

CATARAQUI STREET

CHARLES STREET

JAMES ST

MONTREAL STREET

JOHN ST

BAGLAN ROAD

PATRICK STREET

SYDENHAM STREET

BROCK STREET

PRINCESS STREET

1

WILLIAM STREET

JOHNSON STREET

EARL STREET

CLERGY STREET

WELLINGTON ST

GORE ST

LOWER UNION ST

WEST STREET

c

COWDY STREET

PINE STREET

YORK STREET

BARRIE STREET

ELM STREET

COLBORNE STREET

DIVISION STREET

BAGOT STREET

COURT STREET

A

Frontenac County Courthouse

B

City Park

Bus Station

401

ADELAIDE STREET

HAMPTON ST

DIVISION STREET

UNIVERSITY AVENUE

ARCH STREET

BARRIE STREET

GEORGE ST

MacDonald Park

Murney Tower Museum

ALFRED STREET

ALFRED STREET

FRONTENAC STREET

Queen's University

Agnes Etherington Arts Centre

LWR UNIVERSITY

Victoria Park

FRONTENAC STREET

PRINCESS STREET

ALBERT STREET

LWR ALBERT STREET

QUEEN'S CRESCENT

STUART STREET

UNIVERSITY

Breakwater Park

KING STREET WEST

NELSON STREET

COLLINGWOOD STREET

VICTORIA STREET

CONCESSION STREET

MACK STREET

BROCK STREET

JOHNSON STREET

EARL STREET

BEVERLEY STREET

KENSINGTON ST

EDGEHILL ST

Bellevue House

PARK STREET

DUNDAS STREET

MACDONNELL STREET

CENTRE STREET

NAPIER STREET

WILLINGDON AVENUE

ELLERBECK STREET

LIVINGSTON AVENUE

REGENT STREET

COLLEGE STREET

PEMBROKE STREET

Train Station

500 m

0

ACCOMMODATION
Alexander Henry B&B   C
Hochelaga Inn   B
Rosemount B&B Inn   A

RESTAURANTS & BARS
Chez Piggy   2
Curry Village   1
Kingston Brewing Company   3

131

Hochelaga Inn 24 Sydenham St ☎613/549-5534 or 1-877/933-9433, Ⓦwww.hochelagainn .com. This twenty-three-room inn occupies a good-looking Victorian mansion with a playful central tower, bay windows and a wraparound veranda. All of the guest rooms are en suite, and, despite the rather pedestrian furnishings and fittings, each is very comfortable. Located in a residential area within easy walking distance of the centre. $139.

Rosemount B&B Inn 46 Sydenham St ☎613/531-8844 or 1-888/871-8444, Ⓦwww .rosemountinn.com. An eminently appealing B&B in a strikingly handsome, distinctively Italianate old limestone villa – arguably Kingston's finest. The Rosemount has nine guest rooms, all en suite, decorated in period style. The breakfasts are delicious. $140.

The City

The obvious place to start a visit to Kingston is **City Hall** (free guided tours June–Sept Mon–Fri 10am–4pm, plus Sat & Sun in July & Aug 11am–3pm; 30mins), a copper-domed, stone extravagance which, with its imposing Neoclassical columns and portico, dominates the waterfront just as it was intended to – a suitably grand structure for what was originally scheduled to be the Canadian Parliament. By the time the building was completed in 1844, however, Kingston had lost its capital status and – faced with colossal bills – the city council had to make some quick adjustments, filling the empty corridors with shops and stalls and even a saloon. Things are more sedate today, with municipal offices occupying most of the space, but the **tour** provides a fascinating insight into the development of the city and includes a trip up the **clock tower** via a magnificent circular stairway.

Outside, the **Market Square**, at the back of City Hall, is home to an excellent open-air **farmers' market** on Tuesdays, Thursdays and Saturdays, while on Sundays the square is given over to craft and antiques stalls. Opposite, the site of the original French outpost is marked by the waterfront **Confederation Park**, whose manicured lawns run behind the harbour with its marina and squat, nineteenth-century defensive tower (no access), which is similar to the nearby Murney Tower (see p.134). From the dock at the foot of Brock Street, there are regular **cruises of the Thousand Islands** that confetti the St Lawrence River as it leaves Lake Ontario, ranging from tiny hunks of rock to much larger islands with thick forest and lavish second homes. It's a pretty cruise at any time of the year, but especially so in autumn when the leaves turn. Several companies offer cruises, but the benchmark is set by **Kingston 1000 Islands Cruises** (☎613/549-5544, Ⓦwww.1000islandscruises.on.ca), whose bread-and-butter cruise is a three-hour jaunt in a replica steamboat, the *Island Queen* (mid-May to mid-Oct 1–2 daily; $25), though it's pot luck when it comes to the "live entertainment".

The Cathedral of St George

Back on dry land, it's a couple of minutes' walk from Confederation Park to Kingston's finest limestone building, the Anglican **Cathedral of St George**, at King St and Johnson (mid-April to Sept Mon–Sat 10am–4pm; Oct to mid-April Mon–Fri 1–4pm; free). Dating from the 1820s, the graceful Neoclassical lines of the cathedral are deceptively uniform, for the church was remodelled on several occasions, notably after severe fire damage in 1899. The capacious interior holds some delightful Tiffany stained-glass windows and, attached to the wall of the nave, a plain **memorial** to Molly Brant (1736–1797), a Mohawk leader and sister of Joseph Brant (see p.67).

From the cathedral, it's a brief stroll to the main commercial drag, **Princess Street**, whose assorted shops, offices and cafés stretch up from the lakeshore.

△ Cathedral of St George

Murney Tower Museum

From the corner of Princess and King streets, it's a good ten-minute stroll west to the **Murney Tower Museum**, on Barrie St (mid-May to Aug daily 10am–5pm; $3). The most impressive of four such towers built to defend the Kingston dockyards from an anticipated US attack during the Oregon Crisis of 1846–1847, this one holds incidental military memorabilia including old weapons, uniforms and re-created nineteenth-century living quarters. The design of the tower, built as a combined barracks, battery and storehouse, was copied from a Corsican tower (at Martello Point) which had proved particularly troublesome to the British navy. A self-contained, semi-self-sufficient defensive structure with thick walls and a protected entrance, the Martello design proved so successful that towers like this were built throughout the British Empire, only becoming obsolete in the 1870s with advances in artillery technology. Incidentally, on Christmas Day 1885, members of the Royal Canadian Rifles regiment left the tower equipped with their **field hockey sticks** and a lacrosse ball, skidding round the frozen lake and thereby inventing the sport that has become a national passion.

West of the Centre: the Agnes Etherington Art Centre

Striking inland up Barrie Street, with City Park on the right, it's a ten-minute walk to the top of the park and another grand limestone pile, the **Frontenac County Courthouse**, whose whopping Neoclassical portico of 1858 is fronted by a fanciful water fountain and surmounted by a copper dome. Head west from here, along Union Street, and you'll soon be in the midst of the **Queen's University** campus, whose various sturdy stone college buildings fan out in all directions. The place to aim for is the first-rate **Agnes Etherington Art Centre**, on the corner of University Ave and Queen's Crescent (Tues–Fri 10am–4.30pm, Sat & Sun 1–5pm; $4, but free on Thurs). The gallery has an excellent reputation for its temporary exhibitions, so paintings are regularly rotated, but the first room (Room 1) usually kicks off in dramatic style with a vivid selection of Canadian Abstract paintings (1940–1960), with French-speaking artists on one side and English-speaking artists on the other. Beyond, there is a strong showing for the **Group of Seven**, including a striking *Evening Solitude* by **Lawren Harris** and the carpet-like, rolling fields of **Lismer**'s *Quebec Village*, while **Tom Thomson** weighs in with his studied *Autumn, Algonquin Park*. Other exhibits to look out for are the **Inuit** prints of Kenojuak and Pitseolak – two of the best-known Inuit artists of modern times – as well as heritage **quilts** from eastern Ontario, which date back to 1820, and an excellent collection of West African sculpture.

Bellevue House

Born in Glasgow, **Sir John A. Macdonald** (1815–1891) emigrated to Canada in his youth and settled in Kingston, where he became a successful corporate lawyer, an MP – representing the town for well-nigh forty years – and ultimately prime minister (1867–1873 and 1887–1891). A shrewd and forceful man, Macdonald played a leading role in Canada's Confederation, with a little arm-twisting here and a little charming there, to ensure the grand plan went through.

In the 1840s, Macdonald rented **Bellevue House** (daily: April–May & Sept 10am–5pm; June–Aug 9am–6pm; $4), a bizarrely asymmetrical, pagoda-shaped building located about 2km to the west of the city centre, beyond the university campus, at 35 Centre Street. The idea was that the country air would

Algonquin Provincial Park

A giant slab of untamed wilderness, **Algonquin Provincial Park** (🌐www .algonquinpark.on.ca) boasts dense hardwood and pine forests, canyons, rapids, scores of lakes and, amongst a rich wildlife, loons, beavers, moose, timber wolves and black bears. The nearest entrance is a slowish 260km north of Toronto, too far for a day-trip, but worth considering for a longer excursion. To get there, make your way to Huntsville on Hwy-11 and then continue 45km along Hwy-60 to the park's west gate, where there is a visitor centre (☎705/633-5572). Canoeing and hiking are the big deals here, and several Toronto companies offer all-inclusive wilderness packages, including meals, permits, guides, equipment and transport to and from Toronto. The pick of the bunch is **Call of the Wild**, 23 Edward St, Markham, Ontario (☎905/471-9453 or 1-800/776-9453, 🌐www.callofthewild.ca), which runs a varied programme that includes three-day ($350) and five-day ($580) canoeing trips deep into the park.

improve the health of Macdonald's wife, Isabella, whose tuberculosis was made worse by the treatment – laudanum. Isabella never returned to good health and died after years as an invalid, leaving Macdonald alone (with the bottle). Both the house and gardens have been restored to the period of the late 1840s, when the Macdonalds lived here.

Eating and drinking

Chez Piggy 68 Princess St at King St E ☎613/549-7673. Kingston's best-known restaurant is housed in restored stables dating from 1810. The patio is packed in summer and the attractive interior has handcrafted pine and limestone walls. The wide-ranging menu features all manner of main courses, from Thai and Vietnamese through to South American and standard North American dishes. Main courses average around $19.

Curry Village 169A Princess St ☎613/542-5010. Popular, reasonably priced Asian Indian restaurant above a shoe shop and just north of Bagot St. Serves all the Bangladeshi favourites, with main courses beginning at $9. Reservations recommended.

Kingston Brewing Company 34 Clarence St. The best pub in town, serving natural ales and lagers brewed on the premises, as well as tasty bar food. Outside patio area, too.

Listings

Listings

6

Accommodation

A s Toronto's popularity as a travel destination increases, so too does the variety of **accommodation**. During peak season (late June to Aug), and especially around popular summer events like Gay Pride, Caribana and the Toronto International Film Festival it is essential to book well in advance. Rack rates will differ from the rates available through online bookings, special offers and various package deals, but in general, a clean, centrally located hotel room starts around $150.

A recent spate of **boutique hotel** openings has added some spice to the scene, as well as played a part in neighbourhood rejuvenation. Particular mentions go to the **Drake Hotel** and its same-block neighbour, **The Gladstone**. When the *Drake* reopened its doors on Valentine's Day 2004, following a multi-million-dollar renovation, it simultaneously shed its sketchy, flophouse past and became part of the hip regeneration of the Parkdale neighbourhood. Both properties are independently owned by socially aware adventurers in inn keeping (Jeff Stober and sisters Margaret and Christina Zeidler, respectively).

Although many **bed-and-breakfasts** are not as central as the city's hotels, they tend to be slightly cheaper and take you off the beaten path into some of Toronto's quaint, leafy neighbourhoods. Budget-conscious travellers might want to consider Toronto's **hostels**, but the best deal in town is the **summer residences** at local universities. They only offer the essentials, but the rooms are cheery, campus ambience is always pleasant and prices are rock bottom.

Hotels

Downtown is the epicentre of Toronto's **hotel** scene. With the exception of some new boutique hotels, properties outside the downtown core are mostly chains catering to business travellers. Any downtown hotel will be sufficiently close to all the main attractions and easily accessible by public transport. Some, like the *Delta Chelsea* in particular, (see overleaf) offer special features and packages geared toward families. Rates quoted here reflect the cost of a standard double room in high season, in Canadian dollars, before tax. Prices can vary depending on season, and differing weekend and weekday rates may apply, so always confirm them before making reservations.

Downtown

Bond Place 65 Dundas St W, at Victoria St
☎416/362-6061 or 1-800/268-9390, ⍵www
.bondplacehoteltoronto.com. Subway: Dundas.

A favourite of the tourist-bus crowd, this place is just steps away from the Eaton Centre and Dundas Square. $140.
Cambridge Suites Hotel 15 Richmond St
E ☎416/368-1990 or 1-800/463-1990,

www.cambridgesuiteshotel.com. **Subway: Queen.** High-end comfort, style and discretion in the heart of Downtown, close to theatres, shops and restaurants. Caters mainly to a business clientele (and the odd sports and movie star). $180.

The Cosmopolitan Hotel 8 Colborne St, at Yonge St ☎416/350-2000, www.cosmotoronto.com. **Subway: King.** Toronto's first declared feng shui hotel offers amenities such as shampoo and body gel that represent the eight chakras, as well as en suite natural gemstone fountains. Other room features include full kitchens, balconies, air purifiers and 32-inch plasma screeen TVs with a special meditation channel. Guests receive a complimentary continental breakfast, plus a gemstone instead of a mint on their pillows at night. $199.

Delta Chelsea Inn 33 Gerrard St W, at Yonge St ☎416/595-1975 or 1-877/814-7706, www.deltachelsea.com. **Subway: Dundas.** With 1590 **guest rooms, this is** reputedly Canada's largest hotel. It's replete with bars, restaurants and a health club with a pool, plus kid-friendly offerings like day care, a water slide, a family pool and play centres. The rooms are as varied as the guests, ranging from bachelor-pad modern to apartment-like suites for families. Very central location. $189.

Drake Hotel 1150 Queen St W, at Beaconsfield Ave ☎416/531-5042 or 1-866/372-5386, www.thedrakehotel.ca. **Streetcar: Queen (#501).** An eclectic, Bohemian-inspired hotel with a lounge, dining room, sky bar, café and hip performance space, as well as installation art, yoga classes and a house poet. The "Crash Pads" feature vintage furniture, handmade dolls on the beds, flat-screen TVs and high-speed Internet access. $129.

Fairmont Royal York 100 Front St W ☎416/368-2511 or 1-800/257-7544, www.fairmont.com/royalyork/. **Subway: Union Station.** The *Fairmont Royal York* offers luxury service fit for the Queen of England – in fact, a special suite is kept for her when she comes to town. The lobby is a sight in itself, with mosaic floors, coffered ceilings and massive chandeliers. Dependable quality, unflappable staff and a central location have kept this a favourite for generations. $289.

Gladstone Hotel 1214 Queen St W, at Gladstone Ave ☎416/531-4635, www.gladstonehotel.com. **Streetcar: Queen (#501).** When it

▽ Gladstone Hotel

opened in 1889, the *Gladstone* was the kind of place where one's maiden aunt could respectably stay. Today, owners Margaret and Christina Zeidler are guided by urban philosopher Jane Jacobs's principle of "new ideas in old buildings", though two important *Gladstone* traditions remain vibrantly intact: the Wednesday life-drawing class and the purely mad Thursday to Saturday karaoke nights in the *Melody* bar. Ongoing rennovations of guest rooms by local artists and the transformation of the ballroom into an art gallery give you an idea of the vibe. $140.

Hilton Toronto 145 Richmond St W, at University Ave ☎416/ 869-3456, www.hilton.com. **Subway: Osgoode; Streetcar: Queen (#501).** Don't let the office-tower exterior fool you: this full-service Downtown property has all the sleekness one would expect of a hotel on the edge of the Queen Street West neighbourhood. The on-site restaurant, *Tundra*, is excellent. $264.

Holiday Inn Express Downtown 111 Lombard St ☎416/367-5555, www.ichotelsgroup.com. **Streetcar: King St (#504).** Located on a quiet street in an older part of town near the St Lawrence Market district, and just a ten-minute walk from Downtown. Offers standard amenities and a free continental breakfast. A favourite among travellers looking for good value. $135.

Holiday Inn on King 370 King St W, at John St ⓣ416/599-4000 or 1-800/263-6364, ⓦwww .hiok.com. Streetcar: King St (#504). Especially popular with families and overseas travellers, this 425-room hotel is close to the Rogers Centre (formerly the SkyDome), Roy Thompson Hall, theatres, fine restaurants and fun nightclubs. $185.

Hotel Le Germain 30 Mercer St, at John St ⓣ416/ 345-9500 or 1-866/7345-9501, ⓦwww .germaintoronto.com. Streetcar: King St (#504). The sleek, spacious and open-air design of this boutique hotel makes for a sophisticated yet cozy experience. A critically esteemed restaurant, *Luce* (see p.160), and an attractive, mostly bilingual staff complement the chichi surroundings. $280.

Hotel Victoria 56 Yonge St ⓣ416/363-1666 or 1-800/363-8228, ⓦwww.hotelvictoria-toronto .com. Subway: King. This adorable, affordable boutique hotel, located in the heart of Downtown, is a real find. Complimentary continental breakfast is served daily, and service is excellent. $135.

InterContinental Toronto Centre 225 Front St W ⓣ416/597-1400 or 800/422-7969, ⓦwww .torontocentre.intercontinental.com. Subway: Union Station. Adjacent to the Metro Toronto Convention Centre and CN Tower, and only a few blocks from the Rogers Centre and Financial District, this relatively glitzy hotel is an obvious choice for business travellers as well as families. Air-conditioned rooms are well equipped with the usual amenities, and there is a fairly good spa on-site. $275.

Le Royal Meridian King Edward 37 King St E ⓣ416/863-3131 or 1-800/543-4300, ⓦwww .lemeridien-kingedward.com. Subway: King. This dowager of a hotel, designed by E.J. Lennox in 1903, has had its opulent Beaux Arts exterior and *Victoria Café* buffed and restored, and its rooms updated and refreshed. Famous guests have included everyone from Mark Twain to John Lennon. $400.

Marriott Toronto Eaton Centre 525 Bay St ⓣ416/597-9200 or 1-800/228-9290, ⓦwww .marriott.com. Subway: Dundas. If staying right next door to one of the largest malls in North America is your idea of heaven, look no further. This hotel's best feature is its excellent staff, who are uniformly helpful. $280.

Metropolitan 108 Chestnut St ⓣ416/599-0555 or 1-800/668-6600, ⓦwww.metropolitan.com. Subway: St Patrick. Located directly behind the new City Hall, this small, handsomely appointed hotel is ideally situated for a visit to the nearby Art Gallery of Ontario. $280.

Novotel Toronto Centre 45 The Esplanade, off Front St ⓣ416/367-8900 or 1-800/668-6835, ⓦwww.novotel.com. Subway: Union Station. Part of a Swiss chain, this hotel on the Esplanade offers good, efficient service, a handsome building and comfortably kitted-out rooms. Close to the St Lawrence Market neighbourhood, the Harbourfront and the ever-humming Distillery District. $250.

Pantages Suites Hotel & Spa 200 Victoria St, at Dundas St ⓣ416/ 362-1777 or 1-866/852-1777, ⓦwww.pantageshotel.com. Subway: Dundas. Named for the Pantages theatre (now the Cannon), this hotel-spa combo with an eager-to-please staff offers a complimentary meditation channel to go with the 400-thread-count Egyptian cotton sheets, complimentary breakfasts and modern kitchens. The spa menu includes mostly standard mani-pedi-waxing services, wth a few water massage treatments available. Despite its emphasis on serenity, the Pantages is right next to a major Downtown hospital and the attendant sirens. $400.

Renaissance Toronto Hotel Downtown 1 Blue Jays Way, at Spadina Ave ⓣ416/341-7100 or 1-800/237-1512,ⓦmarriott.com. Subway: Union Station; Streetcar: King (#504). Victim of a seemingly unending series of name changes, this hotel's claim to fame is its location – overlooking the Rogers Centre field. The CN Tower is right next door and the Harbourfront and the theatre district are close by, but baseball fans revel in the delights of dining on-site whilst watching the game below. Rooms facing the ballpark $200; rooms facing the city $300.

Sheraton Centre Toronto 123 Queen St W, at University Ave ⓣ416/361-1000 or 1-800/325-3535, ⓦwww.sheratontoronto.com. Subway: Queen. Beyond the snazzy lobby, which features a waterfall and islands of soft leather couches, the indoor/outdoor pool, interior gardens and terraces, the guest rooms feature incredibly comfortable, ultra body-conforming mattresses that are hard to tear yourself away from. The hotel is connected to the Underground City, and is a short walk from the clubs, restaurants and shops on the Queen West strip. $260.

SoHo Metropolitan 318 Wellington St W
☎416/977-5000 or 1-800/668-6600, ⓦwww
.metropolitan.com/soho. Streetcar: King St
(#504). This chic, high-end boutique hotel
boasts the exceptional *Sen5es* restaurant
(see p.160), a Dale Chiuly-designed glass
entrance, and one of Toronto's very best
concierges. Conveniently located close to
the hive of restaurants, bars, clubs and
theatres between Queen West and King
West. $295.

The Strathcona Hotel 60 York St, at Front St
☎416/363-3321 or 1-800/268-8304, ⓦwww
.strathconahotel.com. Subway: Union Station.
With affordable rates and a great location
– about half a block from Union Station,
across the street from the *Fairmont Royal
York* and five minutes from the Rogers
Centre and CN Tower – this attractive hotel
with all the standard amenities is a great
find. $140.

Travelodge Toronto Downtown West 621 King St
W, at Bathurst St ☎416/504-7441 or 1-800/578-
7878, ⓦwww.travelodgetorontodowntown.com.
Streetcar: King St (#504). No surprises here
at this standard chain hotel. The neighbourhood is filled with good bars, restaurants
and clubs, and theatres and attractions
are also nearby. Check the website for
its "Guaranteed Best Available Rate"
programme. $190.

Uptown

Best Western Primrose 111 Carlton St
☎416/977-8000 or 1-800/268-8082, ⓦwww
.torontoprimrosehotel.com. Subway: College.
You'll find all the basic amenities you'd
expect from this large chain hotel, as well
as a pool, gym, restaurant and bar. Lots
of young people are around too, since the
hotel doubles as a university residence. A
ten-minute walk from Downtown. $175.

Comfort Hotel Downtown Toronto 15 Charles St
E, at Yonge St ☎416/924-1222 or 1-800/221-
2222, ⓦwww.choicehotels.ca. Subway: Wellesley. Centrally located on a leafy side street,
close to the bustling intersection of Yonge
Street and Bloor West. Check the website
for excellent deals. $149.

Courtyard by Marriott Downtown Toronto 475
Yonge St, at Alexander St ☎416/924-0611 or
1-800/847-5075, ⓦwww.marriott.com. Subway:
Carlton. Close to the Gay Village as well
as the restaurants, shops, cinemas and
all-night action of the Yonge Street strip.

Twelve rooms are wheelchair-accessible and
have special features for hearing-impaired
guests. $190.

Days Inn Toronto Downtown 30 Carlton St
☎416/977-6655 or 1-800/DAYS-INN, ⓦwww
.daysinn.com. Subway: College. Located just
up the block from Maple Leaf Gardens and
near the Gay Village and Yonge St strip,
this chain offers a convenient location, with
all-night eateries and a multiplex cinema just
steps away. All the basic amenities, plus a
pool. $110.

Four Seasons 21 Avenue Rd ☎416/964-0411
or 1-800/332-3442, ⓦwww.fourseasons.com.
Subway: Bay (Cumberland exit). In the heart
of the costly Yorkville neighbourhood, this
luxury hotel has a reputation for hosting
some of the city's most illustrious guests.
The restaurants and wine cellar are as stellar
as the impeccable service. $340.

Howard Johnson Yorkville 89 Avenue Rd
☎416/964-1220, ⓦwww.hojo.com. Subway:
Bay. At this small, budget-friendly hotel
tucked away in a busy section of Avenue
Road, the staff is helpful and attentive, and
the large rooms are tidy, comfortable and
equipped for the business traveller. $120.

Madison Manor Boutique Hotel 20 Madison Ave
☎416/922-5579 or 877-561-7048, ⓦwww
.madisonavenuepub.com. Subway: St George.
Located in the heart of the Annex neighbourhood amid the mansions-turned-frat
houses, this cozy inn has 23 comfortable,
affordable, nonsmoking rooms, some with
fireplaces and all with en-suite bathrooms.
A sister property next door is cherished by
locals for its five beer patios. $99.

Park Hyatt 4 Avenue Rd ☎416/924-5471 or
1-800/977-4197, ⓦwww.hyatt.com. Subway:
Museum or Bay. At the edge of the posh
Yorkville neighbourhood, this luxury hotel also
boasts an on-site spa, a rooftop cocktail bar
with spectacular views of the city, two dining
rooms and a Morton's steakhouse (see
p.168). The well-appointed rooms offer high-
end comfort at a premium price. $249.

Ramada Hotel & Suites 300 Jarvis St ☎416/977-
4823 or 1-800/567-2233, ⓦwww.ramadahotel
andsuites.com. Streetcar: Carlton (#506). A
comfortable, small hotel on busy Jarvis street,
with both The Gay Village and Yonge Street
just a five-minute walk away. $140.

Sutton Place 955 Bay St ☎416/924-9221
or 1-800/268-3790, ⓦwww.suttonplace
.com. Subway: Wellesley. Long associated
with the Toronto International Film Festival,

this classy hotel offers luxury service and surroundings for very reasonable prices. It's a favourite with visiting celebrities, and the service and amenities are excellent. Nicely situated for all the Downtown sights, and close to the University of Toronto campus. $169– $200.

Windsor Arms 18 St Thomas St ☎416/971-9666, ⓦ www.windsorarmshotel.com. Subway: Bay. A jewel among boutique hotels, the Windsor Arms is a faithful reconstruction of the 1911 original, which was razed in the early 1990s. What's new are the condominiums on top, the opulent spa, the designer guest rooms with their 300-thread-count sheets and abundant electronic gadgets. The charming little street on which it's located is increasingly precious, alas, but the service is top-notch and the on-site restaurant, the *Courtyard Café* is excellent. $295.

The waterfront

Radisson Plaza Hotel Admiral 249 Queens Quay W ☎416/203-3333 or 1-800/333-3333, ⓦ www .radisson.com/torontoca_admiral. Subway: York Quay. Located right on the waterfront and beside the Harbourfront Marina, this full-service chain hotel divides its attention between families and conventioneers. Not as central or as amenable as other comparably priced hotels, but still only five minutes from Downtown by taxi or ten minutes by public transport. $240.

Westin Harbour Castle 1 Harbour Square ☎416/869-1600 or 1-800/937-8461, ⓦ www .westin.com. LRT: York Quay. This massive, 977-room hotel right on Lake Ontario's edge is a terrific base for forays to the Toronto Islands – ferries dock at the plaza

out in front. The Westin Harbour makes up for its lack of intimate charm by catering to its guests' creature comforts with a gym, indoor pool, restaurants and bars. Nicely furnished rooms have splendid views of either Lake Ontario or Downtown's skyscrapers. Meetings and events are a speciality. $210.

The airport

Delta Toronto West Airport 5444 Dixie Road, at Hwy-401 ☎905/624-1144 1-800/737-3211, ⓦ www4.deltahotels.com. While offering all the things that make airport hotels bearable – a swimming pool, 24-hour room service, a business centre, and in-room movies – this property has something entirely unexpected: a closed-in, northern resort-type garden, screened from the frenetic bustle and overall cinderblock ugliness of the airport strip. $140.

Holiday Inn Select Toronto International Airport 970 Dixon Rd, at Airport Rd ☎416/675-7611, ⓦ www.ichotelsgroup.com. With over 440 rooms, this airport behemoth can handle airbus layovers and passengers waiting for the red-eye special. Standouts include the polyglot staff, indoor and outdoor pools and great family features, notably the restaurant's "Kids Eat Free" children's menu. $120.

Sheraton Gateway @ Toronto International Airport Terminal 3, Toronto International Airport ☎905/672-7000, ⓦ www.sheraton.com. While most airport hotels turn away from the runways they serve with a concrete-and-glass shrug, the *Gateway* is the only hotel directly connected to the Toronto Pearson International Airport. As if the virtue of proximity were not enough, it also offers exceptional mattresses. Free shuttle service to Terminals One and Two. $240.

Bed-and-breakfasts

Often a cheaper alternative to the city's hotels, sometimes, however, Toronto's **bed-and-breakfasts** can be just as expensive as a good Downtown hotel room. What deluxe B&Bs offer that most hotels cannot is an intimate setting and a feel for what it's actually like to live in Toronto. Many B&Bs require a tram or subway ride to reach Downtown, but the city's public transit system is efficient, and none of the places listed here is more than twenty minutes from the city centre; the odd one (or two) are even in Downtown. If there is a particular area you wish to stay in, or if you have special needs as a traveller, contact the Federation of Ontario Bed and Breakfast Accommodation (☎613/515-1293, ⓦ www .fobba.com), or the Downtown Toronto Association of Bed and Breakfasts Guest Houses, ☎416/410-3938, ⓦ www.bnbinfo.com.

Ambassador Inn B&B 280 Jarvis St, at Gerrard St, Downtown ☎416/260-2608, @www.jarvishouse .com. **Streetcar: Dundas (#505).** This property is right on the cusp of being an inn: a Romanesque mansion, replete with stained-glass windows, exposed brick and high ceilings, with twenty guest rooms, all featuring private bathrooms; some have a Jacuzzi and gas fireplace. There is no exterior sign, so double-check the address. $149.

Au Petit Paris B&B 3 Selby St, at Bloor St E, Uptown ☎416/928-1348, @www.bbtoronto .com/aupetitparis. **Subway: Sherbourne.** All four of the guest rooms in this meticulously renovated Victorian house are decorated in a modern style and have hardwood floors, queen beds and en suite facilities. Crepe breakfasts are the house speciality. $115.

The Coach House 117 Walmer Rd, Uptown ☎416/899-0306, @www.thecoachhouse.ca. **Subway: Spadina.** Very, very cute: stay in either the split-level, one-bedroom Coach House or the apartment suite on the third floor of the main house. Located in the groovy Annex neighbourhood, this cozy spot is within walking distance of shopping, museums and the University of Toronto. Minimum two-night stay. $160–$175.

Dundonald House 35 Dundonald St, Uptown ☎416/961-9888 or 1-800/260-7227, @www .dundonaldhouse.com. **Subway: Wellesley.** Popular with the gay community and close to the Gay Village as well as theatres and restaurants along Yonge Street. Fun extras include bicycles and a workout room. $135.

Fourth Street Bed & Breakfast 22 Fourth St, Ward's Island, Toronto Islands ☎416/203-0771, @www.torontoisland.org. **Ferry: Ward's Island.** A place that Torontonians yearn to stay in, this airy cottage on Ward's Island has a stylish interior and is surrounded by lush gardens. Bicycles are available for getting around, and the ferry and beach are just a two-minute walk away. Weekly and monthly rates are negotiable; open all year round. $100.

Jarvis House 344 Jarvis St, at Carlton St, Uptown ☎416/975-3838, @www.jarvishouse.com. **Streetcar: Carlton/College (#506).** A relic of the late nineteenth century, when fashionable millionaires used to live along Jarvis Street. Eleven of the twelve rooms in this renovated Victorian have private baths, and the location is close to popular attractions like Maple Leaf Gardens and Cabbagetown. $110.

Les Amis B&B 31 Granby St, off Yonge St, Downtown ☎416/591-0635, @www.bbtoronto .com. **Subway: College.** This Downtown B&B just a short stroll from the Eaton Centre holds a handful of pleasantly furnished rooms with shared facilities. Vegetarian breakfasts are a speciality, with the crepes being a special treat. $99.

Lowtherhouse 72 Lowther Ave, Uptown ☎416/323-1589 or 1-800/265-4158, @www.lowtherhouse.ca. **Subway: St George.** This Annex guest house offers six rooms with private baths, air-conditioning, cable TV and other conveniences within steps of Yorkville, the Royal Ontario Museum, the Bata Shoe Museum and the University of Toronto's main campus. $95.

▽ The Mulberry Tree

The Mulberry Tree 122 Isabella St, at Jarvis St, Uptown ☎416/960-5249, @www.bbtoronto.com/mulberrytree/. **Subway: Wellesley.** For some people, Toronto wouldn't be Toronto without a stay at the *Mulberry Tree*. This delightful B&B, one of the city's most agreeable, occupies a tastefully decorated heritage home close to the city centre. Each of the guest rooms is comfortable and relaxing – indeed the whole atmosphere of the place is just right, combining efficiency and friendliness. Breakfasts are first-rate too. Highly recommended. $105.

Palmerston Inn 322 Palmerston Blvd, Uptown ⓣ416/920-7842, ⓦwww.lanierbb.com. Streetcar: College (#506). This 1906 mansion with a distinctive, pillared porch and stained glass throughout, is situated on the edge of the trendy College Street strip. It offers six, very feminine rooms with names like Lady Anne, Lady Philipa and Lady Vivien. Four have private baths; extras include bathrobes, afternoon sherry and daily maid service. $130.

Terrace House 52 Austin Terrace, Uptown, ⓣ416/535-1493, ⓦwww.terracehouse.com. Subway: Dupont. Perched high on a hill overlooking the city, this pre-World War I mock-Tudor house is in the same neighbourhood as noteworthy piles like Casa Loma and Spadina House. The three attractive guest rooms are decked out with antiques and North African rugs. It's only a five-minute walk from the Dupont subway station, but it's all uphill – so consider taking a cab if your bags are heavy. Rates start at $150.

University residences and hostels

Two large **universities** are set in the city centre: the University of Toronto and Ryerson University. From the second week in May to the end of August there is an abundance of student residences available on a daily, weekly or monthly basis to budget-wise travellers of all ages; quite often this is the best deal for clean, affordable and relatively private accommodation. Most residences require a night's or week's deposit, depending on the length of your stay. Students with valid IDs can often get a discount of around ten percent; enquire at reception.

Toronto's range of **hostels** has improved in recent years, with several of the more recently opened ones being agreeable options. Most have private or family rooms as well as dormitories, which offer the cheapest rates of all. Discounts are often available with Hostelling International (HI) or student ID cards, so be sure to enquire when making reservations.

89 Chestnut 89 Chestnut St, at Dundas St, Downtown ⓣ416/977-0707, ⓦwww.89chestnut.com. Streetcar: Dundas (#505); Subway: St Patrick. A full-service hotel until fairly recently, this student residence still accepts paying guests from mid-May to late August. $84.

Canadiana Backpackers Hostel 42 Widmer St, at Richmond St, Downtown ⓣ416/598-9090 or 1-877/215-1225, ⓦwww.canadianalodging.com. Streetcar: Queen (#501). For the price of an appetizer at some of the chichi bars nearby, you can crash at this hip, clean hostel. Located steps away from Queen Street West and within easy walking distance of all Downtown. Dorm bed $26; private double $70.

Global Village Backpackers 460 King St W, at Spadina Ave, Downtown ⓣ416/703-8540 or 1-888/844-7875, ⓦwww.globalbackpackers.com. Streetcar: King (#504). This former hotel has four private/family rooms; everything else is dormitory-style with shared bathrooms. The above-standard amenities include laundry facilities, a kitchen and a games room, plus the staff is top notch. Close to the Richmond Street/Queen Street West action as well as the King Street West strip. Dorm bed $26; $59 for a private double.

Neill-Wycik College Hotel 96 Gerrard St E, at Church St, Downtown ⓣ416/977-2320 or 1-800/268-4358, ⓦwww.neill-wycik.com. Subway: Dundas; Streetcar: Dundas (#505). A Ryerson University student residence from fall to spring, this property becomes a hotel in the summer. Fifteen of the building's twenty-two floors contain four hotel apartment units, and each unit has four bedrooms, two bathrooms and a kitchen area. A great option if you are travelling with familiy or friends. The campus itself is scenic and calm, but the youth-magnet intersection of Yonge and Dundas is only a short walk away. Private room $61.

University of Toronto, Massey College 4 Devonshire Place, at Queens Park Circle, Uptown ⓣ416/978-2549, ⓦwww.utoronto.ca/massey/summer.html. Subway: Museum. Apart from being the one-time stomping grounds of author Robertson Davies, beautiful Massey College, designed by architect Ron Thom, reportedly boasts the presence of at least one ghost.

Singles with shared bathrooms and a handful of suites with private bathrooms are available from May to mid-August. Linens, towels, housekeeping services and breakfast (May to July) are provided. $90.

University of Toronto, St Michael's College 81 St Mary's St, at Bay St, Uptown ℡416/926-7296, Ⓦwww.utoronto.ca/stmikes. **Subway: Museum.** Singles and doubles that include housekeeping service are available on a weekly basis. This is a popular option, so call ahead to see about availability. Season ends on August 16th. $154.

University of Toronto, Victoria College 140 Charles St W, at Bay St, Uptown ℡416/585-4524, Ⓦwww.vicu.utoronto.ca/. **Subway: Museum.** Rooms are available in Annesley Hall, Burwash Hall, Law House and Margaret Addison Hall, and up to 800 guests can be accommodated. Single and shared rooms are set up as study bedrooms, where desks and beds have equal prominence. $67.

Cafés and light meals

oronto's thriving **cafés** are the seam in the city's social fabric. Locals head to them for a morning latte, a quick meal, an evening drink or just to meet up with friends. The scene gets especially busy during the summertime, when many cafés roll out onto terraces and sidewalks, providing excellent vantage points for people watching or just hanging about.

One of the latest trends in Toronto's varied food scene is the appearance of **grazing menus** (alias dim sum, tapas, meza) that offer a wide variety of appetizer-sized dishes best enjoyed with at least one other person. Two of the city's most illustrious chefs, **Susur Lee** and **Jamie Kennedy**, have recently opened places specializing in this form of dining.

We've grouped spots into two broad categories: places that are best for beverages and socializing – though you'll find even these places typically serve some sort of food – and places that can be considered for **light meals** (and, at times, even full meals).

Cafés

As in many other cities, a certain ubiquitous Seattle coffee chain is making its presence felt in Toronto's **coffee bar scene**, which is also home to chains like Timothy's and The Second Cup. While these franchises are giving independent establishments a run for their money, they obviously don't offer the charm or authenticity that places like *Moon Bean Coffee* and *Vienna Home Bakery* do. As for **tea**, you'll find everything from high tea, offered in four-star hotels, to bubble tea, a Taiwanese mixture of sweet, iced, technicolour teas with globules of tapioca sitting at the bottom.

Downtown

B Espresso 111 Queen St E, at Mutual St ☎416/866-2111. Streetcar: Queen (#501). A full-on espresso bar that doesn't fool around when it comes to serving up its potent, fragrant caffeine elixir.
Balzac's 55 Mill St ☎416/207-1709. Streetcar: King (#504); Bus: Parliament St (#65A from Castle Frank Station). In the midst of the nineteenth-century Distillery District, *Balzac's* has an Old Montréal look and feel, plus it

churns out nicely presented espresso-type coffees and some sweets to go with them.
Café Bernate 1024 Queen St W ☎416/535-2835. Streetcar: Queen (#501). Once an outpost of café society, this ever-charming neighbourhood spot is now surrounded by galleries, shops and some café competition. The menu offers a wide variety of plump sandwiches for all tastes, and the regular coffee comes with free refills.
Canary Grill 409 Front St E, at Parliament St ☎416/364-9943. Streetcar: King (#504). This

very basic but authentic grill has been in situ since the Great Depression, when workers from the nearby railyards would warm up with a cup of joe. Before the Distillery District got on its feet, it was also a favoured spot among movie stars filming in the nearby area.

Moon Bean Coffee 30 St Andrew's St, at Spadina Ave ☎ 416/ 595-0327. Streetcar: Spadina (#510). A Kensington Market tradition, and one of the few remaining cafés that cares enough to roast its own beans. The patio is a great spot for people watching.

Petite Dejeuner 191 King St E, at Jarvis St ☎ 416/703-1560. Streetcar: King (#504). Deep in the heart of the George Brown College campus, this high-class, low-price little breakfast joint offers up *bonne femme* comfort food and patisserie mainstays like freshly baked croissants.

Sugar Café 942 Queen St W ☎ 416/532-5088. Streetcar: Queen (#501). Out amid all the city's alternative galleries, this little café on the West Queen West strip sits pretty in a bright, Victorian-era storefront. Has all the usual offerings, like espresso coffees, sweets and light fare.

▽ Vienna Home Bakery

🏃 **Vienna Home Bakery** 626 Queen St W ☎ 416/703-7278. Streetcar: Queen (#501). Part of the original, pre-cool Queen West landscape, the *Vienna Bakery* has been providing starving-artists and gallery goers with caffeine, ample sandwiches and sugar rushes for decades.

Tequila Bookworm 490 Queen St W ☎ 416/504-7335. Streetcar: Queen (#501). The exposed brick walls in the front of the café are lined with magazines for sale, while the back section is filled with floor-to-ceiling book-shelves stuffed with old text books, celebrity biographies, romance novels and the odd Penguin classic. Garage-sale armchairs and coffee tables await patrons inclined to plop down and stay a while. Espresso drinks, light meals and simple desserts are served without fussy embellishments.

Uptown

Avenue Coffee Shop 222 Davenport Rd ☎ 416/744-1617. Subway: Bay. One of the few post-World War II coffee shops left in Toronto, this Art Deco sliver on the northern edge of Yorkville keeps its food simple and its coffee straightforward.

Café Doria 1094 Yonge St ☎ 416/944-0101. Subway: Rosedale. The local coffee bar for Toronto's monied elite, the *Doria* nevertheless avoids ostentation and treats all its customers with equal care. Serves up forti-fying espresso drinks for patrons worn out from shopping at the many beautiful antique stores lining this strip near the upscale Rosedale neighbourhood.

The Coffee Mill 99 Yorkville Ave ☎ 416/967-3837. Subway: Bay. This Hungarian establish-ment dates back to Yorkville's coffee house days, when the likes of Joni Mitchell and Neil Young were getting their start in the neigh-bourhood. It serves a variety of potent coffees and is famed for its rib-sticking goulash.

Jet Fuel Coffee Shop 519 Parliament St ☎ 416/968-9982. Streetcar: Carlton/College (#506). One of the oldest independent coffee establishments in town, and the unofficial club house of bicycle couriers. It only serves beverages that can be made with an espresso machine (tea included), and imports a few baked goods for dunking. An excellent choice for relaxing with a huge, inexpensive latte and a newspaper.

Puseteri's Café 57 Yorkville Ave, at Bay St ☎ 416/785-9100. Subway: Bay (Bay exit). Few cafés offer stargazing and valet parking, but this one, attached to the downtown grocery store owned by Toronto's best purveyors of fine food, is the *ne plus ultra* of Yorkville's daytime glam spots. If watching visiting movie stars do their grocery shopping isn't your idea of an interesting time, perhaps the fact that *Pusateri's* only serves lilly espresso coffee will entice you.

Soda Market Café 425 Danforth Ave, Uptown ⓣ416/466-5227. Subway: Chester. In addition to lattes, espressos, cappuccinos and juices, this attractive lunch spot offers a menu of substantial but inexpensive items such as large, fluffy omelettes with a variety of fillings, pizzas and a platter of Greek dips and grilled pitta.

Tim Horton's 1170 Bay St ⓣ416/975-4464. Subway: Bay (Bay exit), Bay St. This Toronto Maple Leaf's eponymous coffee chain, with several other locations downtown, is a Canadian institution, famed for such innovations as the 99-cent-a-dozen "Tim Bits" (doughnut holes). *Tim's* latest gift is its "Steeped Tea", a caffeinated godsend. Sandwiches, soups and stews are served along with crullers, muffins and buns. This location is open 24/7.

The suburbs

Athens Pastries 509 Danforth Ave, Greektown ⓣ416/463-5144. Subway: Chester. True to its name, this café-cum-bakery sells sweet and savoury Greek pastries with coffee, and nothing else. Huge trays of baklava, spanakopita and a delectable custard and filo confection empty out in rapid succession as sit-down or takeaway customers file in for their pastry fix.

Beaver Café 1192 Queen St W, at Gladstone Ave ⓣ416/537-2768. Streetcar: Queen (#501). Stop smirking! The beaver is Canada's national symbol and this spot wears its patriotic heart on its sleeve with kitschy Canadiana decor. The menu, however, has pronounced Mediterranean leanings; panino sandwiches stuffed with a wide choice of fillings are a signature item.

24-hour food

If you find yourself awake and hungry between 3am and 6am, or if you are just heading home after a long night, these establishments will be open to serve you.

7 West Café	p.153
Fran's	p.150
Golden Griddle	p.150
Mars Restaurant (Fri & Sat)	p.150
Tim Horton's	p.149

Iliada Café 550 Danforth Ave, at Pape Ave ⓣ416/462-0334. Subway: Chester. The Greek coffee served here, which comes in a tiny cup three-quarters full of fine coffee grounds, makes espresso seem as tame as baby formula. Regular coffee and espresso-type beverages are also available.

Lakeview Lunch 1132 Dundas St W, at Shaw St ⓣ416/530-0871. Streetcar: Dundas (#505). The sign outside proudly proclaims "Established in 1949", and this Deco diner hasn't structurally changed since. The menu, on the other hand, is up-to-the-moment chic, with paninni, fusion salads and pretty desserts to go with a range of coffees and teas.

Tango Palace Coffee Co. 1156 Queen St E, at Leslie St ⓣ416/465-8085. Streetcar: Queen (#501). Ensconced in an Edwardian storefront amongst a row of antique stores, *Tango* serves up huge cups and even bowls of café au lait, cappuccinos and just plain coffee with a bewildering variety of sweets, all to the strains of jitterbug and doo-wop tunes. Desserts like pecan pies, huge chocolate cookies and sticky sweet buns are the strong suit here.

Light meals

Somewhere in-between Toronto's more casual cafés and its full-blown restaurants are smaller, bistro-type dining spots that serve light and generally inexpensive meals. These are often the best places to sample the diverse cuisines that the city has to offer, at very affordable prices.

American and Canadian

Beaconsfield 1154 Queen St W, at Beaconsfield Ave, Parkdale ⓣ416/516-2550. Streetcar: Queen (#501). A recent addition to Parkdale's hip strip between the *Drake* and *Gladstone*

hotels, the *Beaconsfield* is all dark woods, moody lighting and huge *belle époque*-style mirrors. Gussied-up takes on classics, such as burgers served on brioche ($13), attract a youthful mix and keep the main room and adjoining patio hopping.

Dooney's Café 511 Bloor St W, Uptown ☎416/536-3292. **Subway: Spadina.** This is the David to Starbucks's Goliath. When the latter tried to usurp *Dooney's* lease, the café's regular patrons rebelled and kept the *Dooney* dream alive. The café's interior is cozy with exposed brick throughout, and the full menu features stand-bys like salads, pastas and pizzas, as well as snazzier entrees like duck confit with root vegetables and *rösti* potatoes ($15).

Edward Levesque's Kitchen 1290 Queen St E, at Leslie St, Downtown ☎416/465-3600. **Streetcar: Queen (#501).** In a town of celebrity chefs and tycoon restauranteurs, Edward "Ted" Levesque is one of Toronto's genuine characters. His fans, and they are legion, follow him from place to place, as much to experience his unbridled personality as to enjoy his excellent fare. An ever-changing dinner menu is offered Tuesday to Saturday night, and the establishment's mega draw is Sunday brunch. House specialities include chicken liver pâté with red pepper jelly and grilled foccacia ($9.90). Entrees start around $7.45 and top up at $19.

Fran's 20 College St, at Yonge St, Uptown ☎416/923-9867. **Streetcar: College (#506); also** 210 Victoria St, Dundas St E, Downtown. Just when this venerable Toronto institution had dwindled to one last outpost on College Street, a snazzy, brand new *Fran's* opened alongside Dundas Square. Old favourites such as shepherd's pie and the chicken club sandwich are still on the menu, and a comprehensive breakfast menu is crowned by the "all day, all night Big Breakfast", which features eggs, bacon, sausages, pancakes, home fries and toast for $9.95 on a 24/7 basis.

Golden Griddle 45 Carlton St, at Yonge St, Uptown ☎416/9775044. **Subway: Carlton; also** 11 Jarvis St, at Front St E, Downtown ☎416/865-1263. **Subway: Union Station.** Optimistically billed as a family restaurant, the late-night, early-morning clientele are an attraction all to themselves. This 24-hour chain serves mainly an array of pancakes, but a full menu is also available, with burger, pancake or egg dishes at $4.99.

La Hacienda 640 Queen St W, Downtown ☎416/703-3377. **Streetcar: Queen (#501).** Stalwart *La Hacienda* remains a constant feature on the Queen West strip. Bleary-eyed partygoers swear by the *huevos rancheros* as a hangover antidote, but less damaged patrons can enjoy uncomplicated Mexican fare such as shrimp enchiladas or quesadillas stuffed with your choice of chicken, beef or chorizo ($6.95). If the hair of the dog is required, the margaritas are first rate.

Hello Toast 993 Queen St E, Downtown ☎416/778-7299. **Streetcar: Queen (#501).** The flea-market chic furnishings are your first clue that this place positions itself on the lighter side of serious. It's known for its Sunday brunch, which features the house specialties – French toast and Belgium waffles – but also offers a changing dinner menu with pastas, risottos and roasts ($18–23). The espresso drinks are just right and the cappuccinos pack a wallop.

Insomnia Internet Bar Café Inc 563 Bloor St W, Uptown ☎416/588-3907. **Subway: Bathurst.** This fully licensed Internet café has six computer terminals and a kitchen that stays open until 2am, serving up standards like pizzas, pastas, salads and daily specials ($5–17). There's also a large-screen TV, plus couches on which to snuggle and booths for a tête-à-tête.

Jamie Kennedy Wine Bar 9 Church St, at Front St E, Downtown ☎416/362-1957. **Subway: Union Station.** At this spot, which is particularly good for grazing at either lunch or dinner time, 21 appetizer-sized dishes ($5–15) vie with an excellent wine list for patrons' attention. A highly affordable way to encounter one of Toronto's celebrity chefs. Reservations for lunch only.

Maggies 400 College St, Uptown ☎416/323-3248. **Streetcar: College (#506).** Although *Maggies* has a full lunch menu, with soups, salads, burgers and desserts, the real draw here is the inexpensive, all-day breakfast, featuring omelettes (starting at $7.95) and fancier items like poached eggs with hollandaise sauce and smoked salmon ($11.95). Generous free refills given on regular coffees and tea.

Mars Restaurant 432 College St, Uptown ☎416/921-6332. **Streetcar: College (#506).** Though there is a chain of shiny, kitschy *Mars* diners nowadays, the original restaurant on College Street is still in business. Their all-day breakfast – eggs, rashers and choice of toast or home fries – remains a Toronto cheap-eats classic, and the cheeseburger is still under $5.

Swan Restaurant 892 Queen St W, Downtown ☎416/532-0452. **Streetcar: Queen (#501).** Once an ugly-duckling lunch counter, this little eatery with a warm, wood-panelled interior maintains vestiges of its past – booths, swivel stools at the counter and 1940s light fixtures. A friendly staff serves meal-sized salads ($9), creamy risottos and blue-plate specials like roasted capons on fluffy mashed potatoes ($18). The portions are huge, so bring a serious appetite or a friend or both.

Utopia Café & Grill 585 College St, at Euclid Ave, Uptown ☎416/534-7751. Streetcar: College (#506) The lion lies down with the lamb at this bistro, where most of the meaty menu options are replicated in a vegetarian version, or vice versa depending on your dietary inclinations. Meal-sized salads start around $9.95 and the eclectic selection of dips and appetizers, burgers and tandoori draw a youthful crowd on Toronto's hippest strip.

Asian Fusion

Green Mango 707 Yonge St ☎416/920-5448 and 730 Yonge St, Uptown ☎416/928-0021. Subway: Yonge/Bloor. One of Toronto's early Asian fusion restaurants, this popular establishment offers sit-down dining and cafeteria-style takeaway. Both are perfect for inexpensive, quick lunches. Spicy noodles are dressed up with tofu, chicken or vegetables, and fresh (ie unfried) spring rolls and sticky rice desserts are on the menu as well. Entrees start at $7.95.

Kubo Radio Asian Eatery & Public House 894 Queen St E, at Leslie St, Downtown ☎416/406-5826. Streetcar: Queen (#501). The peripatetic *Kubo*'s arrival on the Leslieville strip of Queen East signals the neighbourhood's slow advance towards trendiness. The menu's goofy names for the fare – "Funga Me Funga You" is an abalone and wood ear mushroom dish on Shanghai noodles for $10.95 – are now balanced with straight-ahead choices like the cilantro salmon ($14.95). Dumplings, broth noodles, curries and grill items don't stray above $16.95, and a selection of the "small plates" ($3.95–7.95) could easily make up a meal.

Red Tea Box 696 Queen St W, at Manning Ave, Downtown ☎416/203-8882. Streetcar: Queen (#501). At this feminine Asian Fusion lunch spot, little tables covered in decorative cloth and an assortment of antimacassared chairs make up the front tearoom. Bento boxes of dainty dishes ($17) are the house speciality,

along with a bewildering array of teas served in china teapots (from $3.50 a cup to $10 a pot). There is also a larger tearoom out back beside a garden patio, and a little gift shop.

Shanghai Cowgirl 538 Queen St W, at Ryerson Ave, Downtown ☎416/203-6623. Streetcar: Carlton/College (#506) Worlds collide at this greasy spoon turned fusion palace, where just about everything falls between the $5–12 price range. Gourmet burgers and spicy Asian noodles are both on the menu, pretty salads juxtapose overwhelming desserts (Jagermeister chocolate mousse, for example) and the retro lunch counter vibe morphs into clubland when weekend DJs arrive. The summer patio is a must on warm, sunny days.

Silk Road Café 341 Danforth Ave, at Hampton Ave ☎416/63-8660. Subway: Chester. On a menu that features meals from Mongolia to Hong Kong and prices that are never over $12, hot, spicy beef dishes from Turfan appear alongside a highly recommended vegetarian appetizer plate for two ($8.95). Family recipes make it onto the list as well, notably Grandma Wong's hot pot – a spicy stew of tofu, vegetables and meat.

Spring Rolls 85 Front St E, at Church St, Downtown ☎416/365-7655. Subway: Union; also at 693 Yonge St ☎416/972-7655 and 38 Dundas St W ☎416/585-2929, Downtown. Various Asian cuisines and influences (Japanese, Chinese, Thai) make up the menu at each of this restaurant's three attractive locations. Eleven different kinds of spring rolls ($3.95–4.25), soups, stir-fries, noodles, satay and salads are the mainstays. Everything except wine list selections is under $12, and nothing should take longer than ten minutes to reach your table.

British

Chippy's 893 Queen St W, at Gore St, Downtown ☎416/866-7474. Streetcar: Queen (#501). Stop by here for some fish and chips, where the fish in question is haddock, cod, halibut or salmon, and the perfect chips are hand-cut and dressed with a luscious variety of savoury sauces. Meals are around $15.

House on Parliament 456 Parliament St, at Carlton St, Cabbagetown ☎416/925-4074. Streetcar: Carlton/College (#506). This excellent pub serves affordable food that makes allowances for a variety of dietary choices (one of the fattest, juiciest vegetarian burgers is served here for $7.95) and features British stalwarts like steak and kidney pie. There is a rib-sticking weekend brunch, plus roast beef dinners with all the trimmings on Sundays.

Caribbean

Ali's West Indian Roti Shop 1446 Queen St W, Parkdale ☎416/532-7701. Streetcar: Queen (#501). *Ali's* is one of the city's best roti shops, featuring succulent *dhalpoori* and *paratha* roti (starting at $5.95) stuffed with your choice of meat, seafood or vegetarian options. Stews and full dinners are also available. Island juices and home-made soursop ice cream are on hand to cool spice-excited palates.

Bacchus 1376 Queen St W, Parkdale ☎416/532-8191. Streetcar: Queen (#501). This tiny restaurant offers a Guyanese version of roti, filled with stuffings such as curried goat, squash, spinach or conch ($4.99–7.99), to name but a few. Feather-light dumplings and fritters, peanut butter cakes and fried plantains can be accompanied by a wide selection of tropical fruit drinks and ginger beers.

Eazy Eats 749 Broadview Ave, Riverdale ☎416/461-9576. Subway: Broadview. The Trinidadian proprietress of this diner is a natural-born cook, offering up treats like firm, cheese-infused macaroni pie ($5.95), perfectly done fresh fish, rice and peas with oxtail gravy and bread pudding that is absolutely sublime.

Irie Food Joint 745 Queen St W, at Bathurst St, Downtown ☎416/366-4743. Streetcar: Queen (#501). A recent addition to the Queen Street strip west of Bathurst Street, *Irie* serves Caribbean-style cuisine in a trendy, upscale setting. Entrees of jerk chicken, beef or pork ($9.95–16.95) and a wide array of roti arrive with sides of island slaw and peas and rice. Surprisingly affordable for such an attractive space.

The Real Jerk 709 Queen St E, at Broadview Ave, Downtown ☎416/463-6055. Streetcar: Queen (#501). The *Jerk* lives up to its name and dishes up platters of hot, spicy chicken and beef with mounds of rice and peas ($4.75–8.95), as well as bottles of Red Stripe beer to take away the heat. Seafood and a few vegetarian entrees round out the offerings, but this is really a place for carnivores.

Ritz Caribbean Foods 450 Yonge St at College St, Uptown ☎416/934-1480. Streetcar: College/Carlton (#506); also 10 Roy Square, at Yonge & Bloor sts, Uptown ☎416/972-7480. The *Ritz* has all the high points – roti, callaloo, saltfish and more – plus Caribbean Chinese food (an Island take on low mein). Service is excellent and the portions are generous; chicken, goat, beef or veggie dinners with peas, rice, coleslaw and rotis go from $4.75–9. Large portions of Kingfish, shrimp curry and jerk fish cost $12–14.

Chinese

Bright Pearl Seafood 346-348 Spadina Ave (upstairs), at Dundas St W, Chinatown ☎416/979-3988. Streetcar: Spadina (#510) or College (#506). You can't miss this seafood and dim sum palace: huge lion statues, paws aloft, seemingly wave to passing streetcars from the entrance. A big draw is the one-hundred-item dim sum lunch ($1.75–4), as popular with locals as it is with tourists. Servers who zip around the huge pink banquet hall with carts of dim sum are happy to explain the contents of the little bamboo baskets, dishes and trays. Tempting items like the spicy, Szechwan *ta chien* chicken ($10.95) are also available à la carte.

Lee Garden 331 Spadina Ave, at Baldwin St ☎416/593-9524. Streetcar: College (#506). Local atmosphere abounds in this unpretentious, Cantonese favourite. Although seafood is high on the list, *Lee Garden* is famous for its grandfather smoked chicken ($14) – a half bird glazed in honey and sesame seeds, with pillowy, moist flesh.

Liu Liu Hot Pot 149 Baldwin St, at Spadina Ave ☎416/593-8858. Streetcar: Spadina (#510) or College/Carlton (#506). No one knows why the *Liu* isn't called "Famous for Sichuan Hot Pot", as that's the only sign in English. Not the place for solitary dining, hot pots are like Chinese fondues and demand group participation. Guests choose the comestibles they desire and cook them at the table in a communal pot of bubbling chicken stock. Prices vary according to the number of diners and the ingredients chosen, but a communal hot pot shouldn't go above $25.

Lucky Dragon 418 Spadina Ave, at College St, Uptown ☎416/598-7823. Streetcar: College (#506). A favourite among nearby university students for three excellent reasons: the food is good, almost everything on the more than 550-item menu is less that $10 and it's open until 4am on weekends.

7

Swatow 309 Spadina Ave, at Dundas St W, Chinatown ☎416/977-0601. Streetcar: Dundas (#505). All of the money saved on decor and atmospheric lighting goes into the food, which is old-style Cantonese costing mostly between $3.50–5.75. Congee, soups, numerous rice dishes, very fresh seafood and chicken are dished up at a frenetic pace to happy diners at communal tables.

Indian

New Arani 402 Spadina Ave, Chinatown ☎416/979-8105. Streetcar: Spadina (#510) or Dundas (#501). Located in the middle of Chinatown, this is one of Toronto's best-loved Indian restaurants. Specializing in aromatic southern Indian fare, in which more subtle spice combinations with occasional fire predominate, the small, narrow dining room here fills up quickly. Its best bargain is the hot lunchtime buffet for $6.95.

Udupi Palace 1460 Gerrard St E, at Craven Rd, Little India ☎416/405-8138. Streetcar: Carlton (#506). This walk-down mall space doesn't win any beauty prizes, but no one pays attention to the surroundings when they bite into the delectable southern Indian-style food, which pairs green chilies with coconut chutney in countless vegetarian ways. Entrees range from $5.25 to $8.95 and tempt first-time diners into ordering more than they can possibly eat.

Italian

7 West Café 7 Charles St, at Yonge St, Uptown ☎416/928-9041. Spread over three floors in a former Victorian house, *7 West Café* offers a bistro-type dining area, an espresso bar/café and a tiny back deck. Enjoy simple food like cheese, onion and sun-dried tomato-laden hot bread ($6.95), as well as pastas and soups and stews with an Italian twist. The desserts are lovely and there is a bargain-basement brunch on Sunday. The café section is open 24/7.

35 Elm 35 Elm St, at Yonge St, Downtown ☎416/598-1766. Subway: Dundas. Only the name has changed at this former *Il Fornello*. The delectable thin-crust pizzas loaded with lucious toppings, such as pear and gorganzola or simple mozzaerella and fresh herbs, are still on the menu (starting at $8.95), as are spelt crusts and vegan options for special diets. Stuffed pastas

and daily mains are also available, if less memorable.

Café Diplomatico 594 College St, at Gore St, Uptown ☎416/534-4637. Streetcar: College (#506). Known locally as "the Dip", this no-nonsense remnant of an earlier time has managed to hold its own among newer, chichi neighbours. Substantial, simple pizzas with a selection of market-fresh toppings, as well as pastas, are served inside or on the packed patio. Pies start at $9.95.

Café Nervosa 75 Yorkville Ave, at Bellaire St, Yorkville ☎416/961-4642. Subway: Bay. One of the few reasonably priced restaurants left in Yorkville, *Café Nervosa* is a great spot for people (and also celebrity) watching. The open kitchen produces salads, ample pastas and delectable thin-crust pizzas ($11.95–15.95), which are excellent. The dinner menu offers grilled strip loin, prepared with a mushroom risotto or as a *bistecca alla fiorentina* (steak and potatoes), grilled sea bass or grilled chicken breast stuffed with goat's cheese and sun-dried tomatoes. Service is unfailingly pleasant.

John's Italian Café 27 Baldwin St, at McCaul St ☎416//5596-8848. Streetcar: College (#506). The Hebrew letters on the front windows of this unpretentious little café are an acknowledgement of the Kensington neighbourhood's Jewish past. *John's* specializes in pizzas and pastas, with Italian sweets to round out the meal. Nibbling gorgonzola-laden bruschetta ($6) or *caprese* salad when the field tomatoes are just in ($6.75) on the summer patio is a great way to unwind.

Kit Kat 297 King St W, Downtown ☎416/977-4461. Streetcar: King (#504). Antipasti ($16.95 for two), pastas ($13.95–19.95), steaks and seafood dominate the uncomplicated menu at *Kit Kat*. Even though it's usually busy, the atmosphere is friendly and the service is attentive. First-timers are invited to pat the tree growing in the middle of the kitchen for good luck.

Terroni 720 Queen St W, Downtown ☎416/504-0320. Streetcar: Queen (#501); also at 106 Victoria St, Downtown ☎416/955-0258. Subway: Queen. A recent expansion doubled the width of this bustling Queen West fixture, and not a moment too soon. The popularity of *Terroni*'s pastas, perfectly structured pizzas ($9.95–13.95) adventurous salads and antipasti and regional desserts put space at a premium.

CAFÉS AND LIGHT MEALS | Light meals

International

Bonjour Brioche 812 Queen St E, at Logan
Ave, Downtown ☏416/406-1250. Streetcar:
Queen (#501). Jewel-like fruit tarts, buttery
croissants, puffy brioche and delectable
pissaladière, a variation on pizza from
Provence, draw hordes from all over the city
to this patisserie/café. The sit-down menu
is a blackboard full of soups, sandwiches,
omelettes and quiche, starting at $8. There's
always a line for Sunday brunch, and almost
everything is eaten by 2pm, so come early.

By the Way Café 400 Bloor St W, at Brunswick
Ave, The Annex ☏416/967-4295. Subway:
Spadina. An eclectic mixture of Middle
Eastern meze standards (a combination
plate of hummus, baba ghanoush and
tabouleh is a mere $9), Jewish delicacies,
Mexican quesadillas and Thai green curry,
along with fortifying soups, salads and
daily specials, keep this spot packed year
round and the patio humming on summer
evenings and weekends. A prime neighbourhood spot for people watching and
conversation.

Epicure Café 512 Queen St W, at Ryerson Ave,
Downtown ☏416/504-8942. Streetcar: Queen
(#501). Unpretentious, funky and comfortable, the *Epicure* serves up a tried and true
combination of Italian and French menu
items. Polenta makes for a nice alternative to pasta, and regulars swear by the
burger menu (starting at $8.95) featuring the

▽ Kalendar Koffee House

Toronto Burger, an update of the famous
Toronto speciality, the banquet burger,
which is topped with cheddar cheese and
bacon. A good selection of local microbrews
and regional wines encourage repeat visits.

Kalendar Koffee House 546 College St, at
Euclid Ave, Uptown ☏416/923-4138. Streetcar:
Carlton/College (#506). Perhaps the loveliest café in town, with dark wood panelling
and intimate booths providing an old-world
atmosphere. This is a popular place to start
an evening's bar and restaurant crawl along
the College Street Strip or end one with a
coffee and dessert. Light daily specials are
served by excellent staff, and a well-stocked
bar complements a full range of espresso
drinks. Naan bread wraps called Nanettes
($6.95–9.95) are a house speciality.

🏃 **Lee** 603 King St W, at Portland St, Downtown ☏416/504-7867. Streetcar: King
(#504). Of maestro chef Susur Lee's two
eponymous restaurants (see *Susur*, p.157),
Lee is the lighter, affordable one. A cross
between a tapas bar and a dim sum palace,
small, treat-size dishes, ranging from $6 to
$15 and meant for sharing, offer up explo-
sions of tastes, textures and daring combinations. The signature Singapore Slaw,
featuring nineteen separate ingredients, is
a must-try – followed closely by the duck
confit. Dinner reservations are advisable.

Olivia's 53 Clinton St, at College St, Uptown
☏416/533-3989. Streetcar: Carlton/College
(#506). Olivia Mizzi turned her Victorian
house into a restaurant filled with intimate
nooks and corners – again. The former co-
owner of *7 West Café* tweaks market-fresh,
family specialties upwards on the Italianate
menu, featurinig dishes like squash gnocci
in sage butter sauce ($17). There are only
twelve indoor tables, with just a few more
dotting the patio and front porch, so reservations are advisable.

Thai and Vietnamese

Pho 88 Restaurant 270 Spadina Ave, at Dundas
St W, Chinatown ☏416/971-8899. Streetcar:
Spadina (#510) or Dundas (#505). The speciality here is pho, a spicy noodle soup with
beef and vegetables that starts at $5.99 and
goes up slightly in price depending on the
numerous additions you might choose.

Pi-Tom's Thai Cuisine 6 Alexander St, at Yonge
St, Uptown ☏416/966-1813. Subway: College.
A perfect spot for pre-theatre dinners and

pocket-friendly lunch specials (only $7.49 for soup, spring roll and daily main), this unassuming space is lightly decorated in Thai tapestries and kittedout with contemporary tables and dinner services. The extensive menu offers a full range of traditional Royal Thai soups, noodles, salads and mains with vegetarian options and the fire adjusted according to taste.

Salad King 335 Yonge St, at Dundas St E, Downtown ☎416/971-7041. Subway: Dundas. A recent renovation has smartened up *Salad King*'s exterior and somewhat tamed the interior, but the food is as good and as cheap as ever, plus the punchy spicing can be quite intense. Vegetarian, chicken or shrimp pad Thais ($7.95), green chicken curry and lime leaf beef dishes ($7.25) make this a favourite Downtown spot for frugal diners.

Vegetarian

Fresh, by Juice for Life 368 Queen St W ☎416/599-4442; also 894 Queen St W, Downtown ☎416/9132720. Streetcar: Queen (#501). *Fresh* lives up to its name with a sleek modernist interior and a varied and health-conscious vegan and vegetarian menu. Rice bowls with names such as "Tantric" and "Warrior" are the speciality and feature delicious combinations of tempeh, tofu, greens and gravies over brown basmati rice ($11). Burgers, sandwiches and wraps have optional sides of fries, and apart from the signature shakes, smoothies ($4–7) and juices, there is a decent selection of wines and microbrews.

King's Café 192 August Ave, at College St, Kensington Market ☎416/591-1340. Streetcar: College (#506). This attractive, blond-wood café, with a Chinese vegetarian bent, is an oasis of quietude in the midst of bustling Kensington Market. The menu has lightened up on "mock meat" dishes and instead centres more on entrees like rice noodle soup with golden cubes of fried tofu and emerald broccoli. Committed carnivores will find the rich desserts and espresso coffees more than enough reason to stop by. Most mains start around $9.

Lotus Garden 393 Dundas St W, at Beverly St, Chinatown ☎416/598-1883. Streetcar: Dundas (#505). A huge fibreglass moose, decked out in vaguely Taoist colours and symbols, stands in front of this little Vietnamese vegan eatery. There are numerous standard "mock" beef, pork and seafood dishes ($5.95–7.95), as well as soups, noodle dishes or stuffed vegetables, but the Vietnamese crepes are a house speciality.

Simon's Wok Vegetarian Kitchen 797 Gerrard St E, at Logan Ave, Riverdale ☎416/778-9836. Streetcar: Carlton/College (#506). An excellent Chinese vegetarian restaurant suitable for vegans on the eastern outposts of Riverdale's Chinatown. Most of the dishes come from the Buddhist tradition of monastic cooking, which not only eliminates all animal products from the kitchen but also anything judged too yin or too yang. Hot pots, mock meat dishes, stir-fries and house specialties like fragrant ginger rice range from $6.95 to a top price of $12.95 (for a king mushroom dish).

Restaurants

Dining out is one of Toronto's most pleasurable experiences, and the passion with which residents embrace gastronomy is readily evident. Two of the city's most popular festivals, **Summerlicious** and **Winterlicious** (see p.219 & p.217) revolve exclusively around gaining access to high-end restaurants that may otherwise be prohibitively expensive to the average diner. Contrary to what you might expect, such interest in fine food is not snobbish: with more than 5000 restaurants in the city, everyone is sure to find a place where they can afford to educate their palates and discover new cuisines. Competition between restaurants is fierce, so the **service** and the quality of the food is usually good to excellent.

In many respects, Toronto's restaurants are very good value. A handy way to sample the fare and enjoy the ambience of pricier establishments is to take advantage of lunch menus, where available. Typically offered from 11.30am to 3pm, lunches can be roughly 25 percent less than the cost of dinner menus. As well, we've listed plenty of places where you can eat light or full meals in a **more casual setting**, usually quite inexpensively, in Chapter 7, Cafés and light meals.

Restaurant **opening hours** and times of peak flow vary, so it's a good idea to call ahead. **Maps**, with all the restaurants in this chapter keyed to them, can be found in the back of the book.

For an up-to-the minute scoop on who the best chefs are and where to dine, consult Ⓦ www.martiniboys.com or the glossy *Toronto Life* magazine, which has a much-coveted annual restaurant review guide also available online at Ⓦ www .torontolife.com.

Celebrity chefs

In Toronto, chefs really are celebrities. Often, these culinary superstars are followed by their fans, who read avidly about them in gossip columns devoted to foodie chit-chat and save up for special occasions at their restaurants. Five-star Toronto chefs, and their respective restaurants, include:

Susur Lee	*Susur* (see p.157); *Lee* (see p.157)
Jamie Kennedy	*Jamie Kennedy Wine Bar* (see p.150)
Mark McEwan	*Bymark* (see p.157)
Claudio Aprile	Sen5es (see p.160)
Guy Rubino	*Rain* (p.157); *Luce* (p.160)

Downtown

African

Sultan's Tent 49 Front St E, at Church St
☎416/961-0601. Subway: Union Station.
This long-time favourite migrated from its
improbable space in an upstairs mall on
Bay Street to a beautiful location in the St
Lawrence Market neighbourhood. The prix
fixe four-course menu – featuring Moroccan delicacies such as pan fried monkfish
or cous cous royale served up in conical
tajines – start at $39.95. Belly dancers
shimmy away seven nights a week.

Asian fusion

Blowfish 668 King St W, at Bathurst St
☎416/860-0606. Streetcar: King (#504). An
excellent venue for people watching, this
Japanese-influenced watering hole has
developed a following for injecting Korean
and Chinese influences into grazing favourites like sushi. The nigiri/sushi ranges from
$4 to $24 and the hot or cold entrees are
$7–35. The tea list rivals the wine list in
selection and scope.
Monsoon 100 Simcoe St ☎416/979-7172.
Subway: St Andrew. Make time to stop for a
martini in the plus chic bar before going on
to the dining room. A leader in the grazing
trend, the menu is simply arranged as Small
($8–24), Large ($24–36) and Sides. Meals
such as Asian salmon tatar with wasabi
cream arrive on delicate raku dishes, and
the light, assured preparation boasts imaginative combinations. An excellent place to
mark a special occasion.
Rain 19 Mercer St ☎416/599-7246. Streetcar:
King (#504). Brothers Guy and Michael
Rubino raised the bar for Toronto's now-
glamorous lounge scene with this sleek
beauty, housed in a former women's prison.
Half restaurant, half lounge, *Rain*'s kitchen
transcends trendy: tasting menus ($85–135)
feature elegant, Asian-inspired dishes that
pair and contrast market-fresh ingredients. The attentive waitstaff offer excellent
suggestions.
🏃 **Susur** 601 King St W ☎416/603-2205.
Streetcar: King (#504). Susur Lee is
consistently ranked as one of the ten best
chefs in the world, and people come to
Toronto expressly for the purpose of eating
at his restaurant – if you ever wondered why

someone would spend serious money for a
meal, make a reservation (well in advance).
The best thing to do is to place yourself
in the chef's hands and order one of four
mystery tasting menus ($55–110); the
extraordinary waitstaff will bring you bowls
of this and little dishes of that. (Menus can
vary night to night, and tasting menus vary
patron to patron.) The underlying sensibility
is more-or-less Chinese, and aspects of the
technique are classically French, but the
absolute purity of taste defies adjectives or
labels. Tasting menus and vegetarian dishes
are available, and other special diets can be
easily accommodated.

Canadian and American

360 CN Tower CN Tower, 301 Front St W, at John
St ☎416/362-5411. Subway: Union Station. You
know you are going to be here anyway, so
why not schedule in a lunch or dinner? The
restaurant, which is in the "donut" three-
fourths up the CN Tower, slowly rotates a
full 360 degrees in 72 minutes, thus afford-
ing an unrivalled view of the city and around.
Other marvels include stoves that heat with
electromagnetic energy and the world's
highest wine cellar. The uncomplicated,
tourist-friendly menu – pastas, seafood,
sirloin au jus with Yukon Gold frites – has
mains ranging from $29 to $39 and rivals
or surpasses similar establishments' (such
as New York's *Rainbow Room*) in verve
and presentation; locals, however, who
can enjoy the view any old day, consider it
expensive.
Boiler House Distillery District, 55 Mill St, at
Parliament St ☎416/203-2121. Bus: Front St
(#72A). The largely Creole influence means
plenty of peppery shrimp offerings and
impressively meaty ribs ($21). The interior of
this former distillery boiler house is long and
dark yet decidedly chic; the outdoor patio
usually has a band to serenade diners.
Bymark in the Toronto Dominion Tower, 66
Wellington St W, at Bay St ☎416/3777-1144.
Subway: King or St Andrew. When chef
and restaurateur Mark McEwan opened
this latest eatery, he immediately gained
notoriety not for the stylish, masculine
decor, or for the verve and nuance of chef
Brooke McDougall's kitchen, but for the $35
hamburger with a side of frites served in a

RESTAURANTS | Downtown

cone. *Bymark* is the scene for carnivorous deal-making in the heart of the financial district, but it is also a very fine restaurant in its own right. In addition to the high-end burger, visitors are encouraged to try the sumptuous grilled cheese sandwich made with aged brie, lobster, pancetta and a daub of citrus aioli ($27).

Canoe in the Toronto Dominion Tower, 66 Wellington St W, at Bay St ☏416/364-0054. Subway: King or St Andrew. The minimalist splendour of Mies van der Rohe's Toronto Dominion Tower provides a dramatic venue for an excellent restaurant. Way up on the 54th floor, *Canoe* has stayed on top of the restaurant game by serving highly imaginative Canadian cuisine (East coast seafood, Quebec cheeses, Yukon caribou, feral greens, wild berries) alongside one of the best wine lists in Toronto – indeed, some of Ontario's best vintages are produced exclusively for this sky-high venue. Six-course tasting menus start at $85.

Montreal Restaurant Bistro and Jazz Club 65 Sherbourne St, at King St ☏416/363-0179. Streetcar: King (#504). Like Montréal itself, the menu is a mishmash of Québecois, French, Italian and American influences, meaning that you can have split pea soup with your huge, moist burger topped with bacon and swiss cheese ($10.95). The real draw, though, is the top jazz acts that perform here. Cover charges, usually about $10, apply, so it's a good idea to call ahead.

Oyster Boy 872 Queen St W, at Dovercourt Rd ☏416/534-3432. Streetcar: Queen (#501). Maritimers homesick for a taste of Down East and those who want to eat like Bluenosers visit *Oyster Boy* for tasty bivalves with names that read like a map of the east coast: Malpeque, Caraquet Vert and Tatamagouches. A half dozen of two each starts at $14.50. Other options include clam fritters, fish and chips in beer batter and lobster. The house-party atmosphere, superior brew list, and rare Ontario vintages like Daniel Lenko and Malivoire also warrant a visit.

Le Papillion 16 Church St, at Front St ☏416/363-0838. Subway: Union Station. Large crepes, plump with sweet or savoury fillings tweaked with Québecois flair, are the house specialties and start around $11. The menu also includes *tortier* (a Québec meat pie), and bistro standards like onion soup and steak and frites. Convivial service in an *auberge* environment.

Chinese

Bright Pearl Seafood Restaurant 346-348 Spadina Ave, 2nd and 3rd floors ☏416/979-3988. Streetcar: Dundas (#505) or Spadina (#510) Two huge Ming lions crouch protectively outside Steve Chan's all-day dim sum palace, and the fish tank near the entrance is like an aquatic zoo. Upstairs, in the enormous dining room, a seeming army of servers zip to and fro with little carts bearing eighty to one hundred different dishes, such as sticky rice in lotus leaves, shrimp, pork or vegetable dumplings, deep-fried taro cakes and, for the more adventurous, steamed chicken feet and various forms of tripe. The à la carte menu offers a full range of Cantonese dishes as well, as Peking duck and vegetarian options.

Champion House 480 Dundas St W, at University Ave, Chinatown ☏416/977-8282. Streetcar: Dundas (#505). This Chinatown favourite is known equally for its Peking Duck and its well-rounded list of vegetarian entrees, starting around $8.95. Even though a few courses have been trimmed, the Peking Duck experience still takes a bit of time and involves some pleasant theatricality in its service.

Golden Court Abalone Restaurant 270 Beaver Creek Rd, at Hwy 7, Richmond Hill ☏905/707-6628. Fresh seafood, specifically abalone, is the big draw here. Dim sum includes barbeque pigeon if you feel adventurous (or vengeful).

Happy Seven 358 Spadina Ave, at Dundas St ☏416/971-9820. Streetcar: Dundas (#505). With over 250 selections on its menu, this bright and spotless Chinatown favourite offers predominantly Cantonese-style cooking and a few spicy Szechwan meals. Attractively presented dishes range from $7–12.99. Open until 5am.

Lai Wah Heen *Metropolitan Hotel*, 108 Chestnut St, at Dundas St ☏416/977-9899. Streetcar: Dundas (#505). The name means "elegant meeting place", which it most certainly is. The high-end dining room atmosphere (place settings include silver chopsticks) is matched by the menu, best described as Hong Kong moderne. Slow-cooked abalone and shredded chicken casserole with egg noodles for two ($28) is a comfort food surprise. The daily dim sum lunch includes exotica like dumplings filled with marinated alligator loin ($3.50 a piece), and the boneless marinated chicken "hugged" by Yunnan cured ham ($28) is a tantalizing blend of regional cuisines.

Pearl Harbourfront Queens Quay Terminal, 207 Queens Quay W, at York St ⓣ416/203-1233. **LRT from Union Station.** It's unclear why this upscale Chinese eatery, prettily perched on the edge of Lake Ontario, would want to serve something called a "hockey puck" (six pieces for $7.85), particularly when the delicate shrimp and scallion dumplings are anything but dark and rubbery. Neverthe- less, all the familiar Cantonese fare is attrac- tively presented in a fine dining atmosphere.

Shanghai Lily 409 Spadina Ave, at Cecil St ⓣ416/596-7309. **Streetcar: Spadina (#510).** Unlike its Chinatown sisters, *Shanghai Lily* is a weekend *boite* that is all about sleek glamour and the clever presentation of delicious Chinese morsels called Chai-pas. Save the oily dim sum for Sunday morning, elsewhere; this place is most definitely for Saturday night. Chai-pas start at $4.

Spadina Garden 116 Dundas St W, at Bay St ⓣ416/977-3413. **Streetcar: Dundas (#505); Subway: Dundas.** The owners here are Hakka Chinese, a distinct branch of the Chinese diaspora living in India. China is the dominant influence on the extensive menu (look for perennial favourites like General Tso prawns), but India holds sway in spicy noodle dishes and stews ($9.50).

French

Brassaii 461 King St W, at Spadina Ave ⓣ416/598-4730. **Streetcar: King (#504).** Tom Dean's sculpture, *Bitch Pack*, which featured at the Venice Biennale, sniffs at passers-by in the courtyard that leads up to this long, skinny space, well worth the extra steps. French bistro favourites like duck confit ($25), salad nicoise with a fat slab of tuna ($25) and a first-rate steak tartare arrive in huge portions. Appetizer half portions, when available, are a cheaper, equally filling alternative. If you can't make it for dinner, breakfast is served at 8am.

Jules 147 Spadina Ave, at Richmond St ⓣ416/348-8886. **Streetcar: Queen (#501).** Tucked between coffee shops and the Fashion District wholesalers, this small French bistro is a real find. Huge bowls of steamed mussels in a garlicky white- wine sauce complement rosemary rubbed chicken, while a daily selection of savoury

crepes or toothsome quiches are a bargain ($9.95–16.95). The wine list is thoughtful if somewhat limited, and the desserts are *comme Mama fait* ("like Mum makes").

Indian

Babur 237 Queen St W, at John St ⓣ416/599- 7720. **Streetcar: Queen (#501).** Rich, buttery sauces, delicately spiced stews and fluffy naan and poori breads are all delivered to your linen-cloth table by a helpful waitstaff. The luncheon buffet ($10.95) is a Queen West bargain.

Bombay Palace 71 Jarvis St, at Richmond St ⓣ416/368-8048. **Streetcar: King (#504).** Mostly northern-style cooking with a nod towards Delhi is served up in perhaps the loveliest dining room in town. Crispy pakoras and samosas are good bets for starters. Main courses à la carte start at $11.95 and include a full range of fish, meat and vegetable dishes.

Dhaba 309 King St W, at John St (upstairs). ⓣ416/740-6622. **Streetcar: King (#504).** *Dhaba*, smack in the middle of the Theatre District, has been winning a dedicated following for its subtle tweaks on standard Northern dishes like saag paneer (spinach and fresh cheese, at $10.95) and bhartha (baked eggplant). Its claim to fame, however, is the sumptuous butter chicken, which is probably too rich to eat before a show.

Gujurat Durbar 1386 Gerrard St E ⓣ416/406- 1085. **Streetcar: Carlton (#506).** In the midst of the East End's Little India, this vegetarian restaurant serves up aromatic dishes from India's northwest Gujrati region. Your best bet is the generously proportioned thali ($6.95) which features a variety of daily curries, dhal, pickles and rice.

Kama 214 King St W (downstairs), at Simcoe St ⓣ416/599-5262. **Streetcar: King (#504).** Handily located across the street from Roy Thompson Hall, *Kama* offers a lighter, modern interpretation of Indian classics like tandoori chicken or vindaloo lamb or beef ($9.95–16.95). Nothing on the menu is too hot or too buttery, making this place a good introduction for those not ready for full- blown Indian cuisine.

International

Courthouse Market Grill 57 Adelaide St E, at Church St ⓣ416/214-9379. **Streetcar:**

8

RESTAURANTS | Downtown

159

King (#504). This building – once Toronto's courthouse, where ringleaders of the 1837 Upper Canada Rebellion (see p.230) were sentenced to death – commemorates its stirring history in a downstairs bar where the jail used to be. Upstairs is a series of beautiful rooms, culminating in a hidden garden patio, each giving way onto one another with the promise of fine dining. In actuality, the mainly steak and seafood entrees ($22–36) don't fulfill the promise of the setting; if you want to stop off for a drink and snacks, however, you can't do better for a backdrop.

Czehoski's 678 Queen St, at Bathurst St ☎416366-6787. Streetcar: Queen (#501). Not too long ago *Czehkoski's* was a Polish deli, and remnants of its decidedly unchic past have been incorporated into its current decor, best described as Central European *belle époque*. Deli-inspired items like smoked trout and pickled sardines remain on the menu; otherwise, the options are decidedly upmarket – with sformato (a savoury potato pudding that is a cross between gnocci and a soufflé), cassoulet and braised lamb with mushrooms. Entrees start around $16.

▽ Ultra Supper Club

🏃 **Ultra Supper Club** 314 Queen St W, at Spadina Ave ☎416/263-0330. Streetcar: Queen (#501). Huge candelabra lit with twinkling pillar candles provide flattering light for the beautiful women and their hipster companions, while opaque silver curtains delicately divide tables for group reservations from the main room. The menu is an update of traditional French classics, such as proscuitto-wrapped veal tenderloin with butternut squash ravioli and shaved foie gras torchon ($36). This is a wonderful place to splash out and celebrate something.

Gypsy Co-op 817 Queen St W, at Palmerston Ave ☎416/703-5069. There are so many reasons to come to *Gypsy*: it's a genuine Toronto experience, the environment is as relaxing and embracing as a big Muskoka chair and the meals are wonderful. The varied menu offers stylish spins on comfort food belonging to various cultures. The squid ink ricotta ravioli ($16) is a house classic.

Sen5es 328 Wellington St W, at Peter St ☎416/935-0400. Subway: Union; Streetcar: King (#501). Chef Claudio Aprile reopened *Sen5es* with a bang when it moved from its Bloor Street West location to the SoHo *Metropolitan* hotel. Aprile is famed for his seafood, and his tasting menu ($120) is an excellent way to experience his signature touches, including deceptively simple preparations that allow for bright, clear taste sensations.

Tomi-Kro 1214 Queen St E ☎416463-6677. Streetcar: Queen (#501). Tucked in a Victorian row of antiques shops on the Leslieville strip, this charming spot offers up a United Nations-like menu selection, with organic salmon prepared with Japanese touches, like soy, wasabi and a hint of maple ($22) alongside Greek meze and French bistro classics.

Verveine 1097 Queen St E, ☎416/405-9906. Streetcar: Queen (#501). When well-decorated restaurants serving contemporary takes on bistro classics – steamed mussels bathed in mango butter, fat sandwiches served with crispy pommes frites (around $15) – pop up in formerly proletarian sections of town, locals cluck their tongues at the gentrification of yet another neighbourhood...and then line up to sample the menu. It's a very popular Sunday brunch spot, so you'd do well to make reservations if that's when you plan to visit.

Italian

Luce 30 Mercer St, at Peter St ☎416/599-5823. Streetcar: King (#504). The Rubino brothers from *Rain* (see p.157) juggle a second kitchen in the stylish *Hotel Le Germain* and leave aside Asian influences for their Italian heartland. Simple fare like stuffed mushroom caps are served atop polenta "stalks for two" ($30), game meats such as venison, boar and rabbit are delicately scented with juniper, citrus and fresh herbs and handmade pastas impress hard-bitten food critics. Portion sizes are small, but the tab won't be. Entrees start at $25.

🏃 **Noce** 875 Queen St W ☎416/504-3463. Streetcar: Queen (#501) This exceptional Italian restaurant is located in a former home. The pasta is rolled by hand, the beef carpaccio ($15) melts on the tongue and the meat from the roasted capon breast ($24) falls right off the bone. Service is personable, as befits such a small place, and although the wine list is short, it is well considered. A wonderful choice for a special occasion.

Romagna Mia 106 Front St E, at Jarvis St ☎416/363-8370. Subway: Union Stn. Elegant antipasti, pastas, soups and mains are found on the menu here, but the real show stopper is the spectacular risotto Parmesan ($26): a huge wheel of Parmesan *reggiano* is blow-torched to melt a layer of cheese, the risotto is tossed on top to inhale it, and this magical fusion is then topped with walnuts and black truffle.

Japanese

Fune 100 Simcoe St, at King St ☎416/599-3868. Streetcar: King (#504). *Fune* serves up perfectly respectable sushi, sashimi, tempura and teppanyaki dinners and features a staggering deluxe assortment for two at $52. Sushi is served Tokyo-style, in little boats that float along a channel from the sushi chef to you.

Hiro Sushi 171 King St E ☎416/304-0550. Streetcar: King (#504). Hiro Yoshida raised the bar for Toronto's sushi establishments when he opened this sliver of a restaurant. It offers unparalleled subtlety in all respects: decor, presentation and the food itself, and many hold it to be the best sushi spot in town. Sushi selections start at $6.

Izakaya 69 Front St E, at Church St ☎416/703-8658. Subway: Union Station. "*Izakaya*" is Japanese for the favourite Spanish word among restaurateurs these days: tapas. This pared down newcomer is focused on the Nipponese art of noodles fried, in a broth, or cold in a salad, for about $12. Long communal tables predominate the seating arrangements.

Nami 55 Adelaide St E, at Victoria St ☎416/362-7373. Streetcar: King (#504). A very fine Japanese restaurant with a dark, suave interior lined with discrete private booths. The sushi bar, which starts at $6.75, serves the

standard fare, but the robata counter, where grilled seafood is prepared in front of you, is the main draw (starts at $11.75).

Latin

Caju 922 Queen St W ☎416/532-2550. Streetcar: Queen (#501). A zingy taste of Brazil on the West Queen West strip. *Caju's* svelte interior is warmly minimal and the compact menu features just eight appetizers and eight main courses, including vegetarian dishes. Distinctive features, beginning at $15, are the varied uses of cassava root (as flour, rosti, in stews, as chips), the hearty soups of the day, and stolid beef entrees. Desserts are attractive and the cocktail list alone is reason to visit.

Seafood

Adega 33 Elm St, at Yonge St ☎416/977-4338. Subway: Dundas or Carlton. For such a small street, Elm boasts a number of fine dining establishments, including this Portuguese charmer. *Adega's* signature platter, the Petisco (meaning a bit of everything), is a great bargain: grilled chourico, gravlax, grilled sardines, grilled squid, fresh Portuguese goat cheese and prosciutto for $29. Low lighting, dark wood accents, discrete booths and excellent service make this a great choice for an intimate evening.

Pure Spirits Oyster House & Grill 55 Mill St, Distillery District, Bldg 52A, at Parliament St ☎416/361-5859. Streetcar: King (#504). Despite being housed in a former industrial building, the interior here is decidedly stylish and attractive. There is a classic bouillabaisse ($28), a succulent roast salmon with mussels and vegetable chowder ($25) and plenty of oysters, clams and scallops done up in a variety of styles that veer from traditional to spicy Asian.

Rodney's Oyster House 209 Adelaide St E ☎416/363-8105. Streetcar: King (#504). Toronto's favourite oyster bar serves more than twenty different bivalves, along with scallops, crab, lobster and shrimp. White plate specials featuring market-fresh grilled fish ($11) are a recent addition. The wine and dessert menus are short, but the selections of beer and Scotch are impressive.

Whistling Oyster 11 Duncan St, at Richmond St ☎416/598-7707. Streetcar: Queen (#501). With seventy starters and an all-day happy hour on Sunday (when appetizers range from

$2.99–18.99) and Monday, this local favourite is always a party waiting to happen. In addition to the oysters, jerked conch fritters are a house delicacy.

Steakhouses

Barberian's 7 Elm St ⊤416/597-0335. Subway: Dundas. *Barberian's* hasn't changed much since it opened in 1959, serving Toronto's first shrimp cocktail (now $19.25) and catering to Richard Burton and Elizabeth Taylor when Burton was starring here in *Camelot*. It continues to offer no-nonsense steak and some seafood dishes ($27–49), and the wine list is excellent.

Harbour Sixty 60 Harbour St, at Bay St ⊤416/777-2111. Subway: Union Stn. Housed in the former Toronto Harbour Commission building, *Harbour Sixty* has had its dining room, downstairs, decked out in that manly, Ralph Lauren-type classique look. The restaurant is serious about steak, which starts at $39.95 for prime cuts, and the attentive waitstaff will help if you don't know your porterhouse from your rib-eye. A wine list the size of a telephone book carries over seven hundred vintages.

Ruth's Chris Steak House 145 Richmond St W, at University Ave ⊤416/955-1455. Subway: Osgoode. This outlet of the Ruth's Chris group has all the bases covered: dark wood booths, tuxedoed waiters and dark red accents set the stage for hand-cut steaks (starting at $35) that arrive at your table in varying shades of pink, sizzling away.

Thai and Southeast Asian

Angkor 614 Gerrard St E, at Broadview Ave ⊤416/778-6383. Streetcar: Carlton/College (#506). Familiar Thai dishes (shrimp and coconut soup; spicy beef salad) coexist alongside less familiar Cambodian fare, which is a beguiling blend of Indian, Thai and French cuisines. Menu items include staples like soups, salads, noodle dishes and simple chicken and seafood options ($7.95–9.95). Vegetarian meals are also available, and various requests are readily accommodated.

Ban Vanipha 638 Dundas St W, at Augusta Ave ⊤416/340-0491. Streetcar: Dundas (#505). Subtle, sophisticated Laotian and Northern Thai versions of dishes that may be familiar by name (fresh spring rolls, shrimp soup, glass noodles) taste nothing like the

▽ Bangkok Paradise

Bangkok Paradise 506 Queen St W, at Ryerson Ave ⊤416/504-3210. Streetcar: Queen (#501). Funky Thai for the Queen West crowd. Informal and usually packed, *Bangkok Paradise* has a goofy thatched-hut motif with an off-centre appeal. The menu features all the satay, noodle and curry classics you'd expect, plus a wide range of vegetarian options, starting at $7.95.

peanut-laden standards found elsewhere. Peppers, ginger and coconut are used with care, not abandon. Delicate eggplant Pad Markua ($8.95) reveals a whole new world of vegetable possibilities.

Diners Thai 395 Danforth Ave, at Chester Ave ⊤416/466-9222. Subway: Chester. Improbably situated in the midst of the Danforth's Greek restaurants, this unassuming, attractive space serves up uncomplicated Thai food that is crisp, fresh and inexpensive. The vegetarian appetizer plate ($12.95) easily makes lunch for two. The satay dinners including chicken, beef, shrimp, squid, lamb and tofu ($8.95–14.95) are a house speciality.

Little Tibet 712 Queen St W, at Bathurst St ⊤416/306-1896. Streetcar: Queen (#501). A move from a Yorkville step-down to a Queen West street-level space has much improved the atmosphere of this pleasing spot. Plenty of specialties from Tibetan Buddhist monasteries, notably the desserts, keep vegetarians happy, while peppery pork and beef dishes lure carnivores. In many ways the spicing is closer to the Indian subcontinent, but the staples, especially stuffed steamed dumplings called *momos* ($8.50–11.95), have a more Eastern character.

Vegetarian

Bo De Duyen 254 Spadina Ave (upstairs), at Dundas St ☎416/703-1247. Streetcar: Spadina (#510). This popular walk-up greets guests with puffs of incense and an ancestral shrine halfway up the stairs. The absence of any animal by-products in its Chinese-Vietnamese cuisine means that even the strictest vegan can eat here with a clear conscience. Pages and pages of selections ($5–12.95) include "mock" meat and seafood items.

Le Commensal 655 Bay St (entrance off Elm St) ☎416/596-9364. Subway: Dundas. The cafeteria-style, pay-by-the-gram setup of this airy restaurant is its only drawback. Otherwise, the place is great, with an excellent variety of offerings; soups, delicious salads, hearty potpies, stews, casseroles and baked goods are clearly marked for vegans or lacto-ovo vegetarians. A large dessert counter tempts with delectables like maple sugar pie, fruit cobblers and sweet pastries. Takeaway is also available. Licensed for beer and wine.

Fressen Herbacious Cuisine 478 Queen St W, at Spadina Ave ☎416/504-5127. Streetcar: Queen (#501). This is Toronto's most upscale vegetarian dining room, which also boasts a great bar. The food and the service, however, are notoriously uneven. When the kitchen is firing on all gas rings it produces excellent, innovative fare, such as cornmeal crusted tempeh with mango coulis ($16). A full meal can also be made of the delicious appetizers, and the juice and smoothie list is extensive.

Vegetarian Haven 17 Baldwin St, at McCaul St ☎416/504-5127. Streetcar: Carlton/College (#506). An attractive, pan-Asian vegetarian restaurant, *Haven* pulls out the stops on the use of meat substitutes: tofu, tempeh (cultured soy beans), seitan (wheat gluten) and TVP (textured vegetable protein). A house speciality is the mock seafood "Souperbowl" ($9.99–11.99), perfect for vegans on the Atkins Diet.

Uptown

African

Boujadi 999 Eglinton Ave W, at Bathurst St ☎416/440-0258. Subway: Eglinton West. This much-loved Moroccan outpost with Sephardic touches has both Kosher and vegetarian options. Celebrate friendship with one of their *plats des fetes*, a multi-course platter meant for sharing, at $41.95 for two.

Ethiopian House 4 Irwin Ave ☎416/923-5438. Subway: Wellesley. A two-storey restaurant with cosy, muralled rooms and food that is graced with aromatic, complex spicing. Moist towelettes and huge discs of sourdough bread called *injera* replace cutlery, and large platters (starting at $8.95) covered with yurt-like raffia caps replace ho-hum dishes. For a nominal fee, a full-blown coffee ceremony replaces a plain cup o' joe at the end of the delicious meal.

Asian fusion

Indochine 4 Collier St ☎416/922-5840. Subway: Yonge/Bloor. The French accent in the Vietnamese dishes is fairly pronounced, especially with the shellfish, while gentle touches of fragrant lemongrass, coriander and curry prevail in the soups and noodle dishes. The pho (beef noodle) soup is the best bargain, and the crab curry – spicy but not too spicy – is much recommended ($11). The really hot yellow chicken curry, however, is not for the uninitiated.

Xacutti 503 College St ☎416/323-3957. Streetcar: College (#506). This deeply hip space (pronounced sha-KOO-tee) makes an immediate impression with a pair of decorative chandeliers made from small handwritten notes in many languages and alphabets. After taking these in, slip to the lounge at the back and order a drink from the innovative cocktail list, or sit down at the long, communal table that slices through the middle of the restaurant. The food is pan-Asian via India (Thai noodles, curries, pakora), with market-fresh ingredients that lend a Canadian touch. A good introduction to the restaurant is to order lots of small dishes or appetizers ($6–16).

Canadian and American

Gallery Grill 7 Hart House Circle, Hart House (University of Toronto campus) ☎416/978-2445. Streetcar: College; Subway. Museum. On the Victorian-Gothic University of Toronto campus you'll find this restaurant, considered a hot find by foodies in-the-know. Offers very well prepared, presented, served and priced lunches and brunches (nothing above $14.95), with seasonal menus that change regularly.

Laurentian Room 51A Winchester (upstairs), at Parliament St ☎416/925-8680. Streetcar: Carlton/College (#506). A second-floor walk-up atop Cabbagetown's old *Winchester Hotel* (about to be transformed from a seedy tap house into a chain coffee shop), the *Laurentian* is the 1930s glam Deco hangout you always wanted to star in, complete with classic cocktails and the building's original long bar. The entrees are upscale comfort food with a distinct Afro-Canadian/American twist and start at $15. Open Thursday to Sunday nights only; reservations recommended after 7.30pm.

Southern Accent Cajun and Creole Restaurant 595 Markham St ☎416/536-3211. Subway: Bathurst. This taste of Louisiana doesn't stint on the full Creole and Cajun experiences, offering psychic readings and a squeeze-box house band called Swamperella. Specialities include hushpuppies, grits, chicken-fried steak, candied yams and vegetarian stews. Newcomers can take the stress out of decision-making and order the prix fixe meal (from $25). Allow time to eat slowly and enjoy the party that surrounds you.

Town Grill 243 Carlton St, at Parliament St ☎416/963-9433. Streetcar: Carlton/College (#506). This well-established Cabbagetown favourite makes guests feel right at home and part of the neighbourhood with carefully thought out, bistro-style entrees such as braised lamb or the signature roast capon ($20). Special dietary needs can be accommodated with a little extra notice.

French and Belgian

Batifole 744 Gerrard St E, at Broadview Ave ☎416/462-9965. Streetcar: Carlton/College (#506). The east-end Chinatown strip is the last place anyone would look for Toronto's hot new French restaurant, but *Batifole*

defies expectations. The Breton-influenced menu features regional favourites like tender braised beef cheeks in a red wine sauce, and a buckwheat galette filled with caramelized onion, brie and egg. Appetizers and mains are a consistent $8 and $15.

Bistro 990 990 Bay St ☎416/921-9990. Subway: Wellesley. Beloved bistro standards like *magret de canard* ($27) or steak tartare ($21), buoyed by an excellent wine list, are served at this cozy favourite of corporate types – and the odd movie star. The superb staff make everyone feel like a valued regular.

Brasserie Aix 584 College St ☎416/588-7377. The Yabu Pushelberg design team that won gold for *Monsoon* (see p.157) tricked out this former neighbourhood joint to make *Brasserie Aix* the glamour queen amongst bistros. A three-course prix fixe meal ($19) is available before 7pm. Vegetarians may prefer to perch at the zinc bar, as the pricey menu is meat-driven, featuring classics like grilled calf's liver ($18.95) or the *specialite du maison*, steak frites with horseradish butter ($22.95).

Café Brussel 124 Danforth Ave, at Broadview Ave ☎416/465-7363. Subway: Broadview. Close your eyes when you walk in the door and when you open them you will have been transported to Brussels circa 1928. Loving attention is paid to the authentic period decor, and the menu showcases simple meals done well: moules et frites with garlic mayonnaise ($21 for a kilo), savoury or sweet crepes and huge fluffy waffles, for Sunday brunch. Service is friendly but not overly solicitous. Like all good Belgian establishments, the beer list is as serious as the wine.

Café Margaux 796 College St, at Roxton Rd ☎416/588-7490. Streetcar: College/Carlton (#506). A recent addition to the predominantly Italianate neighbourhood, this bistro offers simple foods prepared so well you'll think you never had meat and potatoes before. Prix fixe meals start at $25.

Gamelle 468 College St, at Palmerston Ave ☎416/923-6254. Streetcar: College (#506). Every neighbourhood should be so lucky as to have a little Gallic bistro like *Gamelle* tucked in its midst. Touches of Québec and Morocco find their way onto the menu in the form of lentil salads or hearty roast pork. The wild mushroom risotto with dried apples and basil ($22) is inspired. Brunch is popular and space is limited, so be sure to make reservations.

Matignon 51 St Nicholas St, at Charles St ☎416/921-9226. **Subway: Wellesley.** This hidden gem is tucked away on St Nicholas Street, which, with its cobblestone paving and Victorian cottage, seems a world away from nearby gritty Yonge Street. Here, traditional French mains are prepared with a light touch and, speaking of light, *Matignon's* omelettes are perfectly cloud-like, with sides of crisp frites ($11). Lunchtime salads and cheese plates ($9.50) make a civilized alternative to the nearby fast-food.

Provence Delicés 12 Amelia St, at Parliament St ☎416/924-9901. **Streetcar: Carlton (#506).** This renovated Cabbagetown cottage offers a compact but satisfying menu, with pronounced nouvelle cuisine leanings: there's plenty of attention to vegetables and meats served *au jus* rather than in heavy sauces, which saves room for the excellent crème brûlée. The three-course prix fixe meal ($29.95) is an excellent bargain; vegetarian options are available.

Greek

Avli 401 Danforth Ave, at Chester Ave ☎416/461-9577. **Subway: Chester.** Owned and operated by the dynamic duo of Sharon and Lambros, *Avli* is the only Greek restaurant on the Danforth that combines authenticity, friendly service and culinary verve in equal parts. A combination of meze – the Greek version of tapas or dim sum – starts the meal off ($5.95 each or $14.95 for three). Classic seafood dishes like shrimp with ouzo ($12.95), a variety of potpies and sublime baklava round out the meal. The most theatrical dish in the house is *saganaki*, a slab of mozzarella-like cheese doused in brandy and set aflame.

Ouzeri 500 A Danforth Ave ☎416/466-8158. **Subway: Chester.** The later the hour, the more festive the atmosphere in this perennial favourite. A long list of classic meze starters like *skardalia*, taramasalata, stuffed grape leaves, hummus and home-made pitta ($5.95–13.95) vie with entrees such as moussaka, pasta and rack of lamb ($13.95–15.95). A solid wine list, loud music and animated conversation make each visit a party.

Pan on the Danforth 516 Danforth Ave ☎416/466-8158. **Subway: Chester.** Cyrillic script on the sign outside is the most traditional aspect of this restaurant, offering upmarket interpretations of Greek classics best described as nouvelle Hellenic. Their jumbo quail stuffed with sausage, mushroom and shallots ($18.95) is particularly good.

Pappas Grill 440 Danforth Ave ☎416/469-9595. **Subway: Chester.** Very much a family establishment, *Pappas Grill* has two-and-a-half levels and plenty of space for large tables. All the standard items are featured – souvlaki, meze, grilled seafood and roast leg of lamb ($13.95) – and served with rice and potatoes. Everything comes with baskets of pitta and lashings of olive oil.

Indian, Nepalese and Sri Lankan

Indian Rice Factory 414 Dupont S, at Bathurst St ☎416/961-3472. **Subway: Dupont.** Possibly the longest-established Indian restaurant in Toronto, this family-run place has introduced generations to mostly North Indian cuisine. The spicing of the main dishes is on the mild side, while the samosas and pakoras ($4.50–4.95) are perfectly crisp, the mains ($8.95–16.95) are voluptuously rich, and traditional desserts such as *gulab jamun* (fried balls of dough soaked in a rosewater, syrup and honey mixture) are very sweet.

Jaipur Grille 2066 Yonge St, at Eglinton Ave ☎416/322-5678. **Subway: Eglinton.** An unexpected find in the confluence of offices, hi-tech cinemas and singles bars, this quiet hideaway holds its own in the orchestration of spices and textures that characterizes Northern Indian cuisine. Channas, dhals, vegetable and meat stews ($13–19) are skilfully executed and attractively presented.

Mt Everest 469 Bloor St W, at Brunswick Ave ☎416/964-8849. **Subway: Spadina.** Nepalese and Northern Indian dishes fill the menu alongside familiar appetizer and tandoori options like paneer tikka ($10.95), as well as Himalayan specialties like *khasiko maasu* ($9.95), a Nepalese goat dish imbued with heady spicing. The "Mt Everest Special for Two", with chicken, lamb, naan, paneer and more is a great bargain at $25.95.

Nataraj 394 Bloor St W, at Brunswick Ave ☎416/928-2925. **Subway: Spadina.** This Annex stand-by nudges the competition along by proving memorable meals with alchemy-like spicing. Try the peppery stews, near-addictive shrimp pakoras and sugar-rush desserts. Entrees start at $7.95.

Rashnaa 307 Wellesley St E, at Parliament St ☎416/929-2099. Streetcar: Carlton (#506). Intriguing Southern Indian and Sri Lankan dishes are on the menu at this tiny restaurant, crammed into a small Cabbagetown cottage. A red lentil linguine is served with coconut chutney ($6.95–8.95), and dosas, habit-forming Sri Lankan crepes, come with a variety of fillings ($5.95–7.95).

Sidhartha 1450 Gerrard St E, at Craven Rd ☎416/465-4095. Streetcar: Carlton/College (#506). A darling of Toronto's food critics and foodie cognoscenti, this is a top-notch addition to Little India's restaurants. The chicken tikka masala is nonpareil. Trout gives an unexpected Ontario twist to the delectable tandoori options, and vegetarians are wooed with outstanding mali kofta (vegetable dumplings), for $7.99.

International

Goldfish Restaurant 372 Bloor St W, at Spadina Ave ☎416/513-0077. Subway: Spadina. Although the sleek minimalism of this space is so extreme you may feel like you are in an aquarium, *Goldfish* remains a breath of fresh air on the somewhat dowdy Bloor West strip bordering the Annex neighbourhood. The beet pasta ($16) is the picture of pink perfection, while meaty mains ($13–27) range from beef to ostrich tenderloin.

Pony 588 College, at Markham St ☎416/923-7665. Streetcar: College/Carlton (#506). Casual, bistro-style dining at very reasonable prices makes this attractive two-storey former storefront a neighbourhood classic. Delicious repasts like handmade mushroom ravioli ($14.95) and braised lamb shank with navy bean cassoulet ($17.95) make a hearty prelude to a night out on the College Street strip.

Wish 3 Charles St E, at Yonge St ☎41/935-0240. Subway: Yonge/Bloor. When the doyenne of *7 West Café* (see p.153) wanted to broaden her restaurateur horizons, she simply looked across the street. You can dine outside year-round at *Wish* on the covered patio with pillowed benches; the inside is decked out with flea-market treasures. The well-executed menu offers something for everyone, with special attention paid to pasta entrees ($11–14). The small but good wine list is rounded out by a snappy selection of smart cocktails.

Italian

Bar Mercurio 270 Bloor St W, at St George St ☎416/960-3877. Subway: St George. This totally charming bistro focuses on mostly Northern Italian approaches to a range of dishes, including pastas, salads, meat and fish; unexpected flourishes with spicing and presentation keep regulars coming back. A luscious array of desserts, such as tortes, fruit tarts and chocolate confections ($7–10) are paraded like beauty queens at the end of the meal.

Coco Lezzone Grill & Porto Bar 602 College St ☎416/535-1489. Truth be told, there are better places in town for Italian fare, but stargazing over a plate of baked Chilean sea bass ($30) doesn't get any better than here, with the likes of Russell Crowe, Bono, Woody Harrelson and Steven Seagal stopping by when they're in town.

Grano 2035 Yonge St, ☎416/440-1986. Subway: Davisville. The family feel here is no illusion: the Martella family, who owns the place, lives upstairs and works downstairs, and when you step into the restaurant you know you're a true guest, not just a customer. Family recipes make the pastas, seafood and meat dishes a personal slice of Tuscany; the brilliant antipasti – fried zucchini blossoms, golden rice balls with a mozzarella centre, perfectly grilled eggplant – are positively addictive. The charming back patio is closed only during the depths of winter. Pastas start at $14.50; entrees start at $19.95.

Japanese

Rikishi Japanese Restaurant 833 Bloor St W, at Christie St ☎416/538-0760. Subway: Christie. Stuck out among Portuguese, Cuban and Somalian sports bars, this little gem not only serves well-prepared traditional Japanese dishes – either individually or in bento boxes as a prix fixe – but also offers over thirty makki options. Dishes, decor and service are all very authentic, but Western cutlery is available upon request. Waitstaff are extremely helpful and attentive. All entrees below $20.

Tempo 596 College St ☎416/531-2822. Streetcar: College (# 506). This slim, minimalist restaurant continues to draw the hip and beautiful and produce some of the city's most desirable sashimi, while the hamachi tartare can't be beat. Nigiri sushi and maki are $4–14; entrees start at $20.

Latin American, Portuguese and Spanish

Boulevard Café 161 Harbord St ☏416/961-7676. Streetcar: Spadina (#510); Bus: Wellesley (#94). The menu at this popular eatery draws from all over the South American continent, featuring seafood from Peru (quesadilla del mar; $10.95), steak from Argentina and Latin staples like corn, beans and avocados prepared with a
light touch, a little heat and plenty of citrus. Located in a former house, the
cozy setting has upstairs and downstairs dining rooms and tables along a sidewalk terrace.

El Bodegon 537 College St, at Euclid Ave ☏416/944-8297. Streetcar: College/Carlton (#506). Zesty Peruvian seafood and hearty Argentinean beefsteak ($11–19) are the mainstays at this colourful family eatery on the College West strip.

Segovia 5 St Nicholas St, at Wellesley St E ☏416/960-1010. Subway: Wellesley. This long-time favourite does an excellent job with Spanish classics such as tapas ($6–7.50), paella ($35 for two) and grilled seafood, chicken and roast meats ($14–17). A preferred venue for uptown power lunches with the civil service brass from nearby Queens Park, *Segovia* warms up in the evening as diners in search of a slice of sunny Spain generate buzz.

Middle Eastern

Jerusalem 955 Eglinton Ave W, at Bathurst St ☏416/783-6494. Subway: Eglinton West. After delighting diners for three decades, this venerable establishment is still going strong. Everything is ultra fresh with an emphasis on the many small dishes from the Levant (falafel, hummus, baba ghanouj, etc) that can be shared as a memorable meal. Combination platters start at $30.

Kensington Kitchen 124 Harbord St, at Robert St ☏416/961-3404. Streetcar: Spadina (#510); Bus: Wellesley (#94). Another Toronto favourite, this airy, converted house offers upstairs and downstairs dining amid

carefully selected knick-knacks and crimson-ochre carpets. The menu is pan-Mediterranean, with Turkish, Lebanese, Greek and Moroccan classics ($13–17), such as braised lamb stuffed with eggplant and dried fruit, as well as plenty of choices for vegetarians.

Pomagranate 420 College St, at Bathurst St ☏416/921-7557. Streetcar: College/Carlton (#506). You'll be enveloped in the perfume of spices as soon as you open the door to this pretty Persian eatery. The cuisine is poised delicately between Middle Eastern and Indian, both of which it influenced; it's more complex than the former and less assertive than the latter. This balance is evident in the baqali palo, a saffron basmati rice dish studded with fava beans, braised lamb shank, Persian pickles and yogurt ($14.95). There are plenty of vegetarian options and a list of daily specials.

Seafood

▽ Joso's

🏃 Joso's 202 Davenport Ave ☏416/925-1930. Subway: Bay, Cumberland exit; Bus: Avenue Rd (#). This much-loved restaurant, described at length by Margaret Atwood in her novel *The Robber Bride*, is famous for three things: its squid-ink risotto, the plethora of breasts and buttocks in owner Joso Spralja's paintings and statues that decorate the place – along with the odd Dali and Picasso – and the celebrities who can't get enough of the signature Adriatic treatment of seafood. Pastas start at $13; entrees start around $25.

Steakhouses

Bruyea Brothers 640 College St, at Grace St
☎416/532-3841. **Streetcar: College/Carlton
(#506).** While not a steakhouse in the
traditional sense, the brothers Bruyea offer
patrons "extreme meat", as in Alberta beef,
wild boar, elk, venison, buffalo, caribou, veal
and wild fowl such as duck and pheasant.
Their "grazing menu" starts at $7.

Morton's 4 Avenue Rd, at Prince Arthur Ave
☎416/925-0648. **Subway: Museum.**
This outpost of the Chicago-based chain
is all about Big Meat for Big Men. Serving
both prime Alberta and USDA cuts that start
at $42, *Morton's* also offers some seafood
such as lobster and swordfish. Californian
reds are over-represented on the wine list,
but that's a minor beef.

Bars

For a city that didn't serve mixed drinks until 1948 and is still subject to Canada's often puzzling liquor regulations, Toronto has managed to eke out a remarkably vital **bar scene**. You'll find everything from grizzled taverns, some of which still maintain a separate entrance for women, to sleek cocktail bars.

Most bars and lounges featuring entertainment have a weekend **cover charge** after 9pm ranging between $5 and $10. Cover charges may also apply during the week if there is a special act, performance or top guest DJ. The legal drinking age throughout Ontario is nineteen, and **last call** at all establishments is 2am. This doesn't, however, necessarily herald an end to the night's festivities: after-hours bars riddle the city, and the people who will generally be able to guide you to them are the very bartenders serving your last orders. Be aware, though, that speakeasies (known locally as **booze cans** and roughly defined as unlicensed, after-hours clubs serving alcohol) are flat-out illegal and can be raided.

All Toronto bars are required to serve **food**, presumably to soak up some booze – though the quality and service of this is often sorely lacking. As a general hint, if you don't see anyone eating, the food probably isn't worth ordering. **Smoking** is no longer permitted in Toronto bars, but it *is* permitted on **outside patios**, which may be confusing to some and annoying to others. Laws pertaining to **drinking and driving** are strict, so if you end up drinking too much, leave your car in a car park, or, better yet, don't take it along in the first place. **Taxicabs** are far easier to find than parking spots, and **public transportation** roams the city's main arteries 24 hours a day.

Downtown

Apothecary 340 Adelaide St W, at Peter St ☎416/586-9858. Streetcar: King (#504). Back after a brief hiatus, *Apothecary* has lost nothing of its urban neighbourhood charm or effortless cool.

Barrio 896 Queen St E, at Leslie St ☎416/572-0600. Streetcar: Queen (#501). While the west end of Toronto has hip new bars springing up every five minutes, the east end still has this worthy Riverdale competitor. A great spot for a nightcap.

Black Bull 298 Queen St W ☎416/593-2766. Streetcar: Queen (#501). The line of gleaming motorcycles parked outside give an idea of who the regular patrons are at this popular spot, one of the oldest taverns in Toronto. The *Black Bull* also has an excellent summer patio, plus a grill menu heavy on the burgers.

Bovine Sex Club 542 Queen St W ☎416/504-4239. Streetcar: Queen (#501). The *BSC* has held its own for more than 10 years now, and in all that time has never invested in a sign. The exterior is encrusted with layers of industrial scrap and bicycle parts, offering no glimpse of the playground within, which is filled with kinetic sculptures built from old portable record players, as well as a couple of bars and pool tables.

Budo Liquid Theatre 130 Peter St, at Queen St W ☎416/593-1550. Streetcar: Queen (#501). Often thought of as a bar for younger guys about to graduate to full-scale lounges, *BLT* is a worthy spot to add to the pub-hop list, if only to check out the (sort of) Japanese garden interior.

C'est What? 67 Front St E ☎416/867-9499. Subway: Union Station. Over twenty micro-brews are on tap in this St Lawerence Market spot – including the popular house brand, hemp beer – plus there's an impressive selection of single malt Scotches and hearty pub food. The performance space here has seen the likes of Bare Naked Ladies and Jeff Buckley, to name just a few.

Chelsea Room 923 Dundas St W, at Grace St ☎416/364-0553. Streetcar: Dundas (#505). This is a cocktail bar, pure and simple. A couple of rooms with some loungers, a bar with a few stools, a sound system and uncomplicated mixed drinks. Perfect.

Dominion on Queen 500 Queen St E, at River St ☎416/368-6893. Streetcar: Queen (#501). The recently resorted Romanesque building shrugs its massive plum granite shoulders at trends and celebrates its return to being a neighbourhood taproom. Flea market club chairs, beer tasting "flights" and a solid menu draw a steady crowd.

Esplanade Bier Market 58 The Esplanade, at Lower Church ☎416/862-7575. Subway: Union Station. Even though mussels and frites are served here, this place's primary purpose is to pour big glasses of Belgian (and Canadian and French and wherever else) beer to a mostly young, mostly male clientele, usually fresh from viewing a hockey game over at the nearby Air Canada Centre.

Fez Batik 129 Peter St ☎416/204-9660. Streetcar: Queen (#501). The ground-floor restaurant in this barn-like space has a North African look, with coloured glass, pierced metal and rich textiles, but the real attractions here are the dancefloors throughout, the patio out front and a little upstairs club.

Fluid Lounge 217 Richmond St W ☎416/593-6116. Streetcar: Queen (#501). One of the few establishments on the Richmond Street strip that doesn't curl up and die in the middle of the week, this youngish dance bar is also a prime spot to mingle with the locals.

Joe 250 Richmond St W (upstairs), at John St ☎416/971-6563. Streetcar: Queen (#501). Joe makes an effort – some woud say too much of an effort – to be the opposite of its glitzy Clubland neighbours by kitting itself out as a rec room. Very popular with young, straight guys.

The Last Temptation 12 Kensington Ave ☎416/599-2551. Streetcar: Dundas (#505). A change of ownership and a much-needed renovation saved this well-located Kensington Market spot from sheer nastiness. Now, in place of the former grittiness, it has a smooth club ambience inside and a generous patio out front. There's a Middle Eastern/Mediterranean menu as well, but the main reason to pop in is to have a drink and watch the lively street life.

Left Bank 567 Queen St W ☎416/504-1626. Streetcar: Queen (#501). This gorgeously decorated restaurant-cum-dance hall re-imagines Paris circa 1880. The dining room, spacious dancefloor, pool room and remarkable salon *priveé* have a luxurious look that defies the relentless minimalism of so many other properties. The youngish crowd is mainly local. A good place to start the night.

Library Bar in the Fairmont Royal York, 100 Front St W ☎416/368-2511. Subway: Union. One of the few places left in town where the staff knows how to make a good martini and, better still, brings a little flask holding the other ounce of your drink. The bar also sports huge leather wing-back chairs and racks of newspapers, plus it never plays loud music.

Loft 720 King St W, at Bathurst St ☎416/203-2883. Streetcar: King (#504). For some reason, both *Loft* and the *Drake Hotel*'s lobbies have a pommel horse in the middle of the hubbub. Regardless, *Loft* is simply a fun place to grab a drink and catch a bite as one either heads into or winds down after a night on the town.

The Paddock 176 Bathurst St ☎416/504-9997. Streetcar: Queen (#501). Rising phoenix-like from a grotty past, The *Paddock* reclaimed its original, authentic Deco glory when it reopened in 1998. It boasts the world's longest Bakelite-topped bar, and the crowd is mainly smart young filmmakers and TV types, The kitchen produces straightforward, meat-and-potatoes-type fare.

Pravda Vodka Bar 36 Wellington St E, at Victoria St ☎416/306-2433. Streetcar: King (#504). The recent trend in vodka bars finds its expression here in a beautiful old space near the St Lawrence Market.

Reservoir Lounge 52 Wellington St E ☎416/955-0887. Subway: Union Station. An intimate subterranean club with a good selection of wines by the glass and microbrews on tap. Live jazz on the weekends.

🏃 **The Rivoli 332 Queen St W ☎416/504-1320. Streetcar: Queen (#501).** High-backed booths line either side of Queen Street West's venerable temple to fusion cooking. There is a long bar beside the dining room (which serves Wookie balls, Asian noodle soups and a global selection of appetizers), a cabaret space in the back, and a pool-and-billiards room upstairs.

The Rotterdam 600 King St W ☎416/504-1040. Streetcar: King (#504). King Street West's current trendiness has not afflicted the *'Dam*, which is both a downtown brewery and a pub. There are eight home brews to sample at the long bar and, on the weekends, you can take a tour of the brewery.

Savage Garden 550 Queen W, at Ryerson Ave ☎416/504-2178. Streetcar: Queen (#501). Old Goths never die, they just find their way to the *Savage Garden*. The metal sculptures, cages and post-apocalyptic distressed paint finishes perfectly complement the DJ-ed industrial thrash.

Toad in the Hole 525 King St W ☎416/593-8623. Streetcar: King (#504). Once an outpost of sorts for cheap suds and pub grub, today the *Toad* offers much the same but amid the fancy lounges and restaurants that now line King West.

The Wheat Sheaf 667 King St W ☎416/504-9912. Streetcar: King (#504). Toronto's oldest public house, *The Wheat Sheaf* served its first pint in 1849. In the ensuing century and a half since then, not much has changed – except for indoor plumbing, refrigeration and a television permanently tuned to sporting events.

Uptown

Amber 119 Yorkville Ave, at Bellair St ☎416/926-9037. Subway: Bay (Bellair exit). Many beautiful and famous people have been spotted sipping martinis at this very of-the-moment spot.

Andy Poolhall 489 College St, at Palmerston Ave ☎416/923-5300. Streetcar: College/Carlton (#506). If you want the opportunity to sit down – the seats were salvaged from the Concord's VIP lounge at New York's JFK airport – then come early. If you want to see what the buzz is all about, then come early. Named for Andy Warhol, this place, next to *Caio Edie* (see below), gets top marks for its Factory-like retro-kitch atmosphere, great bar action, and excellent DJs. One of the College Strip's best hangouts.

Artful Dodger 10 Isabella St ☎416/964-9511. Subway: Wellesley. This English-style pub looks and feels authentic. A second home for many locals, the *Dodger* also sees any number of social clubs and dart teams hanging out amid its red velvet banquettes and flock wallpaper.

Avenue *Four Seasons*, 21 Avenue Rd, at Yorkville Ave ☎416/324-1568. Subway: Bay (Cumberland exit). The *ne plus ultra* watering hole in town, and the place where visiting movie stars hang out during the

Toronto International Film Festival. The luxurious interior includes a long bar and dark woods, and you can enjoy the excellent wine list and great selections of stylish martinis and aperitifs.

🏃 **Bird 503 College St (upstairs), at Palmerston Ave ☎416/323-3957. Streetcar: College/Carlton (#506).** Perched atop *Xacutti* (see p.163), *Bird* is a tiny, perfect hideaway bar with discreet service and inobtrusive background music. Chocolate leather club chairs, a *belle époque*-style bar and angel-winged chandeliers constitute the decor.

The Brunswick House 481 Bloor St W ☎416/964-2242. Subway: Spadina. This old public house and neighbourhood fixture has been pulling pints and serving pitchers of cheap draught to poets, students and working stiffs since the 1880s. Despite a recent paint job and a few new pieces of furniture, the *Brunswick* has remained true to its proletarian roots and eschews anything faddish or trendy. There is always some community event or other going on in one of the taprooms, and weekends usually see live music. Thursday's cheap-pitcher night is an excellent time to stop by.

🏃 **Ciao Edie 489 College St, at Palmerston Ave. ☎416/927-7774. Streetcar: College**

(#506). Andy Warhol muse Edie Sedgwick was a source of inspiration for this deliberately kitchy but cool lounge, which is unselfconsciously decorated in original Seventies garage finds. DJs spin acid jazz and trip-hop, and Sundays feature the ever-popular singles' night.

Eat My Martini 649 College St ☏416/516-2549. **Streetcar: College (#506).** While it is possible to eat here, the main attraction, not surprisingly, is the extensive martini list, which boasts over eighty concoctions to put you over the top at the end of a long day.

Lava Lounge 507 College St ☏416/966-5282. **Streetcar: College (#506).** Lava lamps and slick red banquettes and booths give this place a Sixties feel. There's a good bar menu that features Middle Eastern, Asian fusion and grill items to sop up the martinis, beer and wine, and DJs usually reign – although the odd live act has been known to perform.

The Madison 14 Madison Ave ☏416/927-1722. **Subway: St. George.** This massive multi-floor pub has two pool rooms, a piano bar and a dancefloor. Popular with students, especially fraternity types, from the University of Toronto.

Myth 417 Danforth Ave ☏416/461-8383. **Subway: Chester.** A cavernous space with a huge suspended TV screen that silently plays Hollywood films with Greek mythological themes, like Jason and the Argonauts. Although you'll find better Hellenic fare elsewhere on the Danforth, *Myth*'s lively late-night crowd is a major draw – as are the massive chandeliers hanging from twenty-foot ceilings, exposed beams and pillars burned with runic symbols and beautiful blonde-wood bar.

Roof Lounge in the *Park Hyatt*, 4 Avenue Rd ☏416/924-5471. **Subway: Bay or Museum.** Long a retreat for establishment literati, the *Roof Lounge* offers a spectacular view of the city and hands down the very best martinis in Toronto. The bartender has been perfecting his method for almost four decades. Sofas, a fireplace and silken smooth service make this spot a treasured oasis.

Smiling Buddha Bar 961 College St, at Dovercourt Ave ☏416/515-2531. **Streetcar: College/Carlton (#506).** If you are looking for a sports bar that serves Chinese food and has a microphone in the corner for people who may (or may not) get the urge to use it, look no further. A great place to get goofy with the locals – and the wonton soup isn't bad either.

🏃 **Souz Dal** 636 College St ☏416/537-1883. **Streetcar: College (#506).** The extensive cocktail list and dark ambience are the main draws at this spot on Toronto's College Street strip. The backroom is really a walled patio, open to the stars and lit exclusively by banks of votive candles. Waitstaff drop by with little dishes of pistachios and keep the drinks coming. A great place to end an evening out.

Umbrella Bar & Lounge 890 College St, at Ossington Ave ☏416/530-4043. **Streetcar: College/Carolton (#506).** A new addition to the ever-extending College Strip. Caters to the hip-hop crowd on weekends.

Yammy the Cat 1108 Yonge St ☏416/515-1729. **Subway: Rosedale.** An appealing neighbourhood hangout whose zebra-print booths, flea market sofas and tiny bar brim with genuine cool. The two people who operate the bar, hot plate and CD player run the place like a 1950s rec room, where it's fine to get a little tipsy and (if there's room) start a samba line.

▽ Pauper's

🏃 **Pauper's** 539 Bloor St W ☏416/530-1331. **Subway: Bathurst.** This former bank has been performing a far more useful function as a two-storey beer hall for about a decade now. Pauper's is rightly esteemed for its rooftop patio, which can tend toward loud boisterousness on the weekend evenings.

Clubs and live music

T oronto's **nightlife**, like its restaurant scene, has blossomed in recent decades, and the city's reputation for rolling up its sidewalks after 10pm is no longer true. Today, there are **clubs**, **lounges** and **discos** for every taste and disposition. During the winter, nightlife is decidedly an indoor phenomena, but the explosion of pent-up energies during those first warm spring nights sees the revellers spill out into the club-lined streets of Downtown until dawn.

Most of the disco-type dance clubs are located on the Richmond Street strip, just south of Queen Street West, which is itself home to a number of **live-band venues**. The College Street strip, west of Palmerston Avenue, is also a likely spot to look for an up-and-coming dance bar amid all the cafés and bistros (although the emphasis here is more lounge-oriented). Also in the mix are trend-defying venues that staunchly support **jazz**, **blues** or **R&B**, and whose clientele bemoan the fact that they can no longer smoke indoors.

Most clubs and all lounges serve **alcohol** and, as with Toronto's bars, last call is at 2am. That means that all drinks have to be consumed and bottles taken away by 3am. On the weekends, however, most clubs will stay open until 4am, though live-music spots tend to wind things down earlier. The **rave scene** of the mid-nineties continues at various spots throughout the Richmond Street strip (known as Clubland), although their main constituents are kids under 19 who can't get into bars. This has led to table signs at places reading "No minors served until after 3am."

For venue **listings**, consult *NOW*, *eye* or *TRIBE*, three free weekly newspapers that are available in stores, restaurants and in newsboxes on the street. *NOW* has the most comprehensive listings, followed by *eye*, while *TRIBE* specializes in dance/rave/house discos. By far the best source of hot club information is the Martini Boys website at ⓦwww.martiniboys.com.

Toronto's **comedy clubs** are another good nightlife option. The city has a proven track record when it comes to showcasing emerging comedic talent, and several venues around town are specifically dedicated to stand-up or improv, with comedy cabarets finding a regular slot in some of the more varied venues.

Live music

Toronto's sizzling-hot **live-music scene** boasts a venerable history. Gonzo guitar god Neil Young is a local boy who got his start in the city's bars, as did The Band's Robbie Robertson and Joan Anderson, who later became known as Joni Mitchell. Other Toronto artists include Gordon Lightfoot, the Barenaked Ladies and cult heroes The Rheostatics, to name just a few.

Toronto's contemporary music scene goes well beyond guitar-based rock, however. **Jazz** in particular features prominently, with all its bebop, acid and classical varieties, and **Latin dance**, whether it's salsa, mambo, tango or merengue, holds a firm place near the top of the trend list as well. On the other end of the dance spectrum is a lively **hip-hop** scene, and the city's large Afro–Caribbean population ensures a fairly consistent offering of **dancehall**, **reggae** and **soca** music.

Venues

Big Bop 651 Queen St W, at Bathurst St, Downtown ☎416/504-6699. Streetcar: Queen (#501). This vast space is actually three clubs in one – *Kathedral*, *Reverb* and *Holy Joe's* – all of which cater to the live alternative rock scene. The main stage was recently decorated with sumptuous mural-sized reproductions of famous nineteenth-century paintings.

Black Swan 154 Danforth Ave, at Broadview Ave, Uptown ☎416/469-0537. Subway: Broadview. A neighbourhood beer joint that brings in Blues performers, especially Canadian ones.

Cadillac Lounge 1296 Queen St W, Downtown ☎416/ 536-7717, ⊛www.cadillaclounge.com. Streetcar: Queen (#501). Half a cadillac hangs above the entrance to this place, which features rockabilly, classic rock, alt country and blaring honky tonk.

Cameron House 408 Queen St W, at Cameron St, Downtown ☎416/703-0811, ⊛www.thecameron.com. Streetcar: Queen (#501). A line of huge metal ants marches up the side of this legendary place, making it easy to spot. The interior is a wondrous clash of Beaux Arts boudoir and honky tonk bar, and the stage at the back of the room has provided a showcase for emerging talent of every genre.

College Street Bar 574 College St, at Bathurst St, Uptown ☎416/533-2417. Streetcar: College (#506). A laid-back jazz bar that often dips into the blues. An excellent alternative to some of the over-hyped, trendier establishments in the area. Open until 2am seven days a week.

El Mocambo 464 Spadina Ave, at College St, Uptown ☎416/968-2001. Streetcar: Carlton/College (#506) or Spadina (#510). The stuff of legends insofar as live acts are concerned, having had visits from luminaries like the Rolling Stones, B.B. King, Blondie, Elvis Costello and hometown faves like Nash the Slash. Ownership changes and hard times have had their toll, but the bands (usually lesser known now) play on.

Healey's 178 Bathurst St, at Queen St W, Downtown ☎416/703-5882, ⊛www.jeffhealeys.com. Streetcar: Queen (#501). A steady diet of jazz and blues is served up in blues legend Jeff Healey's eponymous establishment. The man himself plays at least a couple of sets a week.

Horseshoe Tavern 370 Queen St W, at Spadina Ave, Downtown ☎416/598-4753. Streetcar: Queen (#501). Lots of Toronto bands like the Cowboy Junkies and Blue Rodeo got their start here, and now-famous names still swing by to play a set or one-off concert. The interior is relentlessly unglamorous, but the low (or no) cover charge and music industry promo specials are a major compensation.

Hugh's Room 2261 Dundas St W, at Roncesvalles Ave, Downtown ☎416/531-6604. Subway: Dundas West. An excellent reason to visit the west, west end, and a place to hear cutting-edge world music, folk legends (like John Renbourn) from Britain, Canada and the US and the best up-and-comers in every genre from across Canada. *Hugh's* doubles as a supper club, so be prepared to order (an inexpensive) dinner if you want the best seats in the house.

Lee's Palace 529 Bloor St W, at Bathurst St, Uptown ☎416/532-1598. Subway: Bathurst. *Lee's* continued popularity has nothing to do with the decor, the food or even the draghft beer; its reputation is based entirely on the outré bands it consistently books. An club called *Dance Cave* is upstairs.

Matador 466 Dovercourt, at College St, Uptown ☎416/533-9311. Streetcar: College (#506). This noble institution was memorialized in song by none other than Leonard Cohen in "Closing Time". When everyone else is shutting down, the *Matador* is opening up – don't think about swinging by before 2am. A good place to star-watch and catch great bands trying out new material.

Mod Club 722 College St, at Dovercourt, Uptown ☎416/588-4663. Streetcar: College/Carlton (#506). Possibly the hippest spot for live shows in Toronto right now. This place, with trippy murals, draws the bands with the biggest buzz, and the crowds to match. All that atmosphere means that beer can be expensive and shows sell out very quickly.

Montreal Bistro 65 Sherbourne St, at King St E, Downtown ☎416/363-0179 Streetcar: King. They take their jazz very seriously here. Food is served (see p.158), but while acts are performing patrons make sure they don't speak above a whisper.

Opera House 735 Queen St E, at Broadview Ave ☎416/366-0313. Streetcar: Queen (#501). This former vaudeville theatre is the chosen outpost for hard-core rock acts who like to thrash the night away. Despite the bad sound system, seatless interior and utter absence of decor, the venue books some of the biggest cult rock and electronica bands from England and the US. Additionally, it's a popular venue for the S&M/leather crowd, and is home to Toronto's annual Leather Ball.

The Orbit Room 580 College St (upstairs), at Euclid Ave, Uptown ☎416/535-0613. Streetcar: College/Carlton (#506). Long a favourite of the terminally hip, the *Orbit* features jaw-droppingly good sit-ins, notably internationally celebrated guitarist Kevin Breit (Cassandra Wilson; Norah Jones), who likes to play a set or two Monday nights.

Phoenix Concert Theatre 410 Sherbourne St, at Dundas St, Downtown ☎416/323-1251. Streetcar: Dundas (#505). An imaginative renovation (and equally imaginative booking agents) has made this a popular concert venue. Big-name acts looking for intimate gigs (the Stones broke in material for their 2005 Bigger Bang tour here), guitar legends and world music divas such as Caesara Evora perform on a stage space that looks like a cross between a Wild West saloon and an old vaudeville theatre.

The Rex Hotel Jazz Bar and Grill 194 Queen St W, at McCaul St, Downtown ☎416/598-2475. Subway: Osgoode; Streetcar: Queen (#506). In fierce arguments about which is the best jazz club in town, this one is consistently near the top of the list. A well-primped crowd lounges in the spiffed-up interior, but any reservations about pretensions evaporate once the music – which is always top-notch – begins.

Silver Dollar 486 Spadina, at College St, Uptown ☎416/975-0909. Streetcar: College/Carlton (#506). Self-billed as "Toronto's Premier Blues Club", this somewhat sketchy-looking venue books all the top international blues artists passing through town, and its sound system is worthy of its performers. Arrive early if you want a seat with a good view.

Sneaky Dees 431 College St, Uptown ☎416/603-3090. Streetcar: College (#506). This no-attitude slacker palace has live rock bands, pinball, pool and Tex-Mex grub until 5am seven days a week. Great for sampling Toronto's thriving indy band scene.

Tranzac Club 292 Brunswick St, at Bloor St, Uptown ☎416/923-8137. Subway: Spadina. The name is short for the Toronto Australia New Zealand Club, which was founded in 1931 by Aussies and Kiwis who had relocated here. Long open to the public, the small venue hosts some top Canadian, US and British folk musicians.

Clubs and lounges

New strains of **clubs** are springing up in Toronto like never before, assuring a quality night out whatever your tastes. Weekends tend to be busy, and the more popular spots can have long lines year round. **Cover charges** are usually between $8 and $15, but can be higher if the headliner act is a really big name. Some clubs book live bands on occasion, but most stick to the DJ formula. **Lounges** rarely have live music – space being at more of a premium – but they generally don't have cover charges, either. Check the listings in the free *NOW* or *eye* papers (see p.173) to see which DJs are playing where.

2 Cats 569 King St W, at Spadina Ave, Downtown ☎416/204-6261. Streetcar: King (#504). A cosy little hipster refuge, with a lounge in the front and a long bar in the back.

606 606 King St W, at Spadina Ave, Downtown ☎416/504-8740. Streetcar: King (#504). One of the early lounges on this now trendy strip, the front area is a garage-doored restaurant and the back is a clubhouse-like space with intimate corners.

Bauhaus 31 Mercer St, at John St, Downtown ☎416/977-9813. Streetcar: King (#504). This split-level club is as much about the display of its patrons as it is the actual dancing. Dress special or you won't make it past the bouncer.

C Lounge 465 Wellington St W, at Spadina Ave, Downtown ☎416/260-9393. Streetcar: Spadina. A spa-inspired lounge featuring a South Beach-style deck and a bar carved out of ice. Leather, wood, relaxing down-tempo beats and a sexy vibe make this a nice alternative to the regular club scence.

Camera Bar 1026 Queen St W, at Ossington Ave, Downtown ☎416/530-0011, ⓦwww.camerabar .ca. Streetcar: Queen (#501). Director Atom Egoyan and film distributor Hussain Amarshi (of Mongrel Media) concocted this sleek little martini bar that has a screening gallery in the back for showing the owners' ecclectic selection of favourite films.

Communist's Daughter 1149 Dundas St W, at Dovercourt Rd, Downtown ☎416/647-435-0103. Streetcar: Dundas (#505). There is no better antidote to the chrome-and-glass theatre of the lounge scene than this frayed little bar. The sign above the door reads "Nazzarre", referring to a prior tenant, while "Communist's Daughter" comes from a Neutral Milk Hotel song lyric. Flea market furnishings and a willful dishevelment imported from Ontario's north makes it the trendiest dive in town.

Crocodile Rock 240 Adelaide St W, at Duncan St, Downtown ☎416/599-9751, ⓔparty@thecroc.ca. Streetcar: King (#504). There is only one reason to mention a glorified sports bar with a huge reptile on the roof, and that is their famous 911 Tuesdays. If you have a hetero hankering for a man in uniform, be he a cop or a fireman, this is the place to come to meet an available urban hero once a week. Otherwise you may want to drop in for the beer and nachos.

The Docks 11 Polson St, the waterfront ☎416/461-DOCK. This massive complex – the lakefront patio is 41,000 sq ft – is like a theme park for clubbers. The music veers from old-school disco and R&B to Top 40 and dance, so no one should feel left out. If you get tired of the nightclub, disco or restaurant, you can watch double and triple features at the drive-in movie theatre.

🏃 **Drake Lounge** 1150 Queen St W, at Beaconsfield Ave, Downtown ☎416/531-5042. Streetcar: Queen (#501). Pretty much the front living room of the *Drake Hotel* (see p.140), this wonderful space has been a hit since the doors reopened in 2004. A wet bar serving house tipples like the Dorothy Parker cocktail (vodka, cranberry juice and Chambord) and a sushi bar keep the crowd satisfied as they sprawl on fat sofas, club chairs or loungers. Over the fireplace, a huge flat-screen TV projects live or taped shows held in the basement performance space.

🏃 **El Convento Rico** 750 College St, at Dovercourt Rd, Uptown ☎416/588-7800. Streetcar: College (#506). Walking into this lively joint, replete with red velvet flock wallpaper and baroque spot welding, makes you feel like you've stumbled onto the best party in town – and you may well have. The crowd ranges from earnest suburbanites to dishy Latino drag queens, and the DJs spin Latin and disco classics until 4am six nights a week (until 10pm on Sunday). Make sure to arrive in time for the Midnight drag queen shows and the free Latin dance lessons on Sunday afternoon.

Fluid 217 Richmond St W, at Duncan St, Downtown ☎416/593-6116, ⓦwww.fluidlounge.net. Subway: Osgoode. If you're looking to feel glamourous, *Fluid* is the perfect spot to act out in. Its doormen, line-ups and shower of glass tears suspended from the ceiling are

▽ Guverment

🏃 **Guverment** 132 Queens Quay E, at Lower Jarvis, the waterfront ☎416/869-0045, ⓦwww.theguverment.com. Subway: Union Station. This huge barn of a dance club houses seven distinct venues on the shores of Lake Ontario. Features DJs, live music and special events. One ticket gets you into everything.

The
arts

It may not conjure up visions of New York or London, but Toronto is as thriving and diverse as anywhere when it comes to the arts – fine, performing or otherwise; indeed, seeing a show, gallery-hopping or hitting the big film festival (or one of the smaller ones) has become as much a reason as any to visit. With major museums and avant-garde galleries, fringe theatres and Broadway-style knock-offs, events that range from the sublime to the ridiculous, and energetic neighbourhoods like Queen Street West, Yorkville and the university area, it's easy enough to see why.

Early artists

Lawren Harris's *Above Lake Superior*

The most prominent and accomplished clique of early Toronto artists were the landscape-obsessed **Group of Seven**, which formed in the 1920s. Works by spiritual founder Tom Thomson and others in the original Group – Franklin Carmichael, Lawren Harris, A.Y. Jackson, Frank Johnston, Arthur Lismer, J.E.H. MacDonald and F.H. Varley – as well as those later to join, like Lionel Fitzgerald, A.J. Casson, and Edwin Holgate, dominated Toronto's creative output for quite some time with their attempts to seek out and glorify **nature**; the provinciality of the city didn't seem to offer them much in the way of an outlet. Their work remains a vital contribution to Canadian modern art, despite it having ostensibly little to say about what it was like to live in Toronto at the time; certainly in the Art Gallery of Ontario (AGO) and the McMichael Canadian Art Collection they are what receives pride of place. Some painters today still draw on them for inspiration – after all, nature is still on Toronto's doorstep – but in general the tide has turned, and rather than fleeing to the countryside for inspiration, artists have become more likely to hit the city as a proving ground or to key in to the scene.

Tom Thomson

In May of 1912, **Tom Thomson** (1877–1917) ventured north from Toronto bound for Algonquin Park, where he spent the summer travelling around by canoe and painting the wilderness. Upon his return to the city, Thomson's friends – who were to become the nucleus of the Group of Seven – took a long look at his sketches and paintings and agreed that the wilds of northern Ontario were, as Arthur Lismer expressed it, "a painter's country". Over the next few years, the Group, under the influence of European Impressionism, went on to develop a distinctive **Canadian aesthetic** in their paintings of the outback; Lawren Harris was more or less the leader, and his canvases of Lake Superior are spare and vivid renderings of nature at work. Sadly, Thomson himself, who died under suspicious circumstances during a canoeing trip, only saw the beginnings. There are examples of Thomson's work in all of the major art galleries, but his quintessential canvas, the striking *West Wind*, can be found at the AGO.

Round Lake, Mud Bay

Public and outdoor art

While some of Toronto's exhibition spaces undergo changes – and occasionally close up to paying customers in the meanwhile – you can always count on seeing plenty of eye-catching **public art**: Henry Moore's *Large Two Forms* (corner of McCaul and Dundas St W) and *The Archer* (Toronto City Hall); Michael Snow's *The Audience* (Rogers Centre),

Flight Path (Eaton Centre) and *Red, Orange and Green* (Jarvis St and Bloor St E); and Tom Dean's *Bitch Pack* (*Brassaii* restaurant), to name but a few. Nearly two hundred such pieces exist around the city, oftentimes serving to memorialize some event, person or other, or in some cases just to beautify the surroundings. If poking around for all that art seems a hassle, time a visit with summer's **Outdoor Art Exhibition**, the largest of its kind.

Henry Moore's *Large Two Forms*

Patrons and venues

It's not just the artists who help shape the scene. When **Ed Mirvish**, a latecomer to the theatre world, persuaded his son David to join Mirvish Productions, the glamorous but rocky world of large, lavish theatrical production gained a steady foothold in Toronto. Together, the two not only built the beautiful **Princess of Wales Theatre** in 1993 (Ed bought and refurbished the Royal Alexandra Theatre in 1962), but have staged productions as diverse as Disney's "Beauty and the Beast" and various acts discovered at Toronto's Fringe Festival to their latest venture, the world premiere of "The Lord of the Rings", the musical.

Billionaire and aesthete **Lord Thompson of Fleet** – or just plain Ken Thompson – endowed the **Roy Thompson Hall** and is a driving force behind the Frank Gehry (himself a Torontonian) addition to the AGO, which will house the museum's collection of Tom Thomson and other Group of Seven works. Another big name in architecture, Daniel Libeskind, best known for winning the competition to design the site of the former World Trade Center in New York, is providing the facelift for the **Royal Ontario Museum**.

Toronto's Jack Diamond created the **Four Seasons Centre for the Performing Arts**, which will house the National Ballet and the Canadian Opera Company, and Will Alsop provoked both debate and delight with his (literally) stilted design for the Ontario College of Art and Design's **Sharp Centre**. And following years of wrangling, the only development project deemed acceptable for the historic Gooderam and Worts buildings, collectively known as the **Distillery District**, was a site devoted to the arts and crafts, with no chain stores allowed.

Roy Thompson Hall

Johnny Depp arrives for a screening

The Toronto International Film Festival

In thirty years, the **Toronto International Film Festival** (☎416/968-FILM, ⓦwww.tiffg.ca) has gone from being an obscure celluloid celebration for hardcore film fans to the most important festival after Cannes and the largest public film festival in the world. Oscar-winning films, such as *Ray* and *Sideways*, have had their world premieres here.

A ten-day affair, the festival begins on the first Thursday in September, and its system of passes, coupons or individual tickets allows for maximum viewing flexibility. Single, same-day tickets for Gala screenings (usually the big, star-studded Hollywood efforts) are available from the Film Festival's box offices – or as rush tickets immediately before screenings – for $18 or $31. Lines to get in to the films can be fearsome, but once you do, you'll have the opportunity to see directors and stars introduce their pictures and then make themselves available for question-and-answer periods after a film's first showing (all films screen twice).

The film industry

Mirroring the rise in the city's cultural prominence, the last few decades have seen Toronto turn into a major force in the Hollywood film industry. One of North America's most active **film sets**, with huge production trailers, miles of cable and laconic film crews trawling the urban landscape all year long, the city also serves as one of the film world's busiest **body doubles**, passing for Boston in *Good Will Hunting*, Tangiers in *Naked Lunch*, Yale in *The Skulls*, Chicago in *My Big Fat Greek Wedding* and Depression-era New York in *Cinderella Man*, to name a few. Perversely, local audiences packed the theatres to view the spectacular demolition of their City Hall and the Bloor Street Viaduct when they featured as fictional Raccoon City, of *Resident Evil 2 – The Apocalypse*.

A stroll down **Canada's Walk of Fame** on King Street downtown prove that it's not just the city that's familiar from the screen. Big local names abound, perhaps the greatest proportion in the field of sketch comedy: Jim Carrey (from nearby Newmarket); John Candy (also from Newmarket); the whole of SCTV, a Toronto comedy troupe derived from Chicago's Second City; Mike Myers (from the suburb of Scarborough) and, perhaps most influential of all, Toronto-born Lorne Michaels, of *Saturday Night Live* producer fame. There must be something funny in the water.

Mike Myers on his Walk of Fame star

enough to make the young punters feels special.

Gladstone Hotel 1214 Queen St W, at Gladstone Ave, Downtown ☎416/531-4635, ⓦwww .gladstonehotel.com. **Streetcar: Queen (#501).** Each of this hotel's three venues – The *Ballroom*, *The Melody Bar* and *The Art Bar* – is booked out with something or other worth attending. In homage to its seedy, recent past, it tends to showcase bands, such as perennial Cajun favourite Swamperella, alongside burlesque dancers as the adjunct acts.

Hush/Under Bar 457 Adelaide St W, at Spadina Ave, Uptown ☎416/366-4874. **Streetcar: King (#504).** *Hush's* old, rough exterior gives way to a high-toned, mahogany-stained bar and lounge that is part Rat Pack and part *2001: A Space Odyssey*. If you've nothing else to do in this swank space, you can amuse yourself and an acquaintance with a game of chess played on one of the upright chessboard "pods".

Joker 318 Richmond St W, at John St, Downtown ☎416/598-1313. **Streetcar: Queen (#501).** A stylish behemoth of a club whose weekend patrons are willing to line up around the block. The music is generally heavy-handed techno, with smatterings of hip-hop and R&B in the third-floor disco.

Lula Lounge 1585 Dundas St W, at Duffrin St, Downtown ☎416/588-0307, ⓦwww.lula.ca. **Streetcar: Dundas (#505).** Bastion of all things Latin, this thriving dance palace regularly features top salsa, son and other performances.

This Is London 364 Richmond St, Downtown ☎416/351-1100. **Streetcar: Queen (#501).** Although the entrance is in an alley, it's easy to spot *TIL* by the maddeningly long lines outside. Popular for its DJ's selection of disco, soul and Top 40 beats, perhaps the real draw is the women's washrooms: they take up the whole top floor, and hairdressers and make-up artists are on hand for touch-ups. Not a good choice of clubs if your date already spends too much time powdering her nose. Dress codes apply.

Una Mas 422 Adelaide St W, at Peter St, Downtown ☎416/ 703-4862 **Streetcar: King (#504).** This is hip-hop central, showcasing top DJ and live acts that include major international talents.

Underground Garage 365 King St W, at Spadina Ave, Downtown ☎416/340-0365, ⓦwww .undergroundgarage.ca. **Streetcar: King (#504).** Just when you thought you couldn't stand another stylish martini bar, the *Underground Garage* has emerged as an "urban saloon" with good rock music and no attitude problem.

Comedy clubs

ALT.COMedy Lounge at the Rivoli 332 Queen St W, at Spadina Ave, Downtown ☎416/596-1908. **Streetcar: Queen (#506).** The cabaret space in the back of the *Rivoli* hosts an alternative comedy night on Mondays at 9pm. Acts vary from wobbly stand-up routines to truly inspired silliness, such as Minimalist Puppet Theatre (no puppet, just the hand).

Bad Dog Theatre 138 Danforth Ave, at Broadview Ave, Uptown ☎416/491-3115. **Subway: Broadview.** This former newspaper office regularly hosts Theatresports on Wednesday evenings, in which teams of comics compete in improv showdowns, and at midnight on Fridays, Late Late Horror shows mix Grand Guinol with horror movie spoofs. (Free popcorn is generously thrown in.) Performances are Wednesday, Friday and Saturday, and comedy classes and workshops take up the rest of the week.

The Laugh Resort 370 King St W, at Spadina Ave, Downtown ☎416/364-5233. **Streetcar: King (#504).** A comedy club with nightly bookings; consult *NOW* or call ahead to see who's on and when.

Second City 56 Blue Jay Way, at King St W, Downtown ☎416/343-0011, ⓦwww.secondcity .com. **Streetcar: King (#504).** This Toronto-based company is also a club, having spawned John Candy, Martin Short, Catherine O'Hara and the SCTV crowd. Time has not dulled the troupe's taste for political satire. A good place to learn all you need to know about local as well as global affairs.

The Tim Sims Playhouse 56 Blue Jay Way, at King St W, Downtown ☎416/343-0011. **Streetcar: King (#504).** A co-tenant with Second City, *TTSP* specializes in staging an amorphous, improvisational comedy matrix. It could be about a mob wedding, it could be based on a 1950s game show or it could morph into who knows what.

Yuk-Yuks Downtown 224 Richmond St W, at John St, Downtown ☎416/967-6425. Streetcar: Queen (#501). This is the place where stand-ups have to make it in order to move up the food chain. Everyone has played *Yuk-Yuks* at some point or another, and the top house act these days is the legendary Kenny Robinson.

Performing arts and film

Toronto is internationally recognized as a vibrant centre for **film** and the **performing arts.** At the turn of the twenty-first century the arts are what the city has chosen to stake its claim on, and in the last few years a flurry of construction has seen some of the world's most famous architects take on one cultural institution after another.

Perhaps Toronto's main strength is the diversity of its population, which lends to dynamic and exciting artistic expressions. Visitors can enjoy varied **dance, opera** and **musical performances**, as well as a year-round **theatre scene** that's the third-largest in the English-speaking world (after London and New York, respectively). Additionally, Toronto is justifiably proud of the many arts **festivals** it hosts throughout the year – the most renowned being the **Toronto International Film Festival**, which is the world's largest public film festival and second only to Cannes in terms of its importance in the film industry.

The high season for most of the performing arts is late September to May, bringing cheer to Toronto's long winter months. The summertime is livened by a slew of outdoor festivals and events; for more information, see Chapter 16.

Theatre

Home to more than six hundred opening nights a year, Toronto offers an exceptionally varied array of **theatre** productions, from opulent international hits to idiosyncratic fringe affairs. Classical drama rubs shoulders with edgy improvisational comedy, and big, Broadway-bound musicals coexist with Baroque period pieces.

As if the wealth of choices during peak season were not enough, Toronto also hosts a number of arts-related events at other times of the year. The biannual **World Stage** theatre festival, held at the Harbourfront Centre in April (☎416/973-4000, ⊛www.harbourfrontcentre.com/worldstage) is a major international affair, featuring alternative theatre companies from more than twenty countries, while the annual **Fringe Festival of Toronto** showcases approximately eighty workshops and alternative performances in ten days in early July. Additionally, Toronto's newest repertory company, Soulpepper, bucks the trend of a fall-to-spring season and treats audiences to bracing interpretations of works by contemporary masters, as well as underperformed classical pieces, during the summer months. Lastly, although they aren't within the confines of Toronto proper, the Stratford Festival and the Shaw Festival (see p. 122 & p.117), both held two hours from Toronto in the towns of Stratford and Niagara-on-the-Lake, respectively, are two of the largest and most respected theatre festivals in North America.

Toronto has three main **theatre districts**. The **Downtown** district, encompassing the area around Yonge, Front, King Street West and John streets, is the oldest and includes some of the most established companies; the **East End** district, which occupies the southeast corner of the city, features primarily small, fringe companies; and **the Annex** neighbourhood, east of Bathurst between Dupont and Bloor, holds some of the best alternative companies.

For all theatrical events, **prices** – which range from $17 for shows by smaller companies to $90 for major ones – can be cut in half for same-day performances at **T.O. TIX office** (Tues–Sat noon–7.30pm; ☎416/536-6468 ext 40, ⓦtotix.edionysus.com), located on the southeast corner of Dundas Square, right across from the Eaton Centre. Tickets go on sale at noon, so it's a good idea to get in line a half hour before; cash, credit cards (Visa, MasterCard) and Interac are accepted, and no reservations are made by phone. When deciding on seats in an unfamiliar venue, check the front section of Toronto's *Yellow Pages*, which thoughtfully includes the seating charts for the Hummingbird Centre, Roy Thompson Hall and Massey Hall.

Should half-price tickets still exceed your means, look for PWYC ("Pay What You Can") performances listed in publications such as *NOW*. These have a suggested ticket price of about $15, but the boldest or poorest can get away with offering a few bucks (or maybe even nothing at all).

Downtown

12 Alexander Street Theatre 12 Alexander St, at Yonge St ☎416/975-8555. **Subway: Wellesley.** Tucked away on a tree-shaded side street, 12 Alexander is home to the gay-specialist "Buddies in Bad Times" company. When not showcasing the best in original queer-culture theatre, the space hosts visiting alternative companies and concert performances, and serves as home base for the annual Rhubarb! Theatre Festival (see p.217).

Artworld Theatre 75 Portland St, at King St W ☎416/366-7723. **Streetcar: King (#504).** This intimate,150-seat stage and gallery space features consistently innovative programming that reflects Toronto's many diverse communities.

Cameron House Backroom 408 Queen St W, at Cameron St ☎416/703-0811. **Streetcar: Queen (#501).** Situated behind the much-loved and ever-popular Cameron House (which hosts live bands and DJs), this 50-seat space is best known for its twice-yearly Video Cabaret performances of Michael Hollingsworth's *The History of the Village*

of the Small Huts, which satirizes Canada's colonial history.

Canon Theatre 265 Yonge St, at Dundas St E ☎416/872-1212; box office 244 Victoria St, ☎416/593-1962. **Subway: Dundas.** Just up the street from the Elgin Theatre and Winter Garden, the Canon, formerly the Pantages, was saved from demolition and restored to its former vaudeville glory in 1989 by impresario Garth Drabinsky, who used it for his Toronto production of *The Phantom of the Opera*. These days, the Canon is used for visiting theatre companies and short-run Broadway productions (*The Producers, Wicked*), and special guest acts (Dame Edna Everage).

Elgin Theatre and Winter Garden 189 Yonge St, at Queen St E ☎416/314-2901. **Subway: Queen.** The Elgin and Winter Garden are the last functioning double-decker theatres in the world, with the latter built on top of the former. From 1987 to 1989, the Ontario Heritage Foundation, under the watchful eye of architect Philip Ziedler, fully restored them to their exact original specifications. While the downstairs Elgin is a treat, with its plush, red upholstery and gilt-plaster ornaments, it's the upstairs Winter Garden that really takes your breath away. This tiny gem was constructed to look like a garden, its ceiling replete with real leaves and its pillars clad to look like tree trunks. Tours are given on Thursdays at 5pm, and on Saturdays and Sundays at 11am. Today, the Elgin specializes in dramatic and musical productions, as well as Gala screenings of the Toronto International Film Festival; the Winter Garden uses its more intimate setting to host special events.

Harbourfront Theatre Centre 231 Queens Quay West ⓣ416/973-4000. LRT: Queens Quay. Hosts a wonderful variety of international dancers, musicians and theatrical productions.

Hummingbird Centre 1 Front St E, at Yonge St ⓣ416/872-2262. Subway: Union Station. The Hummingbird kick-started the then-moribund Toronto theatre scene when it opened its neo-Expressionist doors in 1960. At 3200 seats, it's too large for intimate drama, so instead it's the Downtown venue of choice for family-oriented productions. For the past four decades, it has also been home to the Canadian Opera Company and the National Ballet, though both tenants are moving in summer 2006 to the newly built Four Seasons Centre for the Performing Arts.

Panasonic Theatre 651 Yonge St, at Carlton St ⓣ416/8721111. Subway: Yong/Bloor. The old New York Theatre was stripped to the studs and rebuilt in 2004 to accommodate the indefinite Toronto run of the ever-popular Blue Man Group.

Princess of Wales Theatre 300 King St W, at John St ⓣ416/872-1212. Subway: St Andrew. Built in 1993 to accommodate the helicopter in *Miss Saigon*, and currently the expected site of the world premier of the *Lord of the Rings* musical, this beautiful theatre has an intimate feel despite its 2000 seats. The murals and loge reliefs by artist Frank Stella are an added visual treat.

Royal Alexandra Theatre 260 Yonge St, at Simcoe St ⓣ416/872-1212. Subway: St Andrew. The dowager of Toronto theatres, the graceful, Beaux Arts "Royal Alex", as it's known to locals, was designed in 1906 by architecht John Lyle. Today it puts on everything from classical repertory theatre to exuberant Broadway or West End musicals, such as

Mamma Mia. The dramatically cantilevered balcony ensures clear sightlines from every seat.

St Lawrence Centre for the Arts 27 Front St E, at Yonge St ⓣ416/386-3100. Subway: Union Station. The St Lawrence Centre, home to the Canadian Stage Company, contains two stages: the Bluma Appel Theatre, the facility's main stage, where primarily new works by contemporary artists are shown, and the upstairs, studio-sized Jane Mallett Theatre, which presents experimental and workshop productions and is home to the Toronto Operetta (see p.185).

The East End

Alumnae Theatre 70 Berkeley St, at King St E ⓣ416/962-1948. Streetcar: King (#504). Original productions with low-budget charm has long been the Alumnae Theatre's mandate. Low on frills, high on fringe.

Canadian Stage 26 Berkeley St, at King St E ⓣ416/368-3110. Streetcar:King (#504). In addition to being the second stage of the Canadian Stage Company, which presents its more experimental pieces here, this location often houses avant-garde or workshop performances, and is an excellent place to see young talent.

Lorraine Kisma Young People's Theatre 165 Front St E, at Sherbourne St ⓣ416/862-2222. Streetcar: King (#504). This muscular, Romanesque-style building, which used to be a stable, was saved from the wrecking ball in 1977. The innovative productions shown here are geared towards a young audience, but they're often as intriguing as many of the city's more mainstream offerings (see also Kids' Toronto, p.214).

The Annex

Annex Theatre 730 Bathurst St, at Bloor St W ⓣ416/888-6133. Subway: Bathurst. Home to the Tempest Theatre Company and annexed to the Bathurs Street Theatre in a former parish hall.

Bathurst Street Theatre 736 Bathurst St, at Bloor St W ⓣ416/531-6100. Subway: Bathurst. The accoustics in this more than 500-seat venue (formerly a nineteenth-century church) are excellent, and the performances tend towards the fringe side.

PERFORMING ARTS AND FILM | Theatre

▽ Factory Theatre

🏃 **Factory Theatre 125 Bathurst St, at Bloor St W** ☎ 416/504-9971. **Streetcar: King (#504).** This spot, with its pressed-tin decorative ornaments and seemingly fragile balcony, has a special charm. Since opening in 1970, the Factory has played a leading role in staging new Canadian plays and launching many careers, notably those of playwrights George F. Walker and Adam Pettle; additionally, actors such as R. H. Thompson and Eric Peterson take time from their film and television careers to perform here. Its downstairs sister, the cabaret-like Factory Studio Café, has nurtured a reputation for innovative contemporary theatre.

Poor Alex Theatre 296 Brunswick St, at Boor St W ☎ 416/923-1644. **Subway: Spadina.** The Poor Alex Theatre has been the launching pad for many a career, and hosts the alternative/bohemian endeavours of Mirvish Productions (better known for Broadway brava). As likely to house productions by Albee and Pinter as it is to show original plays by talented unknowns.

Soulpepper Theatre 55 Mill St ☎ 416/203-6264 ⓦ www.soulpepper.ca. **Streetcar: King (#504).** Albert Schultz's electrifying leadership of the young Soulpepper Theatre Company, which performs a classical repertory, has lured leading talents from the likes of the Stratford and the Shaw festivals (see p.117). The Young Centre for the Performing Arts, which opened in fall 2005 in the Distillery District, is the troupe's new home.

Tarragon Theatre 30 Bridgman St, at Howland Ave ☎ 416/531-1827. **Subway: Dupont.** By consistently presenting challenging, innovative performances, the Tarragon, a renovated factory space, has contributed much to Toronto's thriving theatrical community.

Theatre Passe Muraille 16 Ryerson Ave, at Queen St E ☎ 416/504-7529. **Streetcar: Queen (#501).** The unusual configuration of this historical building allows set designers a lot of dramatic possibilities. One of the best venues in the city for challenging, contemporary drama.

Classical music, opera and dance

Thanks to strong moral and fiscal support from a dedicated fanbase, Toronto maintains a diverse programme of **opera**, **dance** and **classical music**. In the summer of 2006 the city's ongoing attempt to build a permanent opera house will have finally paid off: the 2000-seat **Four Seasons Centre for the Performing Arts** (ⓦ www.fourseasonscentre.ca) is scheduled to open as home of the Canadian Opera Company, and will also serve as a performance venue for the National Ballet.

Single adult **ticket prices** for opera, dance and classical music performances range from $35 to $195 for keenly anticipated performances. As with theatre tickets you can take your chances at **T.O. TIX** (see p.180), at the southeast corner of Dundas Square, which sells day-of-show seats at half price. Additionally, *NOW* magazine has listings for smaller music venues, which feature wonderful performers such as the Orpheus Choir (☎ 416/530-4428), the Music Umbrella concerts series (☎ 416/461-6681) – a loose coalition of classical and, increasingly, world musicians who put together small, professional, inexpensive concerts – and free lunchtime recitals, often organ but sometimes choral, given in different churches throughout the city.

Glenn Gould

In the 1970s, anyone passing the Eaton's department store around 9pm on any day of the year might have seen the door unlocked for a distracted-looking figure swaddled in overcoat, scarves, gloves and hat. This character, making his way to a recording studio set up for his exclusive use inside the store, was perhaps the most famous citizen of Toronto and the most charismatic pianist in the world – **Glenn Gould**.

Not the least remarkable thing about Gould was that very few people outside the CBS recording crew would ever hear him play live. In 1964, aged just 32, he retired from the concert platform, partly out of a distaste for the accidental qualities of any live performance, partly out of hatred for the cult of the virtuoso. Yet no pianist ever provided more material for the mythologizers. He possessed a memory so prodigious that none of his acquaintances was ever able to find a piece of music he could not instantly play perfectly, but he loathed much of the standard piano repertoire, dismissing romantic composers such as Chopin, Liszt and Rachmaninoff as little more than showmen. Dauntingly cerebral in his tastes and playing style, he was nonetheless an ardent fan of Barbra Streisand – an esteem that was fully reciprocated – and once wrote an essay titled "In Search of Petula Clark". He lived at night and kept in touch by phoning his friends in the small hours of the morning, talking for so long that his monthly phone bill ran into thousands of dollars. Detesting all blood sports (a category in which he placed concert performances), he would terrorize anglers on Ontario's Lake Simcoe by buzzing them in his motorboat. He travelled everywhere with bags full of medicines and would never allow anyone to shake his hand, yet soaked his arms in almost scalding water before playing to get his circulation going. At the keyboard he sang loudly to himself, swaying back and forth on a creaky little chair made for him by his father – all other pianists sat too high, he insisted. And even in a heatwave he was always dressed as if a blizzard were imminent. To many of his colleagues, Gould's eccentricities were maddening, but what mattered was that nobody could play like Glenn Gould. As one exasperated conductor put it, "the nut's a genius".

Gould's first recording, Bach's *Goldberg Variations*, was released in 1956 and became the best-selling classical record of that year. Soon after, he became the first Western musician to play in the Soviet Union, where his reputation spread so quickly that for his final recital more than a thousand people were allowed to stand in the aisles of the Leningrad hall. On his debut in Berlin, a leading German critic described him as "a young man in a strange sort of trance", whose "technical ability borders on the fabulous". The technique always dazzled, but Gould's fiercely wayward intelligence made his interpretations controversial, as can be gauged from the fact that **Leonard Bernstein**, conducting Gould on one occasion, felt obliged to inform the audience that what they were about to hear was the pianist's responsibility, not his. Most notoriously of all, Gould had a very low opinion of Mozart's abilities, going so far as to record the Mozart sonatas in order to demonstrate that Wolfgang Amadeus died too late rather than too soon. Gould himself **died suddenly** in 1982 at the age of 50 – the age at which he had said he would give up playing the piano entirely.

Gould's **legacy of recordings** is not confined to music. He made a trilogy of radio documentaries on the theme of solitude: *The Quiet in the Land*, about Canada's Mennonites; *The Latecomers*, about the inhabitants of Newfoundland; and *The Idea of North*, for which he taped interviews with people who, like himself, spent much of their time amid Canada's harshest landscapes. Just as Gould's Beethoven, Bach and Mozart sounded like nobody else's, these were documentaries like no others, each a complex weave of voices spliced and overlaid in compositions that are overtly musical in construction. However, Gould's eighty-odd piano recordings are the basis of his enduring popularity, and nearly all of them have been reissued on CD and DVD, spanning Western keyboard music from Orlando Gibbons to Arnold Schoenberg. One of the most poignant is his second version of the *Goldberg*, the last record to be issued before his death.

Glenn Gould Studio 250 Front St W, at John St, Downtown ☎416/205-5555. Streetcar: King (#504). Named for the great pianist and composer, this small, boxy hall in the Canadian Broadcasting Centre is so sprung for sound that enthusiastic performances leave audiences vibrating. The programming is first-rate and generally showcases Canadian talent. A particularly lifelike statue of the studio's namesake sits on a bench outside the door.

Massey Hall 178 Victoria St, at Young & Dundas sts, Downtown ☎416/872-4255. Subway: Dundas. This turn-of-the-century recital hall with great acoustics has hosted a wide variety of performers – everyone from Enrico Caruso and Maria Callas to Jarvis Cocker. The austere architecture is offset by Moorish details, like the fanciful moulding along the balconies.

The Music Gallery Centre for New and Unusual Music 197 John St, at Queen St W, Downtown ☎416/204-1080, ⊛www.musicgallery.org. Streetcar: Queen (#501). Housed in the new, ecclesiastical space in tiny St George the Martyr, the Music Gallery offers one of the most intense, tantalizing performance schedules in the city and is always up for experimentation. A great place to see Toronto originals such as diva Fides Kruker, thrilling pianist Eve Egoyan or the unusual Glass Orchestra, whose musical instruments, as the name suggests, are made entirely of glass. Guest artists come from around the world, and performances are linked with lectures and workshops.

Roy Thompson Hall 60 Simcoe St, at King St W, Downtown ☎416/593-4828. Subway: St Andrew. Roy Thompson Hall is home primarily to the Toronto Symphony Orchestra (☎416/593-4828), though it also hosts the Toronto Mendelssohn Choir (☎416/872-4255) and visiting superstars such as Cecila Bartoli and Midori. The building, finished in 1982 to a design by Arthur Erickson, looks like an upturned café au lait bowl by day, but at night the place is transformed, as the glass-panelled walls glow, casting light over the reflecting ponds and a public square outside. Inside, the circular hall has excellent sightlines, and its acoustics have been recently improved.

Toronto Centre for the Arts 5040 Yonge St, North York ☎416/872-2222. Subway: North York Centre. The classical wing of the Toronto Centre for the Arts, the George Weston Recital Hall, is an acoustically precise performance hall that competes with the Roy Thompson Hall for top-name classical acts.

Trinity-St Paul's Centre 427 Bloor St W, at Spadina Ave, Uptown ☎416/964-9562 or 416/964-6337, ⊛www.tafelmusik.org. Subway: Spadina. Toronto's riveting Tafelmusik Baroque Orchestra, renowned worldwide for historical performances on period instruments, is gliding gracefuly towards its third decade. Under concert master and musical director Jeanne Lamon's leadership, Tafelmusik (German for table music) performs over fifty concerts a year in Toronto.

Opera

Autumn Leaf Performance various venues ☎416/363-1677, ⊛www.autumnleaf.com. This company bills itself as practitioners of the "x-treme art of opera", and goes for the jugular with its sometimes Dadaist sensibilities and daring approach to performance. Productions include the internationally acclaimed *Kafka in Love*, by Erik Hanson, which was staged in the neo-Gothic swimming pool at Hart House in the University of Toronto, and the provocative *Interactive 05*, a series of interactive performances in public spaces around the city.

Canadian Opera Company The Hummingbird Centre, 1 Front St E, Downtown ☎416/363-6671, ⊛www.coc.ca. Canada's national opera troupe, the COC has dazzled international audiences for years with its ambitious productions, devotion to young talent and the musical erudition of its director, Richard Bradshaw. Seats are often scarce, particularly for the eagerly anticipated season premieres, so reserve as far in advance as possible – ticket prices vary widely, from $35 to $175. Rush tickets are only available to seniors and students, and are not released until two hours before a performance. The company is moving to the Four Seasons Centre for the Performing Arts in 2006.

Opera Atelier various venues ☎416/25-3767, ⊛www.operaatelier.com. Offers sumptuous productions of seventeenth- and eighteenth-century operas, dramas and ballets, though only a handul of times a year. Ticket prices range from $45 to $90.

Tapestry Music Theatre 55 Mill St, The Cannery, Studio 315, The Distillery District, Downtown ☎416/537-6066, ⊛www.tapestrynewopera .com. Streetcar: King (#504). This company is dedicated to supporting and producing new operas by Canadian composers, such as *Iron Road* by Chan Ka Nin, about the Chinese migrant labourers who built the Canadian Pacific Railway, and Nic Gotham and Anne-Marie MacDonald's *Nigredo Hotel*, which tells the story of a man forced to spend the night in a creepy roadside motel. Performances are staged in a variety of venues.

Toronto Operetta Jane Malette Theatre, St Lawrence Centre for the Arts, 27 Front St E, at Yonge St, Downtown ☎416/465-2912, ⊛www .torontooperetta.com. Produces meringue-light operettas, including Franz Lehar's confections as well as rousing renditions of Gilbert and Sullivan.

Dance

Harbourfront Centre Theatre 231 Queens Quay W, the waterfront ☎416/973-4000. LRT (from Union Station): Queens Quay. Part of the Harbourfront Centre, this modern theatre hosts dance recitals, as well as the occasional theatrical or musical performance.

National Ballet Company Hummingbird Centre, 1 Front St E, at Yonge St, Downtown ☎3416/45-9595. Subway: Union Station. This company has proven that it is one of the most accomplished corps anywhere, performing classical ballet and contemporary dance with equal artistry. The prima ballerinas, notably Karen Kain and Veronica Tennant, are revered as national treasures. Moving to the Four Seasons Centre for the Performing Arts in 2006.

Premier Dance Theatre 207 Queen's Quay W, the waterfront ☎416/973-4921. LRT (from Union Station): Queens Quay. A beautiful new facility built specifically for dance performances, this space also hosts a number of dramatic events, including those by Toronto's exciting classical repertory troupe, the Soulpepper Theatre Company.

Toronto Dance Theatre 80 Winchester St, at Parlainment St, Downtown ☎416/967-1365. Streetcar: Carlton (#506). In a city infamous for its repressive "Sunday Blue Laws" – which, among other things, forbade theatrical performances on Sunday – it is fitting irony that this, like many of Toronto's contemporary theatres, is housed in a former church. Tucked deep in the heart of the historic Cabbagetown neighbourhood, the Toronto Dance Theatre and its affiliated school offer daring, original productions.

Film

First-run cinemas in Toronto range from multiplex shoeboxes (invented by infamous Torontonian Garth Drabinsky) to old-fashioned picture palaces – although, as elsewhere, the latter are regrettably dwindling in number.

Most of the city's **second-run or repertory cinemas** are operated under the umbrella of the Festival Group, a coalition of independent theatres that screen film favourites and whatever else might strike its members' fancy. Six-month memberships cost $3 (children and seniors are de facto members), so if

Moviemaking in Toronto

Over the last three decades, filmmaking, animation and television production in Toronto has developed into a billion-dollar industry. Apart from the obvious fact that the Canadian dollar gives an advantage to producers working in US currency, few cities have such a diversity of landscape and architecture to use as a backdrop. Of equal significance is Toronto's status as a theatre town: it has a large pool of talented artists to draw on for costumes, wigs, sets and lighting, plus there is an abundance of classically trained actors to fill various roles. Add to these resources a Canadian genius for film animation and high-grade post-production facilities, and it's no wonder that Toronto is a filmmaking centre of international stature.

you plan on seeing two or more Festival Group movies, there's really no reason not to join. After that, adult admission to a film for members is $6 (as opposed to $8 for non-members). Matinees and Tuesdays are $4 for members. For more information, check their website at ⓦwww.festivalcinemas.com.

First-run cinemas

Beach Cinemas 1651 Queen St E, The Beaches ☎416/646-0444. Streetcar: Queen (#501). A plump suburban multiplex serving the growing number of young families in this East End neighbourhood.

Canada Square 2200 Yonge St, at Eglinton Ave W, Uptown ☎416/646-0444. Subway: Eglington. A sprawling thirteen-screen cineplex offering a mix of foreign, independent and mainstream films.

Carlton 20 Carlton St, at Yonge St, Uptown ☎416/598-2309. Subway: College. When Garth Drabinsky's Cineplex chain muscled in on the Toronto scene, a number of arthouse cinemas closed. To compensate for this, Drabinsky set aside the Carlton to show first-run art films, and its eleven screens are still doing just that. The café and espresso bar offer nice alternatives from standard concessions fare, although that too is available.

Cumberland 4 159 Cumberland St, Uptown ☎416/646-0444. Subway: Bay. Contrary to its name, this multiplex actually has five screens. Located in the heart of Yorkville, this Uptown version of the Carlton caters to arthouse film fans. Larger screens and more leg room make for more comfortable viewing than at the Carlton, however.

Dock's Lakeview Drive-in 11 Polson St, the waterfront ☎416/461-3625. If you have a car and crave that quintessential North American experience of the drive-in movie, the Dock's has double bills nightly at dusk, as long as there's not snow.

Paramount 259 Richmond St W, Downtown ☎416/368-5600. Streetcar: Queen (#501). Perfect venue for filmgoers who want to feel like extras in *Blade Runner*. Half the spectacle is in the theatre itself, with a mammoth pixel-board cube showing film clips to the club-hoppers outside, an almost verticle ride up the escalator to the cinemas and, of course, a sound system that will blast you out of your seat. The complex also houses an IMAX theatre.

Rainbow Market Square 80 Front St E, at Church St, Downtown ☎416/494-9371. Subway:

Union. Another Downtown multiplex; this one is close to lots of restaurants and a few bars for after-film meals and discussions.

Regent 551 Mount Pleasant St, at Davisville Ave, Uptown ☎416/480-9884. Subway: Davisville. Wonderful single-screen Art Deco cinema with a great chrome box office and illuminated marquee. Features mainstream fare.

Silvercity Yonge 2300 Yonge St, Uptown ☎416/544-1236. Subway: Eglinton. Aimed squarely at the youth market – with dazzling banks of video games and a cornucopia of junkfood – this premium-priced movie venue attempts to be an entertainment complex unto itself.

Varsity 55 Bloor St W, at Belmuto St, Uptown ☎416/961-6303. Subway: Yonge-Bloor. A recent expansion has turned this two-screener into an eleven-cinema behemoth, replete with displays of Hollywood costumes, costly full-service amenities (drinks and snacks delivered to your seat) VIP screening rooms and regular cinemas with good sightlines, fancy sound systems and deep, comfortable seats.

Independent and repertory cinemas

Al Green Theatre 750 Spadina Ave, at Bloor St W, Uptown ☎416/924-6211. Subway: Spadina. Housed in the Miles Nadal Jewish Community Centre, this little theatre has an incredibly ambitious agenda. The Jewish Film Festival, Toronto Lesbian and Gay Film and Video Festival, Latin Media Festival, Worldwide Short Film Festival, and many more all have screenings here. Between festivals the menu is strictly foreign and art films, sometimes with director nights or discussion forums.

Bloor Cinema 506 Bloor St W, at Bathurst St, Uptown ☎416/516-2330. Subway: Bathurst. Though this cinema won't win any beauty contests, it's a great place to view films. Frequently plays host to the numerous film festivals in Toronto.

Cineforum 463 Bathurst St, at College St, Uptown ☎416/603-6643. Streetcar: Bathurst or College (#506). An independent among independents, Cineforum is indispensible to

Film festivals

At any given point in the year, someone is sure to be holding a **film festival** in Toronto, whether it's the Latin Media Festival, the Worldwide Short Film Festival, the Jewish Film Festival, or the Toronto Lesbian and Gay Film and Video Festival. The most famous of the group is the Toronto International Film Festival (TIFF); ☎416/968-FILM, ✆www.e.bell.ca/filmfest/2005 or ✆www.tiffg.ca. Many regular TIFF attendees are people who plan their holidays around the event, buying passes or books of tickets in advance, which is a somewhat more economical method. There are a variety of plans to choose from, but, because of the festival's popularity and prestige, bargains are hard to find. For more information, see p.187.

film students and buffs who want to catch up on the history of film without resorting to cropped video and DVDs.

Cinematheque Jackman Hall, Art Gallery of Ontario, 317 Dundas St W, at McCaul St, Downtown ☎416/968-FILM. **Streetcar: Dundas #505.** Cinematheque is a year-round extension of the Toronto International Film Festival. The senior programmer, James Quandt, is so respected that the French awarded him a Chevalier des Arts and Lettres and recently the Japan Foundation awarded him a Special Prize for Arts and Culture. The quality of prints he finds are beyond compare, and the retrospectives on the world's great directors are particularly notable.

The Fox 2236 Queen St E, The Beaches ☎416/691-7330. **Streetcar: Carlton (#506).** This former vaudeville theatre, mentioned several times in Michael Ondaatje's *In the Skin of the Lion*, is an alternative to its multiplex cousin, Beach Cinemas, up the road. There's no glitzy marquee and the popcorn is best avoided – just comfortable seats and a good selection of films.

Kingsway Theatre 3030 Bloor St W, Royal Park ☎416/236-1411. **Subway: Royal York.** This place epitomizes the small theatre experience from the movie-house heyday,

before the chains and multiplex theatres moved in.

Ontario Place Cinesphere 955 Lakeshore Rd W, at Remembrance Drive ☎416/314-9900. **Streetcar: Harbourfront #509 or free shuttle (May–Sept) from Union Station.** Located inside Ontario Place and open year-round, the world's first IMAX theatre, Cinesphere, plays both 35mm and IMAX films on a massive screen. Admission is separate from admission to Ontario Place.

Paradise Cinema 1006 Bloor St W, at Ossington Ave, Uptown ☎416/537-7040. **Subway: Ossington.** This neighbourhood cinema, saved and renovated by the Festival Group, tends toward edgy programming and is a draw for cineastes from across the city.

Revue Cinema 400 Roncesvalles Ave, at Marmaduke Rd, High Park ☎416/531-9959. **Subway: Dundas West.** Well worth the trip, this cinema has long had a reputation for some of the finest programming outside of the festival circuit.

The Royal 608 College St, at Clinton St, Uptown ☎416/516-4845. **Streetcar: Carlton (#506).** Situated in the humming midst of Little Italy, The Royal is one of the most attractive cinemas in Toronto, with its lovingly restored original Art Deco interior and 40-foot silver screen.

⑪

PERFORMING ARTS AND FILM | Film

Gay Toronto

Over the past 25 years, Toronto's relationship with gays and lesbians has evolved from blunt intolerance to enthusiastic celebration. In addition to hosting one of the largest Pride events in the world, the lesbian and gay community here has significant economic, political and social clout, and Toronto now boasts the largest "out" population of any city in Canada.

The neighbourhood at the centre of the activity – known commonly as the Gay Village – is centred on the intersection of Church and Wellesley streets, about one block east of Yonge Street. Gay establishments are not exclusive to this neighbourhood (the influx of galleries on West Queen West has generated a nascent scene in the Parkdale area), but it is where the lion's share of lesbian/gay/bisexual/transgendered (LGBT) community services, bars, clubs and restaurants are located. As is the case in many cities, the gay scene is far more conspicuous than its lesbian counterpart, though this neighbourhood is nothing if not inclusive. Even if the bars seem to be specifically for gay men, lesbian and bisexual women should call for information on dyke nights, women-only events and mixed theme nights.

One of the more interesting developments over the past decade has been the addition of a family element to the neighbourhood. For those who remember the monogenerational lesbian and gay communities of decades past, it may be a welcome change to see supportive parents of LGBT children, along with out parents and their children, sort through the minutiae of day-to-day life in a tolerant, open environment. The passage of Bill C-38, the so-called same-sex legislation (see box, p.189), will undoubtedly contribute to this evolution. There is also strong recognition of transsexual and transgendered people, whose presence in the LGBT community is growing.

Throughout the city, look for the free gay weeklies *FAB* (Ⓦwww.fabmagazine .ca) and *Xtra!*, distributed in newsboxes and in many Downtown bars and restaurants. Several other websites cater to the LGBT community: Ⓦwww.gaycanada .com has extensive listings of what's going on in Toronto; Ⓦwww.outintoronto .com has a basic overview of the gay community; and Ⓦwww.gaytoronto.com and Ⓦwww.gayguidetoronto.com are excellent online resources. The Canadian Lesbian and Gay Archives website, Ⓦwww.clga.ca/archives, focuses primarily on gay rights and advocacy.

Contacts

519 Community Centre 519 Church St, at Wellesley St, Uptown ☎416/392-6874, Ⓦwww .the519.org. Subway: Wellesley. Once a private club, this building in the heart of the gay quarter is now the hub for Toronto's gay outreach and awareness programmes. Over

In 1971, Toronto's first Gay Pride celebration was held at Hanlan's Point in the Toronto Islands – a paltry one-hundred people showed up. Today the event stretches over an entire week at the end of June, and attracts an annual attendance of over 800,000 people. Festivities promoting gay awareness and honouring gay culture culminate with the Gay Pride Parade, which begins at the intersection of Church and Wellesley streets and trucks down Yonge Street before terminating at Church Street. To show solidarity with Toronto's gay population, the mayor rides at the front of the parade, and the premier of Ontario writes warm letters of support in publications like *Canada's Gay Guide*, which is available in bookstores throughout the city.

three-hundred groups, mostly part of the LGBT community, utilize this space. **Pride Committee of Toronto 65 Wellesley St E, Suite 304, Uptown** ☎**416/927-7433,** ⓦ**www.torontopride.com. Subway: Wellesley.**

This is mission control for the annual Gay Pride celebration, an organizational feat that requires eleven months of planning and fund-raising events. A great place to find out about upcoming events in the LGBT community.

Accommodation

Maps, with the accommodations below keyed to them, can be found in the back of the book. All prices here are in Canadian dollars and reflect the cost of a standard double room in high season.

Banting House 73 Homewood Ave, at Wellesley St, Uptown ☎**416/924-1458,** ⓦ**www .bantinghouse.com. Subway: Wellesley.** A

sensitively restored Edwardian house with cosy furnishings and nine guest rooms that have either en-suite or shared

△ Gay Pride Parade

baths. Buffet-style continental breakfast is included. $100.

The Bearfoot Inn 30A Dundonald St, at Church St, Uptown ☎416/922-1658 or 1-888/871-BEAR, ⊛www.bearfootinn.com. Subway: Wellesley. All rooms to this central bear boy inn have en-suite three-piece baths, mini fridges, TVs and safes. Pets are welcome and clothing is optional. "Dens" start at $115.

Cawthra Square Bed & Breakfast Inns 10 Cawthra Square, 512-514 Jarvis St, at Wellesley St, Uptown ☎416/966-3074 or 1-800/259-5474, ⊛www.cawthrasquare.com. Subway: Wellesley. These two very well-run, fabulously furnished Victorian mansions-turned-B&Bs are in the heart of the Gay Village. Amenities include PC access, fax, voicemail and afternoon tea. Choose from a standard room with a semi-private bath ($119–$170) or a deluxe en-suite queen ($199–$269). Both properties are very popular for weddings and honeymoons, so advance bookings are suggested.

Dundonald House 35 Dundonald St, at Church St, Uptown ☎416/961-2120 or 800/260-7227, ⊛www.dundonaldhouse.com. Subway: Wellesley. Five rooms, only one en suite, on a quiet street just north of the Church-Wellesley hubbub. Amenities include an exercise room and sauna and hot or cold breakfasts. $100.

Two Aberdeen 2 Aberdeen Ave, near Ontario & Carlton sts, Uptown ☎416/944-1426, ⊛www.twoaberdeen.com. Streetcar: Carlton/College (#506). Two bedrooms, an en-suite room that occupies the entire third floor and a fully contained, 850 sq ft basement apartment with weekly maid service provide a range of options for gay and lesbian visitors in a Cabbagetown Victorian. $97.

Victoria's Mansion 68 Gloucester St, at Church St, Uptown ☎416/921-4625. Subway: Wellesley. The rainbow flag flies proudly over this Victorian mansion, whose rooms are equipped with fridges, microwaves and coffeemakers. Guests are frequently repeat visitors, giving this establishment a genuine warmth and homeliness. Singles start at $90.

Bars, clubs and restaurants

52 Inc 394 College St, at Bathurst St, Uptown ☎416/960-0334. Streetcar: College/Carlton (#506). This sophisticated *boite* draws a mixed crowd until later in the evening, when the Saphic patrons outnumber the straight ones.

5ive 5 St Joseph St, Uptown ☎416/964-8685. Subway: Wellesley. Sleek and minimalist, this is a great place for smart drinks and getting to know someone.

Bar 501 501 Church St, at Wellesley St, Uptown ☎416/944-3272, ⊛www.bar501.com. Subway: Wellesley. Famed for its Sunday evening "Window Show" drag promenade and the ever popular "Hags on Heels" review, *Bar 501* has gone beyond being a neighbourhood institution and has earned its place as a Toronto icon.

Black Eagle 459 Church St, at Carlton St, Uptown ☎416/413-1219, ⊛www.blackeagletoronto .com. Subway: Wellesley. A popular leather and denim cruise spot, with multiple bars and a rooftop patio where you can cool off when things get too hot. The strict fetish dress code is in effect on Fridays and Saturdays, with an emphasis on leather. Rough Trade Tuesdays is a well-attended event.

Byzantium 499 Church St, at Wellesley St, Uptown ☎416/922-3859. Subway: Wellesley. Equal parts martini bar and restaurant, this stylish spot comprises an extremely long, narrow space that promotes mixing and mingling.

Crews/Tango & The Zone 508 Church St, Uptown ☎416/972-1662, ⊛www.crews-tango .com. Subway: Wellesley. A trio of bars with something for everyone: *Crews* hosts drag kings and queens, *Tango* has taken over the late, lamented *Pope Joan*'s role as Toronto's premier lesbian bar, and *The Zone* is a mellow little cabaret with live torch singers.

Fly Nightclub 8 Gloucester St, Uptown ☎416/410-5426, ⊛www.flynightclub.com. Subway: Wellesley. Recognizable to fans of the *Queer as Folk* TV programme, *Fly* is the neighbourhood's – and the city's – number one gay dance club. Special events are held on Fridays, while the party on Saturday lasts until 7.00am Sunday morning.

Hair of the Dog 425 Church St, at Alexander St, Uptown ☎416/964-2708. Subway: Wellesley. A popular neighbourhood watering hole, *Hair of the Dog* is a two-storey bar and restaurant that leans toward the upscale

Same-sex marriage

Same-sex couples in Ontario have enjoyed the right to marry since June 10, 2003, when the Ontario Supreme Court ruled their exclusion from the Marriage Act was unconstitutional under Canada's Charter of Rights and Freedoms. Two hours after that ruling, Michael Stark and Michael Leshner, a crown attorney, were married in a civil ceremony in Toronto by an Ontario Supreme Court judge. The following day, Toronto became wedding central for same-sex couples across North America. On July 21, 2005, Supreme Court Chief Justice Beverly McLachlin signed into law Bill C-38, which legalizes same-sex marriages across all of Canada.

Gay couples wishing to marry in Toronto can obtain a marriage licence from any municipal office for $110. A marriage application form must be signed by both parties and submitted in person along with a current passport or original birth certificate and one piece of photo ID (drivers licence, health card, etc) for each. Couples are not required to have residency, citizenship, blood tests or medical tests. If you need an interpreter, clergy or anything extra, you must supply it yourself. If a previous marriage was dissolved or annulled in Canada, you must supply the original documents or court certified copies; if the divorce was granted outside Canada, extra paperwork is involved. For more information, check out the following websites:
Ⓦ www.city.Toronto.on.ca,
Ⓦ www.mcctoronto.com,
Ⓦ www.samesexmarriage.ca.

side. A nice place to go on a hand-holding date.

Lo'la 7 Maitland St, at Yonge St, Uptown. Subway: Wellesley. This perfect after-hours spot has surprisingly intimate corners, despite its appearance as a minimalist cube. Since the name has changed a number of times, this place doesn't even bother to get a phone number anymore.

lüb lounge 487 Church St, at Wellesley St, Uptown ☏416/323-1489, Ⓦ wwww.lub.ca. Streetcar: Carlton/College (#506); Subway: Wellesley. Downstairs is a pared-down martini lounge that serves light meals and upstairs is a den with a fireplace, which is pleasantly intimate on weekdays but can get boisterous on weekends.

O'Grady's 518 Church St, at Maitland St, Uptown ☏416/323-2822. Subway: Wellesley; Streetcar: Carlton/College (#506). Though it's no longer called *Wild Oscar's*, you can still enjoy burgers and beers on the great patio all summer long, and the Victorian mansion interior is still great for snuggling in winter. Yeah!

Pegasus on Church 491 Church St, at Wellesley St, Uptown ☏416/927-8832, Ⓦ www .pegasusonchurch.com. Subway: Wellesley. Billiards and pool tables, darts and satellite TV give the distinct impression of your average gay sports bar. A tad cruisey, but that's the point.

Red Spot 559 Church St, Uptown ☏416/967-7768. Subway: Wellesley. *Red Spot* features live music, DJs and comedy nights, and is popoular with the younger LGBT set.

Remington's Men of Steel 379 Yonge St, at Gerrard St, Uptown ☏416/977-2160. Subway: Dundas. A cheesy gay strip bar that took over this spot from a cheesy straight strip bar. Predictably garish.

Tallulah's Cabaret 12 Alexander St, Uptown ☏416/975-8555. Subway: Wellesley. Attached to Buddies in Bad Times' Alexander Street Theatre, this very popular bar/cabaret space hosts a youngish gay and lesbian crowd, in addition to straight theatre-lovers.

🏃 **Woody's & Sailor 467 Church St, Uptown ☏416/972-0887. Subway: Wellesley.** This five-bar locale, which reputedly sells more beer than any other watering hole in the city, has an excellent selection of microbrews and draught ales, daily specials and a popular weekend brunch – not that anyone comes here for the food. There's a men's bare-chest competition at midnight on Thursdays, and a Sunday tea dance with drag performers, singers and outlandish themes.

🏃 **Zelda's Bar and Restaurant 542 Church St, at Maitland St, Uptown ☏416/922-2526, Ⓦ www.zeldas.ca. Subway: Wellesley.** *Zelda's* patio is the place to be for a ringside seat during the Gay Pride celebrations. The food is good in general, and the Sunday brunch in particular is fabulous. That goes doubles for the bar. A party room adds to the general sense of excitement. On occasion, Zelda herself whooshes in to hold court. **Zipperz/Cellblock 72 Carlton St, Uptown** ☎416/921-0066. Streetcar: Carlton/ College **(#506).** Across the street from Maple Leaf Gardens, Toronto's former temple to its hockey team, the exterior here looks like a sports bar for beer-swilling mullet-heads. Fortunately, it's not: downstairs, *Zipperz* is a rather good piano and dance bar for an out clientele, and the *Cellblock*, upstairs, is a dance club.

Theatre

Gay theatre in Toronto makes its home at the 12 Alexander Street Theatre (see p.180), where the Buddies in Bad Times company performs a repertoire of original works showcasing queer–culture. Prized by virtually all Toronto theatregoers, Buddies in Bad Times also puts on the annual Rhubarb! Festival (see p.217).

Shops

Come as You Are 701 Queen St W, at Manning Ave, Downtown ☎416/504-7934. Streetcar: Queen (# 501). A wonderfully matter-of-fact sex-toy shop and bookstore that caters primarily, though not exclusively, to lesbians and bisexual women.

Glad Day Bookstore 598A Yonge St, at Wellesley St, Uptown ☎416/961-4161. Subway: Wellesley. Information central for the LGBT community for over two decades, this bookstore was once the only overt sign that a gay community existed in Toronto. **He & She Clothing Gallery 263 Queen St E, at Sherborne St, Downtown** ☎416/594-0171.

Streetcar: Queen (#501). For work or play, the exuberantly sleazy outfits here are deliberately provocative and loads of fun. There's a full range of stiletto pumps in sizes big enough to accommodate both sexes. **Priape 465 Church St, at Maitland, Uptown** ☎416/586-9914 ⓦwww.priape.com. Subway: Wellesley. Wittily described as Toronto's "gay insight centre", this is more than a boy-toy emporium: books, magazines, costumes and a knowledgeable staff guide customers towards the realizations of their secret and not-so-secret desires.

Gay baths and spas

Cellar 78 Wellesley St E, at Church St, Uptown ☎416/944-3779. Subway: Wellesley. Open 24 hours. Use the back entrance. **Club Toronto 231 Mutual St, at Carlton St, Uptown** ☎416/977-4629, ⓦwww.clubtoronto.com. Streetcar: Carlton/College (#506). Cells, slings, party halls and private rooms, to say nothing of the lounge, pool and sauna. Open 24 hours. **Spa Excess 105 Carlton St, Uptown** ☎416/260-2363, ⓦwww.spaexcess.com. Streetcar: Carlton

(#504). Four floors of a safe environment for casual encounters. **Steamworks 540 Church St, 2nd fl, at Wellesley St, Uptown** ☎416/925-1571, ⓦwww .steamworks.ca. Subway: Wellesley. The proud boast here is that Steamworks is "Toronto's largest legal cruise and play space", with features like a 24-hour gym, a multi-channel XXX digital video system and live DJs every week. Anonymity is assured with a key deposit system; membership optional.

Shops and galleries

Whether you're after computers or couture, antiques or the avant-garde, Toronto – Canada's biggest and most cosmopolitan city – is a terrific place for shopping. **Business hours** are fairly consistent: most shops are open seven days a week from 10am to 7pm, with somewhat longer hours on Thursday and Friday and somewhat shorter hours on Saturday and Sunday. One exception to this rule is the large Downtown music stores, which stay open until 10 pm on weekdays and until midnight on Friday and Saturday.

Toronto is composed of numerous **shopping districts**. The intersection at Yonge and Dundas is a magnet for youth, and teems with teenagers who flock here from the suburbs and beyond. With the Eaton Centre stretching a full city block to the southwest, The Gap's flagship store to the north, and most of the city's major music shops to the east, anything a young person could want is within easy reach.

Trekking north from here – on Yonge, to Bloor Street West – takes you to the cusp of **Yorkville**, a nest of streets that includes Cumberland Avenue, Yorkville Avenue and Scollard Street. Although Yorkville was Toronto's Flower-Power central during the 1960s, today the area is filled with costly boutiques and a large percentage of Toronto's rich and famous. Even if you can't afford to buy anything here, it still makes for a pleasant stroll.

Back down on the lower west side of the city, the expanse of **Queen Street West** between University and Bathurst is an eclectic jumble of shops, galleries and street-side stands. This used to be the place for trend-setting designer duds, though an incursion of chain stores is slowly gentrifying the area. Now, the best of the independent shopping scene has been pushed west of Spadina into an area known as **West Queen West**, which runs to Gladstone. In addition to having the flea market ambience Queen Street West used to possess, this stretch has become known for its galleries, which feature up-and-coming artists and photographers.

Shopping categories

On a final note, visitors from outside Canada are entitled to claim a **refund** of the seven percent federal Goods and Service Tax (GST) on accumulated purchases of a minimum of $200, as long as each receipt is for at least $50 (before tax) and that the goods were taken out of Canada within sixty days of purchase. Mail your receipts and a GST Refund form, which is readily available in hotels, major stores, airports or Ontario Travel Information Centres, to the Summerside address on the form. If you're Canadian, but not an Ontario resident, you can apply for a refund on the eight percent Ontario Sales Tax – but the accumulated purchases must add up to a minimum of $625, and the form isn't as commonly found as the GST form. Call ☎1–800/263–7965 and ask for one to be mailed to you.

Antiques and vintage and modern furniture

507 Antiques 50 Carroll St, at Queen St E, Downtown ☎416/462-9989. Streetcar: Queen (#501). A mammoth cache of architectural salvage, large wrought-iron pieces and garden statuary. Most of the stock isn't particularly portable, but there are rooms of smaller furniture at the back and downstairs in a cavernous basement. Little decorative accessories are scattered throughout.

Absolutely Inc 1132 Yonge St, at MacPherson Ave, Uptown ☎416/324-8351 and 1236 Yonge St at Walker Ave, Uptown ☎415/922-6784. Subway: Summerhill. Stacks of wonderful finds are piled high along the walls and in every possible nook and cranny. Huge sea sponges perch atop delicate Victorian pedestals, antique hat forms adorn Georgian desks and huge *belle époque* gilt mirrors reflect everything, doubling the sense of wondrous clutter.

L'Atelier 1224 Yonge St, at Alcorn Ave, Uptown ☎416/966-0200. Subway: Summerhill. A series of rooms, each filled with treasures, give way to one another. Specializes in French Deco furniture and decorative objects with a somewhat masculine flair.

Horsefeathers 1212 Yonge St, at Shaftsbury Ave, Uptown ☎416/934-1771. Subway: Summerhill. A well laid-out jumble of nineteenth- and twentieth-century pieces that are tasteful but not stultifying; prices can be bracing but quality is never in doubt. Offers in-store upholstery service.

The Paisley Shoppe 77 Yorkville Ave, at Bellaire St, Uptown ☎416/923-5830. Subway: Bay. Housed in the last of Yorkville's Regency cottages, this Toronto institution specializes in furniture, decorative accessories and tableware items from the eighteenth and nineteenth centuries.

Phil'z 20th Century Design 792 Queen St E, near Broadview Ave, Uptown ☎416/461-9913. Streetcar: Queen (#501). Carries surrealist pieces remade by the original manufacturers, such as an exquisite Merit Oppenheim gilt consul with chicken legs. Contemporary masters like Gehry and Jensen can also be spotted.

P.S. Wilde Antiques 86 Parliament St, at King St E, Downtown ☎416/368-8128 Streetcar: King (#504). A large space in a Victorian-era warehouse provides an excellent stage for some fine antiques and a few real bargains. Massive nineteenth-century Italian pieces are a welcome relief from dainty Directoire repros.

Putti Fine Furnishings 1104 Yonge St, at Roxborough St W, Uptown ☎416/972-7652. Subway: Rosedale. Beautiful old and new items in this store include everything from antique boudoir tables and Venetian glass mirrors to Limoge pill boxes and fine writing paper; both the Christmas tree ornaments and a recent garden collection are practically irresistible. Putti is the sole North American representative for several French and Italian cosmetic and perfume lines, which are arrayed in an ultra feminine apothecary.

Queen West Antique Centre 1605 Queen St W, at Roncesvalles Ave, Downtown ☎416/588-2212 Streetcar: Queen (#501). An exceptional boon for knowledgeable bargain hunters searching for everything from Victoriana, Art Nouveau and Deco to Danish modern. Why buy an Eames knock-off uptown when you may find the real thing here for half the price?

Toronto Antique Centre 276 King St W, at Duncan St, Downtown ☎416/345-9941 ⓦ www.torontoantiquectr.com. Streetcar: King

(#504); **Subway: St Andrew.** More than 25 antique dealers, each specializing in a different niche, migrated north from the former Harbourfront Antique Market and settled under one ample roof. Great for browsing before or after a play or concert.

Books

Toronto is a highly literate city. It hosts one of the world's largest literary festival (see p.220), has a year-round authors' reading series at the waterfront, and is home to a large population of authors. Reflecting this bibliophilic disposition are a number of excellent bookstores, both specialist and general.

New

Bookcity 348 Danforth Ave, at Chester Ave, Uptown ☎416/469-9997. **Subway: Chester and 3 other locations around the city.** A solid neighbourhood bookstore with a good range of new-release literature, magazines and children's selections. If you can't find what you're looking for, first-rate staff will make special orders.

Indigo Books, Music & Café 55 Bloor St W, at Bay St, Uptown ☎416/925-3536; also 110 Bloor St W, Uptown ☎416/925-3536 and other locations, ⊛www.indigo.ca. **Subway: Bay.** This Canadian chain of large bookstores decks out its many locations in bleached wood and buffed aluminum. Has the *de rigeur* cafés, comfy seating areas and CD, software and gift

▽ Nicholas Hoare

Nicholas Hoare 45 Front St E, at Church St, Downtown ☎416/777-2665. **Subway: Union Station.** A beautifully appointed store replete with Gothic Folly flourishes, this bibliophile refuge provides comfy chairs and sofas in front of a working fireplace. Their large selection runs the gamut, but the collection of books on all aspects of design is particularly impressive.

sections. High marks for its children's book selection and its championship of Canadian authors.

Pages 265 Queen St W, at John St, Downtown ☎416/598-1447. **Streetcar: Queen (#501).** For almost two decades, Pages has been the bookstore of choice for the sophisticated reader with alternative tastes. The stock is incontestably the edgiest, most comprehensive collection of contemporary literature and art and social criticism in town. There are also good travel, film, music, art and architecture sections, as well as an extensive range of magazines and small-press publications

This Ain't the Rosedale Library 483 Church St, at Maitland St, Uptown ☎416/929-9912. **Subway: Wellesley.** A funky neighbourhood bookstore offering lots of magazines, contemporary literature and an excellent resource/research section with an emphasis on gay and lesbian culture. Features an excellent children's section and some great bargains.

World's Biggest Bookstore 20 Edward St, at Yonge St, Uptown ☎416/977-7009. **Subway: Dundas.** With over150,000 titles, it's easy to spend the better part of a day combing through this barn of a bookstore.

Used and antiquarian

Acadia Bookstore 232 Queen St E, at Jarvis St, Downtown ☎416/364-7638. **Streetcar: Queen (#501).** The neighbourhood is a tad scary, but you'll find high-quality antiquarian books and prints at really low prices here. Other dealers shop for stock at Acadia, and the owner appreciates a knowledgeable customer.

D & E Lake 237 King St E, at Jarvis St, Downtown ☎416/863-9930. **Streetcar: King (#504).** This Dickensian brick building with paned windows and creaky floors is what an antiquarian bookstore and print gallery should look like. The wide selection, which is often a collector's first stop, includes military, art, architecture and medical books, all in excellent condition.

Eliot's Bookstore 584 Yonge St, at Wellesley St, Uptown ☎416/925-0268. Subway: Wellesley. Contains a good general and scholastic collection, and its used magazine selection is particularly strong on the arts and music.

Bakka Phoenix Science Fiction Books 697 Yonge St, at Wellesley St, Uptown ☎416/963-9993 ⊛www.baakkaphoenixbooks.com. Subway: Wellesley. Offers a huge selection of science fiction, fantasy and speculative fiction, plus a solid representation of horror. In its more than thirty years of business, Bakka has nourished its share of authors: Tanya Huff, Robert J. Sawyer and Michelle Sagara West all made change here while penning their novels.

Ballenford Books on Architecture 600 Markham St, at Bloor St W, Uptown ☎416/588-0800, ⊛www.ballenford.com. Subway: Bathurst. For over twenty-five years, owners Susan Ford and Barbara Ballentine have been supplying professionals and enthusiasts with beautiful and frequently rare books about all things architectural.

The Beguiling 601 Markham St, Uptown ☎416/533-9168. Subway: Bathurst. Against all odds, this comprehensive collection of 'zines, illustrated novels and comics (both underground and mainstream) continues to thrive, with some quirky postcards and ephemera thrown in.

The Cookbook Store 850 Yonge St, at Bloor St, Uptown ☎416/920-2665, ⊛www.cook-book .com. Both celebrity chefs and first-timers learning to boil eggs stop by for advice, in-store demonstrations and, of course, the array of cookbooks.

David Mirvish Books on Art 596 Markham St, at Bathurst St, Uptown ☎416/531-9975. Subway: Bathurst. This browser-friendly store has terrifc bargains and exceptional sections on contemporary and Canadian art. A striking, fifty-foot painting by American artist Frank Stella, *Damascus Stretch Variation*, adorns the store's back wall.

TheatreBooks 11 St Thomas St, at Bloor St W Uptown ☎416/922-7175, ⊛www.theatrebooks .com. Subway: Bay. An excellent resource centre for books on the performing arts (theatre, film, opera, dance and media), plus there's a beautiful shop. Housed on a chic little street off Bloor West's Golden Mile in a Victorian brick house.

Toronto Women's Bookstore 73 Harbord St, at Spadina Ave, Uptown ☎416/922-8744, ⊛www .womensbookstore.com. Streetcar: Spadina (#510). Situated comfortably in a Victorian row house, this hub of Toronto feminist literature and activism also has a good selection of novelists and poets who aren't all in the FemLit category.

Clothing

Boutique Le Trou 940 Queen St W, at Shaw St, Downtown ☎416/516-7122. Streetcar: Queen (#501). The only collections featured in this prêt-a-porter shop are Canadian, which is both refreshing for those who wear their patriotic heart on their sleeve and exciting for those interested in discovering a store full of new talent.

Comrages 654 Queen St W, at Palmerston Ave, Downtown ☎416/360-7249. Streetcar: Queen (#501). Local design lionesses Judy Cornish and Joyce Gunhouse are famed for their ongoing interpretations of the little dress, though their collections have expanded to include evening and work wear – the latter featuring garments that are perfect for stylish travel.

Fresh Collective 692 Queen St W, at Euclid Ave, Downtown ☎416/594-1313. Streetcar: Queen (#501). Designer Laura Jean Bernhardson has taken the retail plunge, and in doing so brought in fifteen aspiring Toronto designers under her roof, notably Marmalade and Snowflake. The house label is called Fresh Baked Goods.

Hoax Couture Studio Boutique 163 Spadina Ave, 3rd fl, at Queen St W, Downtown ☎416/597-8264. Streetcar: Queen (#501). Partners Chris Tyrell and Jim Searle have been producing innovative, beautifully crafted eveningwear for men and women for years. The Hoax bustier remains a must for glamour gals, while edgy bridegrooms rely on the duo to take them beyond boring tuxedos for their big day. Lately, retail has been set aside in favour of made-to-measure garments, and if you want something unique, they will sit down with pencil and paper and design something (remarkably affordable) for you. **LuluLemon Athletica 130 Bloor St W ☎416/964-9544; also two other locations. Subway: Bay (Bay exit).** Vancouver original LuluLemon was an instant hit when it stretched into town a few years ago. Unlike other exercise wear, LuluLemon's Yoga pants, warm-ups, hoodies, fleeces and T-shirts have great fits and come in a wide range of colours. Comparable to the big chains in terms of price, but light years ahead regarding quality and design.

Pam Chorley Fashion Crimes 322 Queen St W, at Spadina Ave, Downtown ☎416/592-9001. Streetcar: Queen (#501). This store's new digs is one of designer Pam Chorley's most lovely creations, which is saying a lot! Her romantic dresses – with their exclusive fabrics and exceptional attention to detail – have been described as the most beautiful in Toronto. The Martini Dress, hugely popular among the prom set, is currently her signature silhouette. There is also a full range of idiosyncratic accessories, shoes and fabulous hats.

Y5 5 Yorkville Ave, at Yonge St, Uptown ☎416/920-9173. Subway: Yonge/Bloor. Visionary designer Ula Zukowska continues to hold her own in Yorkville, demonstrating that fans of her inspirational approach to knits, textiles, form and cut are loyal and growing in number. Be prepared to buy if something fits and you want it: items move fast and space is at a premium.

Designer/haute couture

Chanel Boutique 131 Bloor St W, at Bay St, Uptown ☎416/925-2577. Subway: Bay. Purveyors of the ultimate power suit for Ladies Who Lunch, Chanel offers dependable excellence at astronomical prices.

I-cii 99 Yorkville Ave, at Bellair St, Uptown ☎416/925-3380. Subway: Bay. A gallery-like space that displays clothes as if they were sculptures. Regulars really know their stuff and appreciate the selection of Comme des Garcons, Junya Watanabe and Undercover.

Prada 131 Bloor St W, at Bay St, Uptown ☎416/513-0400. Subway: Bay. Prada's Toronto outlet is comparable to the company's other North American stores, stocking the latest pricey clothes, accessories, shoes and handbags.

TNT Woman and TNT Man and TNT Blu Hazelton Lanes, 87 Avenue Rd, at Yorkville Ave, Uptown ☎416/975-1810. Subway: Bay. For the ladies, labels range from Teenflo to Robert Rodriguez and Barbara Bui, while men choose from Zenga Sport, Diesel, Iceberg Jean and the like. At TNT Blu, kids stock up on Juicy Couture and Oliver Twist. The flirty little items and techno-power suits don't come cheap here, and a teensy bit of label obsession is probably necessary to pay full price.

Vintage

Brava 483 Queen St W, at Spadina Ave, Downtown ☎416/504-8742. Streetcar: Queen (#501). Movie stars like Renée Zellweger and Susan Sarandon have been spotted shopping here, where the stock of shoes, handbags, kimonos and 1950s bowling shirts are found in pristine condition.

Courage My Love 14 Kensington Ave, at Dundas St W, Downtown ☎416/979-1992. Streetcar: Dundas (#505). Vintage clothing for men and women augmented with an eclectic selection of beads, amulets and buttons. The clientele ranges from high-school girls looking for funky prom dresses to fashion-magazine editors looking for cheap chic. The most venerable of the Kensington Market schmatta shops.

The local fashion scene

Toronto's fashion design scene has been booming, spurred by the emergence of the Toronto-based **Fashion Design Council of Canada** and its sponsorship of the biannual **Toronto Fashion Week** (Ⓦ www.torontofashionweek.ca). Fashion-forward local houses that have earned widespread success include **Damzels in This Dress** (Ⓦ www.damzelsinthisdress.com) and **House of Spy** (Ⓦ www.houseofspy.com), both found in various stores throughout the city, as well as **Pink Tartan** (Ⓦ www.pinktartan .com), on sale at Holt Renfrew.

Divine Decadence Originals 136 Cumberland Ave, 2nd floor, at Avenue Rd, Uptown ☏416/324-9759. Subway: Bay (Cumberland exit). With its museum-quality accesories and stunning collection of vintage haute couture (Chanel from the 1930s; Dior from the '50s; Pucci from the '60s), it's no wonder this store is a local favourite.

Gadabout 1300 Queen St E, at Leslie St, Downtown ☏416/463-1254. Streetcar: Queen (#501). Top-quality vintage, including linens, shoes, hats and jewellery, with an emphasis on items from the 1950s to the '80s. An excellent source for beaded cashmere sweaters and leather gloves in perfect condition.

Stella Luna 1627 Queen St W, at Roncesvalles Ave, Downtown ☏416/536-7300. Streetcar: Queen (#501). Like the high-quality, low-cost antique furniture stores that surround it, Stella Luna is a secret Torontonians tend to keep to themselves. Bargain hunters slip in here for the killer jet and sparkly jewellery, vintage designers (Halston, Valentino) and marvellous shoes. If you make the trek bring cash – credit and debit cards belong to a different era.

Grrreat Stuff 870 Queen St W, at Crawford St, Downtown ☏416/536-6770. Streetcar: Queen (#501). An end-of-line/sample store filled with label clothing at deeply discounted prices – for men. Hugo Boss, Kenneth Cole and others rub tailored shoulders with a house brand featuring tapered shirts.

Honest Ed's 581 Bloor St W, at Bathurst St, Uptown ☏416/537-1574. Subway: Bathurst. A two-and-a-half-storey neon sign announces Toronto's ultimate discount store, offering housewares, groceries, clothing, toys, crazy little ornaments and the like.

Tom's Place 190 Baldwin Ave, at Kensington Ave, Downtown ☏416/596-0297. Streetcar: Spadina (#510) or Dundas (#505). A Kensington Market institution, Tom's Place offers a huge selection of men's and women's designer clothes at discounted prices. The actual price tags are more or less suggestions for when you're bartering with the deeply courteous Tom: the more he likes you, the better the deal. The staff is top-notch and alterations are speedily performed on-site.

Crafts

Bounty 235 York Quay Centre, on Queens Quay W, the waterfront ☏416/973-4993. Streetcar: Harbourfront/Spadina or LRT: #509/#510. This consignment shop features the output of visiting and resident artisans who produce beautiful stained- and blown-glass, jewellery, baskets, fired clay, ironware, turned wood and much more.

🏃 **The Guild Shop** 118 Cumberland St, at Bellaire, Uptown ☏416/921-1721. Subway: Bay. A Canadian institution, the Guild Shop has been representing Canadian artists and artisans for seven decades. They mix newcomers with collectible veterans and carry glass, ceramics and turned wood. The Guild is also the city's oldest dealer of Inuit and First Nations art. Its Inuit statuary, often very affordable, is exceptional, and the curator is more than happy to expound on the pieces' significance. An excellent place for collectors who are just starting out.

Prime Gallery 52 McCaul St, at Queen St W, Downtown ☏416/593-5750, ⊛www.primegallery.ca. Streetcar: Queen (#501). Canada's leading ceramics gallery, you'll also find adventurous jewellery, textiles and some sculpture.

Department stores and malls

The Bay 176 Queen St, at Yonge St, Downtown ☏416/861-9111. Subway: Queen; also intersection of Bloor and Yonge sts, Uptown ☏416/972-3333. Subway: Yonge/Bloor. With two locations (each takes up a full city block), The Bay has become a formidable retail presence. The name is taken from the colonial fur-trading enterprise known as Hudson's Bay Company, and today you can buy a Hudson's Bay Blanket here. (Furiers traded these wool blankets with Native Americans.) The rest of the basic department-store stock is decidedly contemporary, however.

Holt Renfrew 50 Bloor St W, Uptown ☎416/922-2333. **Subway: Bay.** Toronto's premier couture destination for both men and women, specializing in signature collections from the likes of Jean-Paul Gaultier, Gucci, Sonia Rykiel and Giorgio Armani. Upper-echelon Canadian designers such as Pink Tartan and Lida Baday are also represented. Holt aims to wrap its customers in full-service, and provides a concierge desk by the main entrance, two cafés, a full day spa and a great staff to help you out.

▽ Holt Renfrew

Sears 290 Yonge St, at Dundas St, Downtown ☎416/343-2111. **Subway: Dundas.** Formerly the flagship of Canada's oldest department store chain (Eaton's), this once haughty beauty is now a Sears, carrying fashion, perfume, cosmetics and housewares that one won't find in the average outlet of the utilitarian American department store chain.

Malls

BCE Place 181 Bay St, Downtown ☎416/777-6480. **Subway: Union Station.** One of the most dramatic complexes in the city, this galleria of shops and office space was designed by Spanish architect Santiago Calatrava, who found a way to incorporate, rather than bulldoze, the walls of the Commerce Bank of the Midland District (Toronto's oldest stone building) and a block of Victorian shops into the development. A vaulted ceiling allows sunlight to pour in, which is a welcome antidote to the subterranean fluorescent lighting of the Underground City.

Hazelton Lanes 55 Avenue Rd, Uptown ☎416/968-8680. **Subway: Bay.** This mall is almost too classy to be so labelled. It has high-end clothing stores, home decor shops and Toronto's only Whole Foods market, mixed in with a few restaurants and cafés. A wonderful spot for browsing.

Toronto Eaton Centre 290 Yonge St, Downtown ☎416/598-8560. **Subway: Queen or Dundas.** Anchored at its northern boundary by the Sears department store, this enormous mall covers the distance between two subway stops, contains hundreds of stores on five levels and takes the better part of an afternoon just to walk from one end to the other. This is perhaps the best place to shop if you have limited time, simply because every chain store of any significance is here. The layout follows one general rule: high-end shops are on the third level, mid-price shops on the second and the cheap stuff is on the bottom. Some recent additions, notably a huge H&M for younger shoppers and a reconfiguration of ground-level stores so that they open onto the street, have made the Eaton Centre more relevant to a new generation of shoppers.

The Underground City

The largest mall in Toronto is invisible from the surface, hidden beneath the streets in more than 11km of tunnels known as the **Underground City**, which stretches north/south from Front to Dundas, and east/west between Yonge and Richmond. Entrances are brightly marked with the coloured **PATH** logo.

This subterranean network of plazas co-evolved with the banking towers that dominate the street level, when their developers had the idea of creating shopping environments for the hundreds of thousands of workers who pour into the city's core daily. As a result, today, no matter how bad the weather, you can always go shopping, visit a gallery or find something to eat in the well-planned labyrinths beneath Toronto.

Food and drink

Gourmet

Alex Farm Products 377 Danforth Ave, at Chester Ave, the suburbs ☎416/465-9500. Subway: Chester; also at the St Lawrence Market, Downtown ☎416/368-2415. Subway: Union Station. A cheese fanatic's dream, specialities here include a large selection of sheeps-milk cheeses, an impressive array of goat cheeses regularly flown in from France and raw milk cheeses from nearby artisanal dairies.

Caviar Direct St Lawrence Market, at Jarvis St, Downtown ☎416/361-3422 or 1-800/74-CAVIAR. Subway: Union Station. An emporium for Beluga and Persian caviars, this place also touts the Canadian variety (a golden caviar from the sturgeon of Lake Huron). Be sure to try a piece of "Indian candy" – smoked salmon cured in maple syrup.

Holt Renfrew Gourmet 50 Bloor St W, at Bay St, Uptown ☎416/922-2333. Subway: Bay. One side of this shop is a lunch counter and takeaway deli, and the other is filled with a wide range of condiments and prettily packaged herbs. Especially good for its range of sweets.

🏃 **Pusateri's** 57 Yorkville Ave, at Bay St, Uptown ☎416/785-9100 and 1539 Avenue Rd ☎416/785-9100, ⓦwww.pusateris .com. Subway: Lawrence. Serious food critics have proclaimed this family-run café and grocery to be what New York City's *Balducci*'s once was: foodie heaven – as every item is absolutely top-quality. Chef Andre Walker oversees the kitchen, although the owner's mum and a few aunts have been known to pitch in during tomato season. Home deliveries are possible throughout North America via the website.

Summerhill Station LCBO 10 Scrivner Sq, at Yonge St, Uptown ☎416/922-0403, ⓦwww .lcbo.com. Subway: Summerhill. Probably the coolest, best-stocked liquor store in Canada, this 30,000 square-foot outlet was once a railway station, complete with marble walls and a Venetian clock tower. Today it carries more than 5000 wines, spirits and beers from around the world, with a vintages section, a demonstration kitchen and tasting sections. It also features Ontario microbreweries that are otherwise hard to find.

Bakeries and patisseries

Carousel Bakery St Lawrence Market, at Jarvis and Front sts, Downtown ☎416/363-4247. Subway: Union Station. Absolutely the best place for brioche, Carousel also gets high marks for its speciality breads, focaccia and famous peameal bacon sandwiches.

Daniel et Daniel 248 Carlton St, Uptown ☎416/968-9275. Streetcar: Carlton (#506). Classically French, Daniel et Daniel creates superb cakes, jewel-like fruit tarts and dainty pastries.

Queen of Tarts 283 Roncesvalles Ave, at Dundas St W, Downtown ☎416/651-3009. Subway: Dundas West. Luscious clafoutis, toothsome macaroons, pies and tarts of every description, and a politically informed line of excellent gingerbread people.

Yung Sing Pastry 22 Baldwin St, at McCaul St, Downtown ☎416/979-2832. Streetcar: College/Carlton (#506). Lunchtime crowds throng to this tiny takeaway bakery, which features spicy beef-stuffed buns, pork or veggie spring rolls, lotus-nut shortcake and the richest egg custard tarts you've ever tasted. A complete lunch here won't cost more than $4.

Health food

Big Carrot 348 Danforth Ave, at Chester Ave, the suburbs ☎416/466-2129. Subway: Chester. This holistic supermarket collective provides one-stop shopping for people who don't want chemicals in their food or toxins in their personal hygiene items. Although there are many vegetarian-friendly choices, the Big Carrot also stocks organic meat, poultry and fish. It has a very good vegetarian deli counter/café and has branched out into so many areas that it pretty much engulfed the little neighbourhood square named for it, The Carrot Common.

The House of Spice 190 August Ave, at Baldwin St, Downtown ☎416/593-9724. Streetcar: College (#506). A Kensington Market institution long cherished for its fragrant range of products – spices, coffees, teas, oils, condiments and exotic tinned foods – as well as its exceptional prices. Worth a visit just to savour the sights and smells.

Whole Foods 87 Avenue Rd, at Yorkville Ave,

Uptown ☎416/944-0500, 🌐www.wholefoods .com. **Subway: Bay.** Offers a full selection of natural and organic products, such as produce, fish, meat, and cheese, as well as choclates, baked goods, a vegetarian deli counter and more.

Home and garden accessories

Lily Lee 261 Danforth Ave, at Broadview Ave, Uptown ☎416/461-1017. Subway: Broadview. For nearly ten years Lily has featured affordable, pared-down decorative style with an Asian sensibility. She often showcases local living arts designers (Jane Pham; Sonia Chan) and has a very good, though small, selection of textiles.
Teatro Verde Hazelton Lanes, 87 Avenue R, at Yorkville Ave, Uptown ☎416/966-2227. Subway: Bay (Cumberland exit). Perfect one-stop shopping for the Downtown gardener: you can get a floral arrangement, find the perfect addition to your container garden, pick up some interior accessories for your next dinner party and purchase a really good facial mudpack.
UpCountry 310 King St E, at Sherbourne St, Downtown ☎416/777-1700; also two other locations. Streetcar: King (#504). When UpCountry first made its appearance almost two decades ago it was leading the pack in carrying Canadian design, their Niagara table being an example. Their garden furniture and accessories are a boon for winter-weary horticulturalists.

Inuit and First Nations galleries

In Canada all aboriginal peoples are collectively known as First Nations, and within the First Nations are the Inuit (meaning "The People"). Most Europeans and Americans know them as Eskimos but this is a name the Inuit abhor. The diversity of First Nations and Inuit art is staggering, particularly so in the case of the latter. The vast space of the Canadian Arctic engendered many distinct styles and techniques among the artists, who have a long tradition of working in relative isolation. The shops and galleries below can provide a good introduction to this intriguing art and culture.

Fehley Fine Arts 14 Hazelton Ave, at Yorkville Ave, Uptown ☎416/323-1373. Subway: Bay (Cumberland exit). Fehley's is an international leader in the complex and diverse area of Inuit art, representing artists and sculptors from across the enormous expanse of the Canadian Arctic. Although the sculptures here tend to be the star attractions, don't miss the graphic-art pieces, either.
Isaacs Inuit Gallery 9 Prince Arthur Ave, at Avenue Rd, Uptown ☎416/921-9985. Subway: St George or Museum. Serious collectors of Inuit art have long patronized Isaacs, which carries sculpture, prints, drawings and wall hangings.
Maslak-McLeod Gallery 25 Prince Arthur Ave, Uptown ☎416/944-2577. Subway: St George. This gallery carries some of the most important names in First Nations and Inuit painting, including masters like Norval Morrisseau and Abraham Aghik.

Markets

The Farmers Market 92 Front St E, at Jarvis St, Downtown ☎416/392-7219. Subway: Union Station. Also known as North Market, the vendors here offer up fresh honey, pots of herbs, home-baked goods, fresh cheeses and fruits and vegetables straight off the farm. Open Saturday only, from 5am to 5pm. On Sunday, the same space becomes a rather good flea market.
Kensington Market Dundas St W and Kensington Ave, Downtown. Streetcar: Dundas (#505). This is a United Nations of food: one street is stuffed with Ethiopian, Vietnamese, Trinidadian, Bahamian, Chinese, Portuguese

and Jewish food shops, while around the corner merchants from throughout Latin America line up alongside vendors from the Middle East, the Mediterranean and Central Europe. If you can't find it here, the odds are you won't find it anywhere. In addition to the edibles, the area features vintage clothing stores, over-the-edge designers, pubs, cafés and patios. Closed Sunday.

St Lawrence Market Front and Jarvis streets, Downtown ☏416/392-7219. **Subway: Union Station.** On the site of Toronto's first city hall, this market boasts two levels of stalls, shops and bins filled with tantalizing international goods. Treats specific to Canada, like peameal bacon sandwiches (back bacon coated in a cornmeal crust), fiddlehead ferns, salmon cured in maple syrup, and an astonishing variety of mustards, are available as well. A crafts market, where vendors sell hats, scarves, jewellery and wooden toys, is located on the lower level. The busiest and most festive day to visit is Saturday, when buskers of every description play to the crowds. Closed Sunday.

Museum shops

The Art Gallery of Ontario Gallery Shop 317 Dundas St W, at McCaul St, Downtown ☏416/979-6610. **Subway: St Patrick.** In addition to items themed around current exhibits, the AGO's shop stocks work by local potters, glass blowers and silversmiths. There's also an excellent selection of children's toys, posters, books, cards and multimedia teaching aids.

Gardiner Museum Shop 111 Queen's Park, at Avenue Rd, Uptown ☏416/586-5699. **Subway: Museum.** Perhaps the best place in town to find innovative, one-off ceramics, the Gardiner's gift shop carries consignment items from some of the best ceramicists working in Canada today. An excellent place to start one's own collection.

The ROM Shops 100 Queen's Park, at Avenue Rd, Uptown ☏416/586-5775. **Subway: Museum.** The gift shops at the Royal Ontario Museum carry scarves, jewellery, and charming whatnots themed to major exhibits; reproduction items based on the permanent collection; and emphatically Canadian works by local artists on consignment, including raku, porcelain, textiles and native crafts. The book selection has an excellent range of titles covering Canadian and First Nations history and culture, while the children's shop, located downstairs, is chock-full of educational books and toys themed to the museum's collections, particularly – and predictably – the dinosaurs.

Music

Because many entertainment corporations use Toronto's diverse, cosmopolitan population as a test market for North America, the city has some of the **best prices** for new-release compact discs in the world – frequently half of what they cost in Europe. The standard CD price is $15, up to $21–23 for expensive imports and speciality labels. However, the popularity of downloading music from the Internet has made the smaller, independent store an endangered species.

New

HMV 333 Yonge St, at Dundas St, Downtown ☏416/586-9668. **Subway: Dundas.** The four comprehensively stocked floors here are packed with nearly all musical genres. Listening posts play selections from Top-40 tracks, and if the staff isn't familiar with a title they'll consult their computers to find it for you. Five other franchises are centrally located around town.

L'Atelier Grigorian 70 Yorkville Ave, at Bay St, Uptown ☏416/922-6477. **Subway: Bay.** The wide selection of classical and ancient music here includes many imported labels and hard-to-find titles. Nothing comes cheap, but if you really need that four-disc set of Byzantine liturgical music, this is the place to shop.

Rotate This 620 Queen St W, at Bathurst St, Downtown ☏416/504-8447. **Streetcar: Queen (#501).** A bit further down the Queen West strip – and therefore less likely to be filled with young things from the suburbs on a Saturday afternoon. Diverse selection of many genres.

Sam the Record Man 347 Yonge St, at Gould St, Downtown ☎416/646-2775. **Subway: Dundas.** Rumours of this store's death-by-bankruptcy were apparently exaggerated: this Yonge Street landmark still sells an extensive collections of rock, jazz, classical and world music.

Soundscapes 572 College St, at Manning Ave, Uptown ☎416/537-1620. **Streetcar: College (#505).** Alternative indie labels like Merge and Thrill Jockey, and imports at commiserate prices. No Top-40 here.

Used

Second Vinyl 2 McCaul St, at Queen St W, Downtown ☎416/977-3737. **Subway: Osgoode.** Despite the name, this store carries only a limited selection of records. One side of the store is devoted to used jazz and classical CDs, and the other is filled with rock and alternative titles.

She Said Boom 372 College St, at Bathurst St. Uptown, ☎416/944-3224. **Streetcar: College /Carlton (#506).** An emporium devoted to popular culture and sounds, filled with new and used CDs and books.

Vortex 2309 Yonge St, at Eglinton Ave, Uptown ☎416/483-7437. **Subway: Elginton.** One of the oldest used-CD stores in the city, this second-storey walk-up has a sprawling collection that will delight browsers.

Speciality shops

Kidding Awound 91 Cumberland Ave, at Bay St, Uptown ☎416/926-8996. **Subway: Bay.** A large turning key over the door warms you up for this delightfully goofy store, where you can buy quality rubber chickens, punching nuns, metal lunch boxes decorated with Hindu gods, huge dragon puppets or a variety of keychains.

Northbound Leather 7 St Nicholas St, at Wellesley St, Uptown ☎416/972-1037. **Subway: Wellesley.** Spiffy duds in latex, leather and PVC, with a full complement of masks, whips and

other props for erotic home theatre. Beautiful workmanship, high-quality materials and a broad-minded, attentive staff willing to answer questions or take special orders.

Spytech Spy Store 2028 Yonge St, Uptown ☎416/482-8588. **Subway: Davisville.** Dedicated to electronic surveillance gadgets like bugging or anti-bugging devices, teensy cameras and night-vision goggles. A handy place if you're into espionage, or just plain paranoid.

Sporting goods

Hogtown Extreme Sports 401 King St W, at Spadina Ave, Downtown ☎416/598-4192. **Streetcar: King (#504).** Specializes in skateboarding equipment, baggy clothes and snowboards, though they also do a nice line in bike gear.

Mountain Equipment Co-op 400 King St W, Downtown ☎416/340-2667. **Streetcar: King (#504).** For a nominal fee, an annual membership gets you access to the city's most extensive range of top-flight sports equipment. If you're planning to dog-sled in the Arctic, bike across China, climb mountains or go deep-sea diving, you can buy everything you need here at better-than-average prices. Mountain Co-op also does

daily rentals of bicycles, cross-country skis, canoes and kayaks for the urban outdoors person. The building itself is noteworthy: it's made from recycled materials and has a wildflower garden on the roof.

Pollack's Fly Fishing and Fishing Goods 337 Queen St E, at Parliament St, Downtown ☎416/363-1095. **Streetcar: Queen (#501).** Everything you need for the art of angling, hook, line and sinker.

Varsity Sports Store 55 Harbord St, at Spadina Ave, Uptown ☎416/977-8220. The speciality here is in swimwear and swimming accessories (team orders available) with a nice sideline in racquets.

Sports and outdoor activities

There is no shortage of **spectator sports** and **outdoor activities** in Toronto. Ice hockey, basketball, baseball and Canadian football provide a calendar year's worth of excitement in both the professional and amateur ranks. Historic rivalries between regional and city teams are no longer the political allegories they once were, but partisan sentiment for the home team can make being in the stands almost as exciting as the action taking place on the field.

In the early stages of its urban development Toronto was on the vanguard of the Victorian-era parks movement, and centrepiece **High Park** is the result of that time. Today Toronto is an exception among large cities the world over for the amount of parkland and green space it maintains within the city limits – more than twelve percent of the entire city land mass is a park of one type or another. Within those parameters are some three million trees and 1500 named parks, in addition to numerous playgrounds, community centres, swimming pools, tennis courts, golf courses and even a labyrinth in Trinity Square Park, behind the Eaton Centre. There are also all-night baseball diamonds, soccer pitches, hiking and cross-country skiing trails, greenhouses and gardens and wildlife sanctuaries. To find a facility or to check on opening hours and fees, call the **Toronto Parks and Recreation** (℡416/392-1111, ⓦ www.city.toronto.on.ca/parks) or check the Municipal Blue Pages in the phone book.

Major sporting venues

There are currently two main venues for spectator sports in Toronto, both located downtown:

Air Canada Centre 40 Bay St ℡416/815-5500. Home of the Toronto Maple Leafs hockey team and the Toronto Raptors basketball squad.

Rogers Centre (formerly the SkyDome) 1 Blue Jay Way, at Front St W ℡416/341-3663, ⓦ rogerscentre.com. Subway: Union Station. Plays host to the Toronto Blue Jays baseball team and the Toronto Argonauts football team, as well as numerous special events and concerts. See p.50 for more on the building and tours.

Single tickets to all major sporting events may be purchased through Ticketmaster, ℡416/872-5000 or ⓦ www.ticketmaster.ca.

Ice hockey

Hockey is Canada's national pastime, and with players hurtling around at nearly 50kph and the puck clocking speeds of over 160kph, this would be a high-adrenaline sport even without all the combat that takes place on the ice. As an old Canadian adage has it, "I went to see a fight and an ice-hockey game broke out".

At one time, the **Toronto Maple Leafs** were the only professional sports team in the city; they were also the best team in the National Hockey League (NHL), and were deified by virtually all Torontonians. Though they haven't won the Stanley Cup, the Holy Grail of professional hockey, since 1967, they have managed to maintain a strong hold on the locals, who have a pronounced taste for a rough-and-tumble game style colloquially known as lunch-bucket hockey. These very loyal fans' patience were sorely tested, however, with a players' strike in 2004 and 2005, which caused the cancellation of the NHL season.

The Maple Leafs' old home, the fabled Maple Leaf Gardens, was, like the team, beginning to get a little worn around the edges, and in February of 1999 the squad moved to the **Air Canada Centre** (☎416/815-5500). This state-of-the-art complex, replete with all the pixelboard gadgetry and sound systems any modern arena demands, also hosts the city's professional basketball team, the Toronto Raptors. The ACC is connected to Union Station by an underground walkway and is therefore very easy to reach by public transport.

The regular **hockey season**, which lasts from October to May (and sometimes June) is composed of approximately ninety games. **Ticket prices** range from $42 to $385, but can go even higher if there is the merest chance of the Maple Leafs making it to the playoffs. In the rare years when the Leafs do make the playoffs, tickets are virtually impossible to obtain.

△ Toronto Maple Leafs

Canadian football

Professional **Canadian football**, played under the aegis of the Canadian Football League (CFL), is a much different affair than the American game, played in the United States through the National Football League (NFL). Homegrown Canadian talent does tend to move south, however, in search of fame and money, and the NFL's smaller or older players often come north to fill the ranks – the CFL, at its best, still displays an exuberant love of the game that tends to get lost in larger, more glamorous professional sports franchises.

The CFL and NFL's football games vary only slightly. In Canada the playing field is longer, wider and has a deeper end zone, and there are twelve rather than eleven players on each team. There is also one fewer "down" in each series of the game, meaning that after kick-off the offensive team has three, rather than four, chances to advance the ball ten yards and regain a first down. The limited time allowed between plays results in a more fast-paced and high-scoring sport, in which ties are often decided in overtime or in a dramatic final-minute surge.

Toronto's team, the Argonauts (or "Argos"), share the Rogers Centre (☎416/416/341-3663) stadium with the Toronto Blue Jays baseball team. The **season** takes place between August and November, and culminates in playoffs for the Grey Cup, Canadian Football's championship trophy. The Grey Cup weekend is part of a Canadian tradition, which means lots of large house parties and general revelry throughout the city. **Tickets** range from $18 to $65 for a regular game and over $100 for a Grey Cup match.

Baseball

When the **Toronto Blue Jays** won their first World Series in 1992, more than a million people jammed Downtown to celebrate the victory. When the Jays repeated the feat the following year, Toronto's newfound love for baseball was sealed. The Blue Jays (affiliated with Major League Baseball's American League) play 81 home games a season, which lasts from April to October. Games are played in the afternoon or at night and can last anywhere from two to four hours. Home game ticket **prices** can go as low as $9 for the stratospheric seats or $59 for an infield seat.

Basketball

Canadians are fond of annoying Americans with the fact that **basketball** was invented by a Canadian, James Naismith. It is with less enthusiasm, however, that they acknowledge that it wasn't until Naismith took his game south of the border in 1891 that it actually took off.

Toronto had a professional basketball team in the Thirties and Forties, but when the American divisions reorganized themselves into the National Basketball Association (NBA) in the Fifties, the Toronto franchise was dropped. Toronto didn't rejoin the professional ranks until 1995, when the **Toronto Raptors**, named for the dinosaurs made famous by Michael Crichton's *Jurassic Park*, became part of the NBA.

The Raptors play home games from November to May at the ultramodern **Air Canada Centre**. Ticket prices range from $27 to $175, although the upper range prices are even higher for an all-star game. Currently the Raptors are far from being a top NBA team; however, it is worth attending a game to marvel at the sheer athleticism of professional basketball players.

Lacrosse

Although ice hockey is Canada's national sport, the first and perhaps most truly Canadian game is **lacrosse**, which is enjoying a vigorous resurgence in popularity. This fast, rugged sport was invented by the Iroquois peoples of the Six Nation Confederacy, whose games would include hundreds of players on both sides and were mistaken by the first European sports spectators for battles. The rules of play, simplified and codified in the mid-nineteenth century, state that the objective of lacrosse is simply to send the ball through the opponent's goal as many times as possible while preventing the opposing team from scoring. There are ten players to a team and the long-handled, racket-like implement, called the crosse, used to toss and catch the ball, is the most distinctive feature of the game. As in hockey, players face off in midfield with their crosses touching the ground, and the referee drops the ball between them. Other similarities include body checks and penalties for slashing, tripping and fist-fighting. The local National Lacrosse League team, the **Toronto Rock**, are back-to-back series champions. From January to April the Rock play eight games at the **Air Canada Centre**. Single **tickets** are $31–72.

Soccer

One of the few things almost all the diverse cultures who have settled in Toronto have in common is a passionate love of soccer. The years when World Cup championships are played turn virtually everyone into a soccer expert, and restaurants, coffeehouses and bars stay open straight through the night so fans can watch live broadcasts from around the world. Victories are celebrated with much flag waving, toasting and car horn blowing, usually in the ethnic enclave of a rival team. For a good depiction of Toronto during the World Cup, read Dionne Brand's novel *What We All Long For* (see p.239), set against the 2002 series.

Locally, soccer remains largely an amateur sport, although the Toronto Soccer Association (Ⓦ www.torontosoccer.net) is a feisty organization with ambitions of building a stadium one day. Parks with baseball diamonds also have soccer pitches chalked out for the use of local teams or for neighbourhood pickup matches. Access to the parks is free, but it may be necessary to book ahead for organized matches through the Toronto Parks and Recreation department (see p.204).

Bicycling and inline skating

Bicycles have proliferated in Toronto, both as a means of transportation and for recreation. Indeed, the municipal government even has a Cycling Committee, which devotes itself to protecting the interests of cyclists in the city. The committee also sponsors a variety of group rides and bike-friendly activities; for more information call ☎ 416/392-7592.

Bike lanes have made an appearance on the main traffic arteries throughout Toronto, and there are over 85 kilometres of cycling paths in the city's parklands. A particularly popular route is the Leslie Street Spit (more properly

SPORTS AND OUTDOOR ACTIVITIES | Lacrosse • Soccer

known as Tommy Thompson Park), a car-free zone that stretches out like a skinny finger into Lake Ontario from the foot of Leslie Street beyond Ashbridges Bay.

Various cycling routes can be downloaded from either the Toronto Parks and Recreation website (see p.204) or the Toronto Bike Plan website (Ⓦwww .toronto.city.on.ca/cycling/bikeplan). One of the city's best cycling maps, however, is produced by the Green Tourism Association (see p.210) and is available at bookstores and bike shops.

Because bicycles are considered vehicles, cyclists are subject to the same rules of the road as car drivers. Additionally, cyclists under the age of eighteen must wear a protective helmet. (Adults who choose not to wear helmets, of course, run the risk of very serious injury in the event of an accident.) Bicycles are allowed on streetcars, subways and buses, except during weekday rush hours of 6.30am to 9.30am and 3.30pm to 6.30pm. Rental fees are around $45 a day and an additional security deposit is required; hourly rates vary.

Inline skating, which creates competition with cyclists along Toronto's bike paths, is nevertheless another popular form of recreation and even transportation for locals. As with cycling, it is important to rent adequate safety gear, especially helmets, along with the equipment.

Bicycle and inline skate rentals

The Cyclepath 2106 Yonge St and three other locations ☎416/487-1717. Road bikes and mountain/hybrid bikes.

Cycle Solutions 444 Parliament St, at Carlton St, Uptown ☎416/972-6948. Bikes, clothing, components and accessories.

Europe Bound 47 Front St E, at Yonge St, **Downtown** ☎416/601-1990, Ⓦwww.europe bound.com. Standard and mountain bikes.

Toronto Island Bicycle Rental on Centre Island ☎416/203-0009. Quad, tandem and standard bikes.

Wheel Excitement 249 Queens Quay W, the waterfront ☎416/260-9000, Ⓦwww.wheel excitement.ca. Mountain bikes and inline skates.

Skateboarding, snowboarding and skiing

Although the modernist plazas surrounding Downtown's skyscrapers are a serious temptation for skateboard enthusiasts, boarding those areas is not always looked upon kindly by authorities - not to mention the locals. There are, however, plenty of **skateboarding** parks ringing the city. A popular Downtown skatepark is Shred Central, 19 St Nicolas St, near Yonge and Wellesley (☎416/923-9842 or 416/924-2589).

Skateboarding's winter twin, **snowboarding**, as well as **cross-country skiing**, can be experienced without leaving the city limits. In the hilly northern bounds of Toronto, lessons are available for beginners at the Raven Ski Snowboard Club, 206 Lord Seaton Rd, Willowdale (☎416/225-1551). Two municipal centres that rent equipment and provide lessons are the North York Ski Centre (☎416/395-7931), located in Earl Bales Park at Sheppard and Bathurst streets, and the Centennial Park Ski Hill at Renforth and Rathburn streets (☎416/394-8754). Some city parks also have steep banks and cliffs suitable for beginner snowboarding. In particular, try the Broadview side of Riverdale Park (take the #504 or #505 streetcar to the Broadview station), although on a snowy Sunday you may have to make way for young tobogganers. Rentals, equipment and local skatepark tips can be had downtown, at Hogtown Skateboard & Snowboard Shop, 401 King St W (☎416/598-4192).

Ice skating

From mid-November to sometime in spring, 47 municipally operated indoor and outdoor iced surfaces operate seven days a week during the hours of 10am and 10pm. One of the most popular rinks, which has a skate rental facility, is in front of the New City Hall in Nathan Phillips Square. Another public rink where you can rent skates is at Harbourfront Park (☎416/973-4000). There is no charge to use any of these facilities. For information on the various locations, hours of operation and ice conditions, call the parks service Mon–Fri 8.30am–4.30pm at ☎416/338-7465 or 416/338-RINK.

Hiking and walking

Toronto's parklands, ravines and neighbourhoods can be explored along nine walking trails commonly known as the **Discovery Walks** (☎416/392-1111).

△ Discovery Walk signage

In 2001 a movement towards environmental tourism crystallized in Toronto under the umbrella of the Green Tourism Association (ⓦwww.greentourism.on.ca). The organization produces an excellent city map showing all the hiking routes and cycling paths, and public transit routes but none of the paved roads. It also maintains a website that keeps visitors up to date on environmentally friendly restaurants, bed-and-breakfast establishments, shops and professionally guided or self-guided bicycle, hiking and walking tours. In addition to being good exercise, they highlight the city's natural and cultural history.

Recommended outfits

A Stroll in the Park Walking & Adventure Club ⓣ416/484-9255, ⓦwww.interlog .com/~walktalk. A mobile singles' club that meets on weekends for walks and hikes through city parks and ravines, with optional dinners.

ROMwalks ⓣ416/586-8097. Volunteers from the Royal Ontario Museum lead guided walking tours through architecturally and historically significant Toronto neighbourhoods.

Toronto Bruce Trail Club ⓣ416/690-HIKE, ⓦwww.torontobrucetrailclub.org. Regional segment of the remarkable Bruce Trail, which extends from the Niagara Escarpment all the way up to the Bruce Peninsula in Georgian Bay.

Toronto Field Naturalists ⓣ416/968-6255, ⓦwww.sources.com/tfn/. Offers well-run hiking and walking tours throughout tours.

Urban Expeditions ⓣ416/606-7227 ⓦwww.urbanexpeditions.com. Offers an "Urban Jungle" package featuring a two-day overnight walking tour of Toronto's green spaces, as well as a visit to a yoga class, the Art Gallery of Ontario, a live music performance and plenty of great, tucked away spots you would miss if you were driving.

The meandering routes are peppered with signs that explain the local flora and fauna, as well as the historical significance of the trails.

Following an old rail line north to the pastoral setting of Mount Pleasant Cemetery, the Central Ravines, Belt Line and Gardens Discovery Walk winds through the Don River's wooded ravines. Another favourite, the Don Valley Hills and Dales Discovery Walk, which is particularly popular with young families, weaves through a bird sanctuary before crossing the Don River and heading up into Riverdale Park, whose hills are a tobogganer's dream in the winter. Perhaps surprisingly, the Downtown Toronto Discovery Walk is the most intriguing, as much of the natural landscape features, like the buried creeks, continue to exist beneath the concrete surface. The best coastal paths are the Western and Eastern Ravines and Beaches Discovery Walks, which lead to a shoreline boardwalk through natural ponds, marshes and lakeshore parks. From here – or any of the city's walking paths – it's hard to believe you're still within Toronto's city limits. Other Discovery Walks include the Northern Ravines and Gardens, which rambles along the ravine of Burke Brook in the north end and leads to the beautiful, formal Muir Gardens, and the Uptown Toronto route, which weaves together the midtown parks from Allen Gardens to the Village of Yorkville Park.

One of the more physically challenging (and rewarding) Discovery Walks is the Humber River route that leads from the Old Mill, dating back to 1793, through the ancient Carrying Place Trail, currently known as Riverside Drive. This trail was used by First Nations peoples for millennia and was once the connecting route between Lake Ontario and the upper Great Lakes to the north. This path will also take you along the Humber River Marsh, one of the last river marshes in the Toronto area and a breeding ground for waterfowl, turtles and varieties of fish.

Special walking tours are also organized by the city, and focus on birdwatching, fall foliage, heritage walks and spring gardens. For information on city-run walks call ☎416/392-8186.

Golf

More than two hundred public and semi-private eighteen-hole golf courses exist within an hour's drive of Toronto, some of which, like Glen Abbey (☎905/844-1800), are PGA – in essence, professional-level courses, where a full round can cost hundreds of dollars. More cost-effective options are located within the city, namely five public courses that offer beginners and experienced duffers alike the opportunity to whack a few balls around.

All of Toronto's golf courses have club houses and pro shops with rental equipment. Greens fees typically range from $14 to $19 for nine holes, and from $22 to $46 for eighteen holes; renting equipment is of course extra. To get up-to-the-minute course information, visit ⒲www.city.toronto.on.ca/parks/recreation, ⒲torontogolf.com or ⒲toronto.com.

Golf courses and driving ranges

City Core Golf and Driving Range 2 Spadina Avenue ☎416/640-9888. A privately owned facility that is beside the Metro Convention Centre and only a hop, skip and a jump away from the Rogers centre.

Dentonia Park Golf Course on Victoria Park Aven, just off Danforth Ave ☎416/392-2558. An eighteen-hole, par-three course that hosts a nine-hole Family Golf Night, helps various community groups plan tournaments and even has a well-established Ladies League. Offers enough variety for experienced golfers and novices alike.

Don Valley Golf Course at the intersection of Yonge St and William Carson Crescent

☎416/392-2465. Eighteen-hole, par-71 course. Five-minute walk from the York Mills subway stop.

Humber Valley Golf Course on Beattie Ave, east of Albion Rd ☎416/392-2488. A challenging par-70 course.

Scarlett Woods Golf Course Scarlett Rd and Jane St, south of Eglinton Ave E ☎416/392-2484. A par-62 course suitable for beginners.

Tam O'Shanter Golf Course on Birchmount Rd, north of Sheppard Ave E ☎416/392-2547. The city's premier golfing facility, with eighteen holes ranked at par-70. Can be reached via public transport, on either the Birchmount (#17) or Sheppard East #85 or #85A buses.

Watersports

Situated along the shores of Lake Ontario, Toronto is a port city with an active **waterfront**. Sailing, windsurfing, water skiing and cruise boating are popular summertime pursuits, although swimming in the lake is not recommended, due to pollution. The public beaches, however, are still favourite places for sunning and general carousing.

Canoeing and **kayaking** are popular activities, as Toronto not only has the Toronto Island lagoons and a protected harbour to paddle around in, but also two navigable rivers to traverse. Lessons, rentals and guided tours (twice a week in early fall) are available at The Harbourfront Canoe and Kayak School, 283A Queens Quay W (☎416/203-2277 or 1-800/960-8886, ⒲www.paddletoronto.com). Another urban outfitter worth checking out is

Toronto Kayak and Canoe Adventures (☎416/536-2057, ⓦwww.toronto adventures.ca), which specializes in trips along the Humber River. Voyageur Quest (☎416/486-3605 or 1-800/794-9660, ⓦwww.voyageurquest.com). offers four-hour, naturalist-guided canoe tours of the Toronto Islands with a picnic thrown in for groups of ten, and you can rent anything from canoes and kayaks to cross-country skis at Mountain Equipment Co-op, 400 King St W (☎416/340-2667).

Public marinas

If you happen to be visiting Toronto with your own boat in tow, the city operates four public marinas:

Ashbridge's Bay Park just east of Coxwell Ave ☎416/392-6095. Accessible by car from Lakeshore Blvd E.

Bluffer's Park Marina at the end of Brimley Rd ☎416/392-2556. A 500-slip public marina.

Humber Bay West Park ☎416/392-9715. A public boat launch and moorings are within this waterfront park, which also has fly-casting and model-boat ponds and a fishing pier. It can be reached by car via Lakeshore Boulevard near Park Lawn Road.

Toronto Island Marina between Muggs Island and Centre Island ☎416/203-1055. Charges a nominal fee for overnight stays.

Kids' Toronto

T
oronto does an excellent job of keeping visitors with **children** in good spirits. Its reputation as being both safe and clean goes a long way toward promoting a family-positive image, and many attractions were specifically created with families in mind – a result of urban renewal and development coinciding with the maturing of the Baby Boom generation. In addition, Toronto is unusual in that a significant portion of its population lives within city limits, so parks or playgrounds are always close at hand.

Major **cultural institutions** such as the Art Gallery of Ontario and the Royal Ontario Museum (see p.67 and p.79, respectively), as well as attractions like the Ontario Science Centre (see p.104), have innovative programming specifically designed for children. The annual Milk International Children's Festival (see p.218), provides something different – and usually free – every day through a coalition of city parks and attractions, and the municipal parks system has a wide variety of splash pads, wading ponds and indoor/outdoor swimming pools open throughout the city; call ahead to determine availability and space. More ideas for family fun can be found in Chapter 14, Sports and outdoor activities, as well as Chapter 16, Festivals and events.

Gardens, wetlands, waterparks and zoos

For an account of Toronto Zoo, see p.99.

Allen Gardens Conservatory Jarvis St, at Carlton St, Uptown ☎416/392-1111. **Streetcar: Carlton (#506).** The six greenhouses here are in bloom year-round, but the place is especially alive with children during its Victorian Christmas Flower Show, which runs from early December to early January; opening ceremonies include sleigh rides, carolling and games.

Far Enough Farm Centreville, Centre Island ☎416/203-0405, ⓦwww.centreisland.ca. More of a petting zoo than a farm, this petite collection of donkeys, goats and domestic fowl is a cost-free amusement for the very young. See p.95 for more.

Riverdale Farm 201 Winchester St, Uptown ☎416/392-6794. **Streetcar: Carlton (#506).** A slice of early twentieth-century rural life lives on in the heart of Cabbagetown, in what

was once the city's zoo. The old Reptile House is now flanked by a duck pond filled with turtles, while other farm residents include cows, pigs, rabbits, sheep, horses, donkeys, geese and chickens. Popular all year long, the spring is an especially good time for your new(ish) arrivals to see the farm's new arrivals.

Soak City 955 Lakeshore Blvd W, Ontario Place, ☎416/314-9900, ⓦwww .ontarioplace.com, ⓦwww.ontarioplace.com. **Streetcar: Bathurst (#51) or Harbourfront (#509).** The latest addition to the Ontario Place waterpark is a climbing structure for kids that not only sprays, sloshes and slithers, but also boasts the largest tipping bucket in Canada, which dumps one thousand litres of water on the already soaking children every six minutes.

Indoor activities

The Agincourt Leisure Pool 31 Glen Watford Drive, Suburbs ☎416/396-8343. Subway to Sheppard Station, then bus 85 or 85A. Particularly popular with locals in the depths of winter, the Agincourt Recreational Centre's indoor pool is a wet, tropical playground, complete with water-pouring coconuts and a waterslide designed to look like a pirate ship; there is also a spiralling waterslide for older children and adults. Call ahead for family and recreational swim schedules.

Amazon Indoor Playground 21 Vaughan Rd, unit 108, Uptown ☎416/656-5832, ⓦwww .amazonindoorplayground.com. Subway: St Clair West. The name says it all: this indoor playroom has a jungle theme, complete with huge Amazon tree frogs and vines covering the structural I-beams. Public playtime is Mon–Fri 10am–3pm; weekends are booked for private parties.

The Kidsway 2885 Bloor St W, Uptown ☎416/236-5437, ⓦwww.thekidsway.com.

Subway: Royal York. The theme here is a storybook small town, with the whole place looking like an idealized village. Children can play at having their own hairdressing boutique or service station.

🏃 **Lillian H. Smith Library** 293 College St, Uptown ☎416/393-5630. Streetcar: Carlton (#506). Everything here, from the vast collections to the statues of mythical beasts outside the main door, is dedicated to children's literature. Don't miss the Osborne Collection of Early Children's Books, which has rare and first-edition books dating from as far back as the fourteenth century.

Playground Paradise 150 Grenoble Drive, East York ☎416/395-6014. Bus: route #100 bus from Broadview Station. Toronto Parks converted this former recreation and community centre into an excellent indoor playground crammed with equipment and staffed by teens. Call ahead to confirm public play-times.

Theatre

Casa Loma 1 Austin Terrace, Uptown ☎416/923-1171. Subway: Dupont. When theatrical events are held in Casa Loma, the whole castle becomes part of the stage, and the experience is nothing short of wondrous. Plays and pantomimes are scheduled around predictably kid-focused times, with March break and Christmastime being the two yearly high points.

Dream in High Park High Park ☎416/368-3110, ⓦwww.canstage.com, ⓦwww.canstage.com Subway: High Park. Of all Toronto's summer Shakespeare productions, those by the Canadian Stage Company (see p.181), held in High Park's outdoor amphitheatre, are perhaps the best. Admission is pay-what-you-can; bring a blanket for seating.

Elgin Theatre and Winter Garden 189 Yonge St, Downtown ☎416/314-2901. Subway: Queen. For eleven months of the year, the sumptuous Elgin Theatre is a very grown-up environment. December, however, is booked with the season's annual Panto-mime production, featuring flashy costumes, ridiculous characters and the annual retelling

of one old chestnut after another – in other words perfect entertainment for a young audience.

Lorraine Kimsa Young People's Theatre 165 Front St, Downtown ☎416/862-2222. Streetcar: King at Sherbourne (#504). This large redbrick edifice is home to Toronto's excellent Young People's Theatre Company. Although the company provides theatre that is pure entertainment, it's outstanding in scheduling performances that respect their young audiences' intellect. Some productions are pitched towards early teens. Call ahead for seasons and schedules.

Solar Stage Children's Theatre Madison Center (lower level), 4950 Yonge St, North York ☎416/368-8031, ⓦwww.solarstage .on.ca. Subway: Sheppard-Yonge. Although many Toronto troupes offer productions for children, Solar Stage actually carved out a dedicated company, with its goal to provide excellent theatrical entertainment for children ages 6–12. Summer performances are sporadic, so call for information or check the website.

15

Shops

Clothing

Floriane 38 Avenue Rd, Uptown ☏416/920-6367. **Subway: Bay or Museum.** Some kids exhibit extremely well-defined, possibly expensive taste at an early age. Others simply have parents who can afford to dress them that way. Whichever the case, this boutique is based on the notion that one is never too young for sartorial sophistication.

Get Outside 437 Queen St W, Downtown ☏416/593-5598. **Streetcar: King (#504).** At the very sharp point of cutting edge, this 'tween-to-teen emporium has shoes, clothes and accessories for today's youth. Arguably the best place in town for items by Paul Frank and Emily the Strange, with recent additions of Dish and Second Company. Stay tuned for future trends.

Jacadi 87 Avenue Rd, Uptown ☏416/923-1717. **Subway: Bay.** The Toronto branch of the haute couture Parisian chain, this is one-stop shopping if you want your child to look like a character from the *Madeline* books. The clothes are very well made, very *bon chic bon genre*, and very expensive.

Kol Kid 670 Queen St W, at Palmerston Ave, Downtown ☏416/681-0368. **Streetcar: Queen (#501).** This collection of clothing, books, toys and children's accoutrements are almost as much for parents' nostalgia about childhood as they are for the children themselves. Offers playful playthings for infants to 'tweens.

🏃 **Misdemeanours** 322 1/2 Queen St W, Downtown ☏416/351-8758. **Streetcar: Queen (#506).** Currently sharing space with the big girls' store Pam Chorley Fashion Crimes (see p.197), this is the ultimate in imaginative, girly-girl dresses, forward accessories and playwear for girls up to age 14. Designer Pam Chorley's multi-hued garments and accessories, in everything from filmy gauzes to luscious velvets, exhibit a combination of confidence, whimsy and slightly skewed style.

Roots Kids Eaton Centre, 220 Yonge St, Downtown ☏416/542-1618. **Subway: Queen.** No age is too young for this heart-on-its-sleeve Canadian line of high-quality, casual clothing. The beaver logo is much in evidence on hats, fleeces, hoodies and the signature leather jackets.

Books, toys and furnishings

Magic Pony 785 Queen St W (upstairs) ☏416/861-1684, ⊚www.magic_pony.com. **Streetcar: Queen (#501).** Possibly the edgiest kids store in town, Magic Pony is for urbane, pop-literate kids who still want their toys but are too cool to call them that. Asian and Western figures (DIY Quee, full range of Uglydolls) vie with excellent T-shirts, books, magazines and even some purchasable art.

Mastermind 3350 Yonge St, Downtown ☏416/487-7177. **Subway: Lawrence.** One-stop shopping for toys that have stood the test of time: Lego, Play-Doh, Plasticine and the like. An excellent resource for puzzles and other intellectual games for children.

Nestings 418 Eglinton Ave W ☏416/322-0511. **Subway: Eglinton West.** The mandate of this children's furnishings store is "a stylish alternative for those who don't want to compromise their children's bedrooms", and you know that can't be cheap. Diminutive sleigh beds, little down comforters with *toile de loie* prints and a selection of chenille toys are the kinds of items you'll find here.

Science City 50 Bloor St W, Uptown ☏416/968-2627. **Subway: Bay.** Various branches of scientific enquiry inform the games, toys and puzzles for all skills and age levels in this (literally) underground store.

The Toy Shop 62 Cumberland St, Uptown ☏416/961-4870. **Subway: Bay.** The creative, well-crafted toys sold here come from around the world and are geared towards everyone from infants to teens. Founded in 1908, at least four generations of Canadians have bought their teddy bears from this establishment.

Family restaurants

Old Spaghetti Factory 54 The Esplanade, Downtown ☏416//864-9761. **Subway: Union Station.** Several generations of birthday parties have been held in this cavernous restaurant, which opened in an old factory space in 1971. The decor includes a nineteenth-century carousel and an old streetcar that's now filled with dining tables. The food, not surprisingly, consists of spaghetti and other pasta dishes, and the children's menu options are a consistent $5.99.

Richtree Market 42 Yonge St, at Wellington St, Downtown ☎416/366-8986. Subway: Union Station. An ersatz market where diners visit a variety of food stations and their orders are prepared before their eyes. Selections include pasta, Belgian waffles, stir-fries, pizzas, omelettes and mounds of fresh fruit and fruit smoothies – all of which get high marks for variety, freshness and quality.

Kids can order from a special menu and eat their meals seated at diminutive tables, plus there's a play area for toddlers. Sunday (10am–3pm) is family day, where a clown does face painting, makes balloon animals and performs magic tricks.

Shopsy's 33 Yonge St at Front St; also Yonge St at St Clair, Downtown ☎416/599-5464. Subway: Union Station. Kids have been coming to *Shopsy's* since the Shopsowitz family opened their business in 1922. There have been a few changes over the past century but the basic draws remain the same: good deli food at great prices in a warm, friendly environment.

Festivals and events

oronto boasts a large number of festivals and annual events, particularly in the summer months. From June to September there is something big going on every weekend; even better, most of these happenings are free, or have free components. Although things slow down during winter, the city still hosts a series of free events, and Toronto's historical homes, such as Spadina House, Mackenzie House and Colborne Lodge in High Park, observe holiday dates and special occasions with music, food and open-house activities. Check ⓦ www.toronto.on.ca under special events or parks for details. Meanwhile, places like the Harbourfront Centre host various music festivals throughout the summer, as well as rosters of touring bands; see ⓦ www .harbourfront.on.ca for details.

For further information about various other goings-on, contact Tourism Toronto at ☏ 416/203-2600, or visit their website at ⓦ www.tourismtoronto .com. You can also call Ontario Tourism at ☏ 1-800-ONTARIO (ⓦ www .ontariotravel.net) for a seasonal guide. Note that while actual dates for events may vary from year to year, the months generally stay the same.

January

Niagara Ice Wine Festival second and third weekends of the month Held beside the frozen Niagara Falls, this ten-day festival involves tastings, dinners and midnight frozen-grape picking. ⓦ www .niagarawinefestival.com.

Robbie Burns Day the 25th Traditional Scottish *ceilidh* (house party) on the Caledonian Bard's birthday, held at Mackenzie House and featuring poetry readings, Scottish music and dancing. A haggis is ushered in to the sound of bagpipes. ☏ 416/392-6915.

Winter City Festival late Jan to early Feb For two weeks, right when everyone needs a lift, Toronto becomes the self-designated "world's coolest city" and has a party featuring free outdoor concerts and performances by troupes from around the world, plus online coupons for attractions such as the CN Tower and the Bata Shoe Museum. The hugely popular Winterlicious event offers 120 affordable prix-fixe menus in some of

the glitziest restaurants in town. ⓦ www .city.toronto.on.ca.

February

Asian Lunar New Year last week of Jan or first week of Feb Cultural institutions like the Harbourfront Centre hold special events centring on Chinese and Southeast Asian arts and feasts. The daily newspapers will keep you up to date on the most auspicious things to say, do, wear and eat on any given day of the festival.

Kuumba: African Heritage Month all month long African cultures and histories are celebrated throughout the month. Festivities, including the Kuumba: Jambalaya Jump Up festival, take place at the Harbourfront Centre. Open to all ages, the events include special guest performers, storytelling, arts and crafts exhibits, film screenings and culinary events. ☏ 416/973-3000, ⓦ www.harbourfront.on.ca.

Rhubarb! Theatre Festival three weeks of the month The largest new-works festival curated by a Canadian company, the Rhubarb!

serves as both a theatre lab and launching pad for the best and brightest in Toronto stage. Held at the 12 Alexander Street Theatre (see p.180). ☎416/975-8555, ⊛www.buddiesinbadtimestheatre.com.

Interior Design Show last weekend of Jan or first weekend of Feb Everything you wanted to know about the forward edge living design – from table settings to buildings – with special lectures from leading lights in contemporary design such as home-town stars Karem Rashid and Brian Gluckstein, or lustrous imports like Lady Wienberg Anouska Hempel. ☎416/599-3222, ⊛www.interiordesignshow.com.

March

Canada Blooms Flower Show usually the second weekend of the month This massively popular event features plants, plants, plants. Landscape artists, architects and horticulturalists of every description descend on the Metro Convention Centre and transform it into an oasis of herbaceous wonders. ☎1-800/730-1020, ⊛www.canadablooms.com.

St Patrick's Day Parade the Sunday closest to the 17th On this day, all Torontonians claim to be Irish. Indulge in Irish step-dancing, music, food, poetry and, of course, Guinness. ☎416/487-1566, ⊛www.topatrick.com.

April

World Stage Festival all month long Held every other year, this month-long international festival highlights the best contemporary theatre from around the world. Includes lectures, workshops and special events. Many productions, which take place in theatres and less conventional spaces throughout the city, are world premieres, and play at the Glyndebourne festival later in the season. ☎416/973-3000, ⊛www.harbourfrontcentre.com.

Sprockets International Children's Film Festival usually second and third weekends Children's films from around the world, plus behind-the-scenes events for kids ages four and up, are featured at this event, run by the people responsible for the Toronto International Film Festival. ☎416/967-7371, ⊛www.bell.ca/sprockets.

May

Milk International Children's Festival second and third weekends One of the largest

children's and family events in North America, this annual festival of the performing arts features theatre, dance, music and a guest lecture series, all geared to kids ages four and up. Exceptional programming never patronizes the audience. Held at the Harbourfront Centre; many events are free. ☎416/973-3000, ⊛www.harbourfront.on.ca/milk.

Mother's Day Cream Tea second Sunday Spadina House, one of Toronto's heritage houses, hosts this seasonal event. Tea not only represents a slice of Toronto's past, when virtually all special events were teas of one sort or another, but it is also a nice thing to do with your mum on Mother's Day. There are two sittings and a $10 charge, plus tax. 285 Spadina Rd, ☎416/392-6910, ⊛www.city.toronto.on.ca.

Doors Open Toronto last weekend This is the insider event that everyone can get into: Toronto's historical buildings of note, many of which are normally closed to the public, open their doors for guided tours. A great opportunity to get deep into Toronto history. ☎416/3380496, ⊛www.doorsopen.org.

June

Music in the Village of Yorkville Park from June 1 to September Every weekend, Yorkville shoppers and boulevardiers are serenaded with summery, mostly jazz, music in the park, gratis ⊛www.bloor-yorkville.com.

TD Canada Trust Toronto Downtown Jazz Festival last week of the month More than 1500 international jazz headliners representing all the genre's disciplines play venues throughout the city for free. ☎416/928-2033, ⊛www.torontojazz.com.

Pride Week and Parade last week of the month Toronto celebrates gay pride for a full week with various events, culminating in a massive parade. Rapidly becoming the largest pride celebration anywhere. ☎416/92-PRIDE, ⊛www.pridetoronto.com.

July

Canada Day Celebrations the 1st On this national holiday celebrating Canada's birthday, festivities are held throughout the city, and a full roster of concerts and fun events are held in Queen's Park or at City Hall. ⊛www.city.toronto.on.ca/special_events.

Shakespeare in High Park July through to **Labour Day** The Canadian Stage Company (see p.181) moves to High Park's outdoor theatre every summer with productions of The Bard's most accessible plays, notably *A Midsummer Night's Dream* or *Much Ado About Nothing*. These pay-what-you-can performances are perhaps the best of several similar theatrical events.

Beaches International Jazz Festival and Parti-Gras usually second weekend of the month Toronto's favourite neighbourhood jazz festival has joined forces with the Distillery District's PartiGras (a jazz and Latin music festival) to make more space for more fun for more people. Festivities begin at the Distillery District and move over to Kew Beach to occupy a 2km-long stretch of street party. 55 Mill St, Ⓦ www.beachesjazz .com and Ⓦ www.torontopartigras.com.

The Fringe of Toronto Theatre Festival mid-month For ten days, an international assortment of theatre troupes, aspiring actors and playwrights and some people who just have a story to tell take over the theatres and a few parks in The Annex. Big-time hits (*Two Pianos, Four Hands; Da Kink in My Hair*) got their start here. Ⓦ www.fringetoronto .com.

Molson Indy Car Racing second weekend Formula One fanciers line Lakeshore Blvd to watch top drivers compete in this annual race on the Indy circuit. ☎416/9872-INDY, Ⓦ www.molsonindy.com.

Summerlicious second weekend How could a food festival featuring $20–$15 prix-fixe lunch menus and $25–$35 dinner menus at Toronto's best restaurants not be a huge success? Check online for participating restaurants and availability. Ⓦ www.city .toronto.on.ca/special_events.

Toronto Outdoor Art Exhibition second weekend Nathan Philips Square, outside of Toronto's swooping City Hall, fills with North America's largest outdoor art exhibition, where over five hundred established and emerging artists exhibit their works for juried awards worth more than $20,000. An excellent opportunity to acquire a new piece. ☎416/408-2754, Ⓦ www.torontooutdoorart.org.

Toronto Street Festival second weekend The hot-weather sister to the Winter City festival, this celebration stretches up Yonge St from Dundas Square to Lawrence Avenue with four distinct sites – Dundas, St Clair, Eglinton and Lawrence – and sixteen

△ Caribana

different performance spaces for all the bands, acrobats, aerialists, clowns and celebrants. Ⓦ www.toronto.ca/special _events.

Caribana third week of month through to long weekend at end Begun in 1967 as a community heritage project, this two-week festival of Caribbean culture culminates in one of North America's biggest street parties, with an eye-popping parade featuring hundreds of floats, dazzling costumes, steel bands and jaw-dropping dancing. The 1.5km parade route goes along Lakeshore Blvd and continues on to the Toronto Islands for a huge picnic. Check the daily schedule of events. ☎416/466-0321, Ⓦ www.caribana.com.

August

Masala! Mheendi! Masi! first week This South Asian festival of music, dance, theatre, film and food is gaining international accolades for its sensational programming and introduction of South Asian artists to North American audiences. At Harbourfront Centre ☎416/973-3000, Ⓦ www.harbourfront centre.com/summerfestivals.

Rogers Cup second week See Tier 1 international tennis champions slash, slice and pound their way through a game at the York University courts. Men's and women's championships are held on alternating years. ☎1-877-2TENNIS, Ⓦ www.rogerscup.com.

Taste of the Danforth second weekend By far the largest food festival in Canada, the stretch of Danforth Avenue between Broadview and Donlands attracts over 1 million people with its bands, family activities and "tastes" from over one hundred local restaurants. ☎416/698-9053, Ⓦwww.tasteofthedanforth.com.

Canadian National Exhibition (CNE) second week until Labour Day An annual ritual signalling the beginning of the end of summer for generations of Toronto youth, the CNE is pure carny, love it or leave it. Kids will always enjoy the rides, shell games and junk food, and the Midway at night can still be a thrill. There are many special events such as the air show and the concert series, and permanent on-site pavilions are filled with agricultural and industrial exhibits. ☎416/263-3800, Ⓦwww.theex.com.

September

🎬 **Toronto International Film Festival** ten days following the first weekend The Toronto Film Festival is the only major film festival open to the public, which is why it's so phenomenally successful. Movie stars, living-legend directors, big-time producers and thousands of film nuts take over the city's Downtown cinemas for ten days, making this one of the biggest parties of the year. Passes go on sale towards the end of July and are snapped up quickly, although rush tickets are available fifteen minutes before scheduled screenings. ☎416/967-7371 or 416/968-FILM, Ⓦwww.tiffg.ca.

Annual Vegetarian Food Fair second weekend North America's largest vegetarian celebration is held at the Harbourfront Centre. Features cooking demos, activist booths and lots of free food to sample. ☎416/973-3000, Ⓦwww.harbourfront.on.ca.

Cabbagetown Cultural Festival second weekend The oldest and largest of Toronto's many neighbourhood festivals, this one includes its own film festival, pub crawl, arts-and-crafts fair, tour of homes, folk dancing, musical performances and a slew of children's events. The epicentre of activities is Riverdale Park and its little farm. ☎416/921-0857, Ⓦwww.oldcabbagetown.com.

Niagara Grape and Wine Festival last twenty days of month Other wine festivals have come and gone, but for three decades the oenophilic St Catherines and Niagara Falls region has honoured the grape. ☎905/688-0212, Ⓦwww.niagarawinefestival.com.

October

Toronto Marathon and Half Marathon second weekend The largest athletic event in town hits the road in the cool of autumn. Ⓦwww.runtoronto.com.

Thanksgiving second Sunday Americans celebrate it at the end of November, but Canadian Thanksgiving, which entails the same family gatherings and food, is held in mid October.

International Festival of Authors third week One of the world's largest and most prestigious literary events, held at the Harbourfront Centre, features on-stage interviews, special events, a lecture series and readings of fiction, poetry, drama and biography. ☎416/973-3000, Ⓦwww.reading.org.

Hallowe'en the 31st As is perhaps fitting for a town very fond of its Gothic elements, Hallowe'en is a holiday everyone likes to indulge in. Private residences outdo one another in constructing chilling lawn tableaux, children are escorted from house to house to trick-or-treat, and the closest Saturday to the 31st is an occasion for costumed adult revelry and impromptu parades up and down the Yonge Street strip.

November

Royal Agricultural Winter Fair from the first weekend, for two weeks The Royal has promoted agricultural and equestrian excellence for more than seven decades. City folk flock to see languorous bovines, exotic poultry, giant vegetables and butter sculptures, while horse lovers thrill to events like the Royal Horse Show and the National Showcase of Champions. ☎416/263-3400, Ⓦwww.royalfair.org.

Santa Claus Parade first weekend Superlatives abound: the first ever department store parade, the oldest parade for children in the world and the unofficial beginning of the Christmas shopping season. This tradition features clowns, brass bands, animated floats, hundreds of costumed paraders and, of course, the jolly old man himself. Check for route specifics and dates. ☎416/249-7833, Ⓦwww.thesantaclauseparade.com.

Remembrance Day the 11th On the eleventh day of the eleventh month at the eleventh

16

FESTIVALS AND EVENTS

hour traffic stops, bells toll and citizens are silent as the men and women of the armed services are honoured; official civic ceremonies are held at the cenotaph outside Old City Hall. The symbol of Remembrance Day is a red poppy lapel pin, which refers to Canadian officer John McCrea's great poem about the burial fields of Flanders during World War I (see p.79).

Canadian Aboriginal Festival last weekend Held at the Rogers Centre (formerly the SkyDome), North America's largest, multi-disciplined aboriginal arts event features theatre, music, arts-and-crafts, dancing competitions, fashion shows, educational programmes and a marketplace where First Nations peoples from across North America can sell their wares. ☎519/751-0040, ⓦwww.canab.com.

One of a Kind Craft Show and Sale end of the month What started as a neat idea for craftspeople and artisans has blossomed into a remarkable celebration of creativity, innovation and idiosyncrasy. A great place to look for a Christmas gift for that hard-to-shop-for friend. Held at the National Trade Centre. ☎416/393-6000, ⓦwww.OneOfAKindShow.org.

December

Victorian Christmas all month The sights, sounds and tastes of nineteenth-century Toronto Christmases past are recreated in the city's heritage properties of Colborne Lodge, Spadina House and Mackenzie House. Yuletide concerts, activities and baked goods are all part of the historically accurate festivities. ☎416/392-6916, ⓦwww.city.toronto.on.ca/special_events.

The Christmas Story every weekend until Christmas A tradition since 1937, this nativity pageant is held in the charming Church of the Holy Trinity in Trinity Square, behind the Eaton Centre. The Biblical Christmas story is told through mime, narration, organ music and carols sung by an unseen choir. ☎416/598-4521, ⓦwww.holytrinitytoronto.org.

Kensington Festival of Lights on the winter solstice Founded as a neighbourhood event to celebrate the diversity of Kensington's residents, this lantern-lit neighbourhood pageant begins at dusk on the solstice and incorporates images and traditions from Hanukkah, Christmas and other celebrations from around the world. ☎416/598-2829.

Hogmanay! Happy New Year! the 31st A New Year's Eve party at historic Mackenzie House at 82 Bond Street, with traditional Scottish music, holiday food and gaslit tours of the house. ☎416/338-3888, ⓦwww.city.toronto.on.ca/special_events.

FESTIVALS AND EVENTS

Directory

Airlines The best place to get face-to-face service from any of the large airlines is within the airport itself. For airline contact information, see Basics p.21.

Airport car services Aeroport Services ☎416/255-2211; Airline Limousine ☎416/675-3638; Air Flight Limousine Services ☎416/445-1999.

ATMs Automated Teller Machines can be found throughout the city. US and overseas visitors can use their ATM cards at most of them, if their cards are linked to the Cirrus or Plus systems, but confirm with your bank before your trip.

Banks Bank of America, 200 Front St W ☎416/349-4100; Bank of China, 130 King St W ☎416/362-2991; Bank of Montréal, 55 Bloor St W ☎416/927-6000; Bank of Nova Scotia/Scotiabank, Scotia Plaza, 40 King St W ☎416/866-6777; Bank of Tokyo-Mitsubishi, Royal Bank Plaza, 200 Bay St ☎416/865-0220; Canadian Imperial Bank of Commerce (CIBC), Commerce Court, King St W, at Bay St ☎416/980-2211; Citibank, 123 Front St ☎416/947-4100; Deutsche Bank, 222 Bay St ☎416/682-8400; Royal Bank, Royal Bank Plaza, 200 Bay St ☎416/974-3940; TD Canada Trust (main branch), 55 King St W ☎416/982-2322.

Car rental Avis, Hudson Bay Centre, Yonge & Bloor sts ☎416-964-2051 or 1-800-879-2847 worldwide; Budget, 150 Cumberland St ☎416/927-8300; Discount, 595 Bay St ☎416/597-2222; Hertz, Yonge & Bloor sts ☎416-961-3320 or 1-800-654-2280 worldwide; National, Union Station, 65 Front St E ☎416/364-4191 or 1-800/227-7368 worldwide; Thrifty, Union Station, 65 Front St W ☎416/947-1385 or 1-800/847-4389 worldwide.

Consulates Australia,175 Bloor St E, ☎416/323-1155; New Zealand, 225

MacPherson Ave ☎416/947-9696; Republic of Ireland, 20 Toronto St, suite 1210 ☎416/366-9300; United Kingdom, 777 Bay St ☎416/593-1267; United States, 360 University Ave ☎416/595-1700.

Currency exchange Most large Downtown banks will change currency and traveller's cheques. American Express cheques should be cashed at their Downtown office, 50 Bloor St W (Mon–Fri 10am–6pm, Sat 10am–4pm, closed Sun) ☎416/967-3411. Other currency exchange offices include Thomas Cook, 10 King St E (Mon–Fri 9am–5pm) ☎416/366-1961; and Calforex, main branch 170 Bloor St W (Mon–Fri 8.30am–8pm, Sat 9am–6pm, Sun 10am–5pm) ☎416/921-4872).

Dentist For emergencies, call the Academy of Dentistry hotline (daily 8am–12pm) ☎416/485-7121.

Emergencies ☎911 for fire, police and ambulance. Other emergency numbers include the Assaulted Women's Helpline ☎416/863-0511; the Child Abuse Hotline ☎416/924-4646; and the Rape Crisis Hotline ☎416/597-8808.

Film and photography Henry's, 119 Church St ☎416/868-0872; Japan Camera, 777 Bay St, College Park ☎416/598-1133; Korner Color, 1200 Bay St ☎416/928-1008; Vistek, 496 Queen St E ☎416/365-1777.

Hospitals and clinics Toronto General Hospital, 200 Elizabeth St ☎416/340-3111; Toronto Western, 399 Bathurst St ☎416-603-2581; Hospital for Sick Children, 555 University Ave ☎416/813-1500; St. Michael's, 30 Bond St ☎416-360-4000. For minor medical injuries and illness visit: Bay College Medical Centre, 777 Bay St ☎416/977-8878; First Canadian Medical Centre, 100 King St W ☎416/368-6787 or the Walk-In Medical Clinic, 1910 Yonge

St ☎416/483-2000. Canadian citizens are covered by a national health plan; foreign visitors will require health insurance to cover direct fees for medical services. Emergency health care cannot be refused for lack of funds.

Internet access Cyber Orbits, 1 Gloucester St ☎416/920-5912; Cyber Village, 449 Church St ☎416/413-0455; Internet Café, 370 Yonge St ☎416/408-0570; Net Effect, 12 Isabella St, ☎416/964-0749; Netropass, 834 Yonge St ☎416/920-5042; Webstation 2, 575 Yonge St ☎416/922-5104. If you have a laptop with wireless capability, coffee chains like the *Second Cup* and *Timothy's World Coffee*, as well as many smaller establishments, are known as WiFi Hotspots, meaning they offer wireless Internet access.

Laundromats The Laundry Lounge, 531 Yonge St ☎416/975-4747; 24-hour Coin Laundry, 566 Mt Pleasant Ave ☎416/487-0233; St. Lawrence Super Coin, 222 The Esplanade ☎416/363-1223.

Left luggage Union Station, 65 Front St, has lockers (24-hour maximum), as does the Toronto Coach Terminal, 610 Bay St (at Dundas), the Bloor-Yonge subway station or the Metro Reference Library, 789 Yonge St. Most lockers cost a mere 25 cents.

Library The main Downtown branch is the Toronto Reference Library, 789 Yonge St (Mon–Thurs 10am–8pm, Fri & Sat 10am–5pm, Sun during winter 1.30–5pm, closed Sun during summer) ☎416/393-7131. Library Answerline ☎416-393-7131.

Parking Public parking lots are identified by a large "P" in a green circle. The rates vary upwards the closer you are to the Downtown centre. Payment at both public lots and street parking is made at meters. Older street meters require coins, but the newer, solar-powered meters accept both change and credit cards. Time limits will apply in busy areas.

Pharmacies Shopper's Drug Mart, 700 Bay St (24 hours) ☎416/979-2424, and 728 Yonge St (until midnight) ☎416/920-0098. For a holistic pharmacy, including herbal and traditional treatments, try the Big Carrot Wholistic Dispensary, 348 Danforth Ave ☎416/466-8432.

Police stations Toronto Police Service ☎416/808-2222. For emergencies call ☎911. The Downtown area is covered by 52 Division, with central stations at 40 College St and 255 Dundas St W.

Public restrooms Try the lobbies of Downtown hotels, any shopping centre, subway stations (particularly Union Station) or the Toronto Reference Library.

Taxis Beck Taxi ☎416/751-5555; Co-op Cabs ☎416/504-2667; Diamond Cabs ☎416/366-6868; Maple Leaf Taxi ☎416/465-5555; Metro Cab ☎416/504-8294; Yellow Cab ☎416/504-4141.

Time Toronto is on Eastern Standard Time (EST), the same time zone as New York City, which is five hours behind Greenwich Mean Time. Daylight Savings Time runs from the first Sunday in April to the last Sunday in October.

Travel agents The Flight Centre has four Downtown locations: 382 Bay St ☎416/934-0670; 335 Bay St ☎416/363-9004; 130 King St W ☎416/865-1616 and 1560 Yonge St ☎416/923-1899. For full-service assistance for cruises, air, rail and tours, try Carlson Wagonlit at 1248 Yonge St ☎416/929-1980.

Traveller's aid Downtown, go to Union Station, room B23 (☎416/366-7788 from 9.30am–9.30pm) or the bus terminal at Bay and Dundas (☎416/596-8647 from 9.30am to 5.30 pm). At Toronto Pearson International Airport, kiosks at terminal 1 (☎905-676-2868), terminal 2 (☎905-676-2869) and terminal 3 (☎416-776-5890) are open daily 10am–9pm. Traveller's aid kiosks rely on volunteer staff, so evening hours may be curtailed.

(17)

DIRECTORY

Contexts

Contexts

History

Colonial in conception, **Toronto** only emerged as a major international metropolis in the 1950s. Since then, Toronto has made up for lost time, dimming the lights of its Canadian rivals – primarily Montréal – to become one of North America's most invigorating cities.

Beginnings

In prehistoric times, the densely forested northern shore of **Lake Ontario** was occupied by nomadic hunter-gatherers, who roamed in search of elk, bears, caribou and perhaps mammoths, supplementing their meaty diet with berries and roots. Around 1000 BC, these nomads were displaced by **Iroquois-speaking peoples**, who gained a controlling foothold in what is now modern-day southern Ontario, upper New York and Québec. The settlers of this period (usually called the **Initial Woodland** period – 1000 BC to 900 AD) differed from their predecessors only in so far as they constructed burial mounds and used pottery. In the **Terminal Woodland** period (900–1600 AD), however, these same Iroquois-speakers developed a comparatively sophisticated culture, based on the cultivation of corn (maize), beans and squash. This agricultural system enabled them to lead a fairly settled life, and the first Europeans to sail up the St Lawrence River stumbled across large communities, often several hundred strong. Iroquois villages were invariably located on well-drained ground with a reliable water supply. They comprised a series of longhouses, up to 50m long, built of saplings covered in bark and heated by several open hearths situated in a line down the middle. Pits were dug around the longhouses for food storage, and a timber palisade encircled each village. Archeologists have discovered the remains of over 190 Iroquois villages in the Toronto area alone and the restored settlement of Sainte-Marie among the Hurons (see p.127) illustrates all these features.

Iroquois society was divided into matriarchal clans, which were governed by a female elder. The clan shared a longhouse, and when a man married (always outside his own clan), he moved to the longhouse of his wife. Tribal chiefs (*sachems*) were male, but they were selected by the female elders of the tribe and they also had to belong to a lineage through which the rank of *sachem* descended. Once selected, a *sachem* had to have his rank confirmed by the federal council of the inter-tribal league – or confederacy – to which his clan belonged. These **tribal confederacies**, of which there were just a handful, also served as military alliances, and warfare between them was endemic. In particular, the Five Nations confederacy, which lived to the south of Lake Ontario, was almost always at war with the Hurons to the north.

The coming of the Europeans

In the sixteenth century, **British and French fur traders** began to inch their way inland from the Atlantic seaboard. The French focused on the St Lawrence River, establishing Québec City in 1608. From their new headquarters, it was a fairly easy canoe trip southwest to **Toronto** (the Huron word for "place of meeting"), which was on an early portage route between Lake Ontario and Georgian Bay. The French allied themselves with the Hurons, and in 1615 **Samuel de Champlain** led a full-scale expedition to southern Ontario to cement the alliance and boost French control of the fur trade. When he arrived, Champlain handed out muskets to his allies, encouraging them to attack their ancient enemies, the Five Nations. He also sent **Étienne Brulé**, one of his interpreters, down to Toronto with a Huron war party in the first recorded visit of a European to Toronto.

In the short term, Champlain's actions bolstered France's position, but the Five Nations never forgave the French for their Huron alliance, and thirty years later they took their revenge. In 1648, Dutch traders began selling muskets to the Five Nations to enhance their own position. The Five Nations were duly grateful and the following year they launched a full-scale invasion of Huron territory, massacring their enemies and razing the settlement of Sainte-Marie among the Hurons to the ground.

The rise of the British

The destruction of Sainte-Marie was a grisly setback for the French, but it didn't affect their desire to control southern Ontario. In the second half of the seventeenth century, they rushed to encircle Lake Ontario with a ring of forts-cum-trading posts. The British did the same. Initially, the French out-colonized the British, and they also crushed the Five Nations confederacy in the 1690s, forcing them deep into New York State. Furthermore, in 1720, the French established a tiny fur-trading post at Toronto, the first European settlement on the site, and although it was soon abandoned, the French returned thirty years later to build a settlement and a stockade, **Fort Rouillé**, on the lakeshore. This was to be the high-water mark of French success. During the Seven Years' War (1756–63), the British conquered New France (present-day Québec) and overran the French outposts dotted around the Great Lakes. The Fort Rouillé garrison didn't actually wait for the British, but prudently burnt their own fort down and hightailed into the woods before the Redcoats arrived. The site lay abandoned for almost forty years until hundreds of Loyalist settlers arrived following the American Revolution.

Early Toronto (1793–1812)

In the aftermath of the American Revolution (1775–83), thousands of Americans fled north to Canada determined to remain under British jurisdiction. These migrants were known as the **United Empire Loyalists**, and several hundred of them settled along the northern shore of Lake Ontario. The British parliament responded to this sudden influx by passing the **Canada Act** of 1791, which divided the remaining British-American territories in two: Upper and Lower Canada, each with its own legislative councils. Lower Canada was broadly equivalent to today's Québec, and Upper Canada to modern-day Ontario. The first capital of Upper Canada was Niagara-on-the-Lake, but this was much too near the American border for comfort, and the province's new lieutenant-governor, the energetic **John Graves Simcoe**, moved his administration to the relative safety of Toronto in 1793. He called the new settlement **York** in honour of Frederick, the Duke of York and a son of George III, and he began his residence with an elaborate imperial ceremony, complete with a 21-gun salute from the warship on which he had arrived. Eton- and Oxford-educated, Simcoe was a man of style and vim, who brought his home with him in the form of a large "tent" (which included wooden walls, insulating boards and proper doors and windows) that had originally been made for Captain Cook's Pacific trips; Simcoe's soldiers were much impressed. Simcoe's wife, Elizabeth, made a marked impression of her own: her witty diaries remain a valuable source of information on colonial life, and her watercolours are among the first visual records of Native American life along the Lake Ontario shoreline.

Lieutenant-Governor Simcoe promptly arranged for the surrounding area to be surveyed, but his enthusiasm was skin-deep. He had wanted the new capital to be established further inland in a much more benign location, but his superior, Governor Dorchester, vetoed his choice with the wry comment that the only way of getting to Simcoe's chosen site was by hot-air balloon. Simcoe had decided to make a go of things, and he certainly thought York's harbour was first-rate, but he became increasingly exasperated by the marshy conditions, writing, "the city's site was better calculated for a frog pond…than for the residence of human beings". Three years later, Simcoe had had enough and sailed off back to England, leaving control in the hands of **Peter Russell**, a one-time British soldier, slave owner and compulsive gambler. Despite his checkered history and his relatively advanced age – Russell was 63 when Simcoe left – Russell proved a good administrator, improving Toronto's roads and setting land aside for a church, a courthouse and a market. Nonetheless, nicknamed "**Muddy York**", the capital failed to attract many settlers, and twenty years later it had just seven hundred inhabitants. The main deterrent to settlement, however, was the festering relationship between Britain and the US, which culminated in the **War of 1812**, whereby the Americans hoped to eject the British from Canada. The Americans thought this would be a fairly straightforward proposition and expected to be greeted as liberators. In both respects, they were quite wrong, but they did capture York without too much difficulty in 1813. Most of the American casualties came when the garrison of Fort York (see pp.54–55) blew up their own munitions and incidentally pulverized the approaching US army. The Americans stayed for just twelve days, and returned for an even shorter period three months later. Neither occupation was especially rigorous, with the Americans content to do a bit of minor burning and looting. Even this, however, was too much for the redoubtable **Reverend John Strachan**, who bombarded the Americans with demands about the treatment of prisoners and the need for the occupiers to respect private property. The **Treaty of Ghent** ended the war in 1814, and under its terms the US recognized the legitimacy of British North America.

The Family Compact

The Canada Act had established an Upper Canada government based on a Legislative Assembly, whose power was shared with an appointed assembly, an executive council and an appointed governor. This convoluted arrangement ultimately condemned the assembly to impotence. At the same time, a colonial elite built up chains of influence around several high-level officials, and by the 1830s economic and political power had fallen into the hands of an anglophile oligarchy christened the **Family Compact**. This group's most vociferous opponent was a radical Scot, **William Lyon Mackenzie** (see p.64), who promulgated his views both in his newspaper, the *Colonial Advocate*, and as a member of the Legislative Assembly. Mackenzie became the first mayor of Toronto, as the town was renamed in 1834, but the radicals were defeated in the elections two years later, and a frustrated Mackenzie drifted towards the idea of armed revolt. In 1837, he staged the **Upper Canadian Rebellion**, a badly organized uprising of a few hundred farmers, who marched down Yonge Street, fought a couple of half-hearted skirmishes and then melted away. Mackenzie escaped across the border and two of the other ringleaders were executed, but the British parliament, mindful of their earlier experiences in New England, took the hint, quickly liberalizing Upper Canada's administration instead of taking reprisals. In 1841, they granted Canada responsible government, reuniting the two provinces in a loose confederation that pre-figured the final union of 1867 when Upper Canada was re-designated Ontario as part of the British **Dominion of Canada**. Even Mackenzie was pardoned and allowed to return. His pardon seemed to fly in the face of his portrayal of the oligarchs as hard-faced reactionaries - indeed, this same privileged group pushed through a range of comparatively progressive social measures.

Victorian Toronto

Toronto boomed in the second half of the nineteenth century, consuming and exporting the products of its agricultural hinterland and benefiting from its good harbour and excellent maritime connections. Soon, Toronto had become a major manufacturing centre and, as a result, a railway terminus as well. Like every industrial city of the period, Toronto was further characterized by a discordant mixture of slums and leafy residential areas, its centre dotted with proud Victorian churches, offices and colleges.

Politically, the city was dominated by a conservative mercantile elite, which was exceedingly loyal to the British interest and maintained a strong Protestant tradition. This elite was sustained by the working-class **Orange Lodge**, a sectarian fraternal order that originated in Ireland and sought to advance Protestant interests in government. The Lodge's reactionary influence was a key feature of municipal politics – spurring Charles Dickens, for one, to write disparagingly of the city's "rabid Toryism" when he visited in the 1840s. That said, the Protestant working class was enthusiastic about public education, as were the Methodist-leaning middle classes, who spearheaded social reform movements like Suffrage and Temperance.

The Victorian period came to an appropriate close with a grand visit by the future **King George V**, who toured Toronto in 1901 with his extravagantly dressed entourage – all bustles and parasols, bearskins and pith helmets.

The early twentieth century

In the early twentieth century, Toronto's economic successes attracted immigrants by the thousands: in 1850, the city had 30,000 inhabitants, 81,000 in

1882, and 230,000 in 1910. Most of these immigrants came from Britain, and when **World War I** broke out in 1914 the citizens of loyalist Toronto poured into the streets to sing "Rule Britannia". Thousands of volunteers subsequently thronged the recruiting stations – an enthusiasm which cost many their lives: no fewer than seventy thousand Torontonians fought in the war, and casualties amounted to around fifteen percent.

Immediately after the war, Canada hit the economic buffers and just when it appeared that matters were on the mend, the economy was hit by the stock market crash of 1929. During the **Great Depression** unemployment reached astronomical levels – between thirty and thirty-five percent – and economic problems were compounded by the lack of a decent welfare system. The hastily established Department of Welfare was only able to issue food and clothing vouchers, meaning that thousands slept in the streets. Fate was cruel too: Toronto experienced some of the severest weather it had ever had, with perishing winters followed by boiling hot summers.

At the start of **World War II**, thousands of Torontonians rushed to join the armed forces once again. The British were extremely grateful and Churchill visited Canada on several occasions, making a series of famous speeches here. The war also resuscitated the Canadian economy – as well as that of the United States – and Toronto's factories were speedily put to war production uses. Boat-loads of British kids were also shipped to Toronto to escape the attentions of Hitler's Luftwaffe. After the war, Toronto set about the process of reconstruction in earnest. There was a lot to do. The city's infrastructure had not kept pace with the increase in population, and the water, transportation and sewage systems were desperately in need of improvement. Political change was also needed. A jumble of politically independent municipalities now surrounded a burgeoning core, with industries strung along the lakeshore and residential districts spreading beyond. The need for an overall system of authority was self-evident. Vigorous horse-trading resulted in the creation of **Metropolitan Toronto** in 1953, its governing body an elected council comprising 24 representatives, 12 apiece from the city and suburbs. The dominant figure of Metro politics for the first ten years was the dynamic **Frederick G. Gardiner**, aka "Big Daddy", who authorized the construction of the Gardiner Expressway.

The latter twentieth century

Nevertheless, for all its status as the capital of Ontario, Toronto remained strikingly provincial in comparison to Montréal until well into the 1950s. It was then that things began to change, the most conspicuous sign being the 1955 defeat of the incumbent mayor, Leslie Saunders, by **Nathan Phillips**, who became the city's first Jewish mayor. Something of a bon viveur, Phillips was often criticized for neglecting city business in favour of banquets and festivals, but he was very popular, being elected no less than four times between 1955 and 1962. Other pointers were the opening of the city's first cocktail bars in 1947 (there'd been taverns before, but none that sold liquor), and, three years later, a closely fought referendum whose result meant that public sporting events could be held on Sundays. Up until then, Sundays had been preserved as a "day of rest", and even Eaton's department store drew its curtains to prevent Sabbath-day window-shopping. The opening of the **St Lawrence Seaway** in 1959 also stimulated the city's economy, though not quite as much as had been anticipated – only after its completion did it become obvious that road transport would render much waterborne traffic obsolete.

In the 1960s the economy exploded, and the city's appearance was transformed by the construction of a series of mighty, modernistic **skyscrapers**. This helter-skelter development was further boosted by the troubles in Québec, where the clamour for fair treatment by the Francophones prompted many of Montréal's Anglophone-dominated financial institutions and big businesses to up-sticks and transfer to Toronto. Much to the glee of Torontonians, the census of 1976 showed that Toronto had become **Canada's biggest city**, edging Montréal by just one thousand inhabitants, and the gap has grown wider by the year. Meanwhile, Toronto's **ethnic complexion** was changing too, and by the early 1970s Canadians of British extraction were in the minority for the first time.

In the last twenty years, Toronto's economy has followed the cycles of boom and retrenchment common to the rest of the country, though real estate speculation was especially frenzied in the 1980s until the bottom fell out of the property market in 1988. In the mid-1990s, the **Progressive Conservatives** took control of Ontario, and their hard-nosed leader, **Mike Harris**, pushed through another governmental reorganization, combining the city of Toronto with its surrounding suburbs. This **"Mega City"**, as it has come to be known, has a population of around 4.5 million and covers no less than 10,000 square kilometres.

Toronto today

The change in status to megalopolis was deeply unpopular in the city itself, but Harris still managed to get himself re-elected in 2000 with the large-scale support of small-town and suburban Ontario. A hated figure amongst the province's liberals and socialists, Harris's conservative social policies are often blamed for the dramatic increase in the number of homeless people on the city's streets. Harris passed the premiership over to another Progressive Conservative, **Ernie Eves**, the province's 23rd premier – a less divisive figure perhaps, but one who has maintained his predecessor's conservative policies, albeit in a rather less confrontational (some would say less decisive) fashion.

In 2003, the Liberals, with a strong urban base of support, finally ousted the provincial Conservative government and elected an energetic, progressive, young city councilor named David Miller as mayor. By the end of the year the Liberal Finance Minister Paul Martin, who had used a strong Toronto base to challenge his boss, replaced **Jean Chrétien** as Prime Minister. For the first time in two decades, all three levels of government were in accord, and set about to address the long-term needs of Canada's cities, and Toronto's in particular.

Today Toronto is one of the world's favourite capital cities, sporting a flamboyance, self-confidence and vibrancy that would have amazed earlier generations. It is also a thoroughly cosmopolitan metropolis, with a strong environmental lobby that trains a beady eye on developers – often serving to stave off hare-brained schemes that might otherwise pulverize their surroundings.

C

CONTEXTS | History

Literary Toronto

Although there has been a literary scene in Toronto since the mid-nineteenth century, Toronto as a theme in Canadian literature has emerged only in modern decades. From the diaries of Elizabeth Simcoe in the late eighteenth century to the fiery editorials of William Lyon Mackenzie and the fond sketches of Henry Scadding at the turn of the twentieth century, early writings about Toronto were almost entirely non-fiction. When writers did delve into fiction, their subjects were often lofty discussions on matters of church and state, not the pastoral aspects of Toronto life. As early Canadian novelist Sara Jeanette Duncan (1861–1922) wrote of the fictional Ontario town of Elgin in *The Imperialist*, "Nothing compared with religion but politics, and nothing compared with politics but religion." These were the topics worthy of serious discussion.

Social realism

Social realism became a popular literary theme in the aftermath of World War I, but this gritty real-world writing style was slow to take off in Canada, where people preferred historical romances and small-town settings. Two important exceptions were **Morley Callaghan** (1903–1990) and **Hugh Garner** (1913–1979), who wrote about their native Toronto from a class perspective, focusing on aspects of life that had none of the high moral tones or Gothic romance associated with nineteenth-century novelists. Garner and Callaghan also tended to hover on the left of the political spectrum, far from the peculiarly Canadian Red-Tory brand of social satire best captured by humorist **Stephen Leacock** (1869-1944). The overwhelming emphasis was on small-town Ontario, which obscured the fact that the urban population of Toronto was awash in a sea of change. In Callaghan's *Such is My Beloved* (1934), a description of the demographic shift in a Toronto parish between World Wars has a contemporary ring, even though it describes a social construct that no longer exists:

The Cathedral was an old, soot-covered, imitation Gothic church that never aroused the enthusiasm of a visitor to the city. It had been in that neighbourhood for so long it now seemed just a part of an old city block. The parish was no longer a rich one. Wealthy old families moved away to new and more pretentious sections of the city, and poor foreigners kept coming in and turning the homes into rooming houses. These Europeans were usually Catholics, so the congregation at the Cathedral kept getting larger and poorer. Father Anglin really belonged to the finer, more prosperous days, and it made him sad to see how many of his own people had gone away, how small the collections were on Sunday and how few social organisations there were for the women. He was often bitter about the matter, although he should have seen that it was really a Protestant city, that all around his own Cathedral were handsome Protestant Churches, which were crowded on Sunday with well-dressed people, and that the majority of the citizens could hardly have told a stranger where the Catholic Cathedral was.

The Hugh Garner Co-operative Housing Development on Ontario Street is named in testament to Garner's novel *Cabbagetown*. The book is set in the

Depression and takes its name from the Toronto neighbourhood that Garner famously described as the largest Anglo-Saxon slum in North America. An unexpurgated version of the novel did not appear until 1968, by which time the streets he described had either been turned into tracts of sanitized public housing or refurbished as upscale Victorian residences for moneyed professionals. The improbable transformation of the Cabbagetown neighbourhood (see p.84) is documented in Garner's 1976 novel *The Intruders*.

The 1950s and 1960s

In the late 1950s and early 1960s, Toronto was the home base for a remarkable flowering of prose, poetry, painting and theatre. Many of Canada's leading poets, essayists and novelists, most notably **Margaret Atwood**, emerged from the milieu that crowded into the all-night poetry readings at the Bohemian Embassy on St Nicholas Street. Other major talents from that era were **Milton Acorn**, known across Canada as "The People's Poet", **Gwendolyn MacEwen**, and **b.p. nichol** and **Paul Dutton**, both of whom belonged to the Four Horsemen, a poetry performance group. These artists and their contemporaries set up awards to encourage new writers and sustain established ones; they mentored one another at every opportunity, and took many newcomers under their wings. They encouraged a school of writing that considered place, in this case Toronto, to be fundamental to storytelling. For them, Toronto was not, as Robert Fulford said, "a place to graduate from", it was a place to stay. In this passage from *In the Skin of a Lion* (1987), by **Michael Ondaatje** (who came later, though the passage still applies), Commissioner Harris, who built Toronto engineering feats like the Bloor Street Viaduct and the Water Filtration Plant, describes a vision:

One night, I had a dream. I got off the bus at College – it was when we were moving College Street so it would hook up to Carlton – and I came to this area I had never been to. I saw fountains where there used to be an intersection. What was strange was that I knew my way around. I knew that soon I should turn and see a garden and more fountains. When I awoke from the dream the sense of familiarity kept tugging me all day. In my dream the next night I was walking in a mysterious park off Spadina Avenue. The following day I was lunching with the architect John Lyle. I told him of these landscapes and he began to laugh. "These are real," he said. "Where?" I asked. "In Toronto?" It turned out I was dreaming about projects for the city that had been rejected over the years. Wonderful things that were said to be too vulgar or too expensive, too this, too that. And I was walking through these places, beside the traffic circle at Yonge and Bloor, down the proposed Federal Avenue to Union Station. Lyle was right. These were real places. They could have existed. I mean, the Bloor Street viaduct and this building here are just a hint of what could have been done here.

In 1965 Stan Bevington and Wayne Clifford took over a back-lane carriage house space where Marshall McLuhan had lectured and founded **Coach House Press**, which became the incubator for all that was new and adventurous in Canadian literature. In addition to publishing the early works of Atwood and Ondaatje, whose *In the Skin of a Lion* is perhaps the definitive Toronto novel – Coach House began a tradition of giving talented new writers their first break:

Paul Quarrington, Susan Swan and anthologist Alberto Manguel are just three examples. The company continued to expand its interests, putting out textbooks and a Québec translation series featuring emerging Québecois authors like Jacques Ferron, Nichole Brossard and Victor-Levy Beaulieu. A turbulent period of conflict on the editorial board and financial difficulties caused the press to be dissolved in 1996, but in 1997 Bevington announced the birth of Coach House Press Books, an establishment devoted to beautiful, handmade limited editions and, way at the other end of the publishing spectrum, online novels for the Internet.

The 1970s and 1980s

More prominent Toronto-based authors followed in the wake of this particularly fertile period, including **Timothy Findley** and **Robertson Davies**. Findley's third novel, *The Wars* (1977), established him as a major literary talent, and more recent novels such as *Headhunter* (1993) and *The Piano Man's Daughter* (1995), both set in Toronto, make great use of local history, lore and settings.

Robertson Davies, one of the most significant novelists of the postwar era, uses quirky, thinly veiled descriptions of Toronto institutions such as the University of Toronto in novels like *The Rebel Angels* (1981), which is imbued with a strong sense of place. Both Davies and Findley have a knack for recognizing the rich stories that have yet to be told about the people and the city of Toronto. Rather than portraying Toronto as a stuffy, provincial town, the characters of a Findley or Davies novel are flamboyant, mystical, and are often based on obscure events in Canadian history.

In the Seventies and Eighties, new voices continued to find their way into Canadian literature. The **immigrant experience** in Toronto has been covered since the early nineteenth century, but early writers usually saw themselves as importing values and mores, and they shared similar cultural backgrounds and religions. Writers like **Austin Clarke**, who was born in Barbados, **Michael Ondaatje**, who was born in Ceylon, and **M.G. Vassanji**, who is originally from Kenya, contributed a different perspective of immigrant life in Toronto. In Vassanji's *No New Land*, customary activities become strange, and the landmarks native Torontonians see as everyday landmarks become exotic:

What would immigrants in Toronto do without Honest Ed's, the block-wide carnival that's also a store, the brilliant kaaba to which people flock even from the suburbs? A centre of attraction whose energy never ebbs, simply transmutes, at night its thousands of dazzling lights splash the sidewalk in flashes of yellow and green and red, and the air sizzles with catchy fluorescent messages circled by running lights. The dazzle and sparkle that's seen as far away as Asia and Africa in the bosoms of bourgeois homes where they dream of foreign goods and emigration. The Lalanis and other Dar immigrants would go there on Sundays, entire families getting off at the Bathurst station to join the droves crossing Bloor Street West on their way to that shopping paradise.

The 1990s and beyond

By the edge of the millennium, a full generation of Torontonians had grown up surrounded by different cultures and was fully equipped with the language of diversity that an earlier generation had struggled to create. For example, novelist **Dionne Brand**'s recent work, *What We All Long For*, explores the weave of personal relationships and social histories among Toronto's visible minorities – a phrase increasingly outdated – who are Canadian born or raised. Brand uses the metaphor of locales and buildings that are always changing from one reality (a bank, a pizza parlour, a house) into another (a pub, a boutique, a parking lot) to illustrate her city's fluid demography. And while there has always been an ambiguity about Toronto that has made capturing the city's essence difficult, poet-turned-novelist **Anne Michaels**, beautifully explored the city's many faces in *Fugitive Pieces* (1996):

Like Athens, Toronto is an active port. It's a city of derelict warehouses and docks, of waterfront silos and freight yards, coal yards and a sugar refinery; of distilleries, the cloying smell of malt rising from the lake on humid summer nights.

It's a city where almost everyone has come from elsewhere – a market, a caravansary – bringing with them their different ways of dying and marrying, their kitchens and songs. A city of forsaken worlds; a language a kind of farewell.

It's a city of ravines. Remnants of wilderness have been left behind. Through these great sunken gardens you can traverse the city beneath the streets, look up to the floating neighbourhoods, houses built in the treetops.

It's a city of valleys spanned by bridges. A railway runs through back yards. A city of hidden lanes, of clapboard garages with corrugated tin roofs, of wooden fences sagging where children have made shortcuts. In April, the thickly treed streets are flooded with samara, a green tide. Forgotten rivers, abandoned quarries, the remains of an Iroquois fortress. Public parks hazy with subtropical memory, a city built in the bowl of a prehistoric lake.

The above description would have confounded earlier generations of the city's writers, who lived in Toronto but uniformly placed their poems and novels elsewhere. Likewise, the perspective of outsiders who came to Toronto in the nineteenth and early twentieth centuries almost always stressed the city's perceived rigidities. From Charles Dickens to Ernest Hemingway and Wyndham Lewis, literary visitors often took Toronto's social and political milieu to be narrow and provincial. With the city's social and cultural maturation in the latter half of the twentieth century, however, the city has come to recognize a new literary pride; one that has allowed Toronto's artists to describe the city with passion, compassion and lyricism.

Books

Though all the books below have something to recommend them by, we've marked titles we highly recommend with a ⚡. Wherever possible, books are listed by their most recent edition and most accessible imprint. If unavailable in bookstores, most can be ordered directly from the publisher. Out-of-print titles are indicated by o/p.

Impressions and memoirs

John Bently-Mays *Emerald City: Toronto Visited* (Viking Press). Thoughtful critical essays about the city, its architecture and its inhabitants.

C.S. Clark *On Toronto the Good: A Social Study* (Coles Canadiana Collection, o/p). Originally published in 1898, this is one of the city's earliest urban studies, exploring the evolution of the many aspects of city life that have made Toronto what it is today.

John Robert Colombo *Haunted Toronto* (Houslow Press). Colombo is a poet, novelist and indefatigable anthologist of Canadiana. This collection of Toronto hauntings highlights the city's interest in the weird and fantastic.

Wayne Grady *Toronto in the Wild: Field Notes of an Urban Naturalist* (Macfarlane, Walter & Ross). Toronto has a wide assortment of flora and fauna living in its ravines, parks, empty lots and rooftops. Grady chronicles them all in this picture-filled book.

William Kilbourn (ed) *The Toronto Book: An Anthology of Writings Past and Present* (Macmillan of Canada, o/p). A collection of over a century of imaginative descriptions of Toronto.

David McFadden *Trip Around Lake Ontario* (Coach House Press, 1988; reprinted in Great Lakes Suite, Talon Books). Part of a trilogy detailing the author's circumnavigation of lakes Ontario, Erie and Huron written in a deceptively forthright style.

⚡ **George Rust D'Eye** *Cabbagetown Remembered* (Stoddart and Company). An intimate portrait and historical account of this popular Toronto neighbourhood, its people and its landmarks. Wonderful photographs.

William White (ed) *The Complete Toronto Dispatches, 1920–1924* (Charles Scribner's Sons). Ernest Hemingway's first professional writing job was with the *Toronto Star* as both a local reporter and a European correspondent. This is a collection of his dispatches for the paper.

History

Carl Benn *The Iroquois in the War of 1812* (University of Toronto Press). In 1812 the United States, at war with Canada, invaded and briefly occupied York (which later became Toronto). The role played by the Five Nations and Iroquois peoples in the war was pivotal to Canada's survival, and the ramifications of the war affected the aboriginal people of Ontario for years to come.

William Dendy *Lost Toronto* (Oxford University Press). This book documents the unfortunate loss of countless historically important Toronto buildings to the wrecking ball, fire and neglect. An eye-opener for those who only think of Toronto as a modern urban landscape.

🏃 **Harold Innis** *The Fur Trade in Canada: An Introduction to Canadian Economic History* (University of Toronto Press). Words like dramatic, sweeping and engaging are not usually associated with books on economic history, but in this case they fit the bill. Innis's study is invaluable for the insight it gives to pre-European Canada, and its trading customs with Ontario's native peoples.

Anna Jameson *Winter Studies and Summer Rambles in Canada* (Coles Publishing Company). Originally published in 1839, these tart observations of early Toronto's colonial society are marked by a sense of wonderment at the vastness of Canada's untamed land.

Kenneth McNaught *The Penguin History of Canada* (Penguin). A concise, annotated analysis of Canada's economic, social and political history.

Henry Scadding *Toronto of Old* (Oxford University Press, o/p). Originally published in 1873, and written by a member of one of Toronto's founding families, these sketches and pen-and-ink illustrations have an immediacy and charm that give insight to Toronto's early years.

🏃 **Elizabeth Simcoe** *Mrs. Simcoe's Diary*, Mary Innis, editor (Macmillan of Canada). The wife of Upper Canada's first lieutenant-governor and an early resident of York (Toronto), not only did Simcoe give detailed observations of the landscape and the city's way of life, but she was also an astute political observer, offering portraits of major historical figures like Chief Joseph Brant.

Randall White *Toronto The Good: Toronto in the 1920s* (Dundurn Press). A detailed portrait of the evolution of a modern city and its people. Stuffed with intriguing facts, observations and photographs.

George Woodcock *A Social History of Canada* (Penguin). An erudite and very readable book about the peoples of Canada and the country's development. Woodcock is the most perceptive of Canada's historians.

Architecture and arts

🏃 **Eric Arthur** *Toronto: No Mean City* (University of Toronto Press). One of the earliest and best-known studies of Toronto's architectural heritage, written by the father of the city's architectural conservancy movement.

Robert Fulford *Accidental City* (Macfarlane, Walter & Ross, o/p). This entertaining book on the vagaries of the city's development pokes around in some unlikely nooks and crannies. The central thesis is somewhat bogus (almost all cities

develop haphazardly), but it's a good read all the same.

Greg Gatenby *Toronto, A Literary Guide* (McArthur). This walking-tour guide of Toronto is a wonderful way to get to know the city. Gatenby is the founder or the marvellous International Festival of Authors (see p.220).

Glenn Gould *The Glenn Gould Reader*, Tim Page, editor (Lester & Orpen Dennys, o/p). Sometimes chatty, sometimes pompous, Gould's voice and erudition shine through this collection of essays, articles and letters written from early adulthood to the end of his short life.

Liz Lundell *The Estates of Old Toronto* (Boston Mills Press). A pictorial study of nineteenth-century domestic architecture in Toronto, as well as a social history. Most of the buildings, unfortunately, have been lost to time.

Dennis Reid *A Concise History of Canadian Painting* (Oxford University Press). Not especially concise, this

book is a thorough trawl through Canada's leading artists, with bags of biographical detail and lots of black-and-white (and a few colour) illustrations of major works.

Harold Towne and David P. Silcox *Tom Thomson: The Silence in the Storm* (McClelland and Stewart). A study of the career and inspirations of Tom Thomson, one of Toronto's best-known artists. Towne, the co-writer, was also a major Canadian artist.

Travel and specific guides

Katherine Ashenburg *Going to Town: Six Southern Ontario Towns* (Macfarlane, Walter & Ross). A terrific day-trip guide to a variety of towns within driving distance of Toronto.

Green Tourism Association of Toronto *The Other Guide to Toronto: Opening the Door to Green Tourism* (Green Tourism Association). This

perfect guidebook imparts useful and intriguing information about Toronto's green spaces. Sure to contain surprises even for life-long Torontonians.

Elliott Katz *The Great Toronto Bicycling Guide* (Great North Books). A useful guide to Toronto-area bike paths as well as background information about the region itself.

Fiction

Margaret Atwood *The Robber Bride* (McClelland and Stewart). Toronto-nian readers had a field day with the thinly veiled descriptions of famous and infamous locals. A snap-shot of time and place, this book lives up to Atwood's high storytelling standards.

David Bezmozgis *Natasha: And Other Stories* (Harper Perennial). Seven razor-sharp short stories about Toronto's Russian Jewish community.

Dionne Brand *What We All Long For* (Alfred A. Knopf Canada). Covers the entwined lives of four friends, Jackie, Carla, Oku and Tuyen, and Tuyen's older brother, Quy, who was separated from the family in 1970s

Vietnam. Set in the summer of 2002 with the World Cup series as the backdrop.

Austin Clarke *The Origin of Waves* (McClelland and Stewart). Two Barbadians meet in a Toronto blizzard after a separation of almost fifty years. A warm novel of two lives and the journeys each has made.

Robertson Davies *The Cunning Man* (McClelland and Stewart). Jonathan Hullah is a Toronto doctor befuddled by the death of one Father Hobbes, some twenty years earlier. As he recalls the circumstances surrounding the priest's death, Hullah also finds time to ruminate on theatre, art, God

△ Margaret Atwood

and the strange secrets of a doctor's consulting room.

🏃 **Timothy Findley** *Headhunter* (Harper Collins). A sombre, futuristic novel that brings aspects of Conrad's Heart of Darkness to

contemporary Rosedale, an haute bourgeois Toronto neighbourhood.

Lawrence Hill *Any Known Blood* (Harper Collins and William Morrow & Co). Canadian novelists and their readers love books about dynasties, and *Any Known Blood* is an exceptional addition to the multigenerational novel. Extremely valuable in giving a portrait of African-Canadian history.

Gwendolyn MacEwen *Norman's Land* (Coach House Press, o/p). MacEwen once called Canada the most exotic place in the world, and she defends her thesis admirably in this enormously creative novel about a character she first introduced in her short-story collection *Norman*.

Michael Ondaatje *In the Skin of a Lion* (Vintage Books). This is the novel that introduces readers to the characters in the more famous *The English Patient*. It spans a period between the end of World War I and the Great Depression in East End Toronto.

Nino Ricci *Where Has She Gone?* (McClelland and Stewart). The third in a trilogy that began with *Lives of the Saints*, this book is about an Italian-Canadian family's sometimes tragic attempts to find its identity.

Robert J. Sawyer *Calculating God* (Tor Books). Hollus, an alien scientist, comes to earth, specifically Toronto, believing that the fossil collection at the Royal Ontario Museum will prove the existence of God. Hollus enlists the assistance of the ROM's human palaeontologist, a life-long atheist dying of cancer. Nominated for a coveted Hugo Award.

Russell Smith *Muriella Pent* (Anchor Canada). An Oxford educated Caribbean poet is billeted in the nouveau riche mansion of a Toronto socialite. Smith addresses Toronto's heterogeneity through the protagonist's frequently brittle relationships.

Susan Swan *The Wives of Bath* (Alfred J. Knopf). At a Toronto girls' school in the Sixties, the protagonist, Mouse, struggles with notions of feminine beauty as her best friend struggles with gender identity. A wry novel written in a genre the author describes as "sexual Gothic".

ugh Guides To World Of Music

the reliable Rough Guide series' *The Guardian (UK)*

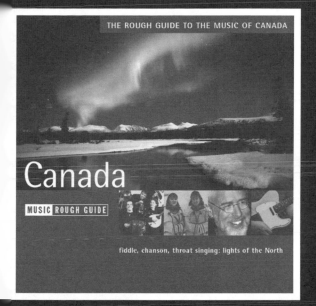

THE ROUGH GUIDE TO THE MUSIC OF CANADA

Canada

MUSIC ROUGH GUIDE

fiddle, chanson, throat singing: lights of the North

every imaginable kind of music, which somehow seems only fitting for such a vastly land. As a new nation built on immigration and cultural mixing, it is one where artists defy traditional boundaries. Including Celtic fiddle traditions of Cape Breton, Québécois throat singing and more, *The Rough Guide To The Music Of Canada,* focuses on some tanding roots music traditions created in established cultural communities, together he newer hybrids those styles have created.

und sampler at

w you can visit www.worldmusic.net/radio to tune into the exciting Rough ide Radio Show, with a new show each month presenting new releases, erviews, features and competitions.

m book and record shops worldwide or order direct from
Network, 6 Abbeville Mews, 88 Clapham Park Road, London SW4 7BX, UK
252 020 7498 5353 post@worldmusic.net

Small print and

Index

A Rough Guide to Rough Guides

Published in 1982, the first Rough Guide – to Greece – was a student scheme that became a publishing phenomenon. Mark Ellingham, a recent graduate in English from Bristol University, had been travelling in Greece the previous summer and couldn't find the right guidebook. With a small group of friends he wrote his own guide, combining a highly contemporary, journalistic style with a thoroughly practical approach to travellers' needs.

The immediate success of the book spawned a series that rapidly covered dozens of destinations. And, in addition to impecunious backpackers, Rough Guides soon acquired a much broader and older readership that relished the guides' wit and inquisitiveness as much as their enthusiastic, critical approach and value-for-money ethos.

These days, Rough Guides include recommendations from shoestring to luxury and cover more than two hundred destinations around the globe, including almost every country in the Americas and Europe, more than half of Africa, and most of Asia and Australasia. Our ever-growing team of authors and photographers is spread all over the world, particularly in Europe, the USA and Australia.

In the early 1990s, Rough Guides branched out of travel, with the publication of Rough Guides to World Music, Classical Music and the Internet. All three have become benchmark titles in their fields, spearheading the publication of a wide range of books under the Rough Guide name.

Including the travel series, Rough Guides now number more than 350 titles, covering: phrasebooks, waterproof maps, music guides from Opera to Heavy Metal, reference works as diverse as Conspiracy Theories and Shakespeare, and popular culture books from iPods to Poker. Rough Guides also produce a series of more than 120 World Music CDs in partnership with World Music Network.

Visit www.roughguides.com to see our latest publications.

Rough Guide travel images are available for commercial licensing at www.roughguidespictures.com.

SMALL PRINT

Rough Guide credits

Text editor: Amy Hegarty
Layout: Jessica Subramanian, Amit Verma
Cartography: Jasbir Sandhu, Katie Lloyd-Jones
Picture editor: Jj Luck
Production: Katherine Owers
Proofreader: Amanda Jones
Cover design: Chloë Roberts
Photographer: Enrique Uranga
Editorial: London Kate Berens, Claire Saunders, Geoff Howard, Polly Thomas, Richard Lim, Clifton Wilkinson, Alison Murchie, Karoline Densley, Andy Turner, Ella O'Donnell, Ruth Blackmore, Keith Drew, Edward Aves, Nikki Birrell, Helen Marsden, Alice Park, Sarah Eno, Joe Staines, Duncan Clark, Peter Buckley, Matthew Milton, Tracy Hopkins; **New York** Andrew Rosenberg, Richard Koss, Steven Horak, AnneLise Sorensen, Hunter Slaton, April Isaacs
Design & Pictures: London Simon Bracken, Dan May, Diana Jarvis, Mark Thomas, Harriet Mills; **Delhi** Madhulita Mohapatra, Umesh Aggarwal, Ajay Verma, Ankur Guha

Production: Julia Bovis, Sophie Hewat
Cartography: London Ed Wright, Maxine Repath; **Delhi** Manish Chandra, Rajesh Chhibber, Jai Prakash Mishra, Rajesh Mishra, Ashutosh Bharti, Animesh Pathak, Karobi Gogoi
Online: New York Jennifer Gold, Kristin Mingrone; **Delhi** Manik Chauhan, Narender Kumar, Shekhar Jha, Rakesh Kumar, Lalit K. Sharma, Chhandita Chakravarty
Marketing and publicity: London Richard Trillo, Niki Hanmer, David Wearn, Demelza Dallow, Louise Maher; **New York** Geoff Colquitt, Megan Kennedy, Katy Ball; **Delhi** Reem Khokhar
Custom publishing and foreign rights: Philippa Hopkins
Manager India: Punita Singh
Series editor: Mark Ellingham
Reference director: Andrew Lockett
PA to Managing and Publishing directors: Megan McIntyre
Publishing director: Martin Dunford
Managing director: Kevin Fitzgerald

Publishing information

This fourth edition published April 2006 by
Rough Guides Ltd
80 Strand, London WC2R 0RL
345 Hudson St, 4th Floor,
New York, NY 10014, USA
14 Local Shopping Centre, Panchsheel Park,
New Delhi 110017, India
Distributed by the Penguin Group
Penguin Books Ltd
80 Strand, London WC2R 0RL
Penguin Putnam, Inc
375 Hudson Street, NY 10014, USA
Penguin Group (Australia)
250 Camberwell Road, Camberwell
Victoria 3124, Australia
Penguin Books Canada Ltd
10 Alcorn Avenue, Toronto, Ontario
M4V 1E4 Canada
Penguin Group (New Zealand)
Cnr Rosedale and Airborne Roads,
Albany, Auckland, New Zealand

Typeset in Bembo and Helvetica to an original design by Henry Iles.

Printed and bound in China.

© Phil Lee and Helen Lovekin 2006

No part of this book may be reproduced in any form without permission from the publisher except for the quotation of brief passages in reviews.

256pp includes index

A catalogue record for this book is available from the British Library.

ISBN-13: 978-1-84353-596-6
ISBN-10: 1-84353-596-3

Help us update

We've gone to a lot of effort to ensure that the fourth edition of **The Rough Guide to Toronto** is accurate and up to date. However, things change – places get "discovered", opening hours are notoriously fickle, restaurants and rooms raise prices or lower standards. If you feel we've got it wrong or left something out, we'd like to know, and if you can remember the address, the price, the time, the phone number, so much the better.

We'll credit all contributions, and send a copy of the next edition (or any other Rough

Guide if you prefer) for the best letters. Everyone who writes to us and isn't already a subscriber will receive a copy of our full-colour thrice-yearly newsletter. Please mark letters: "**Rough Guide Toronto Update**" and send to: Rough Guides, 80 Strand, London WC2R 0RL, or Rough Guides, 4th Floor, 345 Hudson St, New York, NY 10014. Or send an email to **mail@roughguides.com**.

Have your questions answered and tell others about your trip at **www.roughguides.atinfopop.com**.

Acknowledgements

Phil Lee would like to extend a special thanks to Diane Helinski of Ontario Tourism for all her help and kindness. Many thanks also to Paul and Carol Buer of the Mulberry Tree for their charming hospitality and company and to Ellen Flowers of Tourism Toronto. Last but certainly not least, three cheers for my co–author, Helen, who, as ever, was a pleasure to work with on this new edition, and to my persevering and patient editor, Amy Hegarty.

Helen Lovekin would like to offer many, many thanks to the legion of friends, colleagues, store owners, restaurateurs, artists and impresarios whose creativity and hard work have given Toronto all the

wonderful facilities detailed here. Also a word of gratitude to my dear friend and co-author Phil Lee. And thanks to David Falconer for his photo in "About the authors". Finally, deepest thanks to John Harnden, whose support, advice and love make all things possible.

The editor would like to thank Phil Lee and Helen Lovekin for all their hard work and for being good sports throughout. Additional thanks goes to Jessica Subramanian, Amit Verma, Umesh Aggarwal, Jj Luck, Katie Lloyd-Jones, Jasbir Sandhu, Diana Jarvis, Nikki Birrell, Katherine Owers, Amanda Jones, Chloë Roberts, Enrique Uranga and Andrew Rosenberg.

Readers' letters

Thanks to all the readers who took the trouble to write in with their comments and suggestions (and apologies to anyone whose name we've misspelt or omitted):

Xavier Balducci, Chris Clayton, Philip Nyman, Tom Petch, David Saville.

Photo credits

All photos © Rough Guides except the following:

Cover
Front cover: Skating in Nathan Phillips Square © Image Ontario
Inside back cover: Neighbourhood grocery store © Alamy
Back cover: Waterfront © Image Ontario

Title page
Toronto © David Noton Photography/Alamy

Introduction
Kensington Gardens © Atlantide S.N.C./age fotostock
Toronto Islands © David Trevor/Alamy
Kew Gardens courtesy Kew Gardens

Things not to miss
01 Ice skating at New City Hall © Jon Arnold Images/Alamy
02 Monet, Claude French, 1840-1926 *Vétheuil en été*, 1879 Oil on canvas 67.7 x 90.5cm Art Gallery of Ontario, Toronto Purchase, 1929
06 Courtesy of Toronto Symphony Orchestra
11 Courtesy of Toronto International Film Festival
12 High Park © Bill Brooks/Alamy
15 Kensington Market © Brian Atkinson/Alamy
16 Georgian Bay Islands National Park © Richard Olsenius/National Geographic/Getty Images
17 Mummy case courtesy of the Royal Ontario Museum
19 The Royal George and the Festival Theatre © Andrée Lanthier

Black and whites
p.160 Courtesy Ultra Supper Club

p.176 Courtesy of Guverment
p.189 Gay Pride parade © Jorge Uzon
p.199 Courtesy Holt Renfrew
p.205 Toronto Maple Leafs © Dave Sandford/Getty Images
p.219 Toronto International Carnival Parade © J.P. MOCZULSKI/AFP/Getty Images
p.240 Margaret Atwood © Colin McPherson/Colin McPherson/Corbis

Colour insert: The arts
Harris, Lawren S. Canadian 1885-1970 *Above Lake Superior* c.1922. Oil on canvas 121.9 x 152.4cm Art Gallery of Ontario, Toronto. Gift from the Reuben and Kate Leonard Canadian Fund, 1929.
Thomson, Tom Canadian 1877-1917 *Round Lake, Mud Bay*, fall 1915. Oil on wood 21.5 x 26.8cm Art Gallery of Ontario, Toronto. Gift from the J.S. McLean Collection, Toronto, 1969. Donated by the Ontario Heritage Foundation, 1988.
Sculpture by Henry Moore © Atlantide S.N.C./age footstock
The Toronto Symphony at Roy Thompson Hall in Toronto © Kelly-Mooney Photography/Corbis
Johnny Depp at the Toronto International Film Festival © Mario Anzuoni/Reuters/Corbis
Mike Myers on Canada's Walk of Fame © Reuters/Corbis

Colour insert: Ethnic Toronto
Toronto International Carnival Parade © J.P. MOCZULSKI/AFP/Getty Images
Dim sum © Bruce Burkhardt/Corbis

Index

All map entries are listed in **colour**

N

O

P

Q

R

I

INDEX

Map symbols

maps are listed in the full index using coloured text

▬▪▬▪	International boundary	Ⓢ	Streetcar station
⟹✦⟸	Canadian highway	✉	Post office
⟹⑤⟸	US interstate highway	◉	Accommodation
⟹⑤⟸	US highway	▣	Restaurant
⟹⑤⟸	Provincial highway	⚠	Campsite
═══	Major road	✈	Airport
═══	Minor road	🌂	Lighthouse
-----	Path	⚲	Church (regional maps)
▬▬▪▬	Railway	▬	Building
⟿⊕⟿	Metro line	⊞	Church (town maps)
───	Coastline/river	⬭	Stadium
─ ─	Ferry	⊡	Cemetery
ⓘ	Information office	▦	Park

MAP SYMBOLS

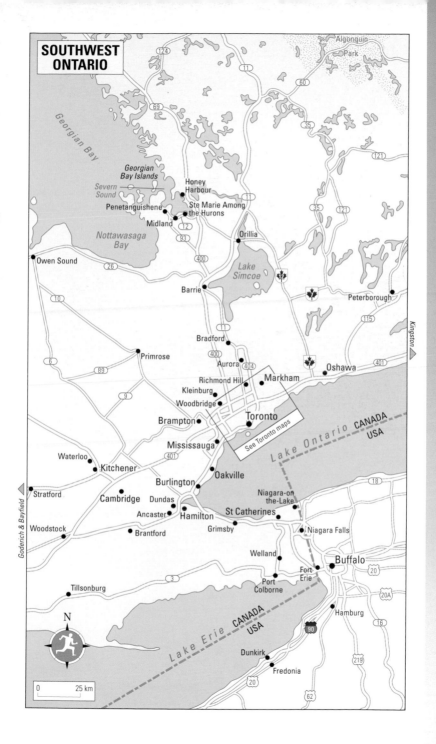

SOUTHWEST ONTARIO

Algonquin Park

Georgian Bay

Georgian Bay Islands

Severn Sound

Honey Harbour

Penetanguishene

Ste Marie Among the Hurons

Midland

Nottawasaga Bay

Orillia

Owen Sound

Lake Simcoe

Barrie

Peterborough

Primrose

Bradford

Aurora

Oshawa

Richmond Hill

Markham

Kleinburg

Woodbridge

Brampton

Toronto

See Toronto maps

Waterloo

Kitchener

Mississauga

Lake Ontario   CANADA
USA

Stratford

Burlington

Oakville

Cambridge

Dundas

Niagara-on-the-Lake

Ancaster

Hamilton

St Catherines

Woodstock

Brantford

Grimsby

Niagara Falls

Welland

Buffalo

Fort Erie

Tillsonburg

Port Colborne

Hamburg

N

Lake Erie   CANADA
USA

Dunkirk

Fredonia

Kingston

Goderich & Bayfield

0   25 km

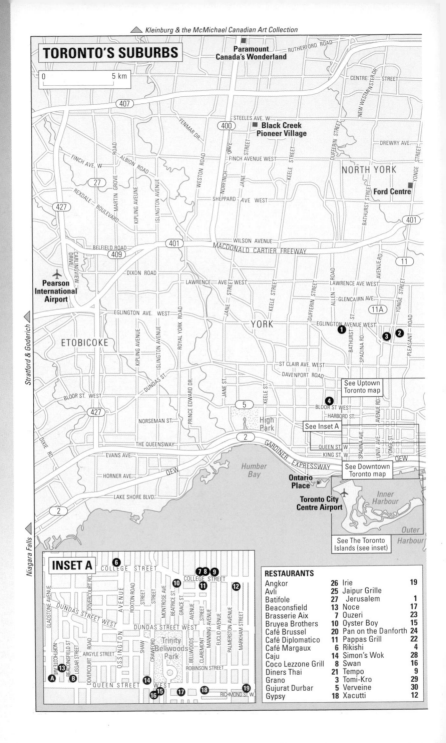

TORONTO'S SUBURBS

0 ——— 5 km

Paramount
Canada's Wonderland

RUTHERFORD ROAD

CENTRE STREET

NEW WESTMINSTER DR.

407

STEELES AVE. W.

400 ■ Black Creek
Pioneer Village

DREWRY AVE.

FINCH AVE. W

ALBION ROAD

FENMAR DR.

WESTON ROAD

OVER

JANE STREET

NORTHFINCH

KEELE STREET

DUFFERIN STREET

FINCH AVENUE WEST

NORTH YORK

YONGE STREET

27

REXDALE BOULEVARD

MARTIN GROVE

KIPLING AVENUE

ISLINGTON AVENUE

SHEPPARD AVE. WEST

BATHURST STREET

Ford Centre

427

401

CARLINGVIEW DRIVE

BELFIELD ROAD

409

WILSON AVENUE

401 MACDONALD CARTIER FREEWAY

AVENUE RD.

11

DIXON ROAD

Pearson
International
Airport

LAWRENCE AVE WEST

LAWRENCE AVE WEST

JANE STREET

KEELE STREET

DUFFERIN STREET

ALLEN RD.

GLENCAIRN AVE.

11A

EGLINGTON AVE. WEST

YORK

EGLINGTON AVENUE WEST
❶

BATHURST ST.

SPADINA RD.

❸ ❷

PLEASANT RD.

YONGE STREET

ETOBICOKE

KIPLING AVENUE

ISLINGTON AVENUE

ROYAL YORK ROAD

PRINCE EDWARD DR.

JANE ST.

KEELE ST.

ST. CLAIR AVE. WEST

DAVENPORT ROAD

See Uptown
Toronto map

BLOOR ST. WEST

DUNDAS ST.

BLOOR ST. WEST

427

NORSEMAN ST.

High
Park

5

BLOOR ST WEST
❹

HARBORD ST.

See Inset A

SPADINA AVE.

AVENUE RD.

UNIV. AVE.

YONG ST.

THE QUEENSWAY

2

QUEEN ST. W

KING ST. W

QEW

See Downtown
Toronto map

Stratford & Goderich ◁

EVANS AVE.

DIXIE RD.

HORNER AVE.

QEW

GARDINER EXPRESSWAY

Humber
Bay

Ontario
Place

Inner
Harbour

LAKE SHORE BLVD.

Toronto City
Centre Airport

Niagara Falls ◁

2

Outer
Harbour

See The Toronto
Islands (see inset)

INSET A ❻

COLLEGE STREET

❼❽❾

GLADSTONE AVENUE

DODGE

DOVERCOURT RD.

COLLEGE STREET

OSSINGTON AVENUE

ROXTON ROAD

MONTROSE AVE.

BEATRICE ST.

GRACE ST.

❿

❶

CRAWFORD

SHAW

AVENUE

CLAREMONT

BELLWOODS

MANNING AVENUE

EUCLID AVENUE

PALMERSTON AVENUE

MARKHAM STREET

⓬

DUNDAS STREET WEST

DUNDAS STREET WEST

BEACONSFIELD ST.

LISGAR STREET

ARGYLE STREET

⓭

Trinity
Bellwoods
Park

ROBINSON STREET

Ⓐ Ⓑ

QUEEN STREET

⓮

WEST

RICHMOND ST. W.

⓰⓯

⓱

⓲

⓳

RESTAURANTS

Angkor	**26**	Irie	**19**
Avli	**25**	Jaipur Grille	
Batifole	**27**	Jerusalem	**1**
Beaconsfield		Noce	**17**
Brasserie Aix	**7**	Ouzeri	**23**
Bruyea Brothers	**10**	Oyster Boy	**15**
Café Brussel	**20**	Pan on the Danforth	**24**
Café Diplomatico	**11**	Pappas Grill	**22**
Café Margaux	**6**	Rikishi	**4**
Caju	**14**	Simon's Wok	**28**
Coco Lezzone Grill	**8**	Swan	**16**
Diners Thai	**21**	Tempo	**9**
Grano	**3**	Tomi-Kro	**29**
Gujurat Durbar	**5**	Verveine	**30**
Gypsy	**18**	Xacutti	**12**

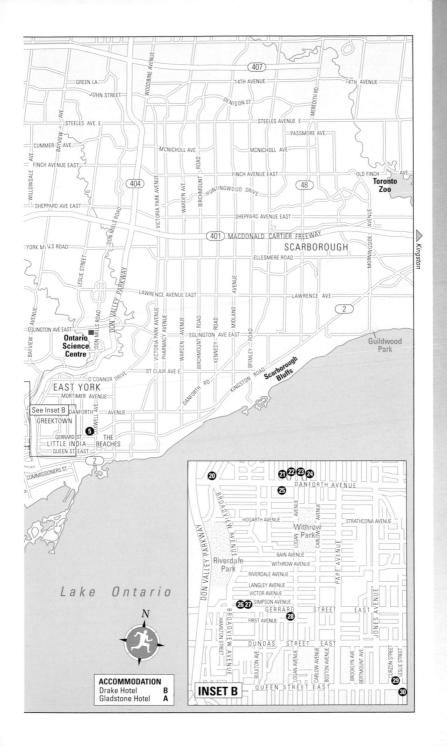

ACCOMMODATION
Drake Hotel   B
Gladstone Hotel   A

INSET B

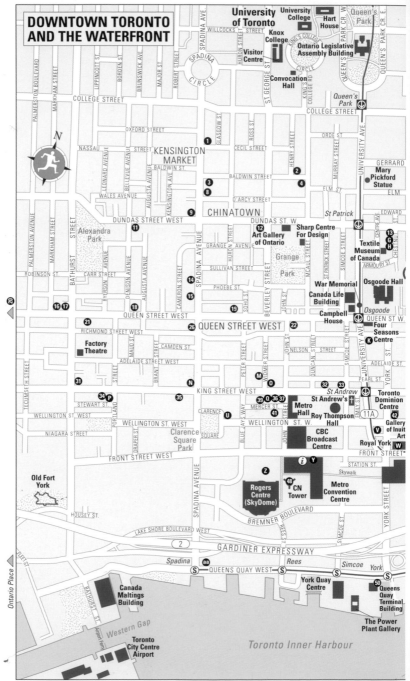

DOWNTOWN TORONTO AND THE WATERFRONT

University of Toronto

University College

Hart House

Queen's Park

WILLCOCKS STREET

Knox College

Ontario Legislative Assembly Building

Visitor Centre

SPADINA CIRCLE

Convocation Hall

Queen's Park

COLLEGE STREET

Queen's Park

COLLEGE STREET

OXFORD STREET

KENSINGTON MARKET

CECIL STREET

BALDWIN ST

ORDE ST

Mary Pickford Statue

GERRARD

ELM ST

ELM

EDWARD

NASSAU

LEONARD AVENUE

BELLEVUE AVENUE

AUGUSTA AVENUE

KENSINGTON AVE

BALDWIN STREET

WALES AVENUE

O'ARCY STREET

CHINATOWN

St Patrick

DUNDAS STREET WEST

DUNDAS ST. W.

Sharp Centre For Design

Textile Museum of Canada

PALMERSTON BOULEVARD

MARKHAM STREET

LIPPINCOTT ST

BORDEN ST

BRUNSWICK AVE

MAJOR ST

ROBERT STREET

SPADINA AVE

GLASGOW ST

ROSS ST

HENRY STREET

MURRAY STREET

COLLEGE STREET

Alexandra Park

Art Gallery of Ontario

GRANGE AVENUE

HURON AVENUE

Grange Park

McCAUL STREET

ST PATRICK STREET

SIMCOE STREET

ARMOURY

Osgoode Hall

SULLIVAN STREET

PHOEBE ST.

SOHO ST

BEVERLEY STREET

War Memorial

Canada Life Building

Campbell House

Osgoode

QUEEN ST. W.

Four Seasons Centre

ROBINSON ST.

CARR STREET

RYERSON AVENUE

DENISON AVENUE

AUGUSTA AVENUE

CAMERON STREET

QUEEN STREET WEST

QUEEN STREET WEST

BATHURST STREET

PALMERSTON AVENUE

MARKHAM STREET

RICHMOND STREET WEST

Factory Theatre

MAUD ST

BRANT STREET

CAMDEN ST.

ADELAIDE STREET WEST

PETER STREET

JOHN STREET

NELSON STREET

STREET

DUNCAN ST

SIMCOE STREET

ADELAIDE ST

PEARL ST

TECUMSETH STREET

STEWART ST.

PORTLAND STREET

WELLINGTON ST. WEST

KING STREET WEST

CLARENCE

MERCER ST

BLUE JAYS WAY

St Andrew

St Andrew's

Metro Hall

Roy Thompson Hall

Toronto Dominion Centre

Gallery of Inuit Art

NIAGARA STREET

WELLINGTON ST. WEST

DRAPER ST

Clarence Square Park

CLARENCE SQUARE

WELLINGTON ST. W.

CBC Broadcast Centre

Royal York

Old Fort York

FRONT STREET WEST

FRONT STREET

STATION ST

Skywalk

HOUSEY ST.

SPADINA AVENUE

Rogers Centre (SkyDome)

CN Tower

Metro Convention Centre

YORK STREET

BREMNER BOULEVARD

LAKE SHORE BOULEVARD WEST

GARDINER EXPRESSWAY

Spadina

Rees

Simcoe

York

QUEENS QUAY WEST

Ontario Place

Canada Maltings Building

York Quay Centre

Queens Quay Terminal Building

The Power Plant Gallery

Western Gap

Toronto City Centre Airport

Toronto Inner Harbour

Hanlan's Point

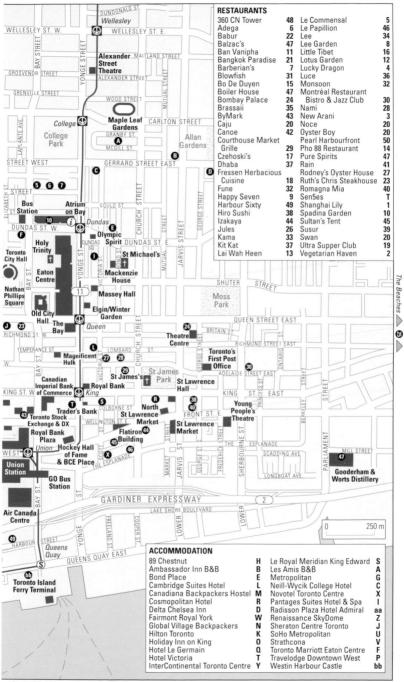

RESTAURANTS

360 CN Tower	48	Le Commensal	5
Adega	6	Le Papillion	46
Babur	22	Lee	34
Balzac's	47	Lee Garden	8
Ban Vanipha	11	Little Tibet	16
Bangkok Paradise	21	Lotus Garden	12
Barberian's	7	Lucky Dragon	4
Blowfish	31	Luce	36
Bo De Duyen	15	Monsoon	32
Boiler House	47	Montréal Restaurant	
Bombay Palace	24	Bistro & Jazz Club	30
Brassaii	35	Nami	28
ByMark	43	New Arani	3
Caju	20	Noce	20
Canoe	42	Oyster Boy	20
Courthouse Market		Pearl Harbourfront	50
Grille	29	Pho 88 Restaurant	14
Czehoski's	17	Pure Spirits	47
Dhaba	37	Rain	41
Fressen Herbacious		Rodney's Oyster House	27
Cuisine	18	Ruth's Chris Steakhouse	23
Fune	32	Romagna Mia	40
Happy Seven	9	Sen5es	T
Harbour Sixty	49	Shanghai Lily	1
Hiro Sushi	38	Spadina Garden	10
Izakaya	44	Sultan's Tent	45
Jules	26	Susur	39
Kama	33	Swan	20
Kit Kat	37	Ultra Supper Club	19
Lai Wah Heen	13	Vegetarian Haven	2

ACCOMMODATION

89 Chestnut	H	Le Royal Meridian King Edward	S
Ambassador Inn B&B	B	Les Amis B&B	A
Bond Place	E	Metropolitan	G
Cambridge Suites Hotel	L	Neill-Wycik College Hotel	C
Canadiana Backpackers Hostel	M	Novotel Toronto Centre	X
Cosmopolitan Hotel	R	Pantages Suites Hotel & Spa	I
Delta Chelsea Inn	D	Radisson Plaza Hotel Admiral	aa
Fairmont Royal York	W	Renaissance SkyDome	Z
Global Village Backpackers	N	Sheraton Centre Toronto	J
Hilton Toronto	K	SoHo Metropolitan	U
Holiday Inn on King	O	Strathcona	V
Hotel Le Germain	Q	Toronto Marriott Eaton Centre	F
Hotel Victoria	T	Travelodge Downtown West	P
InterContinental Toronto Centre	Y	Westin Harbour Castle	bb